... ... human law a woman co...
...e of will or enter into a contract
...f Valentinian. I forbade bequest...
ecclesiastics. By the time of ...
the disabilities imposed upon wo...
...codes had disappeared, and ...
Christianity this change in ...
...e the law of Æthelbert, ...

ANGLO-SAXON
SAINTS AND SCHOLARS

THE MACMILLAN COMPANY
NEW YORK · BOSTON · CHICAGO
DALLAS · ATLANTA · SAN FRANCISCO

MACMILLAN AND CO., LIMITED
LONDON · BOMBAY · CALCUTTA
MADRAS · MELBOURNE

THE MACMILLAN COMPANY
OF CANADA, LIMITED
TORONTO

ANGLO-SAXON SAINTS AND SCHOLARS

BY

ELEANOR SHIPLEY DUCKETT

M.A., Ph.D., D.Lit.

JOHN M. GREENE PROFESSOR OF CLASSICAL LANGUAGES
AND LITERATURES, SMITH COLLEGE,
NORTHAMPTON, MASSACHUSETTS

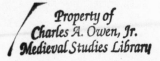
NEW YORK
THE MACMILLAN COMPANY
1947

See p. 111

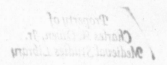

To the memory of
TENNEY FRANK
and
EDWARD KENNARD RAND

PREFACE

It is probably the act of folly to try to follow the footsteps of the Venerable Bede and his contemporaries amid the many snares and mazes through which the learned of Europe and of America have found their way so carefully, lantern in hand. Our debt, so wide and deep, to them and the light they have thrown on our darkness has been to some extent acknowledged in the footnotes and bibliography of this book. This can only put forward as apology for its appearance the words addressed to Bede himself, trembling as he ventured to follow Ambrose in explaining the mysteries of Saint Luke, by his "brother and fellow-priest," Acca, bishop of Hexham: "For, as likewise saith Augustine, there is need of many books on the same subjects, written in different manner but the same Faith, that knowledge of these matters may teach many people, some in one way, some in another. Now truly Ambrose was so scholarly and so deep in his exposition of Saint Luke that only professors could hope to understand him. . . . Get busily to work, then, dear brother, and write your pages very simply, that humbler students may also know of these truths."

It is good to acknowledge here also other aid received from various friends: in Smith College, from Mary Ellen Chase, Professor of English, that criticism of form for which every page cried aloud; from Sidney R. Packard, Professor of History, the ready loan of his books and his detailed knowledge of bibliography; from Harriet D. MacPherson, the Librarian, and her staff, especially from Margaret L. Johnson, Reference Librarian, and from Jessie B. Berwick, of the Circulation Department of the College Library, ready access to books and stacks of other collections; from Elias Claydon, Head Janitor of the Library, the transportation, up and down stairs, of so many monumental tomes; outside my own College, from Keyes D. Metcalf, Director of the Harvard University Library, the freedom of reading therein, and all courtesy of assistance from members of the staff in the Widener, the Houghton, and the Divinity School Libraries; from Georgia D. Kelchner and from Olava A. Ørbeck, of Cambridge, England, the generous gift of many volumes, badly needed; from Charles Lewis, of Frome, Somerset, the kindly imparting of information; from Nevil Shute and his publishers, William Morrow and Company, New York, the passage on page 50 from his book *Pied Piper*.

In regard to the making and publishing of my book I would thank most warmly Harold S. Latham, Vice President of the Macmillan Company, New York, for his constant interest and kindness, and the various supervisors and readers who have efficiently directed and corrected it in its progress through the press. My gratitude is also offered in deep measure to Helen L. Baxter, of Smith College, and Gladys P. Nute, of the Northampton Commercial College, Massachusetts, who skillfully brought its manuscript from illegible drafts toward a readable and ordered whole.

Its many errors are my own. It is, however, bravely dedicated in a spirit of complete humility to those two men of learning from whom long since I caught a vision of what a life of study ideally might mean and be.

E. S. D.

Northampton, Massachusetts
February 2, 1946

CONTENTS

ix

x CONTENTS

.

Chapter I
ALDHELM OF MALMESBURY

ALDHELM OF MALMESBURY

THE FOREST of Selwood was very still. Far away to the north and the east it stretched in its tangled confusion of bracken and fern, dark in the shade of oaks girdled with mistletoe and ivy, of beeches ripening their winter's yield of prickly brown mast, of ash trees standing high as if in pride of their olive-gray branches and gracefully cleft leaves. Pools of water lay here and there, reflecting tall rushes that looked down upon them, and sometimes the sun as it glanced through the trees lingered a moment on some patch of vivid green where moss and matted grass hid the treacherous swampland. Here for a while nothing of moving life seemed to dwell. Then suddenly the silence was broken on the border of some little stream where the beaver was stripping bark to build its home; a squirrel leaped from bough to bough, chattering in wrath, or a wood-dove called to its mate. From the distance a keen ear might catch now and again the bark of a fox, the sound of a deer leaping through the undergrowth, the splash of an otter slinking along the water's edge in search of its prey.

Yet nothing of this reached the thoughts of the man who sat resting upon a fallen tree just where the woods sloped down to meet the river that flowed past them. His body was flung back as though in weariness; his rough girdled frock and sandals were travel-stained; his thin, eager face bore marks of restless seeking, long unsatisfied. At this moment he was looking up intently toward an old half-ruined castle perched, within the masonry that once had guarded it, upon a hill that

3

rose from the forest clearing where he lay. Signs of habitation
marked it, despite its desolation, and by some strange mystic
sense this pilgrim in a distant land felt that here at last he
had come home. The forest, in its vastness, its beauty, its
silence, somehow comforted him, as familiar. Here he would
be alone, cut off from men, alien or enemy, by the waters that
almost surrounded him. He had been travelling along the great
Fosse Way of southwest England, when, he hardly knew why,
he had turned aside and followed a rude path that had led
him here between two streams as to some island refuge. Here,
then, he might rest content; here he might make for himself
a cell under the protecting shadow of this fortress, wherein he
seemed to see marks of a building akin to that of the land
whence he had come. Here he might pray and think; might
study the words of God in peace; here—who knew?—God
might give it him to lighten those who still sat in darkness
of pagan error.

His name was Maelduib; he was an Irish monk, and he
was in truth now reaching the end of his pilgrimage from
Ireland somewhere about the year 635 after Christ.[1] We do
not know from which of the multitude of monasteries that
inspired Irish devotion and learning in the sixth and following
centuries he had come. Perhaps he had been trained at
Clonard on the river Boyne under Finnian the Wise; or under
the other Finnian at Moville on Strangford Lough. Perhaps
he owed allegiance to Clonmacnois, the abbey founded by
Ciaran on the banks of the Shannon; or to one of the monasteries reared by Columba before he left his native land. It
might have been Dair-mag, "Oak-plain," now known as
Durrow, in county Offaly, or Daire-Calgaich, "Calgach's

---

[1] *Gest. Pont.*, 333f., 345; *Eulogium* I, 224f.; III, 279, 328; Leland,
Collectanea I, ii, 302ff.; Camden, 176f.; Dugdale I, 253ff.; Bönhoff, 22ff.;
Plummer II, 149. (Reference, unless otherwise indicated, is made to
pages).

Oak-wood," Derry on the Foyle.[2] Suggestion has also linked his name with the famous monastic school of Lismore, on the Blackwater in county Waterford, where Carthach ruled as abbot in this seventh century.[3]

Perhaps, again, he had learned spiritual discipline from a stay on Belfast Lough at Bangor, in the monastery which held as its founder Comgall, most renowned of Irish abbots in his time. There we could think of him as watching with the Church Celtic in the darkness before the dawn, calling to the heavens and the earth as witness of his prayer:

Audite, coeli, quae loquor; audiat terra verba oris mei;
Concrescat ut pluvia doctrina mea, fluat ut ros eloquium meum, quasi imber super herbam, et quasi stillae super gramina;
Quia nomen Domini invocabo, date magnificentiam Deo nostro. . . .
Audite.

Give ear, O ye heavens, and I will speak; and hear, O earth, the words of my mouth;
My doctrine shall drop as the rain, my speech shall distil as the dew, as the small rain upon the tender herb, and as the showers upon the grass;
Because I will call upon the Name of the Lord; ascribe ye greatness unto our God. . . .
Give ye ear.[4]

There, also, in that time the brethren were repeating with the Church of East and West the Blessing of holy Zacharias and the Song of the Three Children; there on Sundays their choir was singing *Te Deum,* and morning and evening gave its *Gloria in excelsis* to the Lord.[5] There lay-monks chanted the Community Hymn of Bangor, as the line of the priests of the monastery, led by the Abbot, moved slowly toward the altar:

[2] Kenney, 424; *HE* III, c. 4; Ryan, 117ff.
[3] Browne, *Aldhelm,* 47.
[4] *Ant. of Bangor* II, 1ff., 35f.   [5] *Ibid.,* 7f., 40f., 75.

Sancti venite,
Christi corpus sumite,
Sanctum bibentes
Quo redempti sanguinem; [6]

Come, for ye are holy,
Take ye Christ's Body,
Drinking the holy
Blood of your redeeming.

All this, doubtless, Maelduib knew well. Probably he knew also the story that angels first had hymned this approach to the altar, rejoicing at the offering of the Mass in Bangor Monastery, over love restored between Saint Patrick and his friend Saint Sechnall. Had not Sechnall once said of Patrick that he was a good man save for one fault: he failed to preach of charity? And, as all Irishmen could tell, Patrick prized charity above all, and had rushed in wonder to find Sechnall; and Sechnall had left the very oblation upon the altar that he might give answer to his friend. So thus it came to pass, and angels from heaven sang this song as they kept watch within the church till Sechnall should return in peace. [7]

Warm, too, in this pilgrim's mind must have lain the memory of the songs that honoured holy men of the Ireland whence he had come: of the hymn written by Sechnall, it was said, in praise of Patrick; of that in which the monks of Bangor delighted to tell of their Founder, Comgall; of others in which they sang of "the goodly Rule of Bangor" in rich and varied picturing: "a ship riding stormy seas in unbroken calm"; "a bride prepared for her wedding, betrothed to the Lord her King"; or told of the abbots of Bangor "whom the Lord hath called to the seats of His heaven," down to Cronan,

[6] *Ibid.,* 10f., 44f.
[7] Whitley Stokes, *Patrick* II, 394ff.; *ILH* I, 3ff.; II, 3ff.; *Ant. of Bangor* II, 44.

who was still their head in this seventh century, patiently awaiting his own call to rest.[8]

Nor do we know exactly why Maelduib had left Ireland: "a land of calm and wholesome air, far surpassing Britain; where is seen no creeping beast and no serpent may live . . . a land flowing with milk and honey, lacking neither vineyards nor fish nor fowl, renowned for hunting of the deer and the wild goat." [9] It would seem that even while he was still on Irish soil he had gone out from his monastic community to live as stranger and pilgrim. Tradition tells that he had been so beset by attacks of robbers and highwaymen in his own country that he had fled from it and found his way to England. There, commending himself to the will of God, he had wandered, seeking some place in which to dwell, till instinct at length brought him to this remote forest glade. The name of the castle on which he was now looking is given as Caer Bladon, built long before to guard his people by Dunwallo Molmuntius, a heathen British king. But, so the story goes, Saxon enemies had invaded Dunwallo's realm, had destroyed his city and possessed themselves of his castle and his land. To the castle they gave a new name, Ingelborn, and manned it with Saxon soldiers for its safe keeping. A mile or two away Saxon chieftains had made their kingly seat within the little settlement of Brockenburgh, and ruled this neighbourhood from thence.

From the dwellers in Ingelborn fortress Maelduib now asked and gained leave to build his hut beneath their walls. Rough timber, plastered firm with mud, served his purpose well enough, and here, in Wessex, in the land possessed by the West Saxons and in that part of it which we call Wiltshire, he

[8] *Ant. of Bangor* II, 14ff., 28, 33; *ILH* I, 7ff.; Mario Esposito, "The Latin writers of mediaeval Ireland," *Hermathena* XIV, 1907, 519ff.; XV, 1909, 353ff.
[9] *HE* I, c. 1.

settled down to keep his body nourished on the wild life of the woods and his soul on contemplation and prayer.

The Britain to which he had come from his Christian Ireland was not itself a heathen land; Christianity had been widely practised among the British before the coming of the Saxons had for a while driven its knowledge into darkness. There is plenty of witness, also, that tells of fellowship in Christian faith between Britain and Ireland. In the fifth century Patrick of Britain had crossed the sea to become the Apostle of Ireland, head of that First Order of Irish Saints who worshipped in communion with Rome. In the sixth century, Finnian of Moville had been trained at the "White House," the monastery founded long before by the British Ninian on the Isle of Whithorn off Galloway in Scotland.[10] About 565, it was said, Gildas of Britain had preached to the Irish under their King Ainmire, and, with David of Wales, had given a Liturgy of the Mass to the Second Irish Order of Saints.[11] Other ancient tradition tells that David's fellow-countryman, Cadoc, after passing twelve years under the care of an Irish monk in Britain, had journeyed to Ireland's school of Lismore, eager for his perfecting in discipline before he founded his monastery of Llancarfan in South Wales. Men said, too, that his humility found fellowship in Ireland, and that the Irish monks of Finnian of Clonard welcomed eagerly Saint Cadoc's priests.[12] In 563 Columba, disciple of Clonard and himself a founder of Irish schools of sacred learning, had landed on the isle of Hy, later famous as Iona, to set up a mother-house for monks who should teach far and wide among the Scots and northern English.

[10] According to *NLA* ed. Horstman I, 445. On the *Candida Casa* see *HE* III, c. 4; *DCB* IV, 45f.
[11] H.S. II, 292f.
[12] W. J. Rees, *Lives of Cambro-British Saints*, 79.

Thus Irish clergy and monks had sought Britain, as their British brethren had sought Ireland, for the sake of monastic life and scholarship. We may believe, too, that from Britain, as from Gaul, men had fled to Ireland for security from invasion; or, again, that as each belonged to a common race, British and Irish Celts had visited their kindred in either land; or that pilgrims, the Irish especially, had gone into exile across the sea in their yearning to lose all that they might win Christ and His kingdom of all souls.[13]

Then in Britain the terror of pagan Angles, Jutes, and Saxons had sent her Christian people fleeing to the hills and forests to escape "the fierce red tongue" of destroying flame that overran their country from East to West; and Christian religion lay hidden with them in lonely places.[14] It came forth in triumph, when Gregory the Great of his eager and persistent pity sent in 597 to the Jute settlers of Kent the monk Augustine and his companions to teach and baptize them in the fellowship of the Church of Rome. The mission, as we know so well, was fruitful; before long the Roman Church owned a daughter in the Church of Canterbury, whence her faith spread to the Saxons of London and the region of the Thames, to the Angles of the east and the north of England.

In the sixth and seventh centuries, however, the Celtic Churches of Britain and of Ireland had become sharply conscious that their fellowship was not in accord in certain details with that loyalty to the Church of Rome taught in the fifth century by Patrick of Ireland and later on by Augustine from Canterbury. The matters of discord, as concerning external observance, might seem slight. The Romans calculated the date of Easter by one system, the Celts by another; in consequence the Roman and the Celtic celebrations of Easter

[13] Kenney, 142, 160, 180.
[14] Gildas, ed. H. Williams, 57; H.S. II, 292f.

regularly fell on different days; the monastic tonsure prescribed by Rome and obediently followed by the Saxon disciples of Canterbury differed from that worn by British and Irish monks.[15]

In vain Augustine, as Archbishop of Canterbury, had admonished the erring Britons; in vain his successor, Laurentius, had written some time between 604 and 618 to the bishops and abbots of Ireland a letter, also signed by the Roman bishops of London and Rochester, "entreating them to keep the unity of peace and of Catholic observance of the Church of Christ throughout the world." Truly, wrote Laurentius, the missionaries sent by Pope Gregory from Rome had been disappointed in finding that the Britons differed from Rome in their keeping of Easter. They had hoped to find the Irish better. Grievous had been their distress to discover from Dagan, an Irish bishop who had lately visited England, that the Irish Christians not only held the same error in practice as the British, but held it with such vigour that Dagan refused even to eat under the same roof as that which sheltered the Italian priests who served the Church at Canterbury.[16]

To this admonition of Canterbury that of Rome herself had been added. Pope Honorius had addressed to the Irish a letter "prudently exhorting them not to hold their congregation, few in number and domiciled in the farthest bounds of the earth, to be wiser than the Church of Christ universal, both ancient and modern." He had entreated them "not to keep a different Easter, in defiance of Paschal calculations and of the decrees of Bishops assembled in synod from all the world."[17]

It would appear that this letter stimulated the consciences

---

[15] On the complicated history of the Paschal computation in the Churches see Charles W. Jones, ed. *Bedae Opera de Temporibus*, 1943, 6–104.

[16] *HE* II, c. 2; c. 4; Kenney, 218f.

[17] *HE* II, c. 19.

of the Christians of southern Ireland;[18] at any rate, about this time some of them began to keep Easter as commanded by Rome. The story of the change among the southern Irish from the Celtic to the Roman Easter is told in a letter written about 633 by Cummian, possibly abbot of Durrow, Columba's monastery in Leinster, to Segene, abbot of Iona.[19] Cummian writes that when his countrymen first began to change, he himself did not join them, but studied carefully for a whole year this question of Paschal cycles. Then gradually it seemed to him more and more an insult to Mother Church to boast that "Rome is wrong, Jerusalem is wrong, Antioch is wrong, all the world is wrong; only the Irish and the British are right." At last he asked counsel from certain neighbouring abbots for whose judgment he had great respect. In conference they, or their appointed representatives, met near Durrow, where it was decided that all should keep Easter in future with the Church throughout the world.

Not long afterward, however, a "whited wall" ("God, I hope, will smite him in whatsoever way He will," prayed the wrathful Irish Cummian) had brought division into this harmony. Then envoys were sent to ask guidance from the Mother Church at Rome. "In the third year," Cummian continues, "they returned and told us all that they had heard, and gave us witness, even more sure, of their own eyes." In Rome the envoys had lodged in one hostel and had kept Easter together in Saint Peter's with a Greek, a Hebrew, a Scythian, and an Egyptian; all with one consent had solemnly affirmed that this Roman Easter was observed on one and the same day in all their lands.[20]

So Cummian had been converted, and out of his own certainty he wrote to plead with his brother-abbot of Iona just

---

[18] *Cf.* Jones, *ODT* 92, note 4.   [19] *Ibid.,* 89–99.
[20] *Epist. Cummiani, PL* LXXXVII, coll. 969ff.

after the envoys had returned, gravely bidding that he, too, be reconciled in this matter of Rome. This witness of about the year 633 agrees well with that of the Venerable Bede; he tells that some time before 635 the people of the south of Ireland had learned to keep Easter according to the ordinance of the Apostolic See.[21]

The Irish of the north held themselves free to differ from their brethren of the south. Some of their bishops and priests, abbots of the monasteries of Armagh, Clonard, Clonmacnois, Moville, and Iona, had written to Severinus, consecrated Pope in May, 640, concerning their variance from the Roman use, and had received an answer in the same year. Since Severinus had died about two months after his consecration, the Irish letter had been opened by the vice-regents of the Holy See, including the Pope-elect, who was to rule as John IV from 640 to 642. In this reply the Papal See accused the Celts of northern Ireland of being even more seriously at variance with Rome. To rebuke of Paschal error now was added admonition against the Pelagian heresy of self-will and lack of dependence upon Divine grace, which heresy, the Holy See declared, was then spreading its poison among these Irish of the north.[22] The letter, however, was written in vain, and the northern Irish continued with their fellow-Celts in Britain to observe Easter and to wear the tonsure after their own manner.[23]

Such was the position of Celtic Christianity while the Irish

[21] *HE* III, c. 3; Plummer II, 125.
[22] *HE* II, c. 19; Kenney, 221ff.; Plummer II, 112f.
[23] It must be remembered that the Celtic Church was at one with the Roman in sacramental doctrine. "No theological differences parted the Roman from the Celtic Church, for the notion that the latter was the home of a kind of primitive Protestantism, of apostolic purity and simplicity, is without any historical basis": Lloyd I, 173f., quoted by Gougaud, 216. It was Celtic difference from Roman practice which caused the schism of these early centuries; fundamentally the Celts "acknowledged the spiritual supremacy of the successors of St. Peter": Crawford, 9f. For further detail see H.S. I, 152ff.; John A. Duke, *The Columban Church,* 1932, pp. 132ff.

Maelduib was living his first years of exile in Wessex, the land of the West Saxons in southwest England. Whether he came from the Irish of the south or of the north we do not know. But we may think of him among those converted to Roman prescription; we never hear of discord between him and the bishops of Wessex who looked to Rome for guidance, such discord as in the sixth century had so sorely estranged the Irish missionary Columban from Roman bishops of Gaul.

The coming of Maelduib into Wessex was singularly opportune in the annals of its history. This had begun with the name of Ceawlin, who became its ruler in 560 and seventeen years later stood supreme among the Saxon kings of England. He had driven the men of Kent back into their own province, had fought and conquered the Britons in the west, especially at Dyrham in 577, and had held his conquests from the Thames to the Severn.

His fall was as tragic as his glory had been great. Suddenly in 592 he was defeated in a mighty battle, was banished from his kingdom, by whom we do not know, and left his rule to his son Ceolric. Under Ceolric and his brother Ceolwulf, who succeeded him, the West Saxons remained in their pagan tradition. It was not until 635, about the time when the Irish Maelduib began to say his prayers under the castle of Ingelborn in Wessex, that Christianity was first preached within its borders. Ceolric and Ceolwulf were now long since dead, and their nephew Cynegils had been ruling the West Saxons for twenty-five years. Yet not with the glory of Ceawlin; for the chief power among English kings had by this time passed to Northumbria.

The conversion of Wessex came neither from the Celtic Christians, Irish or British, nor from the English Church that looked to Canterbury under Rome. It was due to a certain Birinus, of whom we only know that he had come from Italy, afire with zeal to preach the gospel to the heathen in England; that Pope Honorius had given him blessing and had ordered his consecration as bishop; that this had duly been fulfilled by Asterius, Archbishop of Milan; [24] that he had landed in the country of these West Saxons and had found them utterly pagan and most suitable subjects for the longing of his soul.

Here and there throughout Wessex, from the Thames and the Severn southward to the coast, Birinus preached, and his words bore fruit. Before long King Cynegils himself sought instruction from him, and in 635 was baptized, it is said, together with many of his people.[25]

Birinus was, of course, a loyal son of the Roman Church, and, although he guided and disciplined his people without dependence upon Canterbury, he taught them to observe the Roman usage in all matters, including the "Catholic Easter." Cynegils, together with his overlord, King Oswald of Northumbria, gave to him for his cathedral see the town of Dorchester-on-the-Thames, nine miles from Oxford. Many churches were built under his spiritual governing, many pagans were added to the Lord during the years of his episcopate. About 650 he died, and was buried for the time in Dorchester. Long afterward his relics were laid to rest at Winchester, in the church of Saint Peter which rose under the son and successor of Cynegils.[26]

This prince, who governed the West Saxons after the death of his father in 643,[27] was named Cenwalh, and he began his reign very badly, offending the powers heavenly and earthly alike. He would have nothing of Church and sacraments, and he insulted Penda, king of the Mercians, by divorcing Penda's sister, his own queen, and taking another woman for

[24] HE III, c. 7; Bright, 168f.
[25] ASC ann. 635; T. Scott Holmes, VHS II, 1ff.
[26] Gest. Reg. I, 23.
[27] See Plummer II, 142; Stenton, 66.

his wife. The heathen king of Mercia was now at the height of his power. Promptly he used his advantage to descend upon Cenwalh in 645, driving him from his kingdom to find shelter among the East Angles, dwellers in the valleys of the Little Ouse and the Lark, in the lands of Norfolk and Suffolk.[28]

Here Cenwalh lived in exile for three years, and his exile yielded him reward. For he had fled to a Christian people. East Anglia had been firmly welded to the see of Canterbury under Rome through the labours of its King Sigebert, himself converted during a period of exile among the Franks in Gaul, and by the enthusiasm of a foreign bishop, Felix by name. Felix, like Birinus, had been stirred by longing to preach to the English; he had come from Burgundy and had begged Honorius, Archbishop of Canterbury at this time, to find him a place ready for the garnering of pagan souls. Honorius had suggested East Anglia, and there Felix reaped abundant harvest as bishop of Dunwich.[29]

It was about 631 when Felix had begun his work; about 633 there had come from Ireland into the same region an anchorite named Fursey, who had been "received with honour" by Sigebert and had begun strenuously to aid Felix in his labour.[30] This Fursey loved so well the life within cell and cloister that under his influence, we may think, King Sigebert gradually had been drawn more and more toward the same. Before long Sigebert had gladly yielded his crown to his kinsman Egric, who was already holding some share in its government, and had entered the monastery of St. Edmund, at Bury St. Edmunds in Suffolk. He himself had founded it, and there, forgetful of earthly rule, he "strove rather to fight for the kingdom of eternity." [31]

In his absence Penda had fallen upon his people. In their

[28] R. Hodgkin, 148. [29] *HE* II, c. 15.
[30] *HE* III, c. 19.
[31] *Ibid.*, III, cc. 18f.; Bright. 144f.; Plummer II, 168f.

peril they had begged Sigebert to come from his cell and inspire them, fighting for land and life; when he refused, they
had dragged him forth. But he would neither fight nor bear
sword, "never forgetful of his monastic vow," and had been
killed in the battle that followed, together with King Egric
and all his army.

The exact date of this tragedy is unknown. But the East
Anglians had rallied from the blow, and Anna, a descendant
of their royal house, had been elected king. He, also, revered
religious discipline; he is famed in its annals for giving four
daughters, a step-daughter, and two granddaughters to the
cloister.

The Christian courtesy of Anna and his family, of Felix
and of Fursey, had proved too strong even for Cenwalh, and
in 646 King Anna stood as sponsor for him in his baptizing
by Felix.[32] The ruler of East Anglia seems to have aided his
godson in material ways also; for Cenwalh returned to his
throne in 648. Now, newly converted and newly restored, he
was naturally as enamoured of the Church as he had formerly
been contemptuous. Occasion favoured him; into his land
there arrived shortly after his return another missionary bishop,
one Agilbert, consecrated in his own country of Gaul, but
probably without assignment to any diocese.[33]

Agilbert, like Maelduib, had come to England by way of
Ireland; he had "stayed there no little time for the sake of
reading the Scriptures." In the fifteen years, more or less,
which had now passed since Maelduib had left Ireland, students from Gaul and England had more and more been
travelling to learn of the Irish monks in their religious schools.
Cenwalh was greatly impressed by his visitor's erudition and
keenness for work; Birinus had lately died, and Agilbert of

[32] Stubbs, *DCB* I, 592; *ASC ann.* 646; Flor. Worc. *Chron. ann.* 646.
[33] Bright, 183, note 3.

his own accord began to teach and preach in Wessex. Finally, the king invited him to succeed Birinus as bishop of Dorchester-on-Thames. From about 650, therefore, for nearly thirteen years Agilbert was Father in God to the West Saxons.[34]

And now Cenwalh prospered in battle against the Britons, who still lay encamped in the hills and forests of western England. Frequently they made raids into Saxon territory, and on their side the Saxon warriors always were eager to push forward the line of their advance. Thus gradually Cenwalh enlarged his dominion; in 652 he fought the Britons at Bradford-on-Avon, and in 658 by a victory on the border of Maelduib's forest of Selwood he drove them to the river Parrett.[35] These victories seem to have been of special note; apparently they delivered the British church at Glastonbury into the hands of the Saxons. Be it said to their credit, the conquerors felt so deep an awe of this sacred place that they suffered its monks to continue exactly as before in their round of work and prayer.[36]

Some twenty years had now passed for Maelduib in the clearing beneath Ingelborn in the forest of Selwood. His cell was no longer solitary. The wild life of the woods had not yielded a sufficiency even for the needs of a monk from Ireland, so famed in these days for the stern discipline of her religious zeal. His Irish wit and his sense of necessity were, however, as keen as his devotion. Ireland had planted in him a love of books only second to a love of prayer, and he resolved to try to find pupils whom he might teach in return for some material aid. His retreat had already become well-known to Saxons passing through the forest, and they had learned to respect its kindly hermit. From them news of his erudition

[34] *HE* III, c. 7; Plummer II, 146.
[35] *ASC ann.* 652, 658; R. Hodgkin, 315.
[36] H.S. III, 164.

travelled to others of the Saxon communities settled here and there among the woodlands of Wiltshire and Somerset; their sons, and they for their sons, eagerly heard of this chance of learning. Cut off as they were by swamp and by marsh, by lake and by woodland, by lack of roads and by peril of robbers, from intercourse with the pioneers of civilization in their country, no prospect was facing them but that of growing up into fierce, uncultured soldiers and farmers, hewers of the tangled thickets and clearers of the overgrown soil. Religious schools there were, to be sure, elsewhere in Britain, schools founded for Saxon converts, in Canterbury by Augustine, in Dunwich of East Anglia by King Sigebert and his bishop Felix, following the fashion of Canterbury; older schools of the British, still standing, especially in the fastnesses of Wales : that of Illtyd at Llantwit Major near Cardiff; that said to have been founded by the same saint in Caldey Island, the ancient Ynys Pyr; that of David at Menevia, now St. David's; that of Cadoc at Llancarfan.[37] But these were inaccessible, and one after another of the young men of Wessex must have longed for something—they knew not what—which would satisfy the hunger aroused in them by rumours of books telling in language yet unknown to them of beauty and of wisdom, of a world entirely different from the crude limits into which they had been born.[38]

So Maelduib began to teach, and his school grew, as the Saxon rule opened western land. Presently his woodland glade held a community of young men, living under his patient discipline in rough wattled huts around the wooden chapel to which day by day he called them to prayer. Both community and chapel were dedicated by their founder to the leaders of the apostles, Saint Peter and Saint Paul.[39]

To this place, then, about the year 654, while Cenwalh

[37] Lloyd I, 143ff.; Gougaud, 58f.; Wade-Evans, *Welsh Christian Origins*, 1934, *passim*.
[38] R. Hodgkin, 321ff.   [39] *Gest. Pont.*, 345, 368.

was still gaining new ground for the Saxons in Wessex and his bishop Agilbert was preaching to Wessex souls, came a boy of about fifteen years whose name, Aldhelm, Ealdhelm, "ancient helmet," declared his Saxon birth. Many theories have been spun concerning his home and family; all we know is that he was related to the line of kings of Wessex, descended from Ceawlin, and that his father's name was Kenten.[40] We may imagine, if we please, that he came from the land of Dorsetshire.[41]

Among all the motley collection of lads, gleaning what they could according to their varied intelligence as they sat restlessly listening to Maelduib around the fire during the winter or on the turf in summer time under the forest trees, none could have been more eager than this son of Kenten. Already he must have been dreaming of words—words that could reveal or hide, as one wished, the thoughts in one's mind; words chosen out of a multitude that lay to hand, used for their own sake, alone and in companies, marching and meeting in complex regiment and line, marshalled, each in its appointed place, all under one's own individual control. As a barbarian warrior, yearning for soldiers to carry out his schemes of conquest, as a recruit half fearfully handling the arms that might some day bring him reward of brave and inspired deeds, of such calibre was Aldhelm when he took his place in this company of ignorant West country youth.

Slowly the things of which he had dreamed began to take shape before him. The instruction given by Maelduib, "scholar as well as monk" as the tradition of a later day described him,[42] must have been given through his memory, aided by a few books, of some small part of the material known to monastic schools of Ireland during this seventh century. Irish scholars knew the Bible, in the Vulgate version of Saint

---

[40] *Ibid.,* 333; Ehwald, x f.; Bönhoff, 60.
[41] *Gest. Pont.,* 375.　　　　　　　　[42] *Ibid.,* 334.

Jerome, in Old Latin texts, current before the Vulgate version
was completed in the fifth century, in Irish manuscripts of
these Old Latin texts; [43] apocryphal writings, such as the
Book of Enoch, the *Apocalypse of Moses,* the *Gospel of
Nicodemus* or the *Acts of Pilate,* forbidden to the Roman
Church since the end of the fifth century, but still studied
among Irish Christians; [44] writings of the Greek Fathers in
Latin translation; writings of the four Fathers of the Latin
Church, Ambrose, Jerome, Augustine, and Gregory the Great;
commentaries and interpretations of Scripture, with sermons
based upon the same; lives of saints and martyrs; rules ordering the life of monks; penitentials prescribing penance for
various degrees and kinds of sin; hymns for use during the
monastic offices of the Church; religious poems and prayers.[45]

Concerning Irish writers whose works might have formed
text-books in Ireland of this century we have some knowledge.
The Irish "Augustine" wrote in 655 *Of the Wonders of
Sacred Scripture* with reverent admiration of the saint of
Hippo; [46] a few years later, as it seems, some Biblical scholar,
perhaps this same "Augustine," made a commentary on the
Catholic Epistles; [47] in the same seventh century one Laidcend,
whose monastery stood in the "meadow of graves," founded
by Saint Molua at the modern Kyle, gave to Ireland many
passages from the famous *Moralia,* that mass of allegorical interpretation of the Book of Job so happily devised by Gregory
the Great to solace his dreary years in Constantinople.[48] Of
like character was the *Mystical Interpretation of the Ancestors
of the Lord Jesus Christ* from the pen of Aileran the Wise,
whose death the Irish annals held as due to the Great Plague

[43] Kenney, 625ff.
[44] Crawford, 95ff.; *cf.* M. R. James, *CMH* III, 504ff.
[45] Kenney, 1f.; James, *ibid.,* 501ff.
[46] *PL* XXXV, coll. 2149ff.; Gougaud, 266f.; Kenney, 275ff.
[47] Kenney, 277f.; Mario Esposito, *JTS* XXI, 1920, 316ff.
[48] Manitius, *Gesch.,* 99f.; Gougaud, 267; *Greg. Mag., Moral. Libri:
PL* LXXV, coll. 509ff.

of 665.[49] Celtic imagination gladly followed that tradition of spiritual fancy which the Roman writers had inherited from the Greek; and Aileran himself drew here from Jerome a wealth of interpretation of genealogy in St. Matthew's Gospel.[50] Another commentary possibly known to these Irish monks was that made on the Epistles of Saint Paul early in the fifth century by the daring opponent of Saint Augustine, the British monk Pelagius.[51]

Among Irish Saints honoured in Maelduib's school the greatest, of course, was holy Patrick. He had written during the fifth century the story of his life in his *Confession*: "I, Patrick, am a sinner most uncultured, least among all the faithful, and held for scorn among many. . . . This is my confession before I die."[52] Later witnesses to his memory were the collection of source-material for his *Life*, gathered by Tirechan in the latter part of the seventh century, and a *Life of Patrick* composed during the same period by Muirchu of Armagh.[53] Under the name of Saint Patrick as author there was widely known also in the seventh century, as now, the *Breastplate of Patrick*, a rhythmical litany sung by the faithful in commending themselves to the Lord each morning for protection from evil. It was written in Irish; and its Irish name is "The Deer's Cry"; for tradition told that Patrick and his disciples sang it as they passed in the semblance of wild deer through the dangers of Irish enemies, lying in wait along their path.[54]

Other hymns of Ireland are known to us from the Irish *Liber Hymnorum* and from the *Antiphonary of Bangor*, that collection of Latin songs and prayers once in use at the

[49] Kenney, 279; *PL* LXXX, coll. 327ff.; Gougaud, 269.
[50] *PL* XXVI, coll. 21ff.   [51] Kenney, 661ff.
[52] N. J. D. White, *Libri sancti Patricii, PRIA* XXV, Section C, No. 7, 1905, 201ff.; Whitley Stokes, *Patrick* II, 357ff.; Bury, *Life of St. Patrick*, 1905, 196ff., 225ff.
[53] Kenney, 329ff.; Bury, 248ff., 255ff.
[54] *ILH* I, 133ff.; II, 49ff.

Monastery of Bangor. It was made late in the seventh century; the hymns and collects which it contains had been drawn for the worship of Bangor both from continental and from Irish authorship.[55] In these books we find from the continent the influence of Gaul and Spain and Italy; from Ireland hymns associated with the names of various holy men, Sechnall, Camelacus, Mugint, and others. From Iona had come hymns assigned to its Saint Columba; from Ireland or from Britain another *Breastplate,* given variously to the Irish Laidcend, who wrote on the Book of Job, or to the British Gildas.[56]

Gildas had also given to British monks and clergy in the sixth century his bitter *Complaint on the Miseries of Britain,* reproaching all, spiritual and lay alike, with countless sins of omission and commission in a tumultuous flood of acerbous Latin.[57] Another Latin lament, *On Twelve Evils of the Age,* burst forth in Ireland in the seventh century, bearing, as did the plaint of Gildas, many quotations from the Vulgate Bible.[58] Penitentials for the guidance of confessors in meting out due penance for sin were devised for Britain in the sixth century by Welsh synods and by Gildas; for Ireland in the sixth century by Finnian, probably of Clonard, in the seventh century by Cummean; for Gaul in the sixth century by the Irish Columban, who by the stern clauses of his *Rule* established Irish asceticism in definite shape under countless monastic roofs of continental Europe.[59]

It may be that there were secular Latin books, too, in use among some Irish scholars, one of whom, we may think, was this same Columban. For we possess among his writings cer-

---

[55] Ed. F. E. Warren I, 1893; II, 1895 (*HBS* IV; X).

[56] *Ibid.,* II, xxviff., 19, 44f., 46f., 57f.; *ILH* I, 23f., 66ff., 84ff., 206ff.; II, 242ff.; Kenney, 257, 270f.

[57] Ed. Mommsen. *MGH Auct. Ant.* XIII (*Chron. Min.* III), 1898, 3ff.

[58] Ed. Hartel, *CSEL* III, iii, 152ff.; *PL* XL, coll. 1079ff.; Laistner, *Thought and Letters,* 111ff.; Manitius, *Gesch.,* 107f.; Gougaud, 291.

[59] McNeill and Gamer, 169ff., 174ff., 86ff., 98ff., 249ff.; Le Bras, *s.v. Pénitentiels, DTC* XII, 1160ff.; Watkins II, 587ff.

tain little poems, written in correct Latin metres, hexameter
and lyric, which point to some practice of verse-writing in
Ireland and which are concerned with secular as well as with
sacred themes. From Columban's writings we find also that
he knew the poetry of Vergil, of Horace, of Ovid and of some
of the Christian writers of earlier centuries, including Prudentius, Sedulius, Dracontius, and Venantius Fortunatus.[60]
Yet, at the same time, we cannot tell how much of this Latin
learning Columban gained upon the continent of Europe after
his departure from Ireland. Moreover, the study of Latin
prose writers, and of grammar in the works of Donatus and
Priscian among the Irish in Ireland may well be ascribed in
general to a later date than the sixth and seventh centuries.[61]

On the side of scientific literature, early Celtic scholarship,
Irish and British, was naturally much concerned with arith-
metical and astronomical calculation, on account of the
reckoning of the Celtic Easter; with geographical studies, in
connection with the Celtic longing for missionary work and
exile in foreign lands; with research into the dates and days
of saints and martyrs.

Again, in these early times Celtic scholars loved with a
passion all their own the study of fancies and of rhetoric,
of Latin sentences and passages arranged in manifold fashion
and adorned with all the colour of strange and strangely
sounding words. In nothing is this shown more clearly than in
that wave of literary curiosities which seems to have flowed
from some fellowship of writers in the fifth and sixth centuries,
delightedly concocting a cryptic language of bizarre style and
foreign elements gathered from every known source. Some of

[60] See the notes *passim* of Gundlach, ed. *Columbani Epistolae, MGH
Epp.* III, 1892, 156ff.; cf. Dümmler, ed. *Vitae Columbani, Script. rer.
Merov.* IV, 1902, 21. No doubt Maelduib laid the foundation of Ald-
helm's knowledge of Vergil; cf. Laistner, *Thought and Letters*, 121. For
Muirchu's knowledge of classical literature see Roger, 259.

[61] Roger, 227, 259; Manitius, *Gesch.*, 11; Kenney, 217; cf. Jones,
ODT 78ff.

the literary mosaics put together by these sophisticated men of culture are still to be seen and have been interpreted by modern study; they bear in general the name *Hisperica Famina*, "Western Sayings," and evidence points to Ireland as the land of their birth, an Ireland fostered by the learning of scholars from Gaul and Spain and Britain.[62] Into the maze of their composition were woven wòrds Greek and Hebrew, words of no known derivation, words of far-fetched meaning, words assigned a meaning entirely different from that usually given them, words of native body, adorned with foreign head or tail, technical words derived from Church and monastic usage, poetical expressions, sitting uneasily side by side with words of common and everyday chatter.

This cult apparently flourished not only in Ireland but in Britain and in continental Europe; traces of its fellowship are seen in British and European writings still extant. The British Gildas, who knew well the region round about Maelduib's monastery, seems to bear this mark in his *Lament* over his country's ruin and in the litany of the *Breastplate,* if that indeed be his.[63] So do the *Altus Prosator,* a hymn said to have been written in Iona by the Irish Columba; the letters of the Irish Columban, written in Gaul; and certain poems still conned by students in the Library of the University of Cambridge: the *Rubisca,* religious in character, probably written by an Irishman; the *St. Omer Hymn,* following the alphabet in its rhyming lines; the verses on the life of Christ composed by Juvencus, a priest of Spain.[64]

Akin to these last gropings after poetry were the *Verses of a certain Irishman on the Alphabet,* devised perhaps in Ireland

---

[62] F. Jenkinson, *The Hisperica Famina,* 1908; Kenney, 255ff.; Roger, 238ff.

[63] *ILH* II, 242f.; Manitius, *Gesch.,* 159.

[64] E. K. Rand, "The Irish flavor of Hisperica Famina" (*Stud. zur lat. Dicht. d. Mittelalters, Ehrengabe f. Karl Strecker*), 1931, 134ff.; Kenney, 255ff. For Aldhelm's own borrowing of words from glossaries see W. M. Lindsay, *The Corpus, Épinal, Erfurt and Leyden Glossaries,* 1921, 97f.

in Maelduib's seventh century. Herein we may see the influence of Sedulius, the fifth-century poet, probably of Italy, whose *Carmen Paschale* was read far and wide in the Middle Ages and was honoured in a paraphrase attributed to an Irish admirer. One of the minor poems of Sedulius, still sung in parts by the Church in our days, follows the alphabet, each strophe beginning with one of its letters.[65]

Finally, did the monks of Ireland's seventh century know Greek? The question has been widely debated, and interesting possibilities have been pointed out. So far, however, as Maelduib and his school are concerned, we should be very unwise to imagine any greater attainment than the memory of some few scattered Greek words, such as are found in the *Antiphonary of Bangor* and in the verses attributed to Columba: words found in lists or glossaries, explained by the equivalent term in Latin or Irish.[66]

From Maelduib's memories, then, augmented by passing pilgrims who had studied in Ireland or in Britain, his students drew what they could. They learned of the Bible and of patristic interpretation; of the Saints, their lives and legends. They learned Latin laboriously, as the Irish did, finding it hard that so much of their spiritual training should come to them in foreign dress; they delighted, some of them, in those strange-sounding words, now of Greek or Hebrew tongue, now of Celtic origin, stored away in Maelduib's mind. They learned from him to discuss with some ingenuity what they read, for the Irish always loved dialectic. They learned to write; now and again one of them might be seen painfully trying to copy a text written in the formal rounded half-uncial, which Irish scribes of the sixth century had imitated

[65] Kenney, 275, 281; Baehrens, *PLM* V, 375ff.; Huemer, ed. Sedulius, *CSEL* X, 1885.

[66] See on this question M. R. James, *CMH* III, 502ff.; Roger, 268ff.; Manitius, *Gesch.*, 11; G. T. Stokes, *PRIA*, 3rd series, II (1891–1893), 187ff.

from Roman models brought to Ireland by missionaries and refugees.[67] They learned, too, to say, or roughly to chant with some attempt at accent and rhythm, the psalms and hymns of the Church, and became familiar with her solemn prayers and benedictions. Monastic life now for the first time opened out its fascination before them: the joy and sorrow of the Church's seasons in progressive order. This very order and solemn seemliness of procedure, the alternating round of observance which called into its service body, mind, and spirit, must have held some of them willingly in bond. And, therefore, little by little the forest which once had held a solitary monk's cell saw growing in its shadow a monastery, to which Maelduib as abbot received for permanent allegiance those who felt themselves well and truly called to the obedience of the threefold vow.

Of such was Aldhelm. As time went on, the thought of his noble House of Wessex, its councils of wise men, its battles of warriors, slowly faded before his rising delight in prescription of prayer, of penance and of study, entwined into one fruitful oblation of all his powers. We may think that in his early twenties—tradition says the year 661—he received from Maelduib the monastic tonsure and entered upon a career which in these early days of religious enthusiasm drew to the cloister so many of noble blood, men and women, in Anglo-Saxon England.[68] There, in the forest of Selwood for some ten more years, until 671, we may imagine him continuing to learn things sacred and secular.

The world outside the forest during this time was not standing still. When Aldhelm entered Maelduib's school, about 654, Penda of Mercia was still revelling in heathen conquest of

---

[67] Lowe, *CLA* II, xff.; E. Maunde Thompson, *Introduction to Greek and Latin Paleography*, 1912, 371ff.
[68] See p. 40 *infra*, note 101.

Christian kings, still thirsting for new domination. This he
had sought to gain in attacking Oswy, now king of Northumbria. Were Oswy once slain, Penda might expect to see
all England subject to his power.

Providence disposed otherwise, and in the battle that followed Penda was defeated and killed near the Yorkshire
river Winwaed, unknown in present times. For three years,
from this date of 655, Oswy held supremacy in England. To
his governing of Northumbria he added control of Mercia,
the lands watered by the river Trent in the modern shires of
Nottingham and Leicester. His rule, however, savoured to the
nobles of Mercia of a foreign tyranny, and three of them drove
him from their land in 658, to place upon its throne Wulfhere,
a young son of Penda, whom they had been guarding secretly
against the day of revolt.

It was this Wulfhere of Mercia who in 661, the year of
Aldhelm's tonsuring, caused the turning of the tide of prosperity for Cenwalh of Wessex. He ravaged and laid waste
Cenwalh's lands as far as Ashdown, the low range of chalk
hills in Berkshire; somewhere about the same time he took
from him the Isle of Wight, possessed by Wessex for thirty
years, and handed it over to his own godson, Ethelwalh, king
of the South Saxons.[69] As years went on, Wulfhere gradually
gained chief power in England and caused the fear of his
name to dwell among the "southern nations," including the
West Saxons of Cenwalh's kingdom.[70]

Such reverse was in itself bitter, and Cenwalh had by no
means attained to Christian meekness of heart. Naturally, he
sought an outlet for his temper, and he found it in his bishop,
Agilbert, the partner once so enthusiastically called to work
with him. The cause of his irritation need not surprise us;

[69] R. Hodgkin, 285f., 313; Earle and Plummer I, *ann.* 661; II, 23;
Plummer II, 225; *HE* III, c. 24; IV, c. 13.
[70] Eddius, c. 20; Stenton, 84f.

the king knew only his own Saxon tongue, and in his more serious worries and trials he found it harder and harder to listen to Agilbert's fluent Frankish talk. Like so many others, before and after him, he called this speech he could not follow "a jargon of barbarisms."

At last, about 663, his rising impatience broke such barriers as it had; layman though he was, he secretly invited into his province another bishop, called Wini.[71] Wini, like Agilbert, had received consecration in Gaul; but he did speak decent Saxon. Next, also on his own initiative, the king proceeded to divide his realm into two separate dioceses. Agilbert, bishop of Dorchester-on-Thames, was no longer to hold all Wessex under his jurisdiction; part of it was to pass into the care of Wini, as bishop of Winchester. Tradition has therefore seen in Cenwalh the founder of this great English see.[72] The indignation of Agilbert at this insult to Holy Church and to himself, her prelate, was as great as his astonishment. He promptly left Wessex and retired to Northumbria, where we shall find him an honoured guest early in 664; subsequently, either in this year or shortly afterward, he returned to Gaul, where he was eventually elected bishop of Paris.

This left the see of Dorchester without a bishop and left Wessex under the spiritual oversight of Wini alone, ruling from Winchester. But Cenwalh carried his independence of the Church's authority even further. A few years later, very probably in 666, he dismissed Wini, also, from his bishopric, for some reason unknown to us. The place of refuge this time might be foreseen. Wini fled to Cenwalh's overlord, Wulfhere of Mercia, and, to the horror of the historian Bede, "bought for a sum of money from him the see of London and held it till death." The simony which Gregory the Great had

[71] *HE* III, c. 7; Plummer II, 41, 146.
[72] Plummer II, 143; *ASC ann.* 643; Earle and Plummer II, 22; *CMH* II, 552.

so sternly censured among prelates of Gaul had evidently spread its poison in Britain.[73] Moreover, the secular daring of Wulfhere in disposing of London's bishopric corresponded to the high-handed acts of Cenwalh. The province of Wessex was now without any chief Pastor and remained so for about four years.

With no bishops and with a king of uncertain temper, the West Saxons, like the Israelites of old, suffered comfortless the yoke of oppression year after year. Then bitterness again worked for good in Cenwalh, and a second time he repented of his evil deeds. Conversion to Christianity, he called to mind, had brought him back from exile to his throne; perhaps a second change of heart would induce the Lord to give him back his bishop. Thus his land, again properly shepherded, would surely taste once more of victory. Envoys were despatched to Gaul, bearing humble apology from the king to Agilbert, with, of course, the invitation that he return forthwith to his empty seat at Dorchester.

They travelled in vain. Agilbert was now established on the continent; his own work needed all his care; he regretted he could not come. As the king, however, was so distressed, he would suggest a substitute: his own nephew Leutherius—in the Saxon tongue, Hlothere—a young man, but well worthy of the office of bishop. The king's counsellors, clergy and lay, met in solemn assembly; Hlothere was duly approved, and a petition was sent to the Archbishop of Canterbury that he be consecrated bishop of Wessex, holding his seat at Winchester. So it was done in that same city, and here Hlothere administered rule from 670 to 676; Dorchester after the departure of Agilbert was never again accounted a West Saxon see.[74]

[73] Bright, 247f.
[74] Plummer II, 144ff., 245ff.; cf. Stenton, 134f.

The Archbishop who laid hands on Hlothere in Canterbury is of high importance for this story of Aldhelm, the more so, as his coming was due to a providential course of the un-expected. Honorius, who had held the see of Canterbury while Birinus was converting the West Saxons, and Felix the people of East Anglia, had been succeeded in his office after some interval by its first Saxon holder, Frithonas by name. Frithonas is himself of interest here, as he was a native of Wessex, where Birinus had ministered and where Cenwalh had appointed and dismissed bishops, both in independence of the Metropolitan of Canterbury. Evidently, in spite of this, Wessex stood well with the spiritual and lay authorities in Kent. As an act of reverence toward the Church of Rome, to which he looked for guidance, Frithonas adopted the name of Deusdedit and as such did his best to guide the English Church till 664.[75]

This and the following years saw the Great Plague devastate England and continental Europe; the next nominee for Canterbury, Wighard, a priest of Saxon birth and much knowledge of canon law, was caught in its clutches and died in Rome on the eve of his consecration.

The Pope at the time was Vitalian, and he began at once to search throughout Italy for a candidate whom he might send with confidence to govern this difficult English Church. Before long an excellent monk was discovered and brought to Rome, sorely against his will: Hadrian, born in Roman Africa, but now abbot of the monastery of Niridan near Naples.[76] He was learned in Greek and Latin sacred literature and was an expert in Church law, ecclesiastical and monastic. He possessed, moreover, both humility and a ready mind; respect-

---

[75] Elmham, 192f.; *HE* IV, c. 1. 664 is the date usually given: Searle, 3; Bright, 237; *DCB* I, 822. But *cf. HE* III, c. 20; H.S. III, 99; Stenton, 129.
[76] *Cf.* R. L. Poole, "Monasterium Niridanum": *EHR* XXXVI, 1921, 540ff.

fully he suggested to the Pope another name, that of a man better fitted in years and in talents for so exalted a position. Unhappily, however, for Hadrian, his nominee, a monk called Andrew, although declared by everyone exactly the right person for the choice, was altogether too frail in body to deal with barbarian Celts and Saxons. The abbot of Niridan again found himself facing in terror an honour which he could not refuse.

He begged for a few days of reprieve, and again Providence was gracious. As he was searching in an ever growing anxiety through the churches and monasteries of Rome for some willing and competent soul, he fell upon a holy man who, most fortunately, happened to be on pilgrimage at this moment: a friend of his, suitable in every respect. His name was Theodore, corresponding in Greek to the Latin Deusdedit; he had been born at Tarsus in Cilicia, like the Apostle Paul; the land of his birth had given him the Greek tongue, and he was now widely read in books sacred and secular, Greek and Latin; his reputation for virtue, for discipline tempered with mercy, was as great as his fame for scholarship; he was of a reverend age, but not too old: sixty-six years, in fact.

We can imagine Hadrian carrying off this prize to the Pope's audience. His prayer was granted; Theodore should be Archbishop of Canterbury. At the same time, it had to be remembered that Theodore was a Greek, and Popes of Rome had suffered much through the theological erring and straying of the Greek Constantinople and its Emperor. Let Hadrian, therefore, also leave his monastery; let him escort Theodore to Britain, as one more experienced in travelling and better equipped for the journey; once there, let him stay constantly by Theodore's side to aid the Archbishop in his work, "zealously watching lest Theodore after the manner of the Greeks introduce anything contrary to the true faith into the Church which he is to rule."

The Archbishop-elect, although a monk, was but a layman. He was, therefore, now ordained to the office of subdeacon, which the Church of Rome held as within the requisite degree of the sacred ministry for candidacy such as his. Another difficulty then arose. The Greek monastic tonsure, eager to reverence Saint Paul, required the head to be completely shaven; the Roman Church prescribed for its monks that only the top of the head be shorn and that the hair remain around this bald centre in form of a crown. Theodore was obliged to wait four months in Rome until his hair might grow; it is interesting to read that it would and promptly did! [77]

He was finally consecrated by Vitalian as chief bishop for the English in March, 668, and set out in the company of Hadrian. The see of Canterbury had now been vacant nearly four years. Further delay met the two on their journey, through formalities of passport in Gaul, through visits of courtesy, through rigours of winter, through sickness. In May, 669, Theodore reached Canterbury alone; Hadrian was detained by the hostility of one Ebroin, who under the title of "Mayor of the Palace" was governing Neustria and Burgundy in the name of the Frankish king. At last he, too, arrived, probably the next year, and did his best to aid Theodore while awaiting the call to his own special task among the English. In 671 it came, and he was appointed head of Canterbury's monastery and school of Saint Peter and Saint Paul.[78]

This is not the place to describe the noble work of spiritual organization and discipline which Theodore wrought for England: "the first among Archbishops to whom the whole Church of the English willingly gave obedience." [79] Our con-

---

[77] *HE* IV, c. 1; Bright, 252ff.
[78] He succeeded Benedict Biscop; see Plummer II, 204 and p. 219 *infra.*
[79] *HE* IV, c. 2.

cern here is with his equally magnificent furthering of spiritual and secular education which was to mean so much to Aldhelm. Augustine, "apostle of the English," had sown the seed; [80] his successors had done little save to keep alive his work. But now, from that monastic school which he had founded, concerned almost entirely up to this time with such learning and study as could be held of direct importance for monks and clergy, there grew up a centre of erudition which attracted to its lectures and conferences students flocking in crowds from Britain, from Ireland, from continental Europe. Its development and manner of working were entrusted to Hadrian; Theodore shared in its teaching and watched over its growth with keen approval.

Here secular study was held in regard, as the invaluable handmaid of spiritual wisdom. Professors and students alike without scruple read eagerly in the writings of classical Greece and Rome that they might better interpret and understand doctrine for the soul. Thus Saxon Canterbury departed somewhat from the restricting influence of Gregory the Great,[81] to whom she owed her soul's enlightenment, and followed in this respect other influence from Catholic tradition: of Augustine of Hippo and Jerome of Bethlehem, who in the fifth century had loved pagan reading despite their terror of its poison, steeped in charm; of Cassiodorus, who had carefully separated for his monks in sixth-century Italy the sound grain of instruction from the wind-blown chaff.

News of this higher learning was carried from mouth to mouth throughout England and reached in course of time Maelduib's monastery in Wessex. Aldhelm by now had learned

[80] *Cf.* P. F. Jones, "The Gregorian Mission and English Education," *Speculum* III, 1928, 335ff.

[81] Gregory the Great, an intellectual himself, had to fight against evil and pagan influences: *cf.* Laistner, *History* XX, 1935, 49ff.

what his master could give him of Irish art and science. Already he was striving to realize in himself the student and the
monk; he was longing to reach out to wider fields, in the inspiration of scholarship hallowed and guided by the Church.
This new chance was too good to be missed. The year 671
saw him in Canterbury, a man in his early thirties, absorbing
fresh realities of knowledge hitherto caught only in dreams.[82]

Here once again he listened to teachers, explaining more
closely, more deeply, the mysteries of Holy Scripture, now
drawing from it lessons of spiritual and ethical import, now
building step by step mystic interpretation of metaphor and
symbol. He studied Greek and Latin grammar till he could
read for himself the writings of the Fathers of the Church in
East and West: sermons, allegorical commentaries, explanations of holy texts.[83] Hadrian, compatriot of Augustine of
Hippo, surely knew well the rhetorical art of the *Confessions*
and the *City of God*. The schools of Africa delighted in such,
as did students from Ireland and Gaul. Under expert guidance
Aldhelm also learned to unravel the tapestries of words, brilliant in Hisperic colouring, interlocked in intricate construction, adorned with figures of speech innumerable. He examined
in all their complexity the rules of classical metric; he read
secular authors of Latin classical days.[84] He tried his own
hand at composing: first, in simple forms of prose and verse,

[82] The description *pusio* (*Gest. Pont.* 333) is wrongly inferred from
Aldhelm's words in his letter to Hadrian, *ibid.*, 334: *reverendissimo patri
meaeque rudis infantiae venerando praeceptori*—which refer to spiritual
immaturity: Ehwald, x.

[83] The statement (Fabricius, *Vita Aldh.* ed. Giles, *PEA* I, 357) that
Aldhelm read Hebrew is without support and is probably based on his
borrowing of words from glossaries. His knowledge of Greek seems to
have been elementary; in later days he drew his references to Greek works
from Latin versions: Ehwald, xiif.; James, *CHEL* I, 80, 85.

[84] Especially Vergil, Lucan, Juvenal, and many quotations from other
writers contained in the works of grammarians, as Donatus, Audax, Priscian, etc. See J. D. A. Ogilvy, *Books known to Anglo-Latin Writers from
Aldhelm to Alcuin* (670–804), *MAA*, 1936.

then, in literary designs traced in fantastic shape upon the page; in riddles veiling the things of common usage; in figures of speech created by his imagination. And ever and always he was steeping his mind in the lives of saints and martyrs, in rhythmic hymns and litanies and liturgies.

To the subjects of the medieval *trivium*—grammar, rhetoric and dialectic—was added in his training the fourfold course of the *quadrivium*: arithmetic, geometry, astronomy and music. Arithmetic enabled calculation of the Church's fasts and festivals; astronomy taught of the stars which guided the Church's calendar; both were essential for the understanding of the difference between the Roman and the Celtic computation of the Easter date. Music had constantly been studied in the Choir School of Canterbury since Augustine and his missionaries had brought instruction in chanting from the Rome of Gregory the Great; in Theodore's time the singing of psalms and hymns in churches became generally known and practised throughout England.[85]

Text-books for the principles of the seven liberal arts were found in the encyclopaedic manual of Martianus Capella, who had composed in Africa of the fifth century his famous *Marriage of Mercury and Philology*;[86] also in the monumental work of twenty volumes known as the *Etymologies* or *Origins,* composed in the earlier part of the seventh century by Isidore, bishop of Seville in Spain.[87] From these pages the student also gathered a medley of the world's knowledge on various subjects other than those strictly belonging to the seven arts: religious, political and natural history; geography; the care of land, buildings, clothing, food, furniture; explanations of terms and titles of all kinds; elementary teaching on

[85] *HE* IV, c. 2; Knowles, 547.
[86] Ed. Dick, 1925. See Laistner, *Thought and Letters*, 22f.
[87] Ed. W. M. Lindsay, 1911; *cf.* Laistner, *ibid.*, 92ff.; Manitius, *Gesch.,* 6off.

law and medicine. Theodore himself, as it chanced, had made a particular study of medical science and must have trained his students in "first-aid" classes as a most valuable help for their pastoral ministry.[88] Practical matters—the cure of bodies as well as of souls, skill in organization, details of monastic rule and discipline, fundamentals of Roman law as illustrating the canons of the Church—undoubtedly formed an important part of the training of ordinands under Abbot Hadrian.

Above all, the scholar's day at Canterbury was marked by observance of the monastic Hours of prayer. Theodore and Hadrian were already well acquainted with the Benedictine Rule; and it had also been brought to England long before from Rome by Augustine. The English, therefore, at the end of the sixth century had begun to learn Benedictine living; during the seventh this Rule gradually spread throughout England and became general in Gaul, superseding there the less reasonable or less adaptable constitutions of Columban of Luxeuil and of Caesarius of Arles; in the eighth it was to be known and practised in Germany.

Yet in Aldhelm's time we may by no means think of the Benedictine, or of any code, as uniform throughout the many English monasteries. As on the continent at this time, individual Rules prevailed in England in individual cloisters, assembled from many different places and congregations of Italy and of Gaul. Not even Canterbury is to be regarded as being wholly Benedictine in its usage when Aldhelm was learning there.[89]

We know the names of some other students of its school. One was John, who long afterward was glad he could remember what he had learned of medicine there, as he bent over the bed of a desperately sick nun in Yorkshire: "You have done very foolishly and ignorantly in letting her blood on

[88] *HE* V, c. 3. [89] Knowles, 21f.; Hauck I, 308ff.

the fourth of the moon. For I remember Archbishop Theodore
of blessed memory telling how dangerous is bloodletting when
the moon is waxing full and the sea is flowing to high tide." [90]
Theodore also taught John theology,[91] which stood him in
good stead when in 687 he was appointed bishop of Hexham
in the north of England and later was translated to the see
of York. He was a great prelate. But it is as simple John of
Beverley that he holds his place in the calendar of saints, so
named from the monastery which he founded near Hexham.
There he would retire as often as his duties allowed him, to
study in peace and to say the Hours with a few companions
in its oratory of Saint Michael the Archangel.[92]

Another was Oftfor, who also had come from Yorkshire,
well versed in Holy Scripture under Celtic tradition, until,
"eager for things more perfect," he had sought out Theodore
at Canterbury. Then he went on pilgrimage to Rome and at
last was consecrated bishop of the Hwicce, the people around
Worcester, where he held his cathedral seat.[93] Of a third,
Tobias, consecrated some time after 696 as bishop of Rochester,
it was said that he was as familiar with Greek and Latin as
his own Saxon tongue.[94] The same was declared of Albinus,
another of those who laid, under Theodore and Hadrian, the
foundation of future greatness. About 709 he succeeded
Hadrian as abbot of the monastery of Saint Peter and Saint
Paul at Canterbury, "first of the Saxon race to be chosen for
this office." [95]

Thus learning began and prospered for Aldhelm under
Hadrian. For a brief while he returned to Wiltshire, no doubt

---

[90] *HE ibid.;* Payne, 13ff.
[91] Raine, *HY* I, 244; Bright, 399.
[92] *HE* V, cc. 2ff.
[93] IV, c. 23.
[94] V, cc. 8 and 23; Plummer II, 284; Bright, 429.
[95] V, c. 20; Elmham, 294; Plummer II, 2. For Ceolfrid, another
student at Canterbury, afterward abbot of Jarrow, see p. 221 *infra.*

to report to Maelduib on his progress; very possibly it was then that he was ordained deacon by his diocesan bishop, Hlothere of Winchester. Shortly afterward we find him back again at Canterbury for another term of study. During this second stay, probably in December, 671, he wrote to this same bishop a letter which we still possess.[96] It is a cry of despair: so many things still to be learned, hurtling around the student's head; so little time for learning them. He would so gladly have spent Christmas with his brother monks in Wiltshire; he had so longed to talk with his kindly bishop. But time, he complains, flies so fast, filled with so many studies, as the bearer of the letter will describe. There are the baffling pronouncements of Roman law;[97] there is literature, prose and verse, especially verse, with a hundred different kinds of metre; there is music with its melodies and with words and syllables to fit harmoniously to their measures; there is arithmetic applied in long calculations, producing endless problems; there are the mysteries of the heavens, of the zodiac, of the stars and their meaning to the world of today. Alas! Aldhelm confesses, once I thought I knew something, after all my past toil; but so much more remains to learn that there is not even time to write about it.

Time, indeed, was lacking, for in 672 he was forced by sickness to return to Maelduib. Probably he had worked his mind too hard and cared for his body too little; we read that he obeyed the Irish tradition not only in study, but in the strictest rule of fasting and prayer.[98] Three years afterward, in 675, he wrote to his "most dear and most reverend father Hadrian" that he had ever longed to return to Canterbury

[96] Ehwald, 475ff.; *Gest. Pont.* 341f. (the name Hedda is an error). See also Bönhoff, 49f.; he dates the letter December, 672.
[97] A. S. Cook, "Aldhelm's Legal Studies," *JEGP* XXIII, 1924, 105ff.
[98] *Gest. Pont.* 357. *Cf.* the Anglo-Saxon poem written in praise of Aldhelm, probably at Canterbury: *The Anglo-Saxon Minor Poems,* ed. E. V. K. Dobbie, 1942, xcff., 97f.

since he had had to leave it. But ill-health and "divers other hindrances" had kept him in Wiltshire.[99]

Maelduib was now growing old, and more and more the monks of his monastery were looking to the gifted and travelled Aldhelm for guidance and support. The sacrifice of further study under Hadrian, of the companionship of learners from many different countries, must have cost the young scholar much. No doubt at times, even at Canterbury, he had yearned in curiosity, as Jerome before him, to wander along roads to secular knowledge. But now more and more he was feeling himself called to a life dedicated under monastic rule, and, within this, to the pursuing of sacred truth for the cause of his fellow-men. This thought of his mind is shown in a letter sent, whether during his terms in Canterbury or after his return to Wiltshire, to a Saxon friend named Wihtfrid.[100] Wihtfrid was attracted by Irish learning, which had called so many Saxons from England to Ireland before the fame of Theodore and Hadrian sent the Irish travelling on the opposite way. "Rumour has reached me," Aldhelm writes, "that you are going to study across the sea in Ireland. I pray you, study that you may refute the lies of pagan poetry. How foolish to stray through the tangled and winding bypaths of these legends, to turn from the pure waters of Holy Scripture that you may quench your thirst in muddy pools, swarming with a myriad of black toads, noisy with the guttural bark of frogs! What, think you, does it profit a true believer to inquire busily into the foul love of Proserpina, to peer with curious eyes into things of which it is not even meet to speak —to desire to learn of Hermione and her various betroth-

[99] Ehwald, 478; *Gest. Pont.* 335.
[100] Ehwald, 479f.; from the description of Aldhelm as *vernaculus* we may think it was written before he became abbot. *Cf. Gest. Pont.* 358f., and, for a fragment of another letter from a Withfrid (Wihtfrid), *ibid.*, 332.

als, to write in epic style the ritual of Priapus and the
Luperci?

"Beware, my son, of evil women and their loves in legend;
beware of them, too, in life: of prostitutes lying in wait within
dark houses, insolently decked out in golden anklets and arm-
lets, like magistrates in the official trappings of State.

"Surely it befits you, as a true disciple of Christ, to scorn
all such pride and luxury. True, the cold blasts of Irish
northerly winds call for warm clothing; but let it be of plain
wool or hide, not dyed in costly purple!"

Some time before 675 Aldhelm was ordained priest by
Hlothere. It was probably in this year that Maelduib died and
that he was elected abbot of the monastic settlement,[101] known
at this time as the "enclosure of Maelduib"—"Mailduib-
byrig"—and in Latin "civitas Maldubia." Gradually, however, the name of Aldhelm replaced that of Maelduib, and
we find instead in common use "Ealdelmesburg"—"borough
of Aldhelm." Finally, it would seem, the two forms were
mixed, and the modern name of Malmesbury came into use.[102]

Here from about the age of thirty-six Aldhelm ruled for
thirty years, in a life that was filled with many calls to work,
within and without his monastery. At the centre of all stood
his own practice of prayer and study; as he told of himself,
"when I read I listen to God speaking, when I pray I speak
to God." Fasting subdued such desire for comfort as could
still make itself felt. In the twelfth century the monks of
Malmesbury still pointed out to pilgrims Saint Aldhelm's
spring of water in the valley hard by their walls. He would
plunge into this, so tradition told, and remain immersed to the

[101] *Ibid.*, 347, 385; *Eulogium* I, lxix. Tradition stated that Maelduib
lived 14 years after the tonsuring of Aldhelm, which would date the
tonsuring in 661: Bönhoff, 25ff.; 44, note 7; Ehwald, xiii; Manitius,
Gesch., 135; Giles, *PEA* I, 339.
[102] Plummer II, 310f.; Gover, 47f.

neck, night after night, careless of the winter's frost or of the mist rising in summer from the forest marshes, while he recited the Psalter for his soul's victory. The same eagerness to resist by conquering rather than by shunning temptation was told of him in regard to that terror of the Fathers of the Church, the feminine sex.[103] Like Jerome, he preferred to mock Satan by trusting that the Lord who was calling him to holy conversation and prayer could also free the spirit of women from untimely lusts of the flesh.

For his monastery he desired all things orderly and meet for worship. The little chapel, built by Maelduib, was replaced under him by a noble church, dedicated to the Lord Saviour and to Saints Peter and Paul, patrons of Malmesbury from its beginning. In honour of its consecration Aldhelm wrote a poem of twenty-one hexameters, probably the earliest verses still extant of his composing.[104] To these same days that followed his installing as abbot may possibly belong a "privilege" from his bishop Hlothere, granting in permanent tenure to Aldhelm and his monks the land on which the monastery stood.[105]

There was thought, also, for the people of the village of Malmesbury which had grown up outside the monastery walls. Aldhelm's care for their souls has given us a happy picture in his life, told in one of those passages of instruction and comfort gathered by King Alfred the Great and written down by him in his *Handbook*. The king declares here that Aldhelm was marvellously able to write or chant or sing verses in his native Anglo-Saxon. These were the fruit of his

---

[103] *Gest. Pont.* 357ff.
[104] *Ibid.,* 345; Ehwald, 5; 11f. He dates the poem shortly after 675.
[105] H. S. III, 124, Kemble I, No. xi, Birch, No. 37, Bright, 295, note 4, A. S. Cook, "A Putative Charter to Aldhelm," *Studies in Eng. Philology in honor of Frederick Klaeber,* 1929, 254ff., hold the charter spurious, in whole or in part; for the contrary view see Ehwald, 507ff., Bönhoff, 60, Hahn, 84.

study in Canterbury, and he put them to a practical use. The country folk who lived around Malmesbury in the seventh century were rough and uncultivated people; they could be drawn to the Monastery Church to hear sung Mass, but directly this was over they hurried homewards without waiting for the sermon. To combat this perilous tendency Aldhelm used to stand on the bridge over the Avon, where they must pass to reach their farmlands, and sing merry songs till he had gathered a crowd. Then he would change his gay airs for psalms; little by little the words of his chanting would win those who heard them to a better mood; and they would decide to stay for the sermon in the future. As the story ends, "if he had attempted to use stern measures of Church discipline, he would have done no good at all." In the twelfth century some of this verse of Aldhelm was still to be heard in song.[106]

Beyond Malmesbury he was known far and wide through his kinship with the royal House of Wessex. We last saw this realm of King Cenwalh overshadowed by the supremacy of Wulfhere of Mercia. So it continued until Wulfhere's death in 675, when he was succeeded on the throne of Mercia by his brother Ethelred. One of Ethelred's nobles, Cenfrid, is said to have given to the monks of Malmesbury in 680 some land at Wootton in Wiltshire, and we may believe he did, although the charter of his gift as we have it may not be genuine. Cenfrid was related by birth to his king, and tradition states that Ethelred himself was moved at his petitioning to make in 681 his own gift to the monks, of land at Long Newton in Wiltshire and at Tetbury in Gloucestershire, "for the healing of his soul and for the prayers of the brethren,"

---

[106] *Gest. Pont.* 336; Faricius, ed. Giles, *PEA* I, 359ff. For other lost writings of Aldhelm—sermons, poems, letters—see Ehwald, xvii.

and that four years later Bertwald, a nephew of Ethelred, in the same desire of penitence and intercession, added to the monastery's estate land at Somerford Keynes in Wilts.[107]

In the meantime Cenwalh of Wessex had died—in 672—leaving the reins of government to the hands of a woman, probably the lady he had taken as wife after divorcing the sister of King Penda of the Mercians. Her name was Sexburga, and she apparently administered her realm with great efficiency. "She raised new armies, held those already enrolled faithful to duty, ruled her subjects mildly, threatened her enemies in rage. In fact, she differed from kings of her day in nothing but her sex, and so died, breathing out more than a woman's spirit, barely a year after she had ascended the throne." [108] After her, Aescwine, son of Cenfus, is said to have governed Wessex from 674 to 676, and then Centwine, son of Cynegils, who gradually assumed high sovereignty and "drove the British to the sea." [109]

The year 676, that claims the accession of Centwine in Wessex, saw the death of its bishop Hlothere; and Archbishop Theodore consecrated in London one Haeddi to succeed him in the see of Winchester.[110] Haeddi was Aldhelm's bishop for nearly thirty years; it was he who brought the relics of Birinus, Apostle of Wessex, from Dorchester for permanent burial in the cathedral of Saints Peter and Paul at Winchester, as being the one and only cathedral city of the West Saxons. Miracles were ascribed to the virtue of Haeddi after his death; while

[107] See *Gest. Pont.* 349ff.; Kemble I, Nos. xxiif., xxvi; Birch, Nos. 54, 58f., 65; Stenton, 68, 151; Ehwald, 509f.; Bönhoff, 61ff.; Bright, 295, note 6.
[108] *Gest. Reg.* I, 32; Stubbs, *DCB* IV, 642.
[109] *ASC ann.* 672, 674, 676, 682. Bede (*HE* IV, c. 12) tells that after Cenwalh's death "under-kings" held Wessex in divided rule for ten years. For the difference in narratives see Stenton, 67f.; Plummer II, 221.
[110] *ASC ann.* 676; *HE ibid.;* Flor. Worc. *ann.* 676.

he still lived on this earth, he was held rather a lover of prayer and charity than of intellectual scholarship.[111]

While, then, Haeddi was administering Wessex in spiritual rule, another distant cousin of its royal family, Caedwalla by name, "began to contend for its kingdom." [112] In the conflict of Wessex chieftains he had been at one time driven into exile in the lonely regions of Chiltern and the Weald, where very many of the young Wessex warriors joined him, moved either by sympathy in his banishment or by admiration for the spirit of a man "of boundless ambition, who lost no opportunity of proving his courage." Thus emboldened from within and without, he first fell upon Ethelwalh, king of the South Saxons, killed him, and harried his land up and down, until two nobles of Sussex, Berthun and Andhun, at last drove the invader out and took the rule of their people upon themselves. Then he marched back with his adherents into Wessex, overcame Centwine and took by force the crown. It was the year 685–686.[113]

One of Caedwalla's first acts as king of Wessex was the seizure from the South Saxons of the Isle of Wight, where he conceived the horrible design of massacring all the Jutish inhabitants and replacing them by men of Saxon blood. Moreover, he led another raid into Sussex, bent upon revenge, and this time slew his former victor, Berthun, and ravaged the country far more grievously than before. Henceforth Sussex looked for her orders to this king of the West Saxons, and Wessex again raised her head in pride among the realms of England.[114]

For two years Caedwalla ruled with busy zeal. Then suddenly, pricked into action by the teaching of the Christian faith, his conscience arrested him in mid-career. Soon his fear

[111] *HE* V, c. 18; III, c. 7; Stubbs, *DCB* II, 873f.
[112] *ASC ann.* 685.
[113] *Gest. Reg.* I, 32f.; *Gest. Pont.* 233; *HE* IV, c. 15; Eddius, c. 42.
[114] *HE* IV, cc. 15f.

for his past life filled him with so deep foreboding for his future that he left his kingdom and travelled to Rome; here in 689 he was baptized, by the hand of Pope Sergius, we are told, and died immediately afterward, at the youthful age of thirty. The Church erased from memory his deeds of wrath and bestowed upon him a magnificent epitaph in honour of his forsaking of sin and of the world in which he had sinned. A doubtful tradition connects his name with Malmesbury, and hence with Aldhelm, for he is said to have given to the abbey land in Wiltshire on either side of Kemble Wood, at Charlton and at Purton, where the brethren might catch abundance of fish.[115] Caedwalla's deserted throne passed in 688 to another of his blood, Ine, descended from a brother of King Cynegils. Ine's governing of Wessex was to last until 725. When he, too, left his kingdom for a cloister in Rome, Aldhelm had already departed this earthly life some seventeen years.[116]

The name of Ine as ruler of Wessex is famous in threefold tradition. He extended its dominion and prestige by victories far and wide, in Kent, in West Wales, in Sussex, in Somerset, in Devon. Under his direction its *Witanagemot*, "assembly of wise men," issued a Book of Laws, for the ruling of its own Saxon people and its conquered British subjects alike.[117] Finally, he was a benefactor of its church and clergy. Record states against the year 688 that "he built the minster at Glastonbury"; in reality, he honoured by new and fair building this place of prayer, already long hallowed by its shrine in British and in Saxon days.[118]

[115] *Ibid.*, V, c. 7. Kemble (I, No. xxix) marks the charter spurious; Birch, Nos. 63, 70. See *Gest. Pont.* V, 352f. For the epitaph see Raby, *SLP* I, 159. Aldhelm himself told of Caedwalla's baptism and death: Ehwald, 15.

[116] 726 or 725: *HE* V, c. 7; Plummer II, 281. The MSS of *ASC* give the date variously as 728 or 726; Earle and Plummer I, 42f.; II, 39. *Cf. Gest. Pont.* 332; *Gest. Reg.* I, 34ff.

[117] F. L. Attenborough, *The Laws of the Earliest English Kings*, 1922, 36ff.

[118] Earle and Plummer II, 32f.; Bright, 473, 500; Clark H. Slover, *Speculum* X, 1935, 157ff.

We may well imagine Aldhelm as present about 690 in that *Witanagemot* of Wessex which deliberated and gave out laws for the realm. We do not know where the gathering met. King Ine himself presided, and near him, for his aid in counsel, sat two bishops: Haeddi of Wessex, and Earconwald, bishop of London and of the East Saxons, who were, it seems, under the lordship of Wessex at this time. Beyond and around these chief seats were arrayed all in the kingdom who were noble in blood, in learning and in intellect, in understanding of law, secular, ecclesiastic and monastic, in holiness of life within church and cloister. Aldhelm must have listened for days as one after another rose to debate "of the health of our souls and of the stability of our state; so that just law and kingly dooms may be settled and established throughout our folk." [119]

In later times the memory of Ine was well esteemed by the abbey of Malmesbury. Its monk William, who wrote in the twelfth century our best life of Aldhelm, described the king as of surpassing courage, wisdom, and devotion to the Christian faith; guided, inspired, and sustained by "Aldhelm, our Father." It was Aldhelm, William declared, who moved Ine to rebuild the abbey of Glastonbury, and we need not doubt his word.[120] Another monastic congregation connected with the names of Ine and Aldhelm was that of Abingdon. Early chronicle held it founded by Cissa, who as ruler in Wiltshire and Berkshire under Centwine had granted to one named "Hean" for this founding a goodly portion of land, increased at a later time by King Caedwalla; in this monastery "Hean" himself became a monk. At a later time, however, he was

---

[119] H.S. III, 214ff.; Bright, 410; Attenborough, 34.
[120] *Gest. Pont.* 354. The charter of gift of Ine to Glastonbury which bears Aldhelm's name is spurious: Kemble I, No. li, 58f.; Birch, No. 109. For Aldhelm and William of Malmesbury see also M. R. James, *Two ancient English Scholars*, Glasgow Univ. Publications XXII, 1931.

found asking Ine to help him regain his land, and was finally
released from his monastic vow in the presence of Abbot
Aldhelm and of Haeddi his bishop.[121] The monastery of Abingdon was again connected with Malmesbury; for one of its
abbots, Faricius, who died in 1117, wrote another well-known
life of Aldhelm, also still extant.[122] Above all, we are sure that
Ine was generous in gift toward the Malmesbury of his friend
and kinsman. There is some evidence of this in a charter dated
701, conveying to the monastery land near Corston and Rod-
borne in Wiltshire.[123]

Among royal friends of Aldhelm outside his own Wessex
none was dearer to him, none more welcome for his love of
learning, than Aldfrid, king of Northumbria for twenty years,
from 685 until 705, while Aldhelm was abbot of Malmesbury.
According to tradition Aldfrid was a son of Oswy of Northumbria, born out of wedlock to a British or an Irish mother. He
succeeded Egfrid, lawful son of Oswy and of his queen Eanfled, upon the Northumbrian throne when Egfrid died miser-
ably in 685 at the battle of Nechtansmere, daring to march
against the Picts in the wild mountain passes of Scotland. The
folly of this ambition not only cost Northumbria her rule in
Strathclyde and in the lands beyond the Forth, but it laid
open her own soil to constant raiding of the Pictish warriors.

Aldfrid, Egfrid's younger half-brother, had for long been
living in exile from England among the Irish, attracted by the
fame of Irish scholars and, perhaps, by kinship of Irish blood.
We hear a hint, too, that his absence from Northumbria had

[121] *Chron. Abingdon* ed. Stevenson, *RS* I, 9, 38, 120; II, vff., 495ff.
The tradition, however, is largely spurious; see Stenton, *The Early History
of the Abbey of Abingdon,* 1913, 9–18; 49–51.
[122] Giles ed. Aldhelm, *PEA* I, 354ff.; *PL* LXXXIX, coll. 63ff.; *Gest.
Pont.* 125f., 192, 330. See A. S. Cook, "Sources of the Biography of Aldhelm," *TCAS* XXVIII, 1927, 275ff.
[123] Kemble I, No. xlviii; Birch, No. 103; *Gest. Pont.* 354f.

been encouraged by the hostility of King Egfrid. Whether he
was a student among the Irish in Ireland, or in Iona, or in
both, is not certain; the evidence points to a stay in both
places.[124] At all events, his reputation for scholarship reached
the height of legend in both Ireland and England, and he is
always described as "the Learned" for his knowledge of sacred
and of secular writings.[125] His court was famous far and wide
for its culture, and he must have been a friend and correspondent of the scholars of his day. An attractive conjecture has
imagined the poet of *Beowulf* as living within his court and
writing under his patronage.[126] But he was not only a student;
he was a king, as well; and in his time Northumbria recovered
much of her lost prestige and enjoyed a relative peace.[127]

We may think that Aldhelm had known Aldfrid as a student
at Malmesbury Abbey.[128] They had also a connection by marriage. Aldfrid's first wife was related, as was Aldhelm, to the
royal House of Wessex; she was Cuthburga, sister of King Ine.
But, it was said, from the day of her bridal she pleaded for
her maidenhood, and soon the marriage was annulled that she
might depart in peace to her chosen cloister.[129] A third bond
between the abbot and the king was based on spiritual affinity,
for Aldhelm had stood as sponsor to Aldfrid at his baptism and
confirmation when they were both young men.

These various sympathies, then, and a friendship of twenty
years encouraged Aldhelm, probably soon after Aldfrid entered upon his reign in 685, to send to him a bulky package of

[124] Bede, *Vita Cuth.* (prose) c. 24; *Vita Cuth. Anon.* III, c. 6; *Gest. Reg.* I, 57.
[125] *HE* IV, c. 26; V, c. 12; Plummer II, 263f.
[126] A. S. Cook, "The Possible Begetter of the Old English *Beowulf* and *Widsith*," *TCAS* XXV, 1922, 316ff.; R. W. Chambers, *Beowulf*, 1932, 489. *Cf.* Cook, "Aldhelm and the Source of Beowulf 2523," *MLN* XL, 1925, 137ff.
[127] *HE* IV, c. 26.
[128] Stenton, 89.
[129] Hardy, *Cat.* I, i, 384; *Gest. Reg.* I, 35; *NLA* I, 244ff.; *DCB* I, 730.

written sheets.[130] Upon the top lay a letter, which addressed
the king as "Acircius," interpreted by modern scholarship as
"*a circio*," "from the direction of the west-northwest wind":
a title suggested by the words which follow, describing Aldfrid
as "wielding the sceptre of the northern kingdom." [131]

Mention in this letter of the sevenfold gifts of the Spirit
bestowed in confirmation leads Aldhelm on to a discussion of
the use of the mystic number seven in Holy Scripture. Seven
were the days of creation, a thousand sevenfold shall be the
peace of the blessed hereafter; by sevens did Noah take of
beast and fowl into the ark, seven were the sons of Job and
seven thousand his sheep. And so on till we come to the seven
Catholic epistles which as living streams give life to the City
of God, to the seven grades of the sacred ministry, to the
angels of the seven churches, and to Alpha and Omega, the
first and the last, Who bears in His hand the seven stars and
walks among the seven golden candlesticks. Mystic, also, is the
spirit immanent in Nature and in the culture of man. Sevenfold are the spheres that revolve in heaven, sevenfold the
phases of the moon's waxing and waning; seven the stars of
the Great Wagon and of the cluster that rises in the spring,
the Pleiades; sevenfold the music of the lyre and seven the arts
of human knowledge.

This prologue is followed by a discussion of the different
forms of metrical feet and lines, developed in questions asked
by the disciple and answered by the master. Quotations from
sacred and from pagan Latin poetry illustrate the master's
teaching; sometimes examples are given in metrical lines made
up by Aldhelm himself. Most of this dissertation is of impor-

---

[130] Ehwald (xviii) suggests the date c. 685; Manitius (*Gesch.*, 136)
and Bönhoff (103), c. 695.

[131] Ehwald, 61. Aldfrid lived in the north of England and had come
from Ireland, N.W. of Aldhelm's Wessex. The Latin *circius*=west-
northwest wind.

tance only to the historian of metrics.[132] There is one passage, however, which is good reading for the curious student of nature, as this Latin scholar expounded it. The master is explaining the difference between sounds that can be clearly expressed in meaning, by human voice and pen, and sounds that are confused and incapable of literary expression, such as the characteristic utterances of beasts and birds.[133] He then attempts to reproduce these various sounds in a list that reminds one of the song of French children quoted (in translation) in Nevil Shute's *Pied Piper:*

> "My great-aunt lives in Tours,
> In a house with a cherry tree,
> With a little mouse (squeak, squeak),
> And a big lion (roar, roar),
> And a wood pigeon (coo, coo), . . .

and so on quite indefinitely."

By far the most interesting part of all this mystical and metrical interpretation poured out on the devoted head of the King of the North is a large number of riddles—a hundred, including a prologue—the fruit of Aldhelm's own ingenuity in hexameter verse. Every student of the Anglo-Saxons knows their passion for riddles; in Aldhelm we see the father of this artifice in England. His riddling verses, as befitted the scholar of his day, were written in Latin; but since we know that Aldhelm wrote songs sung to music in his native Anglo-Saxon, he may well have written riddles, also, in that tongue. In him we see the predecessor of the Latin riddles of Tatwine and of Eusebius, as well as of the Anglo-Saxon riddles of the *Exeter Book.* In him we see, too, the pioneer among Latin poets of

---

[132] On his various sources see Manitius, *Gesch.,* I, 136ff., and in *Wiener Sitzungsber.* CXII, 1886, 546ff.; Ehwald, xixff., 61ff.; Roger, 291ff.; Laistner, *Thought and Letters,* 120f.

[133] Ehwald, 179f. On Aldhelm's source (Suetonius) and influence here see Manitius, *Zu Aldh. und Baeda,* 74f.

the Anglo-Saxon race. It is surprising, indeed, that this double merit has not gained for Aldhelm wider renown among students of English literature.

Yet Aldhelm himself acknowledged masters and models in the field of riddle: writers of the Old Testament, "the philosopher Aristotle," [134] and Symphosius, a Latin poet who lived, very probably, in Africa in the fifth century A.D. Of these we must take Symphosius into account, as his riddles are still extant and their influence upon Aldhelm may in some degree be traced.[135]

In Symphosius are found descriptions that cloak the things of nature: fog, rain, and snow become in turn that "which brings darkness in the midst of day"; that "which Earth once held and again receives"; the "dust of the water." Creatures that fly and prowl and swim and crawl are buried here in a veil of words, three hexameter verses for each: the bull, riding the heavens and yet walking upon earth; the pig (*porcus*)—behead him and lo! you have before you Orcus, ruler of darkness; the fox, little of body, greater in craft, most cunning of all beasts; the mole, to whom night is day; the crow with nine lives, black but not through grief; cranes, bearers of bloody war, flying in V formation across the sky—a V that stood for spring (*Ver*) in old legend; the spider, taught by Pallas; the bat, that flies without plumage, yet with wings.

Symphosius played, too, with things of the soil: the apple, that brought death to Troy; the onion, biting its biter, yet toothless; the rose, the violet, the poppy that gives sleep to all save to itself. All kinds of household tools and utensils, large and small, are also wrapped in these tiny poems. Sometimes a human picture is drawn in words: of a rope-dancer, of a one-

[134] See on this Manitius, *Gesch.*, 192.
[135] The best text is that of Riese, *Anthol. Lat.* I, i, 1894, 221ff. For details see PL LXXXIX, 170; Pitman, 1ff.; Tupper, xxviiiff. Translation by E. H. du Bois, *The Hundred Riddles of Symphosius*, 1912.

eyed seller of garlic, of a mother of twins, bearer of three lives within one body.

Other evidence of the old love of riddling verse is seen in the influence of the *Physiologus* or "Naturalist," in which real or legendary creatures were used as illustration of the teachings of the Christian faith. This famous work was first written in Greek about the third century and translated later into various Eastern tongues. As early, perhaps, as the fourth century a Latin version appeared,[136] and subsequently mediaeval renderings were made in a multitude of languages. Among these the Old English version still gives to us in the *Exeter Book* three little poems of allegory: drawn from the panther, from that mysterious behemoth of the sea known as the "asp-turtle," or whale, and from the partridge. Research has suggested that they come from Cynewulf, or from one of his school in the later part of the eighth century.[137]

If this be so, these Old English poems could not have influenced Aldhelm. But surely he wrote in the spirit of the *Physiologus*, which has spread far and wide throughout Christian mysticism the lore of the pelican, the phoenix, the unicorn. And surely he owed to Symphosius much in idea and in form, even though in the spirit in which they wrote they were a world apart. To the pagan Symphosius the form—his three neat verses—was paramount. To him the riddle was the thing to catch his reader's mind, and he wove his web around his chosen objects without any thought save of disguising them as craftily as he might.

We must imagine Aldhelm's spirit here far differently. In him there burned, it is true, the same love of words, and of curious words, which we have seen before; to draw these

---

[136] See Francis J. Carmody, *Speculum* XIII, 1938, 153ff.
[137] Cook, *The Old English Elene, Phoenix, and Physiologus,* 1919, lviiff.; Cook-Pitman, *The Old English Physiologus, Yale Studies in English,* LXIII, 1921; C. W. Kennedy, *The Earliest English Poetry,* 1943, 300ff.

words into the form of verse in his riddles was for him a practical application of his studies in metre. None can doubt, moreover, that he worked hard to gather from every source available to him details of knowledge concerning the things of moving and of still life around which he fashioned his riddling lines. But behind and beyond all this there was found in him that living joy in nature which lights up all Old English poetry. Aldhelm was also a Catholic monk, and all his verses found their root in gratitude to God, Who had given it to man to enjoy freely created things. The Song of the Three Holy Children:

> *Benedicite omnia opera Domini Domino,*
> *Laudate et superexaltate eum in saeculo;*

the cry of the Psalmist:

> *O Lord, how manifold are Thy works!*
> *In wisdom hast Thou made them all;*
> *The earth is full of Thy riches,*

these were the words that sang in his mind as he walked by stream and by tree in the forest of Malmesbury, as he worked with his brethren in the abbey chapel and refectory, in its library and its kitchen. From these in his daily life he chose his subjects, eager by means of humble symbols diligently pictured to give glory to their Maker and his, in verse exactly fashioned to the utmost of his power. Symphosius had tried to conceal in words what he knew of created life; Aldhelm, as he tells in his *Preface*, prayed the Lord:

> *Grant me in lines uncouth to open wide*
> *The hidden mysteries of Nature's work.*

The riddles of Aldhelm are thus more free, more alive than those of Symphosius, and not only in spirit, but in form. For while he kept the hexameter verse of his model, he overflowed the limit of three lines into a number varying from four to

eighty-three. His count of one hundred riddles, however, was
an imitation of Symphosius; and similar convention induced
him to begin and end the thirty-six lines of the *Preface* with
letters forming the words:

> *Aldhelmus cecinit millenis versibus odas;*
>
> *Aldhelm composed poems in a thousand lines.*[138]

Many of these little poems dealt with subjects that were
conventionally treated: sun, moon, and stars; earth, fire, and
water, cloud and wind. Legendary figures appear in some:
the Colossus, Scylla, the Minotaur; many more tell of legends
connected with their names: the diamond, the dragon-stone,
the magnet. Foreign creatures are described: the salamander,
the flying fish and the ostrich, the camel and the elephant.
Much of Aldhelm's material came from the Elder Pliny's
Natural History and from the Christian encyclopaedic works
of Priscian of the sixth and of Isidore of the seventh century.[139]
Holy Scripture in this monk of Malmesbury naturally finds its
place. We read of the raven that was disobedient and of the
dove that did Noah's will when waters covered the earth; of
the apple-tree that took from man his brief early rapture; of
the fig-tree that clothed him in his waking misery; of the palm
of victory borne by martyrs. As in Symphosius, a word may
lose its initial letter to gain a different meaning; *corbus,* the
raven, minus its head becomes *orbus,* bereft of its young. Puns
also appear. Symphosius played upon *Mus,* mouse and name
of a Roman consul; Aldhelm writes of *Cancer,* crab and con-
stellation; of *Camellus,* standing for a camel, and also, somewhat uncertainly, for Camillus, the Roman hero.[140]

Far more interesting are the riddles in which he seems to

---

[138] *Millenis* here means simply a round number: Pitman, 68; Ehwald,
97ff.

[139] See the notes of Ehwald, 97ff.; Manitius, *Zu Aldh. und Baeda,*
14ff.; Roger, 294ff.

[140] Ehwald, 113; 145.

have left to us something of himself. There are the clouds, ever changing in colour as they move across the sky; the wind, howling through the forest in storm, tearing down ancient oak-trees and scouring the open fields in its rush; the forest stream winding along its course, now above, now under the ground, and teeming with tiny life. As he sat by it, Aldhelm watched the spider, poised delicately upon the water; now and again as he walked in meditation along its bank he came upon a beaver, busily gnawing the bark of some tree, and saw the startled little animal disappear into the depths. He noticed curiously the caterpillar of the Emperor moth spinning its web on the spears of the broom, and from the hollows of trees he heard the buzzing of the hornets' swarm. Especially he delighted in the bee, flitting from flower to flower "to fashion with her craft the yellow food of kings." Of strange and marvellous birth she came, Aldhelm told; for he had read his *Georgics* well.[141] In winter he looked long at dark yew trees, tossing in the gales; in summer he knew the scent of elder leaves and in autumn their clusters of black berries. The plant's smell was bitter, but it gave healing to foul eruptions on human bodies. He gazed upon the purple fruit of the hellebore among its rough hairy leaves; he believed that sickness of mind fell on those who ate unwarily of it.[142] Nearer his monastery, perhaps, there was a garden; for he saw the glory of yellow flowers growing on fertile soil and revelling in the sun; he felt, too, the sting of nettles plucked as weeds by the hand.

And there were birds in the forest. Like Alcuin, he heard on summer nights the nightingale trilling outside his cell; like Alcuin he knew its brown humility:

Mean is my colour, but none hath scorned my song.

[141] Riddle XX; *Georgics* IV, 198f.
[142] For explanation of Aldhelm's hellebore as one of the daphnes see Erika von Erhardt-Siebold, *Englische Studien* LXXI, 1936, 161ff.

In spring-time when the forest fields broke into flower, the swallow cried upon the wing; in high summer she left her empty nest and sought the woodland shade.[143]

Sometimes Aldhelm turned to look within his monastery for things of which to tell in verse, and his eye lighted on those he used every day of his life. He told of the bellows that blew sparks into flame; the spindle that spun clothing against winter's cold; the candle of beeswax, the whetstone, the file, the sieve, the cauldron hanging above the kitchen fire, the "double cooker," holding burning fuel below and boiling water above, "locked in peace" within its belly.[144] He marked in his riddling words things to eat: salt, white as ashes or as snow; pepper that seasons soup and tender steak, a royal dish; bread which was baked for the monks' daily food.

From the kitchen he passed to his cell and described his writing-tablets, made of wax and bound with leather, and the metal pen he carried at his girdle with them; his quill pen which "travelled straight, tracing its steps in deep blue across white fields"; the chest that held his books, "ignorant, but full of learning." His love of harmony is shown in his lines on some kind of musical instrument, "vomiting forth from its vital parts a hundred melodies, to silence in wondering fear the music born of strings." Aldhelm mentions this "organ" repeatedly in his writings, and his biographer, Faricius, tells of him that "he was skilled in all kinds of music, both of strings and of pipes, and played thereon every day." [145]

The pipe organ, if such it was,[146] placed in the monastery church, must have been of simple structure. Aldhelm looked

---

[143] Riddles XXII, XLVII.

[144] See Erika von Erhardt-Siebold, *Speculum* VII, 1932, 252ff.

[145] Riddle XIII; cf. *Carmen de Virgin.*, lines 71f., 2788f.; Faricius, *PEA* I, 357.

[146] H. R. Bittermann, "The Organ in the Early Middle Ages," *Speculum* IV, 1929, 390ff.; H. G. Farmer, *The Organ of the Ancients*, 1931, 147, note 3. *Cf.* Bede, *PL* XC, col. 140.

on it as he took part in the abbey's public and private worship, the Mass and the Hours. Perhaps he saw there, too, the chrismal found in one of these riddles, a little casket in which the Blessed Sacrament was reserved. Celtic monks carried the Host in such a vessel, hung around their necks when they went out into the fields for their daily work, or left their monasteries on long journeys; carelessness in guarding this precious burden brought severe penalties. But often, as here, it was larger, fashioned in the shape of a house; and we are fortunate in possessing this description from early mediaeval days.[147] Aldhelm tells of its rich adorning:

> *Ruddy my body shines with clustered jewels,*
> *And yellow gleams with gold my metal sheath.*
> *But fairer far the life I bear within,*
> *Where flames in loveliness the hidden Christ.*

Two other riddles are of special interest, although they differ widely in meaning. One describes a lighthouse:

> *On high and rocky shore, lashed by dark sea,*
> *Where breakers swell upon the ocean's plain,*
> *Man's craft has raised my tower of massive stone*
> *That I may point safe pathways to their ships.*
> *Not mine with oars to traverse ocean fields,*
> *Nor plough the sea in boats with winding course!*
> *Yet, as they labour, driven among the waves,*
> *From my high watch I lead these ships to shore,*
> *Setting within my tower a torch aloft*
> *When clouds and fog blot out the flame of stars.*[148]

Such Aldhelm may have seen, possibly from the jutting point of coast upon the Isle of Purbeck, now known by the name of Alban, but once Saint Aldhelm's Head. Dorset was Aldhelm's

---

[147] Riddle LV; Erika von Erhardt-Siebold, "Aldhelm's Chrismal," *Speculum* X, 1935, 276ff.; Cabrol *s.v. Chrismale, DACL* III, i, col. 1480.
[148] Riddle XCII.

home in later life, and he knew well the country near this point, Wareham and Corfe Castle. The Head was named in later days in his honour. On its summit there still stands a tiny chapel, called also by his name. Coastguards patrol its height, and others walk toward its path along the cliffs from Swanage. There one may look far down upon the waves below, foaming against the rocks as they rush in their swift race. Out to sea there lies the wide scape of the Channel, and nearer at hand the sweep of broken, jagged coast. From there long ago a flare blazed to warn passing ships of the dangers of this sea.

The hundredth riddle, which ends all, tells of Creation. Here Aldhelm lets himself pour out in eighty-three verses something of his feeling for all things great and small which the Lord God hath made, in all the breadth and length of earth and sky: things that fly and run, that walk and creep, in the air and on land, in many waters, by night and by day, in the heights and in the depths; things fair and foul, slender and gross, cold and hot, sweet and bitter; things mighty as the black leviathan that rides the gray-green sea, tinier than the mote which quivers in the sunlight; things that rise up to meet heaven, that creep on their timid path in earth's secret shade. So he sees Nature, wiser than the learning of the sages, yet untaught of any, save of God.

Different, again, were the forty riddles written in imitation of Aldhelm by Tatwine, Archbishop of Canterbury from 731 A.D. He delighted to riddle of churchly things and of questions philosophical. Sixty more, to equal with Tatwine the convention of one hundred riddles, came from Eusebius, in monastic and less learned circles of this same period known to many as Abbot Hwaetbert.[149] His art fell short of Tatwine's form. Later on, Boniface wrote of Christian virtues under the

[149] Wright, *Anglo-Latin Satirical Poets*, RS LIX, 2, 1872, 525ff.; Giles, *Anecdota Bedae, Lanfranci et aliorum*, Caxton Society, No. 7, 1851, 25ff.

guise of these same puzzles, with little merit save of his own scholarly diversion.[150] Around others, possibly also written in this eighth century, many modern pens have waged combat. Such are the Anglo-Saxon riddles of the *Exeter Book,* now assigned to Cynewulf, now denied to him. We are not concerned with them here. Nor need we tarry with the Latin riddles that have come down to us bearing disputed foreign names, of Bern in Switzerland and of Lorsch in Austria. The flood which the Christian Aldhelm both followed and, in his turn, encouraged was, indeed, a copious one.[151]

Some lines of farewell at the end of the treatise beg Aldfrid, "most reverend son," to read carefully that which has cost its author so much toil, grinding and pounding as a miller working at his mill. Many, no doubt, will grudge Aldfrid leisure for such unworldly pursuit; is he not beaten by the waves howling like wild dogs around the steadfast rock of his government in the North? But, Aldhelm pleads, although the glory be all of God, yet none can deny that this work, which he himself has written among the cares of a busy abbot and many interruptions from the outside world, strikes out a new path in Saxon learning and should therefore repay earnest scrutiny.[152]

He now turned to instruction of another kind. In Essex at Barking (*In Berecingum*), eight miles from London, there was a community of nuns, founded by Earconwald some time before the year 675, in which year Theodore of Canterbury consecrated him bishop of London and of the East Saxons.[153] Earconwald "had founded this noble monastery for his sister Ethelburga, who felt herself called to be a mother and nurse of women dedicated to God." [154]

[150] Ed. Dümmler, *MGH Poet. lat. aevi Carol.* I, 1881, 1ff.
[151] See E. von Erhardt-Siebold, *Die lateinischen Rätsel der Angelsachsen, Anglistische Forsch.* LXI, 1925; Tupper, xxxiiiff.
[152] Ehwald, xix, 202f.; *cf. Gest. Pont.* V, 335f.
[153] Perhaps as early as 664; see Plummer II, 218.
[154] *HE* IV, c. 6.

Men, however, as well as women, sought the religious life in this foundation; and the monastery of Barking became one of the "double communities" so famous at the time. The custom that both nuns and monks should follow rule in adjoining parts of the same monastery, under obedience to the same Superior, was prevalent in the seventh and eighth centuries among the cloisters of Gaul. Many of these were ruled by abbesses of royal blood; among them were Ethelburga, daughter of King Anna of East Anglia, and Saethryd, his stepdaughter, who both governed Faremoûtier-en-Brie, and Gisla, sister of Charles the Great, abbess of Chelles, near Paris. In Britain similar foundations were also found in the seventh century up and down the land, of the Celtic and of the Roman obedience; especially renowned was that of Whitby on the Yorkshire coast, ruled by Hild; that of Coldingham in County Berwick, ruled by Ebba, Saint Cuthbert's friend; that of Ely in Cambridgeshire, where Ethelthryd, disciple of Saint Wilfrid, has left her name as abbess.[155]

Upon the death of Ethelburga, whose godly life and excellent guiding brought tradition of miracle to her monastery and to her name its enrolling in the calendar of saints,[156] the office of abbess of Barking passed to Hildilid. A story, which may or may not be true, claims that this lady had passed her novitiate in Chelles and had come to Barking, at the request of Earconwald, to instruct Ethelburga and her friends in religious discipline.[157] Among her nuns was that Cuthburga whom we have seen as bride, in name, of Aldfrid of Northumbria, and as sister of Ine of Wessex.[158] As such, then, Cuthburga was related to Aldhelm, and no doubt it was partly on account of

---

[155] *Ibid.*, III, c. 8; Plummer II, 149. On double monasteries see *ibid.*, 150; Mary Bateson, *TRHS* XIII, 1899, 137ff.; Hilpisch, 44ff.
[156] *HE* IV, cc. 6–10.
[157] Dugdale I, 436; *Gest. Reg.* I, 35; *HE* IV, c. 10.
[158] Plummer II, 264; p. 48 *supra*.

this that he wrote a long epistle to Hildilid and her community at Barking, full of zeal for the virgin life and of exhortation that they hold faithfully to its way. The nuns are addressed by name: "Hildilid, abbess; Justina, Cuthburga and Osburga, Aldgitha and Scholastica; Hidburga and Berngitha, Eulalia and Tecla, adorning the Church in renown of holiness." [159]

"Your letter," Aldhelm writes, "was brought to me just as I was setting out with my brother monks to attend an episcopal conference. How I rejoice that it tells me you are well, that it shows me how thoroughly you have studied holy books, how high a degree of culture you have attained. As spiritual athletes you run well your race in the wide courses of the Scriptures. Or shall I liken you to bees? As bees flit from the marigold to the purple mallow, from the mallow to the yellow blossoms of the willow and the broom, from the clusters of the ivy to the flowering lime, so you gather learning from many a page of scholarship."

We can imagine the Sisters sitting at their sacred embroidery while the Abbess Hildilid essayed to explain to them Aldhelm's interminably complicated periods of minute description. His illustrations were drawn from a multitude of sources: the Bible, the *Lives* of Fathers of the Church, Greek and Latin, of hermits, martyrs, monks, famous and obscure; writings in praise of our Lady, told in mystic language; stories of numberless nuns who had glorified God by chaste life and brave death throughout the centuries of revealed faith.[160]

[159] Ehwald, 228f. This letter (in Latin prose) seems to have been written c. 686. Cuthburga was still queen of Northumbria in 685; shortly afterward she became a nun at Barking, and subsequently abbess of Wimborne: *ibid.*, xviii, 229.

[160] See Ehwald, xxif.; Manitius, *Zu Aldh. und B.*, 14ff., 54ff.; *Gesch.*, 138. The praise of St. Benedict here (prose, c. xxx; verse, lines 842–880) proves that Aldhelm had read Gregory the Great, *Dialogues* II, but not that his monks were exclusively Benedictine: Ehwald, 268, note 1; 389f.; note on line 879.

The letter informs us in detail of the studies of these nuns of Barking. It delights in the curiosity which has carried them from the Old and the New Testament to pore over the Church Fathers, to ponder knotty problems of history, allegory, tropology, and anagogy, "the fourfold norm of sacred study"; in their knowledge of writers of history, and of chronographers who have laboriously handed down the changes and accidents of past times; in their research among systems of grammar and orthography and metrical science.[161]

Once again the bee is brought into service, as both a type of diligence and of chastity, working, untaught by the lure of sexual charm, to produce its honey in well-ordered hives under regular discipline, each one of its own free will in a common society. Such, according to Aldhelm, is of the essence of a monastery. Aldhelm goes back so often to this likeness of bees that we feel sure his abbey possessed rude hives in its garden of herbs and that he must often have watched their citizens going in and out on manifold daily errands.[162]

He now waxes eloquent, as Ambrose and Jerome and Augustine before him, on the glories of the virgin life. In patriarchal days of the Old Testament, he writes, faithful marriage held its special honour; but, as the new dispensation gradually replaced the ancient, marriage became to the virgin life as silver to gold, as wool to silk, as the anvil and the hammer to the things of beauty which they forge. Of course, and be it always remembered, silver and wool, anvils and hammers have their uses, and this is a question of comparative merit; the virgin is not as a lighthouse shining on a lofty crag and looking down upon the lowly married wife. Better to sail precariously through the reefs and whirlpools of secular cares and arrive with battered beams and ragged sails at the haven of

[161] Eckenstein, 113ff.
[162] Cf. A. S. Cook, "Aldhelm at the hands of Sharon Turner," *Speculum* II, 1927, 201ff.

grace, better far, than to journey in false peace under a convent roof remote from this naughty world, deeming oneself whole because one sees no open wounds. The Fathers of the Church may have placed pride last in their catalogue of mortal sins; all the same, warns Aldhelm, pride is the robber that above all steals the grace of virgin souls.

Against the horror of its assaults, vividly described here in a torrent of foaming words, against the peril of those other mortal sins, dashing ever and again to attack while life shall last, let the nuns take to themselves the armour of Cassian's ten *Collations* or the *Morals* of Pope Gregory the Great.[163] "Really," the letter continues, "I am ashamed to tell of the bold and shameless pride, the stupid and arrogant display, seen nowadays among both women and men. Not only nuns and monks, living under monastic discipline in community, but even ordained clergy, subject to episcopal command, are found breaking the canons of the Church and the precepts of the regular life, that they may deck their carnal bodies here, there, and everywhere, with forbidden ornaments and trappings. Satin underclothing, forsooth, blue and violet, scarlet tunics with hoods, sleeves with silk stripes, shoes edged with red fur, hair carefully arrayed on forehead and temples with the curling iron—this is the modern habit. Dark veils yield to headdresses white and coloured, sewn with long ribbons and hanging to the ground; finger-nails are sharpened like the talons of hawks or owls seeking their prey." [164] But let these dedicated maidens keep high their courage. As the sun they shine out against the moonlight cast by those who, albeit married, give themselves to fasting and prayer; far more against the shadow cast by marriage of the average sort.

At the end Aldhelm pleads: "Forgive the faults of this letter, put together, bit by bit, among the distractions of a busy

---

[163] Ehwald, 242. [164] Ch. 58.

life, in fear and peril of error; as a bark sailing treacherous waters, may it escape the fate of those who journey among the solecisms and barbarisms of the ocean of languages, unpiloted by due skill in grammar. May your prayers rise to aid and support me in my labours; for truly I myself struggle among the waves of my own faults while I strive to guide others toward the shore of perfection.[165] And so farewell, flowers of the Church, sisters of the convent, disciples of learning, pearls of Christ, jewels of Paradise and heirs of our home-to-be in Heaven."

The treatise received grateful thanks from Barking and remained to edify later nuns of the Middle Ages. When we consider that it was not only full of material gathered from innumerable learned sources, but was written in Latin for Saxon readers, and a most difficult and elaborate Latin at that, we can understand the respect in which women of the cloister were held in Anglo-Saxon lands. Its reception encouraged Aldhelm to compose a metrical version in hexameter lines, as, indeed, he had promised at the end of the earlier treatise in prose.[166] This copy in hexameters was also sent to the nuns of Barking, with a preface in which the initial letters of the lines, read downwards, and the end letters of the lines, read upwards, form the same sentence, itself, also, an hexameter verse:

Metrica tirones nunc promant carmina castos.

May these verses bring forth pure recruits for God.

It was dedicated to "Maxima Mater," by whom Aldhelm meant our Lady, as may be inferred from the lines which pray

---

[165] *Cf.* Gregory the Great, *Epp.* XI, 2: ed. Hartmann, *MGH Epp.* II, 2, 1895, 261.
[166] *Cf.* Sedulius, *Paschal Song*, in verse and in prose (ed. Huemer, *CSEL* X, 1885, 14ff.), perhaps Aldhelm's model here.

for aid and light in his task. Mercifully his verse is far easier
to read than his prose.[167]

Theodore and Hadrian at Canterbury were, of course, filled
with honourable pride in their pupil. And he gave them full
gratitude. Trained though he had been in boyhood under
Irish discipline, he always looked back with longing to the joy
of his student days in Kent. He was even jealous for the reputation of Canterbury as a place of learning for Saxon youths.
There was excuse, perhaps, for his feeling. During many years
the journeying to Ireland had gone on, as the historian describes, in the pilgrimages "of many Englishmen, both of noble
and of yeoman blood, who had gone there for the sake of
sacred knowledge or of stricter rule of life. Some of these
yielded themselves to keep monastic discipline; others rejoiced
in study, passing from cell to cell of the masters of learning.
All of them the Irish welcomed most gladly and zealously
gave them their daily food, with books and the teaching of
scholars, entirely free of charge." [168] No wonder that the English crowded the ways to Ireland.

A letter written by Aldhelm about this time shows his own
Saxon loyalty. It welcomed home to England a friend, Eahfrid
by name, who had lately returned from long study of six years
in the sister island.[169] The abbot rejoices that his compatriot
has travelled in safety through the fogs of the Irish coast and
the dangers of the Irish Sea; that the praise of his progress in
scholarship rolls like a peal of thunder in English ears. So

[167] Prologue, lines 22f.; Ehwald, 351, note 22. Aldhelm added to this
metrical version a discourse, *De octo principalibus vitiis,* clearly belonging
to the poem but wrongly separated from it afterward as an independent
work: Manitius, *Gesch.,* 139.

[168] *HE* III, c. 27.

[169] Ehwald, 486ff. Others identify this Eahfrid with Aldfrid of Northumbria, but their views are not convincing. See Hahn, 6 and 22; Bönhoff, 99f. Tait's suggestion (*DNB* XVI, 306) that he was Eadfrid, bishop
of Lindisfarne (698–721) is refuted by Ehwald, 486, note 5; see also the
suggestion of Stubbs (*DCB* II, 10) and of A. S. Cook (*Speculum* II,
1927, 363ff.) that he was abbot of Glastonbury.

many students go and come between the two islands, he declares, carrying knowledge as bees carry honey to the hive: the lore of grammar and of geometry, of physical science, of literary interpretation of texts, through allegory and through metaphor. Now, then, let Eahfrid open wide the flood of his newly-acquired science for the refreshing of thirsty minds and the ripening of wisdom's harvest in due season. Let him not hide his light under a bushel nor bury underground the coinage which must increase currency of learning on Saxon shores.

Behind the cordial greeting there lies poised a shaft of good-humoured banter, half whimsical, half mocking; it is pointed by an extraordinary pomp and pageant of Hisperic jargon, unrolled as if in ironic reverence for this young graduate of Irish schools. The point becomes sharp toward the end, in an inquiry why Irish schools are crowded with students from England, why Irish erudition is lauded to the skies. Cannot teachers of Greek and Latin be found in Britain to unravel the knots of scholarship for anxious little minds? No doubt the green land of the Irish boasts cells of learning as numberless as the stars that glitter in the heavens. Yet has not Britain, too, the glory of philosophy's sun in her Theodore, the radiance of rhetoric's moon in her Hadrian? What need to journey the perilous sea to Ireland when one may learn at home of Canterbury? Irish students in throngs might bark questions at Theodore as at a wild boar at bay; the sharp tusk of his dialectic would send them scurrying in terror to their lairs of heresy and pride!

Aldhelm's enthusiasm for works built of words, however, was equalled by his joy in works built of wood and stone, especially when he might combine words and works in the same cause. And so we find him writing poems to celebrate the consecration of churches. As we have seen, the chief church of his abbey bore the names of Saint Peter and Saint Paul. About

685 a second was dedicated at Malmesbury in honour of Blessed Mary: "a garden enclosed, green upon a hill in flower; a sealed fountain of water springing from heaven; a dove trembling under the shadow of the Most High." Thus he wove the *Song of Songs* into his verses, while he told of the work now completed and of its dedication:

> *Femina praepollens et sacra puerpera virgo,*
> *Audi clementer populorum vota precantum.*[170]

> *Lady of mighty power, Holy Virgin, Mother of God,*
> *Pitifully hear the prayers of the peoples who cry to thee.*

A third church mentioned in lines by him has caused much debate among students of his work. It was given by Bugga, a daughter of King Centwine of Wessex, herself another kinswoman of Aldhelm. The simplest view seems to be that Bugga, as would be natural, made this offering for some double monastery, where women as well as men might worship God in His beauty; probably she herself was ruling the monastery as abbess. She would, as naturally, invite Aldhelm to be present at its dedication, and he would rejoice to remember this festival in his verse. He tells in hexameters of the history of the House of Wessex, to which Bugga belonged, and then describes the shrine.[171]

It was indeed very beautiful. The sun shone through its windows of glass, a rare treasure in these days of Saxon England; the altar of our Lady in the apse was adorned with a frontal of golden filament; the chalice was of gold, studded with jewels, the paten of wrought silver. Radiance from all

---

[170] Ehwald, 12f., lines 7f.

[171] *Ibid.*, 14ff.; he dates the poem c. 690. Bugga may best be described as a princess of Wessex, not as a sister of Aldhelm (Bönhoff, 37), nor as identical with the Bugga who was friend and correspondent of St. Boniface (*cf.* Hahn, 108ff., and p. 371, note 55 *infra*), nor with the Bugga who was daughter of Abbess Dunne of Withington near Malmesbury (Browne, *Aldhelm*, 243ff.).

combined, from gold and silver and precious stones, was reflected in the Cross; on a framework supported by low columns hung the thurible which burned incense during the offering of the Mass.[172]

Around the church were twelve lesser altars, of the twelve Apostles,[173] and every year high Feast was kept here on the day of our Lady's Nativity, which we should expect to find marked as the eighth of September. But the date given is the middle day of the month of August. It would seem, then, that at this time in England her Feasts had not yet received the clear dating which was soon to order their observance.[174]

During these days more and more aspirants were knocking at the abbey door, "hastening to Malmesbury by every road." [175] The people, also, of the surrounding country now looked to its churches for the nurture of their minds and souls. But many were the vocations still hidden, many the untaught peasants, and therefore Aldhelm decided to found another monastery in which monks might pray and toil. This was built at Frome in Somerset, the adjoining shire, and dedicated to Saint John the Baptist. William of Malmesbury relates that its church was still there in his twelfth century.[176] The Parish Church which stands there now, midway upon one of the many hills which lead up from the market-place, is well-known for its tradition. It, also, bears the name of Saint John the Baptist, and among the additions and restorations of many

[172] Rock I, 162f.   [173] Line 40; Ehwald, 16.
[174] Ehwald, 17; cf. Duchesne, *Christian Worship*, 1910, 272f. This poem is followed in Ehwald's edition (19ff.) by twelve little poems written by Aldhelm in honour of twelve altars. We do not know in what church they stood, but apparently it was not that mentioned above as built by Bugga. For in her church the apse was dedicated to our Lady (line 41; Ehwald, 16); in this one it was sacred to St. Peter (line 1; Ehwald, 19): see Traube, *Karol. Dicht.* 43f.; Ehwald, 7. Ehwald suggests, from line 1 (p. 26 of his edition), that they stood in the church at Malmesbury dedicated to the Lord Saviour and SS. Peter and Paul (see his page 8, and p. 41 *supra*). A thirteenth poem by Aldhelm (Ehwald, 31) concludes the series of altar poems; a fourteenth (*ibid.*, 32) stands by itself, written for some church of St. Matthias (*ibid.*, 8; Traube, 45).
[175] *Gest. Pont.* 349.   [176] *Ibid.*, 346.

periods it can yet show a fragment of Saxon stone. The stream which runs along Willow Vale near the church holds the memory of converts baptized there by Aldhelm; on the high land surrounding the town Saint Aldhelm's Home trains boys for the Church of England in various arts and crafts.

Much, then, had been accomplished to content Aldhelm's heart in the present. But he was thinking of the future, of the welfare of Malmesbury and of Frome in the days when he should no longer rule them. A great adventure now slowly shaped itself in his thoughts. He must go on pilgrimage to Rome and lay their cause before the Pope himself. Duty, of course, went hand in hand here with desire; to see Rome was the longing of every Catholic monk in Saxon England. Those who could journeyed there at any cost; those who could not always cherished the hope that sometime before they died they might offer their prayers at the shrines of the saints.

But first Aldhelm asked counsel from royal friends and benefactors: from his own king, Ine of Wessex, and from Ethelred, king of Mercia, brother of that Wulfhere who had been overlord of Wessex and supreme in power throughout England.[177] Ethelred, also, was a warrior; he ravaged Kent and fought against Northumbria. There is some ground, moreover, for a theory that he invaded Wessex, as Wulfhere had done before him; that he seized Dorchester-on-Thames, once a see of Wessex, and revived it as a Mercian see under one Aetla as bishop.[178] Like Wulfhere, too, Ethelred revered the Church and gave largely to her foundations, in Gloucester, and in Worcester, as well as in Malmesbury.[179]

Both kings approved of Aldhelm's plan, and he made ready to depart. One of his last acts before leaving was to sign as witness, in company with King Ine, a charter by which

[177] See p. 27 *supra*.
[178] Plummer II, 246; Bright, 351; Stenton, 68.
[179] Kemble I, No. xxxii (marked genuine), xxiif. (marked spurious); Birch, Nos. 60, 75ff.; *Gest. Pont.* 363.

Nothelm, king of Sussex, gave to his sister Nothgith land for a monastery and church within his realm. The signatures of the West Saxons, Ine and Aldhelm, are explained by the fact that the South Saxons, as we have seen, had been subject to Wessex since the invasion of their country by Caedwalla.[180]

On his way Aldhelm went to visit land in his possession, probably property of his family, at and near Wareham in Dorsetshire. The weather over the Channel was stormy, and he was obliged to wait for a calm and favourable wind. The monks he had taken in his company were bidden to look after the travelling arrangements; the abbot occupied himself in building a church on this land of Dorset in which he might pray for the safety of all, in going out and in coming in. Journeys were no light matter in the eighth century; in perils of robbers, in perils of mountain and ravine, of rivers and of the sea, in labour and in hunger, in summer and in winter, beset by care for souls under his keeping, the pilgrim would hasten on.

So Aldhelm made his little church, and William of Malmesbury of the twelfth century told that its ruins were then still standing. The roof had fallen, leaving them open to the sky, except that a fragment of masonry still protected the altar. Yet, he declared, no drop of rain ever fell within those holy walls, however heavy the storm, and peasants of the countryside often ran to take shelter there. They lay near the sea, close by Corfe Castle.[181] Even in our time, Saint Martin's Church on Wareham wall bears traces of Saxon work and is connected with Aldhelm's name.[182]

But now his fervent and oft-repeated prayer was answered. He sailed across to France, travelled over valley and mountain, and at length saw Rome.

[180] Kemble (V, No. 995) holds this genuine (date 692). See also *DCB* s.v. Nothelm (1), and pp. 44f. *supra*.
[181] *Gest. Pont.* 363; M. M. C. Calthrop, *VHD* II, 2.
[182] Baldwin Brown II, 1925, 22, 36, 484.

His gladness was that of countless other pilgrims, then and thereafter; his joy, the forerunner of words of the tenth century, expressed in the triumphant hymn *O Roma nobilis:*

> *Mistress of the world,*
> *Of all cities most excellent,*
> *Red with the blood of martyrs,*
> *White with the lilies of virgins;*
> *Ever all joy to thee,*
> *Ever we bless thee; hail through all ages!*
>
> . . . .
>
> *O Peter, mighty bearer of the keys of Heaven,*
> *Hear ever the cry of those who pray . . .*
>
> . . . .
>
> *O Paul, receive our prayers . . .*
> *That the wisdom which filled thee*
> *May fill us through thy teaching.*[183]

The Pope of Aldhelm's time was the same Sergius who in 689 had baptized King Caedwalla just before he died in penitence. Sergius was very eager to see so learned an abbot and priest; one tradition says that he had himself invited Aldhelm to Rome.[184] His hospitality was most gracious; Aldhelm was received as a guest in the Lateran Palace and every day sang Mass within its church. The chasuble he wore was said to have been his own and to have been preserved for centuries afterward at Malmesbury. It was made of deep red silk, figured in black with designs of peacocks, "evidently of foreign and probably of Eastern workmanship." From its length it was conjectured that Aldhelm had been a tall man, and the same was inferred from his bones.[185]

The days passed, and at last the time of his departure for home arrived. He set out, laden with tokens of good will. Chief

[183] *Anal. Hymn.* LI, 219; Brittain, *The Medieval Latin and Romance Lyric,* 1937, 88.
[184] Faricius, *PEA* I, 360.
[185] *Gest. Pont.* 364f.; Clapham, *ERA*, 60.

of the gifts he carried to his monks was a letter of privilege from Pope Sergius, which we may reasonably date about 693.[186] It granted to the monastery of Saint Peter and Saint Paul at Malmesbury and to that of Saint John the Baptist at Frome exemption from all control, save that of the Holy See of Rome. No bishop or priest or cleric of any degree might at any time exercise jurisdiction therein, nor require nor presume to ask any gifts thereof or privileges, nor make of its church a cathedral for his use nor celebrate Mass therein, except he come by invitation of the abbot and community. Should a priest for the celebrating of holy Mass or a deacon be needed by the monks in either place, let them ask his ordination from the bishop living near them, and let the bishop act in all matters in accord with their monastic rule and require no gift in return for his aid. Furthermore, upon the death of their abbot the monks themselves by common consent were to elect his successor; the same bishop who held rule nearest the monastery would then install this newly elected abbot in his chair of office. So let it be, the letter ended, and let none under direst pain of punishment violate these decrees.

Another of Aldhelm's treasures was more difficult to transport. It was an altar-stone of white marble, 4 feet long, 3 feet wide, 1½ feet high, with a raised border of the same stone running all around, beautifully incised with the figure X, perhaps representing the Greek *Christos*.[187] The poor beast which carried this burden staggered as far as the Alps and there fell exhausted on the steep road; naturally, he was crushed to death, and the stone was broken in half. Both, so the story goes, were wondrously made whole again by Aldhelm's power in prayer; only a zigzag flaw in the marble remained to show the glory of the deed.[188]

---

[186] Ehwald, 512ff.   [187] *Cf.* Baldwin Brown VI, 2, 111.
[188] *Gest. Pont.* 373.

At length the abbot reached his home in Malmesbury. A grand procession came out to welcome him; monks, headed by the crucifer, swung censers and chanted hymns; lay-folk, both students and peasants of the countryside, stamped their feet and tossed their arms in their delight. Both Ine and Ethelred joined in the general thanksgiving, and their hearts were thrilled by the gifts brought them by Aldhelm from Rome. We do not know what Ethelred received, but Ine became the proud possessor of the altar-stone and placed it in the church he himself was said to have built in honour of Saint Mary the Virgin at Bruton, then a royal borough, seven miles from Frome. The two kings marked the occasion by special courtesy; they declared that, whatever relation should exist in days to come between Mercia and Wessex, the monasteries of Malmesbury and of Frome should constantly carry on in peace their work for God.[189]

Once more Aldhelm turned to work in his cell. It will be of interest here, perhaps, to look at that burden of written correspondence which ever lies heavy on priests and monks. As usual, it dealt with body, soul, and mind. There is a letter to an abbess, Sigegyth by name but otherwise unknown, informing her that the bishop, presumably their diocesan, Haeddi of Winchester, has given his permission for the baptism of a nun; the rite must be administered in strict privacy. Doubtless the bishop feared a scandal in this revelation of a religious still unregenerate. Aldhelm begs "his sister" Sigegyth and her nuns to pray for him, as he does on their behalf, and ends: "Farewell, beloved by me tenfold, nay, a hundred and a thousand-fold; God keep thee well."[190]

The language may seem unusual, as there is no proof that

[189] *Ibid.*, 374.
[190] Ehwald, 497; Jaffé, *Mon. Mog.* 31f.; Eckenstein, 113. The reading Sigegyth is preferable to that of Osgitha or Osyth, or to identification with St. Osgyth or Osyth of Essex: Giles, *PEA* I, 90; Bönhoff, 102.

Aldhelm was related in actual kinship to Sigegyth. But it was not uncommon in spiritual correspondence between Anglo-Saxon saints, monks and nuns, who knew themselves united in the Lord by a charity and respect which feared neither temptation nor reproach.

More interesting letters came as requests for intellectual aid, born of Aldhelm's reputation as writer, of his skill in metrical science and in Hisperic prose.[191] Artwil, son of an Irish king, sent his pages of literary work to the abbot in order that "their Irish roughness might be rubbed off by the file of exquisite taste." We know nothing about this prince except that he was accounted a disciple of some talent.[192] Another youthful petitioner of noble rank was Ethelwald, identified by many scholars as the King Ethelbald of Mercia in later days (716–757). "If this theory could be accepted, we might at this point quote a letter of Ethelwald and some effusions of his in verse as the first extant literary productions of an English king, and as evidence that the new learning was affecting the royal House of Mercia." [193]

The theory is, however, more interesting than probable. This problematical Ethelwald writes to Aldhelm in the most turgid Hisperic style of words and conceits, which must have pleased the abbot, whom he addresses with greatest respect and affection as his "dearest teacher of pure learning" from the time he was a little boy. He begs Aldhelm to read and criticize three poems which he encloses; they are his first attempts at composition, and he wants his teacher to see them as soon as possible.[194]

The first of these, in 70 hexameters, is now lost. The second

[191] *Cf.* Karl Strecker, "Aldhelms Gedichte in Tegernsee," *Archiv* CXLIII, 1922, 177ff.
[192] *Gest. Pont.* 336f.; Browne, *Aldhelm*, 81f.; Bönhoff, 98.
[193] R. Hodgkin, 332, 382h; Ehwald, 522f.; Dümmler, *MGH Epp.* III, i, 238f.; Traube, *Karol. Dicht.* 132 and note 2; Hahn, 178ff.; Bönhoff, 73.
[194] Ehwald, 495ff.

tells of three men, two of them brothers, who brave the dangers of a pilgrimage to Rome. There one brother "leaps from the prison of his flesh to reign in the joy of Paradise." The other two travellers return to England, bearing rich gifts for the Church: relics of saints, pictures of the Blessed Virgin, and silk vestments of brilliant and various hues. At this point the writer, whose Hisperic language is almost incomprehensible, seizes the occasion of describing with great detail but little knowledge the process of silk, from the worm to the spinning-wheel.[195] This poem, as Ethelwald remarked in his letter, had already been sent by him to a certain Wihtfrid (or Wynfrid), a friend of himself and of Aldhelm. There is no evidence which might show him to be Winfrid, later known as Saint Boniface; possibly he was the student whom Aldhelm counselled to stick to wholesome books in Ireland.[196]

The third is dedicated to Aldhelm, "the Master," an outpouring in his praise of 78 rhyming eight-syllabled lines, again filled with uncouth Hisperic words and the alliteration so frequent in Celtic verse. Thus, however unimportant these student poems are in themselves, they form for us a notable link between the earlier Irish verse and that written later in Latin upon the continent of Europe.[197] There is a play upon Aldhelm's name in the words *cassis priscus:* "ancient helmet." [198]

[195] Manitius, *Gesch.*, 141f.; Pliny, *Hist. Nat.* XI, par. 76f.; Ehwald, 528ff.

[196] Traube, 131; Ehwald, 497, note 14; Dümmler, 239, note 3. *Cf.* however, Lehmann, *Hist. Vierteljahrschrift* XXVII, 1932, 768.

[197] Raby, *CLP* 144f.; Ehwald, 519ff., 534f.

[198] Line 15. Two other poems (Ehwald, Nos. III and V: 533f., 535ff.; Dümmler, Nos. III and V: 245ff.) are of uncertain authorship. No. III is a prayer to God, ascribed by Ehwald to Ethelwald (Aelthilwald). Bradley (*EHR* XV, 1900, 291f.) and Ehwald (535ff.) think that No. V was written by Ethelwald to a friend called Hova, reading *Hova* in line 5 and *Aethelwaldi* in line 8. Dümmler reads *have* (following Traube, *Karol. Dicht.* 134) and *Aethilwalde;* they believe that the poem was written by Aldhelm to Aethilwald. The verse is of the same Hisperic character as in the other poems here discussed.

More important is evidence of correspondence between
Aldhelm and Cellanus, Irish abbot of Péronne, a monastery
in the north of France. Péronne is of interest here because of
its connection with that Fursey who came, as we have seen,
from Ireland into East Anglia about 633 to preach to its
people under King Sigebert.[199] There, with the king's consent,
he made for himself a little hermitage within the walls of the
old Roman fortification now called Burgh Castle, near Yar-
mouth; in later years Anna, that king of the East Angles who
loved the cloister so well, enlarged this retreat into a noble
monastery.[200]

Very holy was Fursey. It was told of him that in Ireland he
had been granted a vision of the dread things that befall men,
even good men, as they journey from this world toward
Purgatory. In Ireland people had pressed upon him in crowds;
and since he craved time for prayer as well as for preaching,
he had come to England. But neither did his hermitage in
Burgh Castle give him his desire, and he sought it next in the
solitary life of an anchorite.

For a while all was well. But now, instead of the devout
Christians, the pagans disturbed his prayers. This was the time
when England was constantly harassed by Penda and his warriors. Moreover, Fursey had heard of the strict rule of fasting
and prayer followed in Gaul by the disciples of Columban. So
he departed to Gaul, was received with respect by the reigning
king of the Franks, Clovis II, and by Ercinwald, Clovis' chief
minister, made for himself and his companions another monastery at Lagny-sur-Marne, and died there about 649. His
body was carried off by Ercinwald and placed in a church
which he had built at Péronne, on the river Somme. A monastery was afterwards founded near the church and became a
famous seat of Irish devotion and learning; many Irish pil-

[199] Pp. 15f. *supra.*
[200] Camden, 340f.; *HE* III, c. 19.

grims journeyed there to pray beside the tomb of Saint Fursey, their countryman.[201]

From Cellanus, then, abbot of Péronne, came a letter to Aldhelm that aroused his immediate sympathy: "I, an Irishman, living unknown in the further corner of Frankish land, exile from a renowned community, the lowest and most unworthy servant of Christ, in the one and wondrous Trinity I bid you greeting.[202] To my ignorant ears there has come as it were on wings of praise the fame of your skill in Latin, such as the ears of sensitive readers can hear without a shudder; no caricature or feeble imitation, but endowed with the beauty of true Roman eloquence. It has not been given me to hear you face to face, yet I have read your treatises, so well poised, adorned with divers delightful ornaments. If you would comfort the sadness of a stranger in a foreign land, send me a few sermons composed in your own beautiful style, that the streams drawn from this clear spring may gladden the minds of many, in this place where Saint Fursey rests his sacred body, untouched by decay." [203] The letter was addressed to "The reverend abbot Aldhelm, enriched by study of books, gathering knowledge by night as a bee gathers honey, who has found on Saxon shores what some scarcely gain by toil and sweat in a foreign land."

Only a fragment of Aldhelm's answer remains to us. It was equally generous. "I cannot understand," he wrote, "why you, my esteemed brother, who live in that fruitful land of the Franks, should trouble to write to me, such a very little man of Saxon race, and brought up from my cradle under the northern sky." [204]

[201] Plummer II, 173.
[202] *In tota et tuta Trinitate;* Cellanus had the early mediaeval love of alliteration and playing upon words. Text in Ehwald, 498f. See Traube, *Perrona Scottorum, Münch. Sitz. Akad.* 1900, 477ff.; J. P. Fuhrmann, *Irish Medieval Monasteries on the Continent,* 1927, 19ff.
[203] These *sermunculi* are not extant; *cf. Gest. Pont.* 344.
[204] Ehwald, 499; see *Gest. Pont.* 333, 337.

Another letter from an "unknown Irishman," as he called himself, petitioned for teaching from Aldhelm as "one who excels in Latin eloquence, who understands the needs of those who live on the continent of Europe, inasmuch as he has visited Rome and was, moreover, trained in his youth by holy Maelduib of Irish race." If Aldhelm will only consent, this Irish sojourner in a foreign land is confident he can find horses and a servant for his journey. In the meantime, would Aldhelm of his charity lend him, just for a little while, a certain book he longs to read? [205]

Aldhelm's correspondence was not only private. In 705 a synod of Saxon bishops met, probably in Wessex, and gravely considered what they could do for the conversion of the British in the west from their persistent error regarding the monastic tonsure and the date of keeping Easter. Aldhelm was present at this meeting, and a resolution was passed unanimously, which requested him to write a letter of rebuke and exhortation to Geraint, British king in Devon and Cornwall, and to the clergy of these regions. The honour was a great one, for it recognized in Aldhelm the most prominent scholar among churchmen of Wessex.

For once he restrained somewhat his love of ornate discourse, in the thought that he was writing to a Briton, not a Saxon scholar. But his address is most courteous: "To the most glorious ruler of the western kingdom, whom I embrace in brotherly affection." [206] Then follow the four reasons which have caused the bishops to send this admonition:

First, it is known that British priests do not dwell in the harmony of the Church and the following of Holy Scripture, that through their feuds and contentions grave scandal is arising.

[205] Ehwald, 494.
[206] On this letter see Ehwald, 480ff. (he dates it 680); H.S. III, 268ff.; Jones, *ODT* 100f.; Bright, 462ff.; Gougaud, 200.

Secondly, it is widely said that in Devon and Cornwall priests and clerics wear a tonsure of Celtic ordering, refusing that of holy Peter—a Celtic tonsure that follows the example of Simon Magus, the Magician, who himself attempted black art against this apostle. But the Roman tonsure worn in the Church of Christ by Peter and his successors is of the shape of the crown of thorns, the crown of true priesthood.

Thirdly, and this is most serious of all, the Celtic clergy and their people do not follow the rule laid down by the Council of Nicaea, that the method of calculating Easter should be based on a cycle of nineteen years, and that Easter Day should fall between the fifteenth and the twenty-first day of the moon, inclusive. They follow, to their shame, a canon forbidden by Rome. They are "Quarto-decimans," keeping Easter with the Jews on the fourteenth day, and are therefore guilty of heresy.[207]

Fourthly, Aldhelm continues, as a result of this the Celtic priests who dwell beyond the river Severn in South Wales [208] are so alien to the Roman communion "that they will neither pray in church with us, who are Saxons owing allegiance to Rome, nor will they eat at table with us. Worse, they throw out the food left over from our meals to dogs waiting open-mouthed and to foul pigs; they give orders that the dishes and bowls which we have used must be scraped and scoured with sand or with cinders before they are fit to be placed upon their tables. They give us no greeting of peace, no kiss of brotherhood, no basin or towels for washing our hands and feet, as the Lord bade His disciples offer to travellers. If any one of us of the Catholic Church goes to live among them, far from receiving him into their fellowship, they force him to undergo penance for forty days."

[207] Gougaud, 187; Plummer II, 349. For the misstatements of this letter see Bruno Krusch, *Neues Archiv* IX, 1884, 106f., 161f.
[208] Bright, 465, note 1.

The letter ends with an appeal to these Celts of the west to forsake their pride and stubbornness, to return to the Church of that Peter who holds the keys of Heaven and who will surely, according to his commission, bind fast in punishment those who spurn the Roman ritual of the tonsure and the Easter Feast. Let none be confident in that he believes the Christian Faith of God in One and One in Three, of the Incarnation, the Passion and Resurrection of the Lord, of the Judgment of all souls at the Last Day. No! Aldhelm retorts. Faith without works is dead, and there can be no true Catholic who is not living in union with the Truth, which is Christ; and these are the very words of that Truth: "Thou art Peter, and upon this rock I will build my Church" . . .

His words were not fruitless. William of Malmesbury, writing in the twelfth century, maintained that "the British owe to this day their correction to Aldhelm; although because of their inborn villainy they give him no credit and have destroyed his book." [209]

At the same time Aldhelm was still carrying on his work as architect. Perhaps we may attribute to these years the raising of yet another church at Malmesbury, dedicated to Michael, that saint held in honour in England from the time when the hill of Glastonbury received his name. It was placed near the church of Saint Mary, Mother of God, and William tells us that it was still standing in his time, "surpassing in its beauty and its magnitude any English church of ancient days." [210] Doubtless it was adorned with treasures which Aldhelm had brought from Rome.

Another daughter monastery was also built, this time at Bradford-on-Avon in Wiltshire, of stone quarried in the neighbourhood. Concerning this, William wrote that in his time

[209] *Gest. Pont.* 361; *cf. HE* V, c. 18.
[210] J. Armitage Robinson, *Somerset Historical Essays,* 1921, 13f.; *Gest. Pont.* 361f.

there remained here "a little church, said to have been made by Aldhelm, dedicated to Saint Laurence." He goes on to relate sadly that the dwellings of the monks at Frome and at Bradford, like mortal men themselves, have disappeared under the ravages of the Danes or the rioting of the English.[211] As is well-known, Bradford-on-Avon is still famous for its Saxon church, restored from material found at the original site of Aldhelm's monastery; but the architecture of the present "ecclesiola" belongs probably to the tenth century.[212]

The abbot of Malmesbury was now about sixty-six years old. Surely it was natural that his mind should look forward to tranquil meditation in his own home, dwelling serenely upon the land of the morrow and his work in the life to come. Even, however, as he was thinking these thoughts, events were moving to shape far differently the disposing of his last days.

For a long time Theodore, as Archbishop of Canterbury, had keenly desired the division of some of the great dioceses of England into smaller sees. In 673 the first national council of the English Church had met at Hertford under his leadership, and he had proposed that "the number of English bishops be increased as the number of the faithful grow larger." But he had not been able to convince the council, and the matter had lain undecided in theory.[213] Not in actual practice, however, for he was a man of action, and an opportunity had presented itself shortly afterward at Dunwich in Suffolk, the one and only see in East Anglia since the time of Felix. Its

[211] Gest. Pont. 346.
[212] Baldwin Brown II, 1925, 296ff., 445; VI, 2, 178ff.; Clapham, ERA 60, 66, 108 (and Plate 37), 110, 112, 114, 137.
[213] HE IV, c. 5; H.S. III, 120; Plummer II, 211ff.; Bright, 274ff., 281f.; Whitney, CMH II, 531. The date 672 is given by Poole, Studies, 41; Stenton, 133; R. Hodgkin, 305. For the reckoning of time according to the Bedan Indiction see Poole, Medieval Reckonings of Time, 1918, 30f., and Studies, 38ff.; J. E. W. Wallis, English Regnal Years and Titles, 1921, 16; Stenton, 76, note I.

bishop, Bisi, had been forced by ill-health to resign, and Theodore had appointed one Acci as his successor, at the same
time carving out of its diocese another bishopric, with its seat
at Elmham in Norfolk; this he had entrusted to a prelate by
the name of Badwine.[214] Later on, in 678, the Archbishop had
caused much turmoil in the north of England by his decision
to divide the vast diocese of York.[215]

Twelve years later this Theodore, who served England so
well by his administration, yet of whom no miracles wrought
by prayer were recorded despite his vigorous piety, and whom
the Church has, therefore, never distinguished in her calendar
as saint, died at the age of eighty-eight. For nearly two years
no Metropolitan was found to rule at Canterbury; in 692
Bertwald, abbot of Reculver in Kent, was chosen: "a man
learned in the Scriptures and excellently trained in ecclesiastical and monastic discipline, yet in no way to be compared
with his predecessor." [216] Another year passed before he was
consecrated by Godwin, Archbishop of Lyons and Metropolitan of France; and not until the last day of August, 693,
did Canterbury's Church once again receive a ruler.

Bertwald followed the policy of Theodore in regard to the
division of dioceses. We have a letter written to him by Waldhere, bishop of London, concerning grounds of quarrel between the rulers of Wessex and of the East Saxons, in whose
realm of Essex London lay. The letter was written before
July, 705; in it Waldhere reminds the Archbishop of Canterbury that a provincial council of English bishops held in the
preceding year, 704, had warned the clergy of Wessex of sus-
pension from communion with their brethren if they did not
at once appoint another bishop of Wessex in addition to

[214] *HE ibid.;* Plummer II, 214f.
[215] Ch. II *infra.*
[216] *HE* V, c. 8; see J. Armitage Robinson, *Somerset Hist. Essays,* 28f.;
Plummer II, 283.

Haeddi, bishop of Winchester.[217] Most probably Haeddi himself was opposed to the division of his diocese; his opposition
might well spring from the fact that Wessex had been so distracted by warring claimants to its throne during his earlier
years in office.[218]

In July, however, of this year 705 Haeddi died, and with
him passed any resistance to Bertwald's desire. Without delay
a council of the clergy of Wessex decided to divide its charge between two bishops. One was to hold the diocese of Winchester,
including Berkshire, Wiltshire, Dorset, Hampshire, Surrey,
and, most probably, Sussex; the other was to rule "to the West
of the [Selwood] Forest," in practice, perhaps, over the region
of Dorset lying around Sherborne, Somerset and part of
Devon, with the charge of exercising such missionary influence as he might over the Celtic British in Devon and Cornwall. His seat was to be placed at Sherborne in Dorsetshire;
thus bishop would work with king in promoting Saxon rule
among the British.[219]

William of Malmesbury complained that the larger share,
that of Sherborne, was given to Aldhelm and declared it was
unfair. He writes, moreover, that "Sherborne is a village, possessing no attraction in number of inhabitants nor in charm
of situation; it is a wonder, even a shame, that an episcopal
see should have been held there during so many centuries." [220]

The prelate chosen for Winchester was Daniel, a candidate
"born in this west country, not wanting in erudition," and

---

[217] H.S. III, 267, 274f. A decree, quoted in H.S. III, 126f., declaring that the diocese of Wessex was not to be divided during the life of
Haeddi, is of doubtful authenticity; see H.S. *in loc.* and Bright, 462.

[218] *DCB* II, 874.

[219] *ASC* ann. 709. Ethelweard (*saec.* X) writes that the diocese cov-
ered the land commonly known as "Selwoodshire": *MHB* I, 507. For
discussion of the perplexed question of this division of dioceses see F. P.
Magoun Jr., "Aldhelm's Diocese of Sherborne *Bewestan Wuda*," *HTR*
XXXII, 1939, 103ff. He suggests that Aldhelm's diocese lay "west of the
(Hampshire) Weald." *Cf.* also Wildman, 43f.

[220] *Gest. Pont.* 375f., 175.

destined to play an interesting part in the lives of Saint Boniface
and the Venerable Bede. This rather modest praise of William
of Malmesbury for a man who was conspicuous in later days
for his learning and powers of organization was due to comparison with his hero, the founder of his own abbey.[221] To
Aldhelm's consternation he found himself the choice of all,
clergy and laymen of every age and every rank, for the new
see of Sherborne.

Aldhelm as abbot of Malmesbury must have been present
at the council. We can well imagine the thoughts which now
overwhelmed him. He saw his ordered routine, the tranquillity
of his cloister, leisure for prayer over and above the rule of his
monastic duty, time for study and writing, all disappearing
before the demands upon a bishop of unnumbered souls,
Christian and heathen, monastic and secular; in a country
still unsettled in its social life, still disturbed by the resistance
of Celtic rebels against the practice of the Church Catholic.
He pleaded his age, and was told that in this lay a great advantage, the rule of a wiser, more experienced man. As long
as he could, he resisted; finally, fearing to disobey the Spirit
which sounded in all voices around him, he yielded himself,
"colleague for his brother bishops, father for his clergy, protector for his layfolk."

His consent may have been hastened by the pleading of
Bertwald, his Archbishop; tradition tells that they had been
students together and "together had trodden the monastic
path." [222] At Canterbury in the autumn of this same year
Bertwald laid hands upon him for his consecrating, and there
he remained for some time, partly at the desire of the Archbishop who wished his advice in regard to various problems,

---

[221] *Ibid.*, 375. Perhaps, however, Daniel had been trained at Malmesbury. He retired to live there in 744, after resigning his see, troubled by
blindness: *ibid.*, 160; *Epp. Bonif.* 63; Bright, 470.
[222] *Gest. Pont.* 376.

partly, no doubt, in his own longing to pray once more in the abbey of Saint Paul and Saint Peter, the home of his student days, and to talk with Hadrian, his former master, still teaching and administering as its abbot and the head of its school.

There is a story connected with Aldhelm's stay which is worth repeating. One day, it is said, he visited Dover; he had heard that ships had come into its port, and he was hoping that they had brought from France books or other treasures for the Church. When he had examined what they offered, a manuscript containing the whole of the Old and the New Testament especially attracted him, and, as he looked through it with a connoisseur's eye, he asked the price. It was too high for honesty, and the rude sailors jeered when he suggested more reasonable terms. Their insults only brought a smile from Aldhelm, which so enraged them that they thrust him roughly from their boat and put out to sea. Suddenly in the strait, notorious for bad weather, clouds overcast the sky, the wind rose, and a storm broke out in fury. The sailors, unable to row or to steer, were soon tossing at the mercy of the waves, in imminent peril of drowning. As a last hope they appealed with calls and outstretched arms to Aldhelm, who still stood upon the shore. At once he answered. Making the sign of the Cross, he calmed the storm, and all was once more peace. Then he climbed by a ladder to the deck of their ship, where the sailors, their jeers lost in gratitude, offered him the Bible as a gift. This he refused, but bought it at the price he had originally offered. William of Malmesbury, who relates the tale, declares that in the twelfth century this Bible was still inspected by pilgrims to his abbey.[223]

And now came the time for bidding farewell to the monks of Malmesbury and Frome and Bradford-on-Avon. Let them,

[223] *Ibid.*, 376ff. The story illustrates Aldhelm's passion for books: R. Hodgkin, 323f.

Aldhelm bade, now elect an abbot to rule them, one of their own choosing, in accordance with the decree granted by Pope Sergius. Their answer was immediate. As long as he lived, they would have none but Aldhelm himself, whether bishop of Sherborne or not. During his time, at least, they said they would suffer no tyranny, sure of his kindly wisdom and skill. Such pleading at last became irresistible, and once more Aldhelm yielded, promising to remain their abbot until his death, and to use all his influence against any attempt to suppress their liberty of electing whom they would as his successor. A charter embodying these points has come down to us, signed "at the convent of Wimborne." [224]

Four years as bishop of Sherborne Aldhelm laboured in the southwest of England, "constant in preaching night as well as day, diligently journeying to the various parts of his diocese, given to fasting and good works, even as in the prime of his age." [225] We know too little about this period of his life. Probably it was then that he was served as deacon by the young monk Pecthelm, afterward appointed about 730 as the first bishop of the restored see of Whithorn, where Ninian had preached in his *Candida Casa*, "White House," at the end of the fourth century.[226] William of Malmesbury also says that Aldhelm built at Sherborne "a marvellous church" that had lasted through the centuries.[227]

His immediate care was surely given to his *familia* or clergy,

[224] *Gest. Pont.* 378ff. Kemble (I, No. liv) does not accept the charter as authentic. *Cf.* Birch, No. 114 and H.S. III, 276. It tells of the confirming of the action of Aldhelm in a council held near the river Noodr (Nodder), Wilts (*cf.* Ekwall, *English River-Names*, 1928, 297). Ehwald (514f.) holds it genuine; we may, at least, believe in the granting of such privilege.

[225] *Gest. Pont.* 382. The remark of Faricius (*PEA* I, 369) that "as bishop, hindered by secular business, Aldhelm no longer excelled in virtues as before" means that he could not give as much time to prayer as of old at Malmesbury.

[226] *HE* V, cc. 18, 23; *Gest. Pont.* 257; Bright, 444, note 4. Pecthelm may, however, have been under Aldhelm at Malmesbury: Ehwald, xiii.

[227] *Gest. Pont.* 378.

the secular priests and deacons who formed his household
and worked under his direction throughout the west country.[228]
A poem, now described as addressed to Aldhelm by some unknown cleric, may have been written by a member of this
cathedral staff while travelling in such work. The verses,
Hisperically elaborated and filled with strange words, as usual,
tell that the writer has journeyed through Devon and Cornwall; that on his road he was overtaken by a storm of wind
and rain, which he magnifies in language worthy of Lucan's
famous hurricane; that he sought shelter in some monastery
near the sea. There in the winter darkness he sang Matins
with the monks in honour of Saint Paul, for it was the day
of his Feast. The apostle rewarded the weary traveller; for
as monks and guest came out from the church, they saw chaos
before them: uprooted trees, scattered stones and beams, and
the guest-house lying in ruins. But for his devotions he might
have been sleeping there! [229]

Letters, doubtless, were written and received in still greater
number by Aldhelm as bishop. To this time we may perhaps
refer one written to that Ethelwald who had once begged of
him criticism of several efforts in verse. The young man does
not seem to have persevered in study—or even in sober life—
as he grew older. Aldhelm now writes apparently to repeat
what he had already said at some time of a meeting in person.
He exhorts his "beloved son and pupil" that, youth though
he be, he do not indulge to excess in the pleasures of this
world, in daily revels of feasting and drinking, in wild roaming
around the country on horseback, in covetousness of money
and social success. Far better to study spiritual books and say
his prayers; if he must read something different, let it at
least inspire his mind and increase his understanding of sacred

[228] Calthrop, *VHD* 62. See also the interesting discussion by T. S.
Holmes, "The Conversion of Wessex": *EHR* VII, 1892, 437ff.
[229] Ehwald, 523ff.; Traube, *Karol. Dicht.*, 132.

texts. "Please," so ends the letter, "please, keep these written words of mine on the table at which you write and read, that they may be to you as the voice of your master recalling you to duty." [230]

As abbot of Malmesbury, Aldhelm continued to control the monasteries of Frome and of Bradford-on-Avon; advice and aid were asked of him by other congregations, as by that at Glastonbury. Another which he held in mind is also well-known to us, the nunnery at Wimborne in Dorsetshire, where he was said to have signed the charter of freedom for Malmesbury's monks. The extant version, in which the name of the abbess appears as Cuthburga, is spurious, no doubt.[231] But we know that a Cuthburga founded about this time a convent of nuns at Wimborne, to which either she or King Ine in all probability added a congregation of monks, and that from this monastery sprang Wimborne Minster. We may believe, also, that this Cuthburga was the same as that sister of King Ine of Wessex, to whom, as his own kinswoman, and to all her fellow-nuns living under obedience to Abbess Hildilid at Barking, Aldhelm had addressed his prose and verse on the virgin life. Since the writing of those counsels she had left Barking to rule in Wimborne, probably with the aid of her sister, the Princess Cuenburga.[232]

Such were his labours. With the daily care of all parts of his diocese, they were too heavy for a man who was reaching his threescore years and ten and had never thought about his body's comfort. In the spring of 709 Aldhelm knew that his strength was at an end. To his monks, his clergy and his people, he gave his last commission, bidding them keep the bond of charity in the unity of peace, commending all to God as a good shepherd caring for his sheep, and asking the

---

[230] Ehwald, 499f.   [231] P. 86, note 224 *supra*.
[232] *DCB* I, 730.

friends of his household that his body be buried in that place which of all he loved best, the abbey of Malmesbury. His last hour came on the twenty-fifth of May, while he was still at work, visiting his clergy and people at Doulting in Somerset. He asked to be carried into the wooden church, and there, sitting on a stone, "he passed gloriously from this world to the welcome of Michael and all angels in heaven." [233]

At the moment of his passing, the story goes, a vision appeared to one of his friends, Egwin, bishop of Worcester, bidding him hasten to Doulting, where Aldhelm lay dead. Sorrow quickened his way; he offered requiem in that little wooden church for the departed soul and gave command that the body be carried at once to Malmesbury, a distance of fifty miles. As the funeral procession started, a long line of people walked before and behind the bier; "each thought himself the more blessed if he could walk nearer, happy if he could see, were it not possible to touch." [234]

Every seven miles, according to William of Malmesbury, the procession rested for a while, and a stone cross was erected to mark the place, that passers-by might kneel to say a prayer. These crosses, still to be seen in his time, were known as "bishop-stones," and one, he tells us, was standing in the cloister of Malmesbury.[235] We cannot be sure of the route thus marked; perhaps by way of Frome, Bradford-on-Avon, Bath, and the villages of Colerne and Littleton Drew.[236]

With reverent affection the monks of Malmesbury received the bier, torn between sorrow for themselves and joy for their abbot, now in peace. Some days were given to prayer while the body lay guarded by their walls; then it was laid to rest

---

[233] Faricius, ed. Giles, *PEA* I, 369.
[234] *Gest. Pont.* 383f.
[235] *Ibid.*, 384.
[236] See Browne, *Aldhelm,* 150ff.; *cf.* Baldwin Brown VI, 2, 168, on the stone crosses.

in the church of Saint Michael, as Aldhelm himself had desired.[237]

There the sacred relics remained for more than two hundred years. One of the Saxon kings who reigned in the ninth century, King Ethelwulf of Wessex, pupil of Swithin of Winchester and father of Alfred the Great, gave to the abbey a magnificent shrine for their keeping. It was adorned with figures in relief of solid silver and with representations of miracles owed to Aldhelm's prayers; at its end was a crystal headpiece on which his name was engraved in letters of gold. Apparently, however, the monks of Malmesbury did not venture to disturb the bones of their Founder.[238]

In the tenth century a grandson of Alfred, Athelstan, who ruled England from 924 until 940,[239] held Aldhelm in special reverence. Tradition told that in the evening before the battle of Brunanburh, where in 937 he routed the Danes and their Scottish friends, he was taken by surprise and almost slain by Anlaf Guthfrithson, king of the Danes of Dublin. Athelstan's sword had fallen from its sheath by accident; but he called upon God and Saint Aldhelm, and it was miraculously restored to him. The grateful king offered priceless relics as gifts at the shrine of Malmesbury, and after his death his body was buried beneath the altar of its church of Saint Mary.[240]

In the year 955 Eadwig, nephew of Athelstan, came to the throne of England and began his strife with Dunstan, then abbot of Glastonbury. Among other acts of irreverence he expelled the monks from Malmesbury and installed in their

[237] *Gest. Pont.* 385.   [238] *Ibid.*, 389f.
[239] Or 939; see Stenton, 352; Beaven, *EHR* XXXII, 1917, 530f.
[240] *Gest. Reg.* I, 143f., 150f., 157; *Gest. Pont.* 21 (with differing detail), 396f. For the error of William of Malmesbury regarding the Danish leader see Alastair Campbell, ed. *The Battle of Brunanburh*, 1938, 48f.

place secular clergy. And yet, we read, this evil deed had one good result; these seculars removed the bones of Aldhelm to that splendid shrine of Ethelwulf so long awaiting them.[241] The monks were restored to their abbey by Eadwig's brother and successor, King Edgar, under Dunstan's influence.[242]

For Dunstan, too, revered Malmesbury and its Founder. He, also, had been born in Wessex and had been taught by Irish pilgrims to Glastonbury, where he spent as a youth years in study of the Scriptures and of various arts and crafts, including painting, music, and metal work. As abbot of Glastonbury he rebuilt the church which Ine had raised there on earlier foundations; as head of its monastic school he must often have drawn inspiration from Malmesbury in Wiltshire. After he was called to be Archbishop of Canterbury in 960 by Edgar, he, on his part, made his offerings; he gave to Malmesbury Abbey bells of great size and beautiful tone and an organ with pipes of bronze, inscribed:

Organa do sancto praesul Dunstanus Adelmo;
Perdat hic aeternum qui vult hinc tollere regnum:

I, Dunstan, Chief Bishop, this organ give to holy Aldhelm;
Who tries to take it hence, of Heaven's eternal realm be he
  bereft.[243]

The Archbishop was famed in Saxon England for his own knowledge of bells and for the zeal with which he promoted their use; from the Middle Ages to our own days the great bell of Canterbury Cathedral has borne his name. In mediaeval England it was customary to toll a church bell during a storm of thunder and lightning, that the evil spirits, who were thought to work such terror, might themselves flee at its

[241] *Gest. Pont.* 403; *Gest. Reg.* 163; Bönhoff, 95f.
[242] *Vita S. Dunstani auct. Will. Malm.*: RS LXIII, ed. Stubbs, 301f.
[243] *Gest. Pont.* 407; Faricius, *PEA* I, 371.

sound. The "Storm Bell" at Malmesbury Abbey was known as the bell of Saint Aldhelm.[244]

Years afterward, fearing the Danish invaders and their love of spoil, Dunstan, "after long and deep deliberation," removed the relics of Aldhelm from their costly shrine and placed them, wrapped in fine linen and scarlet cloth, in a plain tomb at the right of the altar of Saint Mary's church. This church was now the centre of the abbey, and in it the monks said their Mass and Hours.[245] It was also while Dunstan lived that the Benedictine Rule was fully established in Malmesbury, through his influence and that of Ethelwold, whom he consecrated bishop of Winchester.[246]

Under Ethelred "Lack-Counsel," king of England from 978 until 1016, the Danes did raid the abbey. William of Malmesbury relates that it profited them little, for the monks had diligently removed all the treasures likely to attract them, except that shrine which once had held the Founder's bones. One of these northern robbers, so the story goes, drew near, knife in hand, to scrape off jewels that encrusted the shrine, but he was immediately thrown by unseen force to the pavement. The others fled in terror, and the abbey remained henceforth in peace.[247]

The eleventh century was eventful for Malmesbury's monks. Toward its end, Warin, a monk of Lire in Normandy, came to be their abbot, but his Norman spirit could not abide the sight of all the Saxon relics assembled in their church, of abbots who had died there, of abbots who had been transferred elsewhere but had willed in the hour of death that their bones should rest in the church of our Lady and holy Aldhelm. So

[244] H. B. Walters, *The Church Bells of Wiltshire*, 1927–1929, 128ff.; Aubrey, 76.
[245] *Gest. Pont.* 408; 386; 405.
[246] Cf. *Vita S. Dunstani auct.* B.: RS LXIII, 25; Knowles, 34; 49.
[247] *Gest. Pont.* 409f.

Warin turned them out, even those of Maelduib, decreed that they should be heaped in a corner of Saint Michael's church, and laughed as he did it. Yet his sin was somewhat the lighter in that he highly esteemed Aldhelm, the Founder of his abbey, and determined that his relics should no longer lie hidden in that plain tomb of stone. Long he deliberated, and his monks prayed and fasted with him three full days. Then he petitioned Osmund, bishop of Old Sarum, that they be replaced in their shrine of splendour, and Osmund came to preside at the ceremony of this translation. The year was 1078.[248] Even more magnificent was the decree of Lanfranc, Archbishop of Canterbury from 1070 till 1089, declaring to all the English that Aldhelm should be held and venerated among them as one of the saints of Christendom.[249]

In the earlier twelfth century the church of Saint Mary, which William of Malmesbury looked upon and held as loveliest in the England of his time, was still a Saxon building. Shortly after he wrote, the magnificent Norman church, of which we can still see part, was raised upon the same hill. In the thirteenth century, Abbot William, of Colerne in Wiltshire, rebuilt much of the dwellings of the monks; in the fourteenth, a spire which reached even higher toward heaven than that of Salisbury was added, only to fall about 1541. And not unnaturally, for two years before, the last abbot, Robert Frampton, with his twenty-one monks had surrendered all to Henry VIII. In this very year of the falling spire the church was sold to a Mr. William Stumpe, a rich clothier of Malmesbury; he presented its nave to the congregation of the parish church of the town, and it was at once licensed for public worship by Cranmer. The rest of the monastic buildings were destroyed or allowed to fall into decay. The priceless manu-

---

[248] *Ibid.*, 421ff.; *cf.* Knowles, 118f.; Browne, *Aldhelm*, 209ff.
[249] *Gest. Pont.* 428.

scripts in the library were stuffed into the bungholes of ale barrels or made into covers for school books; as Aubrey, historian of Wiltshire, put it, "they flew about like butterflies." [250] The register of the abbey owed its preservation to the fact that it could serve the Court of Exchequer in defining the exact due of land and tenantry that now fell into the king's hands. Of the Norman church only part of the nave and of the south aisle, with the glorious south porch, stand in the present time overlooking the town. We may take comfort in that this was the last monastery in Wiltshire to yield its inheritance to secular power.[251]

Sherborne Minster was also held in honour after Aldhelm's death. Two kings of Wessex, Ethelbald and Ethelbert, lie buried there.[252] The secular clergy of Aldhelm's household gave place to Benedictine monks toward the end of the tenth century, through the discipline of one of Sherborne's greatest bishops, Saint Wulsige or Wulsin.[253]

The last bishop to rule there was Herman of the eleventh century. In the days of Edward the Confessor he held first the see of Ramsbury, carved for the spiritual charge of Wiltshire out of the Sherborne diocese. His ambition at that time was to hold both the bishoprics of Sherborne and of Ramsbury united in his own hands and to settle his "bishop's stool" at Malmesbury, doubtless intending to rule its monks, also, as their abbot.

But the monks of Aldhelm's Malmesbury had not forgotten their Founder's bequest of free choice of their ruler, and they appealed for aid to Earl Harold, Godwine's son. His support

[250] Aubrey, 79.
[251] Harold Brakspear, "Malmesbury Abbey," *Archaeologia* LXIV, 1913, 399ff.; M. R. James, *Abbeys*, 1926, 26ff.; Ralph Adams Cram, *The Ruined Abbeys of Great Britain*, 1927, 221ff.; Edward Hutton, *Highways and Byways in Wiltshire*, 1928, 352ff.
[252] *ASC* ann. 860.
[253] *Gest. Pont.* 178; *Vita S. Dunstani auct. Will. Malm.: RS* LXIII, 304; *cf.* Dugdale I, 337; James, *Abbeys*, 33ff.; Calthrop, *VHD* 63.

drove the invader from their doors. However, after some years of discontent, Herman saw his aim partly realized, in so far as he held the united sees of Ramsbury and Sherborne under his charge. In 1075 the Council of London required that bishops settle their seats of government in large rather than in small and obscure places; shortly afterward Herman was translated to Old Sarum, and the sees of Ramsbury and Sherborne, no longer known by name, were merged in the Sarum diocese.[254]

Many miracles, of course, were told of Aldhelm in later legend. The four stories best known are those of the beam, of the chasuble, of the baby, and of the trees. To their fame a few words are due.

When Saint Mary's church at Malmesbury was in process of building, beams of wood were assembled with difficulty and at great expense from a far distance. All had been cut to exact measure, except one, which was too short. Operations were stopped, and the worried workmen, after debating to no purpose, reported the trouble to Aldhelm. The abbot not only by his prayer immediately lengthened out the beam to equal its fellows, but in his modesty pretended to scold his workmen for carelessness; in reality, he maintained, this beam had never lacked its proper size. Yet they knew better.[255]

Two marvels are connected with Aldhelm's stay in Rome. One morning at the end of his Mass in the Lateran, his mind was so rapt in contemplation that in taking off his chasuble he let it fall behind him; his server had always been there to receive it. This time, unhappily, the server was not. But the Lord, Who never slumbers nor wanders in thought, was at hand to protect the sacred vestment. He sent through the window a sunbeam, on which the chasuble rested in mid-air until it could be reverently borne away.

[254] Gest. Pont. 67f.; 182f.   [255] Ibid., 362.

The third legend describes the craft and subtlety of the devil at work against the Pope himself. Sergius was accused by a nun, who had forsaken her monastic vow, as father of her nameless child. The horrid tale was whispered from ear to ear, and Rome first smouldered, then blazed with indignation of quick credulity. Aldhelm, guest of Sergius at this moment, publicly exhorted the people to come to their senses, but in vain. Then he ordered the baby to be brought into church, where, to the intense enjoyment of the crowd, he baptized it, nine days old, and then commanded it to declare the truth. The infant promptly cleared the Pope of all evil thought, word, or deed in this matter; and the people who came to mock remained to give glory to God and His priest.[256]

The village of Bishopstrow near Warminster in Wiltshire holds the fame of the fourth story. Once, when Aldhelm arrived there to preach to its people on the open green, he drove, as was natural, the point of his long ashen staff into the ground by his side before he began. In his fervour he preached so long that the staff took root, and he left it there as a living memorial to the power of the Lord of Nature. Gradually it grew into a tree, and many trees sprang from its roots; at last the village received the name of *ad Episcopi arbores*, Bishop's trees: in the Saxon form which still remains, Biscopestreu, Bishopstrow.[257] Its present church is dedicated in honour of Saint Aldhelm; so is the church at Doulting in Somerset, and that of Broadway in the same shire.[258]

Tradition, sacred and secular, still keeps alive Aldhelm's name at Malmesbury. Here long ago were guarded his copy of the Psalter and the chasuble in which he chanted Mass; here its folk strolled across Saint Aldhelm's meadow and made merry year by year at Saint Aldhelm's Fair in his own month

[256] *Ibid.*, 365ff. [257] Gover, 151.
[258] Arnold-Forster I, 406.

of May. Here still they linger by Saint Aldhelm's well, and journey half a dozen miles or so to Hilmarton, recorded in Domesday Book as Adhelmertone.[259] Here, in the town nearly surrounded by the streams of the river Avon and of Newnton brook, pilgrims still cross a bridge and walk its streets. Many now connect them with other names. Philosophers remember that strange legend of John the Scot: how men told that he taught in Malmesbury School in the ninth century, and was slain there by his own students, "thrusting and strikking hym with their table pointelles." [260] More reasonably, they recall that Thomas Hobbes was born here in 1538. Historians look back upon Sir Walter Raleigh, living here in comfort upon his own estate between expeditions and adventures overseas; with greater gratitude they recall William, monk of Malmesbury, for his "deeds of kings and of bishops in England."

Fewer there may be, perhaps, who, as they climb the hill that leads to Aldhelm's shrine, think of him as the first Saxon who is known for his Latin verses and his study of their mysteries; who strove hard to hand on to his Saxon students the culture that Ireland and Italy—the Celt and the Roman— had inextricably entwined in him; who wrote his pompous and pedantic elaborations, yet was withal a beloved abbot and teacher; who, like Gregory the Great, left the peace of his abbey that he might minister to a restless world; who loved his books only less than he loved his holy Church.[261]

[259] Gover, 268.   [260] Hutton, *ibid.*, 354.
[261] The name of St. Aldhelm appears in the Scottish Calendar and was included in the proposed Anglican Calendar of 1928.

Chapter II

WILFRID OF YORK

WILFRID OF YORK

THE FLOWERING hedges and trees of the English country-side, which had seen Aldhelm's funeral procession pass by in May, 709, were heavy with the green of late summer as two men rode their horses along the public way near Lichfield in the Midlands. The elder of the two journeyed slowly and with effort, for his years had long reached the count of seventy. Yet his eyes were still quick and eager, his bearing noble and confident, as of one well accustomed to command; his dress was plain, marked only by the rounded tonsure, token of his monastic calling, and by the jewelled ring on his finger which showed his rank of bishop. His companion wore a like tonsure; but the reverence of his manner was evidently not only that of a younger to an older man, but of a spiritual son to his well-loved Father in God.

As they rode, Wilfrid, bishop of Hexham and abbot of Ripon, related, as his biographer Eddius tells us in his description of their travels, the story of his life to his kinsman and constant companion, Tatbert, monk and priest of the Church in the north of England.[1]

His story began in that year 633–634, "evil of fortune and hateful to all good men, both for the apostasy of Saxon rulers, wherein they had thrown off the sacraments of the Christian faith, and for the raging tyranny of the British king." The apostate rulers had been Osric, king of Deira, one of the two provinces into which Northumbria was divided at

[1] Eddius, c. 65.

this time, and Eanfrid, king of Bernicia, the other province. Both had succeeded the great Edwin, who had held Deira and Bernicia united under his single governing.[2]

The reign of Edwin is remembered because it saw the first conversion to Christianity of Northumbria, the land stretching northward from the Humber to the Forth. Even before he came to its throne, he had learned something of Christian teaching. Welsh tradition told that in his young days the two provinces, Deira and Bernicia, had also been under separate rule; that Edwin, driven from Deira by Ethelfrid, king of its neighbouring state, had sought the protection of King Cadfan of North Wales, who with his subjects adhered to the Celtic Christian Church of Britain. Afterward he had fled to Redwald, king of the East Angles, who was trying to serve Christ and pagan gods at the same time by putting up in his church altars to the glory of both.[3]

But it was still as a professed pagan that Edwin with the aid of his friend Redwald had at last worked his revenge by slaying King Ethelfrid in 617 on the bank of the river Idle,[4] a tributary of the Trent, and in his turn had forced into exile Ethelfrid's seven sons, of whom three are of note in this history: Eanfrid, Oswald, and Oswy. Not until after he had asked and gained in marriage the devout Ethelberga, daughter of Ethelbert, king of Kent, did Edwin yield to the Church. Three agents had moved him slowly forward: first, his queen; secondly, her confessor, Paulinus, who as a simple monk had ventured with Augustine from Rome into Kent at command of Pope Gregory the Great and had been ordained bishop at

---

[2] HE III, c. 1.
[3] Ibid., II, cc. 12 and 15; Plummer II, 93, 114; Rhys, Celtic Britain, 1908, 128.
[4] The year is given variously as 616 or 617. See Plummer II, 66; Stenton, 79; R. Hodgkin, 729; ASC ann. 617; HE II, c. 12; III, c. 1; Sim. Durh. I, 363. For Edwin's conversion and marriage with Ethelberga (in 625) see HE II, cc. 9f.; for his marriage with Cwenburga, ibid., II, c. 14.

Canterbury that he might go to the pagan north as chaplain of this Christian bride; thirdly, a letter from the Pope of this time, Boniface V. The Princess Ethelberga had come as a second wife to Edwin; during his long exile he had stayed, it seems, some time in Mercia and had first married a daughter of its King Cearl. Her name was Cwenburga, and she had borne his son Osfrid.

Among all the events that had drawn Edwin toward conversion two are of special interest here. On Easter Day, 626, he had been suddenly attacked by an assassin in the pay of Cwichelm, who was ruling some part of Wessex under his father Cynegils. Only the prompt action of his thane Lilla had saved him from death, when Lilla thrust his own body between the king and a poisoned sword. The same night, in the midst of this excitement, Queen Ethelberga, "safely and without sore pain," had given birth to a girl child. Paulinus had bidden the king to see in both these mercies the grace of the Lord Christ, and Edwin had been so impressed that of his free will he had given this little daughter Eanfled to Christian baptism upon the eve of Pentecost, "first of all the people of Northumbria," with eleven others of the royal house.[5]

Soon a meeting of the king's wise men had been held, assembled to debate a change of the religion of Northumbria from paganism to Christianity. Here another of his thanes had spoken those unforgettable words which likened the life of man on earth to the passage of a sparrow in winter-time through the brief warmth of the king's high hall, entering from the darkness without and swiftly flying forth again into the dark unknown: "And thus appeareth for a little while this our present life; but what followeth or what hath gone before, truly that we know not. Wherefore if this new teaching hath brought us aught more sure, do we not right to follow it?"

[5] *HE* II, c. 9.

Coifi, chief of Northumbria's pagan priests, had yielded his will, and Edwin and all his nobles with very many of the humbler sort had been baptized by Paulinus on Easter Eve, 627, in a little wooden church of Saint Peter at York. York itself had then been made a bishop's see by Edwin and Paulinus appointed as its bishop. The king had also begun to build there a splendid church of stone which was to enclose within itself the little wooden one made at his command for his baptism.

For six years from this time the two had worked well together: Edwin for the state and Paulinus for the church of Northumbria. The business of conversion went on apace. At Yeavering in Glendale Paulinus once spent thirty-six days, teaching the people of Bernicia from dawn till night and baptizing them near Kirknewton in the river Glen and in Bowmont Water; with the same zeal he baptized the people of Deira in the river Swale at Catterick near Richmond in Yorkshire. Here, there, and everywhere, day after day, his tall, bent figure, his black hair, his face worn with fasting and his sharply hooked nose impressed into silent awe those who listened as he bade them flee from the wrath to come. To him Pope Honorius sent the pall of metropolitan authority over northern England. To him at Lincoln, where he was preaching and building another church of stone, another Honorius came to be consecrated Archbishop of Canterbury. In all his work Paulinus was aided well by his deacon James, who also had come from Canterbury afire with longing to convert these two provinces of the north.[6]

Throughout his reign Edwin held supremacy among English kings so effectually that it was told: "from sea to sea a woman might walk with her newborn child in her arms and

[6] *Ibid.* II, cc. 13f., 16ff.; Ekwall, *EPN* 518; Mawer, *Northumberland*, 221.

none dare to do her harm." [7] Then tragedy fell swiftly. Defeat and death overtook him and his son Osfrid and very many of his priests and people in 633 on the marshy plain of Heathfield, held to be Hatfield Chase near Doncaster, at the hands of heathen Penda, king of Mercia, and of the "British tyrant," Cadwallon of North Wales. Cadwallon professed himself a Christian, but outdid even Penda in his cruelty. "So barbarous was he in mind and manners that he spared neither women nor innocent children, but gave them all over like a savage beast to torture and killing. Long time possessed by devil's fury he roamed all the provinces, seeking to root out wholly from the length and breadth of Britain all the English race."

In his terror Paulinus fled from the north back again to Canterbury in Kent, taking with him to her old home Edwin's widow, the Kentish princess Ethelberga, with his children, a girl and a boy, and his grandson, born to Osfrid. The two boys died soon afterward in France; but the Princess Eanfled, then seven years old, lived to grow up in Canterbury in spiritual obedience to the see of Rome and under the secular protection of her uncle Eadbald, who had succeeded his father Ethelbert as king of Kent. Paulinus was soon made bishop of Rochester; his deacon James had remained at his post in Northumbria, to comfort, teach, and convert the people under his charge.[8]

They needed him; for more dismay and panic were to come. Now that Edwin their enemy was dead, the sons of Ethelfrid came marching back from exile. As we have seen, one of them, Eanfrid, assumed rule over Bernicia; a cousin of Edwin, named Osric, made himself king of Deira. Once again Northumbria stood divided. The division, however, lasted but a short while. Both Osric and Eanfrid, who had forsaken the

[7] *HE* II, c. 16.   [8] *Ibid.* II, c. 20; Bright, 146ff.

Christian faith into which teaching had initiated them, were killed by Cadwallon in 634, Osric by a sally from York which Cadwallon then was holding with armed power, Eanfrid in cold-blooded murder, when he had come to Cadwallon to plead for peace.

Once more a change, and panic turned to joy. Another son of Ethelfrid decided to avenge his brother Eanfrid's death. His name was Oswald, a man far different from Eanfrid, "dear to God, and strong in the faith of Christ." Before the year had ended he raised at Heavenfield, near Hexham and the Roman Wall, his standard of the holy Cross. Saint Columba of Iona, appearing to him in a vision as he slept, bade him go forth and conquer on the morrow; at its dawning he marched out to victory, and Cadwallon, as he fled, was caught and killed near Rowley Burn.[9] Northumbria, then, was again a united kingdom under Oswald when in this same year 634 Wilfrid of York was born within it. The child who was to serve so passionately the faith of Rome in this northern England came into the world as the knowledge of this same faith was waning among its people through the hurried departure of their bishop, Paulinus. In spite of the faithful shepherding of James the deacon, of necessity many were left untaught and unbaptized.

The new king, Oswald, was of the Celtic Church. When he had been driven into exile by Edwin, he had spent some time with the brethren of Columba's island monastery; and now he sent to ask his former instructors, these Irish monks of Iona, to send him a Father in God who should teach the faith throughout his far-reaching land. They quickly granted his petition; for soon there arrived from Iona a bishop of whom it could be said even by the English under obedience to Rome

[9] *HE* III, cc. 1f.; Reeves, 112f. For differing dates of the battles of Heathfield and Heavenfield see Stenton, 80f. and p. 81 *supra*, note 213.

that "he was a man exceeding gentle, holy and self-controlled, having the zeal of God, even if not fully in accordance with knowledge." His name was Aidan.

From this time Christianity spread throughout northern England. Bishop and king laboured hand in hand for the glory of God and the increase of their faith; churches were built and filled with hearers; monks came in numbers from Ireland and Iona to help the cause; monasteries were founded; children and their elders were alike baptized into the Church.

As a faithful pastor Aidan led his flock, observing in his own life the rigid rule of prayer and fasting, of study and of government, of that mingled sternness and charity which Irish monks had practised in the schools of Ireland in the sixth century and which they were still teaching far and wide, independent of Canterbury and of Rome. As his bishop's seat, he chose the isle of Lindisfarne, known today as Holy Isle. It lies two miles off the coast of Northumberland, separated from it by a strait from five to seven feet deep; at low water it is reached by a track through the level sands. There the bishop, "lover of silence and of holy poverty, fleeing the crowds and the pageantry of York," once the seat of Paulinus, would retire to refresh his soul in secret meditation and in common prayer with the monks he had settled amid its peace. From there he came forth to walk on foot through all parts of his diocese of Northumbria, bidding his people, monk or lay, to read the Bible and to learn the Psalms, hastening away as soon as courtesy allowed from the banquets to which now and again he was called by the king, encouraging young men to enter upon preparation for the priesthood, full of kindness to the ignorant and the hard of heart, gravely exhorting those who had once known the light of truth to pursue it at any cost.

In all, so far as he could, King Oswald diligently followed

his bishop's example. Often, since the Celtic Aidan could not speak Saxon very well, the king would translate for him when he was preaching; for Oswald had learned to speak his language well in Iona. The royal treasury, even the royal meals, were always ready for the Lord's poor; strangers were welcomed in hospitality. Bernicia and Deira were again one in government; four peoples, the British and the Picts, the Scots and the English, owned the firm rule of this "most Christian king." [10]

In this harmony of crown and church Wilfrid lived as a young boy; so far as he thought at all about the matter, it must have seemed to him the most natural thing in the world. He came of proud blood. His father was intimate with the king and court; often nobles from the royal household visited his home and stopped for a passing word with an attractive youngster who was always ready to run an errand and make himself useful in any way he could.

But no child of these years could escape their tragedy. No doubt even in his nursery Wilfrid had been subdued by tales of the dreadful Penda, heathen and savage. So wicked was it to be a heathen that the very names of the "apostate" Osric and Eanfrid were never mentioned without horror, as names of evil kings; Penda and Cadwallon must have been to him as were Pharaoh of Egypt and Herod of Galilee in his early Scripture lessons. He was nearly nine when a messenger rode to his father's house one summer day in 642 with word that King Oswald himself had been struck down in battle at Maserfield by Penda and his soldiers. In after days he must have been deeply impressed by tales of marvels that came to pass in the place where Oswald had been slain: of the horse that suddenly sprang into new life on the very spot; of the young girl, the inn-keeper's granddaughter, who was brought

[10] *HE* III, cc. 3, 5f., 25, 14ff.

there on a cart, sick to death of the palsy, and returned gaily to her home upon her own feet; of the post saved from burning by dust from the holy ground; of the pilgrims who often journeyed there in hope of healing.[11]

At the moment, however, all was full of fear and foreboding in Northumbria; Ethelwald, son of Oswald, was too young to govern, and the kingdom was again divided into its former two provinces. Oswy, brother of Oswald, was chosen by the people of Bernicia as their ruler; the crown of Deira went to Oswin, a son of that Osric whom Cadwallon had killed. Both rulers were Christian, and both held Aidan as bishop over their realms; Oswy, like Oswald, had learned the Celtic faith during exile in Iona.

Oswy had much to contend with during these earlier years, for Penda with his Mercians was always invading the land, bent on robbery and further conquest. At last he reached the city of Bamburgh on the Northumbrian coast, once the fortress of Ida, ancestor of Bernicia's kings, and now the royal seat of Oswy himself. Bamburgh yielded neither to Penda's swift descent nor to his prolonged besieging; finally in his rage he destroyed the villages far and wide, carried off the ruins of their wooden houses—beams, débris of wattled walls and of thatched roofs—gathered all his plunder in a mass on the side of the city that faced inland, and when the wind served, set fire to this huge kindling pile. Aidan happened at the time to be in retreat on one of a group of tiny rocks called the Farne Islands, about five miles from the coast, where he used often to go by boat for the peace of his soul. Now, as he looked across to Bamburgh, he saw on the horizon the glow of flames and curling clouds of smoke. Quickly casting his prayer in this direction, like water playing upon the fire, he called to heaven:

[11] *Ibid.* III, cc. 9f.; *cf.* cc. 11ff. Maserfield is very probably Oswestry in Shropshire: Plummer II, 152f. On the miracles attributed to Oswald's relics see Colgrave, in Thompson, 218f.

"See, O Lord, how great evil Penda is working!" The cry was heard, the flames turned back upon the soldiers who fed them, and Oswy's city was saved.[12]

Young Wilfrid surely listened to this story of the Lord's power in Aidan, talked of by all around him; perhaps he had himself watched far off the reddened sky. No doubt he had heard the bishop preach, and probably he had knelt to receive his blessing at home. All had its effect on a mind already prepared by the religious training of childhood, rooted and quickened amid the daily devotion to prayer and churchly rule of those in his own house. Gradually, as he grew older, he became conscious of longings within him, strange and yet familiar. The dawning of new life in his body, of a more serious purpose in his mind; dreams and visions of an end, a dedication to which he somehow felt himself to be called—these all seemed to be pulling him, half-willing, half-reluctant, away from the world of Northumbria, from a world constantly interrupted by war, a world of invasion and of struggle for land and power, of transient triumph and pageant, in which things were always changing and no abiding goal stood fast. Moreover, his mother was now dead and in her place a second wife had come to make the household unhappy with her hard rule and unkind ways.

After long thought one hope seemed best for both problems, for the escape from a home which was becoming daily more difficult for his spirited temper, and for the satisfying of a desire which, however dim in precise shape, day by day grew more insistent. King Oswy had lately married that princess whom Paulinus had carried from Northumbria in his flight southward, Eanfled, niece of Eadbald of Kent. As we have seen, she owned allegiance to the Roman faith of Canterbury, and Oswy had sent the priest Utta there to ask for her as wife.

[12] *HE* III, cc. 14, 16.

Wilfrid had heard, too, about this journey: how Utta had
begged Aidan as bishop of the land to pray for him and his
companions, sailing among the dangers of a rocky coast; how
Aidan had foretold a fierce storm that should strike their ship
and had given Utta blessed oil to cast upon the raging of the
waves; how, when the ship was on the point of sinking, Utta
had remembered the bishop's words and had poured this oil
upon the sea; how its fury had speedily been broken. The
queen was known among all as very gentle and utterly devoted
to religion; perhaps, the boy thought, she would be friendly
to him and help him decide what he should do.

He was now fourteen, old enough to tell his father of his
plans. His stepmother must have scorned them, even if she
did feel glad to be rid of another woman's child. But the
father readily understood and gave the boy his blessing. At
this time to profess service in the Church militant was held
as exalted a career as to fight for king and country, and many
men of royal and of noble birth were giving themselves to the
vows of priestly and of monastic life. In the meantime from
the queen or from her household his son would surely gain
wise counsel.

Consent once given, Wilfrid busily looked forward to his
high adventure. We need not be scornful when we read that,
boy as he was, he wanted "arms and horses and clothes for
himself and his servants that he might make a proper appearance in the royal court." Naturally he did want to make a
good impression, for his home had always taught him
that respect concerns itself even with outward show.
This early training was never forgotten by the man of later
years.

His father's friends welcomed him at Eanfled's castle and
soon presented him to the queen's audience. He won her heart
at once. The friendly child had grown into a handsome youth

of intelligence and ready wit, mingling his natural courtesy and reverence for a queen with frankness in telling all his thought. He had come, she told him, at the right moment. One of the king's friends, a noble named Cudda, was feeling exactly as he did, although, it was true, Cudda was much older and was lame through sickness. But he was going to try his vocation as monk in the community which Aidan had founded at Lindisfarne; if Wilfrid wished, he should go with Cudda and find out something of what its life really meant.[13]

It might seem strange that Eanfled, loyally submissive to the Roman discipline of Canterbury and to Romanus, the chaplain who had come with her from Kent, should not have handed Wilfrid over either to him or to the deacon James for training in the teachings of Rome. Aidan of Lindisfarne was, indeed, bishop of the land ruled in secular matters by her husband Oswy; moreover, the remoteness of Lindisfarne appealed to Wilfrid's enthusiasm. But, in the last decision, we may like to think that respect for Aidan's saintly character influenced the queen in approving the Celtic island. Even if Aidan did not keep the feast of Easter on the date commanded by the Church of Rome and followed by Eanfled and her household, yet he was no "Quartodeciman," as Aldhelm had declared of the British priests; he always kept Easter on a Sunday and reverenced the Lord's Resurrection in spirit as well as any Roman. Despite his erring tonsure, "he did all that lay within his power to obey the precepts of the Gospels, the apostles and the prophets," as one who loved God and man with all his heart and soul.[14]

To Lindisfarne, then, Wilfrid went, and there he lived some four years, from 648 until about 652, under the strict Irish

[13] Eddius, c. 2; *HE* III, c. 15; V, c. 19.
[14] *Ibid.*, III, c. 17.

rule which its monks had learned in Iona. His home by night and by day was a tiny cell, roughly put together of boughs and twigs entwined and made fast by clay, with roof of thatched reeds, one of many such clustering around a small church of the same rude fashion. He was dressed in coarse woollen stuff, girdled by a rope; he walked from cell to church barefoot and slept in his clothes upon a plank covered with an osier mat. Every Wednesday and Friday, except in the weeks from Easter Day until Pentecost, he fasted till three in the afternoon; in Lent only one meal awaited him each week day. Bread, made from barley or corn, fish, and eggs were his daily fare, save when the Rule bade him rejoice on festival days in beef or mutton; nothing was allowed for drinking at any time but water or milk. Five times a day an iron bell called him to prayer of the Hours in the chapel, Prime, Terce, Sext, None, Vespers; in the night he rose twice from sleep at its clang; he joined the monks hurrying from their cells for the Vigils of Nightfall, of Midnight, of Morning. On Sundays and other Feasts of the Church he shared with the brethren their Mass and Communion. The rest of the time he spent in meditation in his cell, in manual labour among the fields and buildings of the monastery, in reading, mostly from Holy Scripture and the Lives of saints, and in writing.[15] The boy who could think of the array by which he should show reverence to the Northumbrian court must have had eyes and mind open to any invitation offered him by art; the writing and its adornment practised on Lindisfarne must have attracted him immediately.

At this time, it is true, the writers of the island monastery were still some fifty years behind the achievement of the Lindisfarne Gospels, if we date that book shortly before

[15] On the Irish-Scottish monastic life see Kenney I, 288ff.; Gougaud, *CCL* 78ff., and *RB* XXV, 1908, 167ff., 321ff.; XXVIII, 1911, 86ff.; Reeves, *passim;* Montalembert IV; Ryan, 193ff.; *HE* III, c. 5.

700 as the work of Eadfrid, bishop of Lindisfarne from 698 till 721. The making of its complex loveliness is yet a question for discussion among the scholars who look upon its patterns of spiral and plait, its forms of trumpet and wheel and key, interlaced and woven and knotted in panel and in border; on the hounds and birds and serpents whose tongues and tails and bodies are lengthened into bands and ribbons; on the human figures that are wrought as part of its geometrical designs, in no way resembling the curves and lineaments of life; on the colours, red, yellow, green, violet, brown, and blue, standing out against the rich black ink of its insular half-uncial script, whether of the Irish or the English type.[16] We may imagine Wilfrid, however, fifty years before, watching the monks of Aidan as they laboured on a script and its illuminating that were progressing even then toward the glory of the Book of Lindisfarne. They may best be described by the words of a modern historian: "Contemplating interminably the elements of sea and sky around them, their minds were filled with adoration of the Creator and of His works, the earth and its living things. In their illuminations they gave expression to their love for the birds and the hounds whose necks they twisted and whose bodies they elongated into those tortuous designs; and through it all was a sense that living beings also were entangled into strange patterns, that life was twisted like these labyrinthine interlacements which crossed and turned, leading you out into puzzling complications and then bringing you back to the place or almost to the place from which you had set out. Life was like these pictures in the Lindisfarne

---

[16] For the history and for varying theories as to the provenance of the art of the Lindisfarne Gospels, see E. G. Millar, *The Gospels of Lindisfarne*, 1923, 3ff.; Baldwin Brown V, 332ff.; J. A. Herbert, *Illuminated Manuscripts*, 1912, 73ff.; J. Brønsted, *Early English Ornament*, 1924, 92f.; A. W. Clapham, *Antiquity* VIII, 1934, 43ff.; Lowe, *CLA* II, xiii, 20; T. D. Kendrick, *Anglo-Saxon Art to A.D. 900*, 1938, 104ff.; C. R. Morey, *Mediaeval Art*, 1942, 187f.

Gospels. It was a maze; it was full of mazes; but in all there was design. The labour of these artist-monks was prayer—a form of worship. They expressed in colour and pattern, with plait and interwoven bird, the mysteries of this tangled world and the wonder of the universe." [17]

Over all the life of the island, common and private, Aidan ruled supreme after the Irish manner, as abbot of its monastery, an office which he united with his overseeing of Northumbria as its bishop. As abbot he was responsible for the training which should prepare his monks, his spiritual sons, for their true home in heaven; to him Wilfrid, together with all the professed brethren, was bound under God in obedience of body, mind, and spirit. It was Aidan who appointed for each dweller in the community that individual priest, the "soul friend," to whom in particular and in secret each should render account of his days and make confession of his misdeeds; from whom he should receive as from God the forgiveness he desired, the penance he should carry out in private, the direction he needed for the future.[18]

The time—from his fourteenth to his eighteenth year—that the boy spent under this discipline must have been a hard testing. Its bare simplicity called for endurance from one accustomed to the abundance of a noble house; its rigid routine laid no little burden of restraint upon a nature eager and impulsive, intensely alive to all the beauty of sea and sky even while struggling against the discomfort they brought in many days of fog and cold and drizzling rain. But the will which had brought Wilfrid to Lindisfarne carried him through all its demands. He faithfully fulfilled the biddings of its life; he ran, as he had done for the high-born guests of his father's house, to serve the wish of its older monks, of whatever class

[17] R. Hodgkin, 360.
[18] Bede, *Vita Cuth.* (prose) c. 16.

or culture; he worked happily with boys of his own age who were studying under Aidan's care for the tonsure and the priesthood. All were his friends, and at times they wished greatly that this brilliant youth would devote his life to permanence with theirs. On him himself, no less, these years left a lasting mark. The combining of the spiritual and the intellectual, of the ascetic and the artistic, which he saw in daily practice there, the lonely stillness of his cell, the nearness of Nature in all her moods were to influence him in the stormy times to come far more than he then dreamed.

Meanwhile, the outside world was still travailing in battle, murder, and sudden death. The monks of Lindisfarne must have fallen to their prayers in horror when they heard that Oswin of Deira had been murdered by the treachery of Oswy of Bernicia, his neighbour in rule. Oswy had longed to hold both kingdoms in his hands, as his brother Oswald had done; he was also, no doubt, jealous of the noble mind and kindly heart, the handsome face and commanding presence which attracted all to Oswin. It is fair to say that their bishop Aidan, zealous as he was for both and for their peoples, loved Oswin the more, "a man deeply pitying, helper of those in need and, as it were, a father to the sorrowful." Just a little while before Oswin's untimely death Aidan spoke a sad prophecy to one of his priests: "I know," he said, "that the king will not live long, for never have I seen a man so humble." He was betrayed by one of his own subjects and struck down by order of Oswy on the twentieth of August, 651. Oswy lived to repent his evil deed by giving to his wife Eanfled, a cousin of the dead king, land at Gilling, near Richmond in Yorkshire, for the founding of a monastery in which prayer should be made perpetually for both the slayer, her own husband, and the slain, her kinsman.[19]

[19] *HE* III, cc. 14, 24.

Eleven days after this sorrow, word came to Wilfrid and the community of Lindisfarne that Aidan, their beloved abbot and bishop, had passed away in a village near Bamburgh. He was seized with sickness while visiting this place, one of the holdings of the crown of Deira, and died under an improvised shelter placed against the wall of its church. He drew his last breath as he leaned for support upon a buttress of the church itself, glad in this moment to cling to that which had been his mainstay throughout his life. His body was brought to Lindisfarne, and his monks carried it to rest in the burial ground of the community. Soon a new leader arrived to follow Aidan both as bishop and as abbot; his name was Finan, and he, too, came from Iona and its Scottish-Irish tradition.[20]

This Finan, in his greater austerity, seems to have been widely different from the more gentle Aidan. Of Aidan it was told that, before he had even been thought of as bishop of Lindisfarne, another priest from Iona had been sent to the people of Northumbria, in answer to Oswald's petition, a man of stern and forceful nature who utterly failed to influence them. He returned home to Iona, reporting that they would neither hear nor obey. The monks of the island monastery were summoned in chapter to deliberate what should now be done, and Aidan, turning to his dour fellow-priest, mildly observed: "I think, brother, that you were harder than you need have been with your untaught listeners in Northumbria, and did not prepare them with the milk of gentler teaching till such time as they should be well nourished, ready to obey the higher commands of God." Immediately Aidan had found himself elected to the work.[21]

Perhaps Finan held in a manner somewhat harsh the precepts of ritual taught by his Celtic Church. We read of hot controversy on the questions, so important at the time, how the

[20] *Ibid.*, c. 17.   [21] *Ibid.*, c. 5.

tonsure should be worn, when Easter should be kept, between Finan and a Celt, Ronan by name, instructed on the continent in the Roman discipline. The more vehemently Ronan argued for Rome, the more bitter and determined grew Finan's answering, and the dispute left him an open adversary to the teaching of Rome on these points.[22]

It may be that this change of spiritual leadership had its part in fulfilling Wilfrid's destiny. Certainly, at the time when he lost the bishop and abbot he had known so long, he was being troubled by new doubts and problems which, once sown within his mind, could not but grow. Doubtless he missed sorely his trust in Aidan's holiness; perhaps, much as he esteemed his new abbot, he found Finan in these first years of office lacking in time or in desire to discuss with a youth, strange to him and not yet even admitted to his novitiate, vexed and complicated matters of Paschal cycle and monastic rule.

Moreover, there still beat strongly within him that pulse of vivid imagination which had brought him to Lindisfarne. From his reading he had learned increasingly of the glory of Rome, of her churches and her shrines, where lay the relics of apostles, saints and martyrs, whose histories were filled with adventure. The very pilgrimage to Rome was still a dangerous crossing over land and sea; how wonderful to go forth and risk even life itself for a few months of reverence in touch with Heaven! Could he but once reach Rome, he might also talk with learned priests of her Church concerning the doubts which were troubling him; at Rome he could see and learn at the centre of Catholic teaching the evidence for her opposition to the practices he had always known in his Celtic childhood.

Finan, if determined, was also wise. The boy was restless

[22] *Ibid.*, cc. 21f.; 25.

and hungry for new knowledge; better to let him go with the abbot's blessing than to try in vain to keep him on the island. Wilfrid had never desired of Lindisfarne official entrance upon its monastic life; his head was still unmarked by the Celtic tonsure; a perplexed and questioning guest yielded no good to an ordered monastery, however attractive in character and quick in mind he might be.

So once again Wilfrid returned to take counsel with his father and with Queen Eanfled. She, of course, was delighted to hear that he longed to visit Rome. The decision was easy. She would send him south, accompanied by messengers bearing letters of introduction to her cousin Erconbert, successor of his father Eadbald on the throne of Kent. No doubt Erconbert would be able to find in Canterbury some prelate or layman of sufficient standing about to start on this same journey to Rome, one who would be willing to take her young friend under his care.[23]

Like his royal kinswoman, Erconbert was delighted to do all he could. He, also, wholeheartedly followed the Faith. First, among all kings in England, he had decreed that pagan idolatry should be banished from his realm and that images of heathen gods should be everywhere destroyed; further, he had obliged all his subjects under dire penalty to keep the Lenten fast of forty days. He now rejoiced in this promise of a notable convert from the obdurately Celtic north, especially when he found in Wilfrid one given to prayer and study, fasting and watches of nightly devotion. The welcome of Canterbury's Archbishop Honorius must have been equally

---

[23] For Wilfrid see, in general, his *Life* by Eddius Stephanus, ed. Colgrave with trans. and notes; the same *Life,* ed. Levison, *MGH Scr. rer. Merov.* VI, 163ff.; the same *Life,* ed. Raine (with other *Lives*), HY 1; *HE passim,* with Plummer's notes and index; *DCB* IV, 1179ff. (Raine); *DNB* LXI, 238ff. (Hunt); Bright, *passim;* Poole, *Studies.* The narrative of Bede in *HE* V, c. 19, borrows largely from Eddius.

sincere, for Honorius had greatly respected Aidan, Celtic though he was in his adherence.[24]

Here, then, in Kent we find Wilfrid about the year 652. Unfortunately no traveller to Rome was at hand, and he waited with an impatience ever harder to control day after day. He was, however, among monks who could answer questions regarding the Faith and its discipline; he could study literature and art in the school founded by Augustine. We know that he gave much time to the Psalms, which he had read on Lindisfarne in Jerome's second revision, the "Gallican Psalter," made from the Septuagint about 390. Now he learned by heart the former edition, "the Roman Psalter," which Jerome had made some years before, in 383, at the request of Pope Damasus, in amendment of the "Old Latin" text.

The school of Canterbury under Honorius, "a man deeply versed in matters ecclesiastical," remained very much as it had been under Augustine, devoted to the study of Scripture and teachings of the Church, but in no sense the centre of learned culture which Aldhelm was to find it nearly twenty years later under Abbot Hadrian. Among its interests to a student was the Roman chanting; and Wilfrid must have listened with eagerness at Canterbury to music unpractised on Lindisfarne.[25]

Canterbury, moreover, possessed its own school of writing, which differed widely from the Irish forms known in northern England. Its uncial script and rustic capitals followed the Roman book-hand and had been brought, like the Gregorian chant, by missionaries from Rome. It remained a foreign use and never took root on English soil; English writing was formed upon the Irish models, and the Canterbury script modelled upon Rome's use seems to have disappeared at an early time. Wilfrid, however, was able in this seventh century

[24] *HE* III, c. 8.
[25] *Ibid.* V, c. 19; II, c. 20; Plummer II, 118f.

to compare it with the insular script he had pored over among Lindisfarne's monks.[26]

Thus a whole year went by, probably that of 652–653. At last to his joy he saw arriving in Canterbury another young man, about twenty-five years of age, some six years older than himself, now nineteen. The new arrival was also from the north of England. Like Cudda, he came of a noble family, and had served under King Oswy; he had received from his king land sufficient to maintain him in the estate fitting his rank. But, again like Cudda, he desired the life of monastic religion; like Wilfrid, he was longing to visit the holy places of Rome. In him Rome already had an ardent disciple, and he was afire to enrich her daughter Church in his native England with things such as he loved, of art and beauty, script, illumination, painting, work in precious metals and in embroidery. Such were, he had heard, to be seen by him, even to be procured, among the treasures of Rome, and there he was going without delay or fear. His name was Biscop, afterward increased to Benedict Biscop, and he had plenty of money for carrying out his plans.[27]

The two students must have talked long and eagerly. During this year under the influence of the south of England Wilfrid had been drawing nearer and nearer to the break with the Celtic training of his life at home and under Aidan's rule; it only needed the enthusiasm of Biscop to complete it and bind him to a new allegiance. Henceforth, as for Biscop, so for him also, the Church of Rome and her prescriptions were to be all in all.

Without delay they set out together in 653, and travelled across the Channel and through France as far south as Lyons. The great city fascinated Wilfrid: the rushing waters of the

[26] Lowe, *CLA* II, No. 126; Maunde Thompson, 384f.
[27] *HE* V, c. 19.

two rivers which girdled it, the Rhône and the Saône; the rugged heights rising above it, of Fourvières, of Saint Irenée, of Saint Foy and of Saint Just; temples, theatres, baths and aqueducts, here standing in their pride, here fallen into ruins; Christian churches rich in shrines and relics of the saints. He remembered now what he had heard, and quickly learned more of the city's traditions. Once it had been the centre of heathen cults of Augustus and of Rome, then it had become the source from which the Christian faith had spread throughout Gaul; it had known persecution, was even hallowed by the blood of martyrs. There, on Fourvières, its amphitheatre had rung in 177 A.D. with shouts of an enormous crowd, honouring Rome and her Emperor, Marcus Aurelius, by torture of Christian witnesses. There Maturus and Sanctus and Attalus had been faithful to the end; there the slave girl Blandina had forced the very heathen themselves to declare that never had they known a woman to endure as she had done. In the prison of the same days had lain Pothinus, first bishop of Lyons, dead through violence of the mob. The glory of these "Martyrs of Lyons" had been sealed by a letter sent from the Christians of Lyons and of Vienne to their brethren in Asia, thereby inscribing, as it has been said, "the baptismal certificate of Christianity in France." [28]

There Saint Irenaeus, Doctor and martyr, had succeeded Pothinus as bishop; there in the fifth century the faithful had come to say their prayers at the shrine of Saint Justus of Lyons; in the same time Eucherius, bishop of its cathedral, had written his well-known homilies and preached solitude for prayer; there in the sixth century Saint Nicetius had been Archbishop for twenty years, so holy that miracles were said to have been wrought at his tomb; there another bishop,

[28] Eusebius V, 1ff.; Gwatkin, *Early Church History to A.D. 313,* I, 1909, 157ff.; *Cath. Encyc. s.v.* Lyons (Goyau); *DACL s.v. Lyon* (Leclercq); Bardenhewer II, 674f.

Ætherius, had received and answered many letters from that Pope Gregory who had sent Augustine to preach in Kent. As he walked from place to place, Wilfrid felt the fervour arising anew within his heart.[29]

To the outward spell of the old city was added warmth of hospitality. The Archbishop of Lyons at this time was Annemund; his brother was Count Dalfinus. Annemund, also, in his turn was readily conquered by the young man's charm of face and manners, united with his enthusiasm and a purpose unusually mature and resolved. Wilfrid's stay was made most pleasant. The Archbishop, like the brethren of Lindisfarne, delighted in such company; unlike Lindisfarne, he deliberately schemed how to keep with him this desirable guest. "If you will stay with me," he said, "you shall marry my brother's daughter, and we will make you governor over a goodly district of Gaul. You shall be to me as a son and look to me for ready and sure aid in all your needs." [30]

Wilfrid might honourably have accepted this magnificent offer, for he was as yet neither priest nor monk. But it did not tempt him in the least. Not for this had he left England and entered upon his travels. He therefore courteously put it aside and prepared to set out again. His companion, Biscop, had already gone, probably impatient of delay. Annemund was as generous as he was reluctant; he provided guides and all things necessary, and only asked that this son in the Lord would visit Lyons once more on the way home to England. The rest of the journey passed quickly enough. Soon Rome burst upon his eyes, as it had for Aldhelm, and its manifold treasures lay within his reach. Which should he visit first? He chose, naturally enough, the "Oratory of Saint Andrew the

[29] *Gallia Christiana* IV, coll. 4ff.
[30] For the error of Eddius, c. 4, followed by Bede, *HE* V, c. 19, see *ibid.* IV, coll. 43f. For the theory that the name Dalfinus also belonged to Annemund, see Levison, *Scr. rer. Merov.* VI, 197.

Apostle," which seems surely to have been that "most sacred place to any pilgrim from England," [31] the monastery on the Caelian Hill. There Gregory the Great had once ruled as abbot; from there afterward as Pope he had bidden its prior Augustine go forth to convert the heathen English. Now young Wilfrid knelt before the altar on which lay the four Gospels of Christ and humbly asked Saint Andrew to intercede for him with the Lord God that his mind might be quick to read and to teach among the heathen the lessons which they held.

His prayer was answered. Day after day he made his revei ence here and there; and at length he met the man who was to be his friend and teacher in Rome, Boniface, Archdeacon and Counsellor to the Holy See. At the moment it was probably without a Pope, since in June of this same year, 653, Pope Martin had been seized in his own city and forced to begin a long and painful journey to Constantinople. This was the work of the Emperor in the East, Constans II, and of Paul, Patriarch of Constantinople, in their wrath at the Pope's action against their heretical views. Martin never returned to Rome, as he died under duress in the Crimea two years later, and the Holy See held no Pope until Eugenius was consecrated in 654, while Martin was still alive in exile.

For many months Wilfrid studied in Rome, turning all the intentness of his will to those four Gospels and their interpretation, and absorbing further details of Roman rule on the date of Easter and many other matters. Boniface, a priest both learned and enthusiastic, instructed him with all care and at last presented his pupil to the Pope—Eugenius, we may believe. The desired end had now been attained; Wilfrid had no more doubts and no valid reason for tarrying longer in Rome. With a mind at rest concerning his problems, bearing the Papal blessing on his heart and holy relics on his person, he

[31] Raine, *HY* I, 8.

left the city and made his way back to his friend, the Archbishop of Lyons.[32]

Annemund was as gracious as ever. He heard all the story and thanked God for this youth he had come to love so well. His welcome was so real and the professors of Lyons were so willing to teach that almost before he realized it Wilfrid had stayed in their city three happy years. At his own wish he received from the Archbishop the Roman tonsure, shaped in form of a crown; with this cutting of his hair doubtless he offered himself to religion. Once more Annemund prayed the Lord in his secret heart that Wilfrid might remain this time with him as the heir of his house. But, as Wilfrid's biographer wrote, "God foresaw something better for our race." Tragedy suddenly swept down upon this peaceful household; some accusation, now unknown, was brought against the Archbishop, and he was condemned to death.[33] Early record laid this crime to the account of Baldhild, wife of Clovis II, king of the Frankish realm of Neustria, and, after his death in 656, queen-regent for their son, Chlotar III. Clovis had been nothing but a figure-head, one of the degenerate Merovingian boy-kings who had held a puppet dynasty in France since 639, when Dagobert I had died and with him all semblance of merit in his royal line. On the other hand, tradition has told of this Queen Baldhild details of great honour: that she excelled in gifts offered for the glory of the Lord; that she lived her last years and died in the monastery of Chelles, near Paris; that she was canonized by the Church. She does not seem, therefore, to merit necessarily the terrible charges hurled against her as a Jezebel, slaying in her wickedness the bishops of the Franks. It is perhaps more likely that the fate of Annemund was due to the real power in the land of Neustria from

---

[32] Duchesne, *Lib. Pont.* I, 340ff.; J. B. Bury, *History of the Later Roman Empire* (ed. 1889) II, 294ff.; Eddius, c. 5; Bright, 219.
[33] Eddius, c. 6.

656 until 681, that of Ebroin, "Mayor of the Palace," in other words, prime minister, and ruler in fact over king, state, and people.[34]

If Annemund must be executed, Wilfrid would, of course, go, too, declaring cheerfully that "nothing could be better than that Father and son should die together and be with Christ." The bishop's protests availed nothing, and the martyr-elect almost gained his end. He was already standing in his shirt awaiting the executioner when the Frankish nobles presiding over the scene asked, "Who is that good-looking young man getting ready for death?" "A foreigner from England," they were told, "of British race." It may have occurred to them that he was a compatriot of their queen-regent Baldhild, also Anglo-Saxon by birth. At any rate, they quickly ordered that no harm be done him; and Wilfrid lived to watch the burial of this Archbishop who had offered him an honoured name and estate among the Franks. Now that his Father in God was dead, nothing called him to remain in Gaul under the threat-

---

[34] Frankish history in this period may be roughly summarized thus: Its most important provinces were Neustria. land of the Western Franks; Aquitania; Austrasia, land of the Eastern Franks; Burgundy. After the death of Brunhild in 613 Chlotar II, son of Fredegund, and, after him, his son Dagobert, were in theory kings of all the Franks. In 639, upon Dagobert's death, a line of *rois fainéants*, so feeble of soul and body that they died young, held nominal sovereignty until 751. The real power lay in the hands of their prime ministers, the administrators or "Mayors" of their palaces; among these the most important were those of Austrasia, especially (1) Pepin I, of Landen in Belgium, (2) his son, Grimoald, and (3) his grandson, Pepin II, of Heristal, also in Belgium. The seventh century saw fierce struggles for power between Mayors, nobles, and bishops of the Franks. Most notable were the rising in 656 of Grimoald against his boy king Dagobert II, resulting in Grimoald's death, and the terrible war between Ebroin, Mayor of Neustria, and Leodegar, bishop of Autun, who held control over Burgundy. Leodegar was murdered by Ebroin, who was himself assassinated in 681. In 687 Pepin II of Austrasia defeated the Mayor of Neustria at the battle of Tertry (Textry), near St. Quentin, and established the ascendancy of the mayoralty of Austrasia among the Franks. He ruled all their land, except Aquitaine, until his death in 714.

For Baldhild see Eddius, c. 6; Colgrave, *Eddius*, 154f.; Plummer II, 322, and her *Life: MGH Scr. rer. Merov.* II, 475ff.; Mabillon, II (1936), 775ff.

ening shadow of Ebroin. With deep regret his friends saw him embark on his return "to a haven of safety" in England.

Much water had flowed on the tide of history since he had left his monastery of the north country. The power of heathen Penda, king of Mercia, had reached its highest mark. To his own kingdom proper he had added the rule of the "Mid-Angles" dwelling on its south-eastern border; henceforth their territory was accounted part of Mercia. Penda had handed them over to the rule of his son Peada, "a most excellent youth, right worthy of the name and standing of a king."

At this point Christianity first penetrated Penda's realms. For this son Peada promptly asked of King Oswy his daughter Alchfled in marriage; he declared his desire to forsake his father's pagan creed for the Christian faith and was baptized by the Celtic bishop Finan of Lindisfarne at *Ad Murum, aet Walle,* possibly Wallbottle in Northumberland.[35] The year was 653.

Penda himself regarded character as of more importance than creed. He had no objection to the preaching of Christianity in either his son's kingdom or his own. He did object to Christians who took no heed to practise what they professed, "saying that such men who scorned to obey the God of their belief deserved both pity and contempt." But his mind was full of other things. Since 645, when he had driven Cenwalh of Wessex from the throne in revenge for Cenwalh's divorcing of his sister, he had held under his power this land of the West Saxons. In 654 he won revenge at last for the offence which King Anna of East Anglia had given him by harboring the exiled Cenwalh, when he defeated and killed Anna in battle. Then the East Angles bowed so deeply to his domination that Ethelhere, who succeeded his brother Anna as their

[35] Mawer, *Northumberland,* 205.

ruler, was fighting for Mercia when at last Penda's pride was crushed.[36]

Meanwhile, the North was also kept in turmoil by his lust for conquest. When in 651 Oswy of Bernicia had murdered Oswin, ruler of the province of Deira which marched with his, Penda had worked to keep Oswy from gaining kingship over a united Northumbria. It even seems that in his zeal to prevent union of its two provinces he had supported Ethelwald, nephew of Oswy, upon the throne of Deira for some years. Since he ruled supreme from the river Humber southward to the coast of Wessex, from the Welsh border to the East Anglian shore, it vexed him bitterly that Northumbria still remained in other hands. Again and again he sent his men across its border to seize its cattle and plunder its fields. At last Oswy, driven to the point of despair, offered as the price of peace "gifts from his royal treasury, innumerable and passing belief," if only Penda and his freebooters would go home.

He offered in vain, and decided to risk all in one great effort. When he saw that the barbarian would be content with nothing but surrender, he ordered his little force to march out against the Mercian soldiers, said to be thirty times more numerous and led by thirty royal chieftains. But his courage was high and he swore a mighty oath: "If the heathen knows not how to accept our offerings, let us hold them up to Him Who knoweth, even the Lord our God!" He vowed, too, to give his baby daughter Elfled to a convent cloister, and rich lands for the founding of monasteries, should he by the grace of God prevail over his enemy. Prevail he did, on the bank of the river Winwaed in Yorkshire, and pursued and killed the heathen ravagers, including Penda himself and nearly all those thirty warrior princes. Nature aided his courage; far more

[36] *HE* III, cc. 21, 7, 18; Plummer II, 168f.

were drowned in the river, raging in flood through torrents of
rain, than were put to death by the sword.

From this year, 655, Oswy ruled a united Northumbria in
peace. He also succeeded Penda in supreme power among
English kings. A more important consequence was the increase
of the Christian faith throughout England, now that this powerful old pagan was dead.[37]

Among those who had faced Penda on the Winwaed was
young Alchfrid, son of Oswy. It seems that his father rewarded him afterward for his share in its victory by making
him king of Deira under his own overlordship. He was an
earnest Christian, brought up in the Celtic faith of Northumbria under Aidan, and a friend of Penda's son, Prince Peada,
whom he himself had urged toward Christianity when Peada
was asking Oswy's daughter Alchfled in marriage. The next
year, 656, however, brought him sudden grief in the murder
of this friend and brother-in-law during the feast of Easter.
Moreover, rumour, whether true or not, declared guilty of
the crime his own sister Alchfled, the murdered man's
wife.[38]

Perhaps this grief turned Alchfrid's thoughts more seriously
toward the faith he had professed. At any rate, some two years
later he gave to Eata, abbot of the Celtic monastery of Melrose
in Scotland, land at Ripon in Yorkshire for the building of a
daughter house of religion; when the house was ready, Eata
became its abbot. One of the monks at Melrose had been
Cuthbert, known to us as the Saint of Lindisfarne, and Eata
now installed Cuthbert in Ripon as guest-master.[39]

Even as he made this gift, the thoughts of Alchfrid were
straying outside his own Celtic fold, like those of Wilfrid on

[37] *HE* III, cc. 23f.; Plummer II, 179, 184.
[38] *HE* III, cc. 21, 24; Plummer II, 189.
[39] Bede, *Vita Cuth.* (prose), cc. 6f. See also Mabillon II (1936),
877ff.

Lindisfarne. Not long before, he had been talking earnestly with young Biscop at the court of King Oswy, and had suddenly felt that he wanted to journey south with Biscop to Canterbury and then "to travel on to Rome and worship at the shrines of the apostles." He would hardly have longed to travel with Biscop, so keenly devoted to the Roman Church, had he not wanted to learn of the same. But Oswy, as a Celtic Christian, forbade his son to depart, and Alchfrid had remained in Northumbria when Biscop set out for his meeting with Wilfrid in Kent.[40]

Alchfrid was also a friend of Cenwalh, king of Wessex. Perhaps Wilfrid visited Wessex when at last, in 660 or 661, he landed in England; for Cenwalh wrote to Alchfrid that he must certainly talk with this young man fresh from Rome. Alchfrid, too, as Oswy's son, may have listened while Wilfrid, now once more home in Northumbria, poured out the story of his travels to that queen of Oswy, Eanfled, who had made them possible by her generous enthusiasm and who now rejoiced to see him bound to the service of her own Church. The young king of Deira would again have felt a wave of excitement surging within him as he heard of that mother-city of saints and scholars, home of the Holy Father himself, which was casting steadily her charm upon him.

An invitation was despatched, and readily accepted. It would be more profitable for Wilfrid, burning with zeal for the conversion of his northern country, to talk with this enthusiastic prince than to linger with his father Oswy and with Oswy's Celtic bishop Finan, whom he himself had once obeyed in the following of the Celtic Church. That Church he now held poisoned by schism of deed and discipline.

Only a few words from Wilfrid were needed to bring the rising desire of Alchfrid to its crest. Soon he was on his knees,

[40] Bede, *VA* c. 2.

humbly begging for the blessing of this wonderful teacher, "for it seemed to him as though an angel of God were speaking." Long they sat, while one asked unnumbered questions for his enlightening on Roman faith and ritual and the other gave freely of all he had learned under Annemund and Boniface. Perhaps it was in York that they talked; they may have visited together the church of stone which King Edwin, Alchfrid's great-uncle, had begun and which his uncle, King Oswald, had enlarged. Edwin and Paulinus, his bishop of York, had planned it as a shrine of Catholic faith and dedicated it to Saint Peter; under Oswald it had been turned to Celtic use for Aidan. It had fallen in glory when Aidan had changed his bishop's seat from York to Lindisfarne; since Oswald's death it had been neglected and its fabric was now showing evident signs of decay. Very possibly even at this time Wilfrid and the prince of Deira as they looked at its mouldering walls planned a time when the city of York would again be Deira's episcopal see.[41]

Meanwhile Wilfrid must make use of his energy, of his learning, of that power of winning friends which had hitherto aided him. All these gifts would find their place, he believed, in a community of monks, whom he should rule and train as abbot. In revealing to his friend Alchfrid that truth which he had himself sought and gained, he had found that, whatever else he might be or do, he was, above all, to be a teacher. Henceforth throughout his long life he was to preach with all the ardour of his passionate nature, wherever he could find hearers, at any and every cost of suffering and peril to himself, the Faith he had learned step by step in Canterbury and Lyons and Rome.[42]

[41] Eddius, c. 7.
[42] Bede, who certainly appraised Wilfrid with justice and charity, but not with excess of zeal, described him as one "who could not be kept back from his ministry of preaching the gospel": *HE* IV, c. 13.

Alchfrid not only talked. In his gratitude he presented to this new friend land for a monastery at Stamford, and, as more and more men gathered there for training under Roman discipline, offered him the abbey of Ripon, settled on a far larger estate. As we have seen, it had lately been granted to Eata and his monks. However, the zeal of Alchfrid for the Roman Church now placed before Eata and his community a simple and definite choice: let them either forsake Celtic tradition and submit to that of Rome, or leave Ripon to those who did. They chose the latter; Eata and Cuthbert returned to Scotland, and Wilfrid was at once made abbot in Eata's place. Both had been trained under Aidan at Lindisfarne; but probably they had known little of one another, as Eata was already abbot of Melrose in 651 when Wilfrid was only seventeen years old.[43]

The new abbot had not yet been ordained priest, because no Catholic bishop was at hand. The Celtic bishop of the diocese, Finan of Lindisfarne, had died shortly after Wilfrid's return to Northumbria, and had been succeeded by another, called Colman, who was now ruling this diocese of Northumbria from the same see of Lindisfarne according to the same Celtic dispensation. Wilfrid and his royal benefactor would have none of him.[44]

Two years passed. In 663, we may think, Agilbert, bishop of Dorchester, shook off the dust of Wessex in his anger against Cenwalh, his king, and hurried north to seek Alchfrid's sympathy. Alchfrid was doubtless his friend as well as the friend of Cenwalh; and Agilbert would naturally seek a Catholic court as refuge in the need of deciding his future. He richly repaid the hospitality given him, and at Alchfrid's

---

[43] Eddius, c. 8; *HE* III, cc. 25f.; Bede, *Vita Cuth.* (prose) cc. 6, 8. The site of "Stamford" is unknown. Suggestions have given Stamford Bridge or Stainforth in Yorkshire.
[44] Bright, 221f.

request ordained Wilfrid priest at Ripon. Colman's permission, apparently, was not asked.[45]

We need not be surprised, therefore, that the presence of Bishop Agilbert helped to bring to a climax in Northumbria the long discord in regard to the shape of the monastic tonsure and the date of keeping Easter. So greatly had the Celtic manner of calculating Easter differed from the system practised by Rome that in one year of Oswy's reign he and his Celts were celebrating Easter while Queen Eanfled and her Roman clergy were still within Holy Week.[46] The Christian tact and charity of Aidan had kept both sides in common tolerance of each other while he lived, for he had been held in as great love and respect by the English who obeyed the Roman Church as by his own Celtic followers. Finan, as we have seen, however, was a man of very different temper, and under his successor, Colman, matters became unbearable. Day by day discussion raged more fiercely, till many fell into soul-searching fear lest, after all, they were outside the true fold of Christ. At last it was decided that a synod should be called for the full debating of these questions at the monastery of Streanaeshalch on the Yorkshire coast, known now as Whitby, the name given it by the Danes.

Whitby was one of the most renowned of the "double monasteries" of this age; its monks and nuns in this year 664 were ruled by the Abbess Hild, famous for her holiness, her energy, and her genius in administration of cloistered schools.[47] She was of royal race, as might have been expected in a re-

[45] Eddius, c. 9; Plummer II, 146.   [46] HE III, c. 25.
[47] The traditional date is 664; Stenton, 122, 129, prefers 663. Note also the argument of C. W. Jones (Bedae ODT 103; cf. Speculum IX, 1934, 413): "although the synod was called to consider the Irish Easter . . . it was called in the year 664 because of an incipient confusion between the Victorian and Dionysiac tables. For eighty-five years, or during the whole period of English conversion, the two tables had been used with reasonable satisfaction side-by-side; but in the year 665 they would diverge in a wholly new fashion."

ligious leader at this time, a great-niece of King Edwin; on Easter Eve, 627, as a child of thirteen, she had been one of the multitude baptized with him by Paulinus at York. This had so impressed her that henceforth she gave her time to prayer and works of charity, meanwhile secretly longing for some definite and formal call to religious life. But convents for women were little known in England during the earlier years of this seventh century, and the Celtic north held out no hope. Further south, women of royal lineage were passing over into France to seek training at monasteries already established there. Hild's own sister, Hereswith, wife of King Ethelhere of East Anglia, had retreated to live under religious rule at the monastery of Chelles, near Paris. Her example had inspired in Hild a desire to enter the same house, and with this in mind she had gone southward to East Anglia,[48] where she had lived for a year amid strong Roman tradition.

It is a witness to the character of the Celtic Aidan that at the end of the year she had answered his appeal for women who should serve under monastic rule in his vast northern diocese. She was now some years past thirty, and he had placed her in a tiny convent on the north bank of the river Wear. After another year, in 649, he had installed her as abbess of the monastery of Heruteu, Heortesig, Isle of the Hart, the modern Hartlepool in the county of Durham, where she had succeeded Heiu, a nun dedicated by Aidan, first of all women in Northumbria, it was said, to take upon herself the vows and habit. Hartlepool was a "double" monastery; and both Bishop Aidan and "all religious and learned men who knew her" had frequently visited Hild there, had loved her for her wisdom and devotion, and had given her their counsel on the many problems confronting an abbess placed over men and women in these difficult days.

[48] Raine, *DCB* II, 879; *HE* IV, c. 23; Plummer II, 244f.

Later on, when Aidan had passed to his reward and Finan was in charge in Northumbria as bishop of Lindisfarne, it had fallen to her to found and organize as its first abbess the monastery of Streanaeshalch, or Whitby, some seven years before the calling of the famous synod known by its name. This she ruled with equal skill, and her renown reached far outside its bounds through the young monks who received under her their preparation for the future. No fewer than five bishops afterwards looked back to the sound learning and practical experience which they had gained through her discipline: Bosa and a second Wilfrid, both of the see of York; Aetla, bishop of Dorchester; John, bishop of Hexham and saint of Beverley; Oftfor, bishop of Worcester. We have already seen the last two as students with Aldhelm in Canterbury.[49]

Such was the woman who was hostess to this conference, who sat with her nuns around her to watch on the Celtic side as men debated in her great hall high above the North Sea. She saw in their due places the champions of the Celtic church in Northumbria: King Oswy, presiding over all; Colman, since 661 bishop of Lindisfarne; Colman's monks and clergy; Cedd, bishop of the East Saxons, interpreting the speech of the Celts to those who listened for the cause of Rome. Chief among these were Alchfrid, subject to his father Oswy as prince of Deira, but opposed to him in this matter of religion; his guest, Bishop Agilbert from Wessex; monks and priests of high and low degree, of whom we know by name Agatho and Wilfrid, James the Deacon, once assistant to Archbishop Paulinus, and Romanus, confessor of Queen Eanfled.[50]

It is not necessary to repeat here in detail the story of this debate, so vividly described in the Latin narrative of con-

[49] Pp. 36f, and 69 *supra.*   [50] *HE* III, c. 25; Eddius, c. 10.

temporary writers: how Agilbert, still suffering through his lack of fluent Saxon, requested that Wilfrid might speak for the Roman usage; how Wilfrid declared this usage to be universal throughout all lands, Africa, Asia, Egypt, Greece and the whole Christian world, save only those of the Picts and British, who still held obstinately to their foolish ignorance, against all civilized mankind; how Colman sought Saint John for the Celtic cause and Wilfrid confronted him with Nicaea; how both argued around the canon of Anatolius, not knowing it to be a forgery;[51] how Colman appealed to Columba, Father of Iona's island church, and Wilfrid flung back at him the Lord's commission to "the most blessed chief of the Apostles"; how Colman himself in his honesty would not deny that to Peter, not to Columba, had been given the keys of the Kingdom of Heaven; how the Church of Rome held fast her witness that from Peter she traced her authority as head of the communion of the faithful everywhere.

With this the audience was deeply moved, and Oswy spoke "with a smile." Was he rejoicing in new light, or pleased that things had gone as he wanted them to go? "And I say unto you, that here is found a door-keeper whom I would not oppose. Nay, but so far as I have knowledge and power, I desire in all things to obey his commands; lest when I come to the doors of the Kingdom of Heaven, there be none to open unto me, through displeasure of him who hath been declared holder of the keys thereof."[52] To Oswy's judgment the Celts who were assembled in the hall now gave assent, promising that for the future they would follow the Church of Rome as leader in the surer way; in particular they would adopt the Roman tonsure and the Roman Easter.

A minority, however, still held out and refused to conform. Chief among them was Colman, who with many of his monks

---

[51] On this see Jones, *ODT* 82ff.   [52] *Cf.* Stenton, 123.

from Lindisfarne went home to Iona, leaving Northumbria deprived of a bishop and Oswy of a valued friend. His place was filled by one Tuda, who had been trained and consecrated bishop among the Irish of southern Ireland after their conversion to the law of Rome. Those of the community of Lindisfarne who chose to remain on the island under Roman discipline were given a new abbot in Eata, who here accepted the obedience from which he had fled three years before as abbot of Ripon.[53]

Wilfrid had thus made one step forward into the light of public affairs in Church and State. It was a definite beginning, and from now on we find him taking more and more that active part in the life of his century to which the natural force of his character called him. Alchfrid was ready for this moment. His court and people of Deira needed a bishop; Wilfrid was undoubtedly the right man. His urgent petition won consent from his father, Oswy; probably the king found it a convenient arrangement that Wilfrid should serve Deira, while Tuda remained in charge of Bernicia with that titular precedence which Oswy himself as king of all Northumbria held over Alchfrid as vassal prince of the province of Deira.

Then suddenly Tuda fell victim to the Great Plague of this year 664, and Northumbria was left without any bishop at all.[54] Alchfrid's hopes for his friend and bishop-elect increased enormously. In his own mind he saw him sole ruler of Northumbria's great diocese; no doubt he also dreamed more and more frequently of his young monk seated in the cathedral chair of York, capital and royal seat of his own Deira.

First, however, Wilfrid must be consecrated to this office. In the Roman Church the laying on of hands by three bishops

[53] *HE* III, c. 26.
[54] *HE* III, c. 27; V, c. 19; Plummer II, 323.

was prescribed. But where to find them? Probably the natural choice, of Deusdedit of Canterbury and of Damian of Rochester, was impossible; it would seem that both had died shortly before. Wini of Wessex, another natural suggestion as the bishop of Wilfrid's friend, King Cenwalh, was *persona ingrata* since he had indirectly caused the flight of Wilfrid's patron Agilbert from his see of Dorchester. Other bishops, such as Cedd of the East Saxons and, most probably, Jaruman of the Mercians, had received their ordering from the Celtic Church, and were therefore judged inadmissible. Wilfrid himself raised the complaint that bishops of valid orders were lacking for his consecration in England.[55]

There remained another resource, far more attractive to him. He might cross the Channel once again to France, the land that had trained him for his work. Agilbert was now there, happily restored to his own country; and of Gallic bishops there were many. Moreover, and this was important, the Gallic Church understood right well all the glorious ritual and tradition attending this high ceremony; far better to be consecrated there than in the ruder England he was to serve and instruct. Throughout all the varied fortunes of his life the abbot of Ripon knew well how to abound and how to want. But undoubtedly he preferred to abound, not only because of his inborn love of beautiful things of art and architecture, but because of a deep sense of the dignity of the Church he represented. If Pope Gregory the Great would not willingly ride upon an ass for the single reason that he was the Pope of Rome, so Wilfrid desired to see around him as her abbot and bishop all the splendour properly due to his office.[56] Accordingly, he asked Alchfrid and his father, King Oswy, now himself allied with Alchfrid in loyalty to Rome, that they send him under their protection to France. They willingly

[55] Eddius, c. 12.　　　　　　[56] Gregory, *Epp.* II, No. 32.

agreed, and made generous provision of a ship, sailors, soldiers
and money; certainly their candidate must arrive properly
escorted. No doubt Wilfrid also brought with him to the
Frankish Church some gift of Northumbrian art.[57]

All went well, and this year 664 saw his consecration by
goodwill of the Frankish king of Neustria, Chlotar III, at the
royal town of Compiègne. While the choir chanted psalms
and hymns, twelve Frankish bishops carried him according
to the custom of their Church to the high altar of its cathedral,
seated upon a chair of gold. Before a great congregation of
people he avowed allegiance to the Faith and received the
laying on of hands from all the twelve, among them his friend
Agilbert.[58]

More than two years passed before he saw Northumbria
again. Perhaps various hindrances arising from custom or
courtesy held him in France; if so, we may feel sure that he
did not chafe overmuch at the delay. After the austere usages
of religion in northern England his soul may have rested all
too gladly on the outward beauty of ritual. Here in France he
once more felt at home, secretly reluctant, in spite of his longing to teach, when he faced the duty of returning to churches
rugged and unadorned, to priests and people new and un-
proved in their conversion to Rome, to brother bishops of
dubious Celtic consecrating, to the uncertain matter of his
own see, wondering perhaps whether, like Tuda, bishop of
Northumbria, he would be required to rule from that Lindisfarne whose loneliness he already knew so well.

Meanwhile, trouble was striking him from that very home.
First of all, his friend and patron Alchfrid mysteriously disappears at this point from the records of history. For some

[57] Baldwin Brown (VI, i, p. 21) suggests that he may have taken the
Franks Casket. For Oswy's consent see *HE* V, c. 19.

[58] Bright, 241, gives 664 or 665; but *cf.* Plummer II, 317. For the
ceremony see Eddius, c. 12, and Colgrave's notes.

reason unexplained he led a rising against Oswy, his father and overlord, and seems to have incurred death or exile as penalty.[59] With him the Church in Northumbria lost his energetic devotion, rallying point of the adherence to Roman precepts. Now its many clerics who still loved Celtic usage, behind their submission to Rome, seized their chance. A successor to Tuda must be promptly appointed, lest the people suffer unshepherded and religion come upon neglect. Before Wilfrid should return, might not some bishop be elected who would be true, indeed, to the decision made at Whitby, but far more ready than Wilfrid to sympathize with Celtic desire for simplicity in the building and serving of churches, one who would look back to Iona as mother of saints and combine observance of Roman rule with the Irish passion for ascetic and penitential living?

Such a man was at hand in the abbot of Lastingham, a monastery on the wild Yorkshire moors overlooking the sea near Whitby. It had been founded by Cedd, bishop of the East Saxons, after the model and tradition of Lindisfarne. There he had lately died of the plague and had bequeathed its governing to his brother Ceadda, better known as Chad, who had himself been one of twelve boys specially trained on Lindisfarne by Aidan for work in the north.[60]

Thus encouraged, the tide of feeling slowly rose. At last it reached the court and found Oswy in no way disposed to resist. If his son could be busy in electing a bishop for his own people in Deira, so could he, for his greater kingdom, choose one to rule in greater power. Not only would he appoint this Chad whom all held "right holy and learned, a faithful practiser in deed of all that he professed," but he

[59] HE III, c. 14. An inscription on the Bewcastle Cross in Cumberland has been thought to indicate that it was set up in memory of Alchfrid: Baldwin Brown V, 119, 202, 314. But cf. CMH III, 555 (Lethaby).
[60] Stenton, 125; HE III, cc. 23, 28.

would establish him in York as well. It would be better to have his bishop in this old and royal city of the ancient Northumbrian faith than on Lindisfarne, which Aidan had chosen as his see for his own love of solitude. If Alchfrid was ruling in Deira, it was under himself as supreme king of Northumbria. With this entirely reasonable argument other thoughts may have been working in Oswy's mind. Resentment against a disloyal son may well have moved him to prefer his own pastor to higher office than that of Deira's elect, so openly championed by Alchfrid. Chad himself was doubtless more congenial to Oswy, friend and disciple of the Celtic Aidan, than this Wilfrid, consecrated abroad in a foreign land and lingering there in apparent heedlessness of his duties in Northumbria.

In due course Chad was consecrated bishop of York, not at Canterbury, for its see was empty, but in Wessex, and by Wini, the bishop who had ousted Wilfrid's friend Agilbert. Here, again, we might perhaps descry a touch of malice on Oswy's part. But far worse to the friends of Wilfrid in his following of Rome was the news carried north that, in the lack of prelates of Roman ordering, two British bishops of Celtic consecration had actually taken part with Wini in the laying on of hands. Neither Oswy nor Chad himself saw in their recent submission to Rome any reason against this act of communion between two Churches which held the same sacramental faith.[61]

In truth, as he began his pastorate, Chad was not thinking of the manner of his tonsure or of the date of Easter. His portrait in this year, 664 or 665,[62] has been drawn for us by one born eight years later: "So Chad, now ordained bishop,

---

[61] Plummer II, 198; *HE* III, c. 28; *cf.* p. 12 *supra*, note 23.

[62] *HE* V, c. 24 gives the date 664; *ibid.*, V, c. 19, we read that Chad was bishop of York "for three years." But he did not leave York until 669; see Plummer II, 324; Bright, 246.

at once strove for pureness and true knowledge within the
Church, for humility, sober living, and study of books.
Through towns and countryside, to cottages, villages, and
castles he journeyed, preaching the Gospel, not on horseback
but on foot, after the custom of the apostles; for he was one
of the disciples of Aidan and endeavoured to train his hearers
in the same ways and manners after the example of Aidan
and of his own brother Cedd." [63]

Not until 666 did Wilfrid at last set sail from France,
escorted by one hundred and twenty men. So far all had gone
well for him; but a mystic mind might see in the storm which
now suddenly rose over the Channel some dire omen of the
days to come. A furious wind drove his sailors far from their
course, upon the land of Sussex, another incident prophetic
of the future. Stranded high upon the shore by the surf, while
the sea rushed back, they fled to dry land, only to fall into
peril among the savage heathen dwellers along that coast, who
held everything cast up by the sea as their own by right of
wreckage. Their chief priest, standing upon a high dune,
opened his mouth to bind the drenched and shivering strangers
by curses of his magic and was at once killed by a stone from
a wrathful Christian hand. Then, as the priests of the company
knelt in prayer, the crew threw themselves upon the heathen
that swarmed around and beat them into flight, with the loss
of only five of their own number. After this a miracle: the
sea came riding back to carry their ship, and all came safely
to haven at Sandwich in Kent. [64]

Not with humility, but at least with fortitude Wilfrid met
the shock of finding another man ruling Northumbria as chief
Pastor and in the see of York. No other place was desired
by him, nor would he rest content in a lower bishopric of
Deira. Chad was working hard and steadily to the satisfaction
of all, king, clergy, and people; Alchfrid, Wilfrid's friend, was

[63] *HE* III, c. 28.   [64] Eddius, c. 13.

dead or gone; he had better retire for a while from this scene and hope for happier fortune. He was only thirty-two, and the inspiration of Compiègne was still very much alive.[65]

The natural retreat was his monastery of Ripon, where his monks had keenly missed their abbot. He made it again his home, threw himself vigorously into his former work, and waited. Soon, through that same personal attraction which attended all his encounters, he was using his new episcopal powers in the service of other kings. One of these was Wulfhere, that son of Penda whom the Mercian nobles had placed upon his father's throne in 658, rising in revolt against Oswy's determined tenure of their land after his conquest on the Winwaed. Like his brother Peada, Wulfhere was a sincere Christian, although we do not know where and by whom he had been converted; he must, however, have submitted to the Roman Church, for he frequently invited Wilfrid into his kingdom for the fulfilling of various episcopal rites. His bishop, Jaruman, as it seems, had lately died.

Often, also, in the lack of an Archbishop of Canterbury

[65] It is very difficult to decide between conflicting views with regard to this period of Wilfrid's life. Bright (241ff., 320ff.; *cf. Gest. Pont.* 220) maintains that Theodore and Egfrid had not originally intended to deprive him "of the see of York, and the charge of part, probably the larger part, of Deira"; that it was his appeal to the Pope and his departure for Rome which caused his deprivation in Deira and York. Poole (*Studies,* 64f.) and Stenton (124, 132) hold the view that in 664 Wilfrid became bishop in western Deira, with his episcopal seat in his church at Ripon, while Chad presided as bishop over the rest of Northumbria, with his seat at York; that the situation continued thus until 669, when Chad was removed from York by Theodore as of invalid consecration and Wilfrid took Chad's place there, now for the first time bishop of all Northumbria. The difficulty lies in the differing narratives of Eddius and of Bede. Undoubtedly to Eddius Wilfrid was a hero who could commit no wrongs but suffered many; undoubtedly Bede was in character a far more reliable historian; undoubtedly Eddius was guilty both of prejudice in his interpretation of facts and of lack of scruple in his omission of evidence. Yet the long and close association of Eddius with Wilfrid is in favour of Eddius as narrator of factual detail. See also for discussion of these matters Levison, *Scr. rer. Merov.* VI, 167ff.; Colgrave, *Eddius,* c. 14, note on Chad, and xff.; R. Hodgkin, c. IX, note 2, pp. 382f.; Plummer II, 198f.; *CMH* II, 556f. (Corbett); Browne, *Theodore,* 34ff., 94ff.; B. W. Wells, *EHR* VI, 1891, 539f.

after the death of Deusdedit, the king of Kent made use of
Wilfrid for the ordination of priests and deacons. His name
was Egbert, and Wilfrid must have met him fifteen years
before at the court of his father Erconbert, during those days
in Canterbury, on the road to Rome. Now once again Canterbury offered her treasures for study and possession, and his
heart grew glad within him as he bore northward from his
visits skilled craftsmen for the enriching of Ripon Abbey and
other churches in Northumbria, workers in stone and glass
and metal, chanters who could train choirs in the art of song.
This had already been taught in Northumbria by James the
Deacon in the time of Archbishop Paulinus, but it had fallen
into neglect after his death. Now Wilfrid brought from Kent
two other masters of choral music: Aedde, also called Eddi
Stephen, author of that *Life of Wilfrid* from which we glean
valued material amid much verbiage of fervid admiration,
and Aeona, of whom we know nothing but his name.[66]

Another gift of Wilfrid to his abbey at Ripon had probably
been made at his first installation as abbot there about 661.
This gift was the instituting of the Benedictine Rule which he
had learned to know in France and in Rome. In this he saw
the forging of another link to bind securely the Church of his
remote island to the universal Church of all the civilized
world, ruling all men and nations from one city and one
head, holding in her hands all those treasures of solidity and
unity, of order and method, of learning and artistry which he
craved to find in Britain in place of Celtic detachment, stubborn individuality, passion for stark asceticism in inner and
in outward form. He infinitely preferred to be reasonable in
discipline with Benedict than to be extreme with Columba
and Columban of the Celts. The Rule of Saint Benedict had,
of course, been long known to Canterbury; we may think that

[66] Eddius, c. 14; *HE* III, c. 24; II, c. 20; IV, c. 2; Bright, 208.

at Ripon Wilfrid was the first formally to introduce it to northern England.[67]

Thus nearly three years passed, peacefully on the whole. They were, perhaps, marked by one disappointment: Wilfrid's friend Egbert, king of Kent, after consulting with King Oswy, husband of his patroness Queen Eanfled, chose in 667 another man to fill the metropolitan see of Canterbury, now vacant these three years. Wighard, the nominee, although "a good man, worthy to be a bishop," was not apparently a monk; he had served at Canterbury as priest under Deusdedit. When he, too, died in Rome just before his consecration, Pope Vitalian took the matter of an Archbishop for England into his own hands and, as we have seen, finally appointed Theodore.[68]

Yet from what may possibly have been bitter to Wilfrid's sense of power there soon came to him fruitful result. Theodore, the born organizer, stayed only a short while in Canterbury on his arrival in 669 before he set out to visit and inspect this England to which he had come as stranger. He travelled through the length of its country, examining into all matters concerning the churches, rectifying what was wrong and supplying what was needed for all, monks, clergy and layfolk. In due time he arrived in the north, and at York he promptly unearthed the fact that two Celtic prelates had taken part in the consecrating of its bishop Chad.

Here was a distinct flaw in the eyes of one whom the Pope had newly sent forth with Hadrian to bring Britain more perfectly into discipline. The bishop of York was summarily called to account. But to Chad a sense of power meant nothing. In all humility he answered that if his consecration was not recognized as valid, he would willingly yield his office of

---

[67] Eddius, cc. 14, 47. This does not mean, however, that Wilfrid insisted upon a usage wholly Benedictine in all points; cf. Knowles, 22.

[68] *HE* III, c. 29.

bishop; he had never felt himself worthy of it and had only assumed it under obedience. As proof of his sincerity he left York and retired to his abbey of Lastingham. Theodore decided that a man of this character was needed in the councils of the Church; he had heard, too, of the splendid work begun in the northern diocese. Just at this time Wulfhere of Mercia was asking for a bishop in place of Jaruman, lately dead; it offered a solution for at least part of the problem. The Archbishop asked Oswy, as Chad's king, to allow his departure from Northumbria; he laid his own hands upon him in the due and formal completing of consecration; he sent him to Mercia as its bishop. In Mercia Chad placed his see at Lichfield and worked as hard as ever he had done among the Yorkshire hills and dales. A pleasant story recounts that Theodore ordered him to ride on horseback about his diocese, as was the habit of bishops in Saxon England, and that when Chad protested against such luxury, he lifted the bishop with his own hands upon a horse.

By these means the Archbishop did his best to justify what he had already planned while Chad was in retreat at Lastingham; he placed Wilfrid of Ripon as bishop in the see of York. Chad was a very holy man; but a man of Wilfrid's culture and personal attractiveness, of his experience at home and abroad, might well be, reasoned Theodore, a more intelligent choice for ruler of the see second in importance in England.[69]

In York from this year of 669 onward Wilfrid found a task of necessity both to the northern Church and to his own sense of the fit and decent. As he looked at his cathedral of Saint Peter, his heart sank within him. Not only had it been raised in the solid, unimaginative manner of Saxon builders, for whom any skill which the Italian Paulinus might have brought from Kent had been lost by King Edwin's untimely

[69] *Ibid.* IV, cc. 2f.; Eddius, c. 15.

death, but even this Saxon work was crumbling in ruin. The roof leaked, birds flew in and out of the empty window-frames, placing their nests where they would; the walls inside and outside were dank and mouldy through many English rains.

Its bishop did what he could. He put a new lead covering on the roof, filled the windows with glass made by foreign craftsmen he had brought from Italy and France and Kent, cleansed the walls, re-adorned the altar and furnished it with seemly vessels. Finally, he endowed the cathedral with rich revenues from the lands given him by devout persons for this use. Unfortunately, no details are left for us of its appearance in his time.[70]

It was now 671, and King Oswy drew to the end of his eventful life. Long before, he had accepted Wilfrid as his pastor in chief. When his last sickness had come upon him, he had earnestly desired to follow the example of other Saxon kings and to die at Rome among the shrines of the saints. Would not Wilfrid his bishop take him there, he had asked, and receive in return generous offerings for the glory of the Church? Death, however, left him no time to go on pilgrimage; and in this year his son Egfrid succeeded him as king of Northumbria.[71]

The tide of prosperity for Wilfrid was now reaching its high-water mark. The land was at peace; the new king was his friend; all his priests and people welcomed him with enthusiasm as one who was to inaugurate a new and glorious era. Once again men saw and felt that in truth a bishop ruled them, conscious of his high office and using its occasions to the full. Not simply, as Chad, but in all the outward dignity which marked a prince of the Church he rode throughout his diocese, baptizing and confirming in the splendour of the

[70] Eddius, c. 16, with Colgrave's notes.
[71] *HE* IV, c. 5; Plummer II, 211.

Roman rites; he preached before king and clergy and people with irresistible force and charm; he entertained friends and strangers with comfort and ease in his episcopal hall, surrounded by his staff and servants, as befitted his state. None dared to refuse him reverence; few met him who did not depart fascinated by his winning courtesy. With all this we need not doubt that, in his magnificence as bishop, he did not relax as man and as monk the monastic discipline to which he was vowed; his magnificence was of the Church, even if he did enjoy it. His fastidious sense of the beautiful and seemly, united with his fervour for the precepts of his religion, kept him free from earthly indulgence of grosser sort. We are told that he never allowed himself more than one cup of wine at meals, summer or winter, and that every night even in the coldest weather he washed himself thoroughly in cold water, a penance symbolic of cleanliness of soul. Moreover, his people trusted him; abbots and abbesses yielded their monasteries and lands into his keeping; laymen of high rank brought their sons to him to be trained either for the cloister or for the service of arms. Also, we are told, Wilfrid "was always giving gifts and presents both to laymen and religious with such generosity that none was found to equal him." [72]

He now turned to a labour perhaps even happier, to enlarging the glory of Ripon, where he built a new church on his own site, probably a short distance from the monastery. It was formed of dressed stone, supported by columns for which he may have been indebted to Roman remains in Yorkshire or to material from Hadrian's Wall; on the north and south sides were small aisles or porches, probably containing altars and used as chapels, hallowed by relics of the saints. Underneath it lay the crypt, approached by antechambers, passages and steps, and covered with barrel-vaulting in correct

[72] Eddius, c. 21.

Roman style. The purpose of such an underground chamber or *confessio* in Italy was the guarding of sacred relics and tombs; such may have been Wilfrid's purpose also here. At the present day a little opening, known as "Saint Wilfrid's Needle," still recalls his memory.[73]

When all was finished, he held high ceremonial of dedication. King Egfrid of Northumbria was present, with his brother Aelfwine, perhaps ruler of Deira under Egfrid, as Alchfrid under Oswy; also dignitaries of many ranks and kinds in Church and State. They looked with mingled feelings—admiration, wonder, envy—on Wilfrid as he stood arrayed as bishop and abbot before the high altar in its purple and gold, to dedicate the church and all within it to the glory of God in honour of Peter, chief of the apostles; as he entreated of the Lord that He would hearken to His people when they should pray within that place. And then they all cried "Amen." After this he read the names of those lands round about the abbey which kings and benefactors had given for the maintenance of this house of God and for the good of their own souls, together with those of the deserted shrines of the British, left to fall in ruin after their flight before the Saxon invaders. These he now purposed to recall to their former use. At the end there was a sumptuous feast in which the whole company was entertained; it lasted three days and three nights.[74]

One wonders what the little community on Lindisfarne felt about it all, when they heard of this prodigal rejoicing of body and soul under the roof of their bishop. Their prior at this time was that same Cuthbert who with his abbot Eata and many of their fellow-monks had left Ripon rather than forsake

[73] Colgrave, 163; *Memorials of the Church of SS. Peter and Wilfrid, Ripon,* I, ed. Fowler, 1882, *SS* 74, 8ff. and *passim*; Baldwin Brown II, 1925, 148, 153, 160ff. *Cf.* W. T. Jones, *YAJ* XXXI, 1934, 75.
[74] Eddius, c. 17.

the Celtic tradition of their fathers. They had first returned to the monastery of Melrose in Scotland, of which Eata was still abbot. When he was made abbot of Lindisfarne, he seems to have held rule over both monasteries, sending Cuthbert to be prior of Lindisfarne.

On the island Cuthbert, who was of the same age as Wilfrid, was now living a life of utter self-denial and hardness, both through his own devotion to monastic austerity and through the discontent of some of his monks who longed for their former Celtic calendar and tonsure. He himself had submitted to Roman use after the synod of Whitby and had found this in practice at Lindisfarne upon his arrival. But he was often attacked in chapter by these unhappy brethren, and only his marvellous patience and calm carried him on in the face of irreverence, even insult. The abbot, Eata, was often absent in his other monastery of Melrose, and Cuthbert was practically ruler. It was difficult for him to combine that bare and strict simplicity, for which this house of Aidan, of Finan, and of Colman had been famous, with a Roman ritual hitherto unpractised there.[75]

But perhaps the most ambitious plans in Wilfrid's thoughts of building were carried out by him in Hexham on the river Tyne. On land given him from her marriage portion by Queen Ethelthryd, wife of Egfrid, he raised there, some time between 672 and 678, a monastery whose church in its elaborate construction far exceeded any other of its century. It was remarkably high and long, built of stone hewn square and polished, which, as in the case of Ripon, had been brought in its rough state from some Roman foundation in the neighbourhood, probably the old town of Corstopitum or Corbridge. The walls, three stories in elevation, were supported by many columns; at different points there stood

[75] Bede, *Vita Cuth.* (prose), c. 16; ed. Colgrave, 7, 324.

rounded towers up which winding stairs led to hidden chambers far above; aisles on either side held many chapels, with altars of Saint Mary, Mother of God, of Saint Michael the Archangel, of Saint John the Baptist and other holy confessors, martyrs, and virgins. At the end rose the arch of the sanctuary; this and the walls and the columns were adorned with carved images, with sculptures in relief, with paintings in combined colours and in a great variety of surface designs. Below the floor ran other flights of steps leading to underground passages and chapels and a large crypt with barrel-vault, vestibule, and steps for descent. This chamber and, in all probability, the similar one at Ripon are the only structures of Wilfrid's foundations which still remain to us.[76]

No building, it was declared, on this side of the Alps could compare with this church of Wilfrid, and pilgrims from Italy who saw it could well believe that they were looking upon some shrine of Rome. It was dedicated to Saint Andrew, in memory of Wilfrid's prayer in that city. Tradition told that fugitives from secular judgment sought sanctuary here from far and wide; in fact, that the church was set apart in privilege as a house of protection for sinners who might find penitence and healing under its shadow.[77]

For use at Holy Mass upon the altar at Ripon Wilfrid gave special order to skilled artists for the making of a text of the four Gospels in lettering of purest gold inscribed on parchment of purple colour, adorned with illumination. The cover was also of gold, set with jewels. Such treasures were known on the continent, but new in England.[78]

[76] Eddius, c. 22; Raine, *The Priory of Hexham* I, 1864, *SS* 44, xxviiff., 10ff., 19; II, 1865, *SS* 46, xxviff.; Clapham *ERA* 44ff., 72f., 154f. and Plate 65; Baldwin Brown II, 1925, c. VI, 149ff.; Short, 124.

[77] *Gest. Pont.* 255. For the reverence given to St. Andrew in England see A. S. Cook, "The Old English *Andreas* and Bishop Acca of Hexham," *TCAS* XXVI, 1924, 249ff.

[78] Eddius, *ibid.: inauditum ante seculis nostris quoddam miraculum.* See Maunde Thompson, 42.

The high tide of success lingered for some years. Perhaps it had already imperceptibly begun to turn when in 673 Theodore as Archbishop of Canterbury summoned bishops and learned priests and abbots to meet at Hertford, in that council which was the first national Church assembly held in England. It is, therefore, somewhat surprising that Wilfrid did not attend as bishop of York but instead sent his accredited delegates to represent him. It looks as though some trouble were already brewing.[79]

At any rate, this was true at the time when the council dispersed. The ninth of the ten rulings proposed by Theodore, "That more bishops be appointed as the number of the faithful increase," embodied his earnest desire and policy for the English Church. The assembly, as we have noted, did not pass this for formal action, and there is little doubt that Wilfrid's known opposition to it influenced his delegates and others.[80] He was efficient; he knew it, and he chose to rejoice in presiding over a vast tract and countless souls rather than relinquish part of his charge to an associate or a suffragan. Who knew? He might be parting with churches and people to another who did not see eye to eye with him in his working for the glory, outward and inward, of the Church; let priests and monks obey him throughout the north country; his energy was sufficient for all.

Gradually Theodore turned the policy which had been refused general consent into action, in individual cases, upon his own responsibility. Thus he carved the see of Elmham out of the diocese of Dunwich; [81] later on he was to carve that of Sherborne out of the diocese of Winchester. This was to give pain to Aldhelm; but Aldhelm was of a different charac-

[79] *HE* IV, c. 5; H.S. III, 118ff.; Bright, 284. For the date *cf.* p. 81 *supra,* note 213; Stenton, 133.
[80] Browne, *Theodore,* 114; Bright, 275f.
[81] *HE* IV, c. 5; Plummer II, 108.

ter. Besides, Aldhelm, in a way, would gain; Wilfrid faced
loss. He must have known that Theodore would not go on
his way without subdividing the enormous diocese of York.

There were, however, other elements that were dangerously
active, especially in the court of Northumbria. As we have
seen, King Egfrid upon his succession in 671 was on friendly
terms with his bishop of York, as his father Oswy had been
before him. Unfortunately his queen Ethelthryd for many
years had been longing to live in cloister as a nun; although
she had been given to two kings as bride, she had consistently
in both cases refused consummation of the marriage bond.
Her first husband, Tondbert, ruler over the fens of Cambridgeshire, had died soon after their wedding, and she remembered him chiefly in gratitude because he had bestowed upon
her as marriage gift the Isle of Ely. For five years she had
lived there as widow in religious seclusion, cut off from the
world by marshes and pools of water, until she was asked
again in marriage, this time by the king of Northumbria, and
compelled by her family to accept so splendid an honour.[82]

As Egfrid's wife she had spent twelve years in keen reluc-
tance, always thinking wistfully of the joy and peace that
gladden the brides of the Lord. Her chief comfort had been
found in the bishop of York, her spiritual director. Wilfrid
knew his canon law very well; no prohibition of the Church
prevented a woman who was wife only in name from assuming
a nun's vows, provided her husband gave consent. Moreover,
how glorious for Ethelthryd to follow the lead of so many
others of Saxon royal blood into the better life of contemplation and charity! Again and again the queen begged Egfrid
to release her, but for a long time he refused; she was, save in
this essential matter, all he wished as queen and consort. At

[82] For Ethelthryd see *Liber Eliensis* I, ed. D. J. Stewart, 1848;
Mabillon II (1936), 738ff.

last, however, her prayers could no longer be denied; he yielded her freedom and she went off with a glad heart to the monastery of Coldingham in County Berwick, ruled by Ebba, an aunt of Egfrid. The picture of the king trying in vain to resist his queen, his bishop, and his aunt as they strove to lead him to virtue at the cost of his wife is somewhat pathetic, even if circumstances placed Ethelthryd within technical permission of the Church's law.[83] At any rate, we can understand his feelings when after a short while she received the religious habit from the hands of Wilfrid himself. She spent a year in training at Coldingham; then she built on her own Isle of Ely a "double" house of prayer and became abbess in course of time over very many monks and nuns. Wilfrid declared afterward that King Egfrid had offered him broad lands and much money if only he would bring the queen to understand her part as a wedded wife. "I know," the king added, "that she thinks of no one in the world more than she does of you." [84]

The marriage was annulled as incomplete, and Egfrid took a bride named Ermenburg; her sister was wife of that Centwine who in 676, about the same time, became king of Wessex. The new queen for several reasons was roundly opposed to Wilfrid. He ranked the honour of the wedded life markedly below that of the cloister; doubtless he did not show her any but necessary respect and disallowed Egfrid's re-marrying. She found, however, her most subtle point of attack in what was externally obvious: "the magnificence displayed in matters of this world by Wilfrid as bishop; his wealth, the multitude of his monasteries, the great buildings he had raised, the army of those who attended him, too many to number, decked out in vestments or in arms proper for the court of a king."

Apparently in her eyes the bishop had little right to reli-

---

[83] Colgrave, *Eddius*, 167: note on *Iurminburg*.
[84] *HE* IV, c. 19.

gious ceremonial in his surroundings. She went further, for his Palace in its splendour of hospitality threatened to eclipse her husband's royal state. "His table," she indignantly declared, "is served with gold and silver dishes; throngs of clients decked out in proud array crowd about him as he sallies forth." Undoubtedly she was bitterly jealous. On the other hand, according to tradition, after Egfrid's death she, too, became a nun.[85] It may be that she was genuinely distressed by what seemed to her extravagance neither monastic nor Christian, compared with the austerity of Aidan and his followers, as well as that of Chad and of Cuthbert, whom she deeply admired. Here, indeed, lay one of the most important reasons for the quarrel of many good men against Wilfrid in the days to come. Even now Ermenburg found it easy to awaken the same feeling in her husband, and soon both Egfrid and his queen were calling Archbishop Theodore north to hear from their own lips of the unseemly conduct of their bishop of York.

Theodore arrived without delay, for the summons coincided with his own conviction regarding this diocese. It may be justly borne in mind that he did hold chief ecclesiastical authority in England. Pope Gregory the Great had, indeed, purposed two archbishoprics, of London and of York, in his plan for the English Church; but Wilfrid had never received the pallium, that vestment sent by a Pope to signify metropolitan authority for its recipient.[86]

Yet concerning Wilfrid the Archbishop of Canterbury acted here neither wisely nor well. It was unwise to ally himself, even outwardly, with an angry pair of secular rulers; it was wholly wrong to take any step concerning a diocese without telling its bishop beforehand exactly what he meant to do.

[85] Gest. Pont. 219f.; Liber Vitae, SS 13, 1841, 3; Eddius, cc. 24, 40.
[86] HE I, c. 29; Dudden, Gregory the Great II, 1905, 129f.; Plummer, II, 117.

Perhaps, however, Theodore did call Wilfrid into conference, and he either refused to appear or showed himself so entirely opposed to the proposal made him that further conversation seemed useless. There is no satisfactory evidence of one or the other, although we are told in words said to be those of Wilfrid himself that Theodore assembled other bishops to confer with him on this business, yet none consented.[87]

The fact remains that in Wilfrid's absence Theodore appointed three new bishops for the diocese he had governed as bishop of York. It consisted in this year, 678,[88] of the provinces of Deira and Bernicia and of a third, Lindsey, which still bears its old name in the northern division of Lincolnshire. This district was shuttled forth and back in the seventh century between Northumbria and Mercia; some years before this time it had been wrested in battle from King Wulfhere by Egfrid and was now under Northumbrian rule.

With his own hands alone Theodore consecrated his three officiants-elect: first, Eata, whom we have seen as abbot of Lindisfarne and of Melrose in Scotland, to govern Bernicia as bishop, with his see either settled in the monastery of Hexham, Wilfrid's own beloved possession, or in Lindisfarne; secondly, as bishop of Lindsey, one Eadhed, a Northumbrian priest who at Oswy's desire had accompanied Chad on his journey into Wessex for consecration; thirdly, as suffragan bishop for Wilfrid in administering Deira, the monk Bosa, once of Whitby.[89]

Wilfrid was still chief bishop over Deira and still in possession of his cathedral of York. Nevertheless, he was shorn of much of his former power, and his wrath was hot. It grew hotter when he heard that these suffragans who were to rule

---

[87] Eddius, c. 30: ed. Colgrave, 168; Bright, 321.

[88] Poole (*Studies*, 48, 65) and Stenton (135f.) place the consecration of the three bishops by Theodore and Wilfrid's departure from England in 677, his stay in Frisia in 677–678.

[89] *HE* IV, c. 12; III, c. 28. Consecration by Theodore alone is attested here by Wilfrid, on the authority of Eddius, c. 30, and by Eddius himself, c. 24: *solus ordinavit*.

in his diocese had been ordained in his absence by Theodore in his own cathedral. At once he hastened to the court, where Theodore was still staying, to ask him and King Egfrid why, without cause on his part and against his will, they had robbed him of the rights with which he had been duly and justly invested by King Oswy and by Theodore himself. But his indignation availed him nothing. Theodore had made up his mind, sure of his supreme power over north as well as south in England, and Wilfrid left the royal hall amid the jeering laughter of its courtiers.[90]

For some time he remained idle, unable in his bitter resentment to imagine any hope of healing. Then suddenly a bold thought entered his mind. If England held no redress for one insulted and deprived as he had been, he would take his case to Rome, the mother Church of England and all the world. He remembered how Pope Eugenius had laid his hands upon him, praying that God would keep him evermore; he remembered the good Boniface and all his friends in Rome's many churches and monasteries. Surely they would understand and help to right this wrong. There were some, too, in England who already sympathized with him, among them those bishops who apparently had been unwilling to take part in the consecration of Theodore's new prelates in spite of the rule requiring three to officiate. Perhaps Theodore had relieved them of embarrassment by holding that as Archbishop of Canterbury his hands alone sufficed for the work.[91] Now these friends

[90] Eddius, c. 24.

[91] They were apparently willing to assent to the division of the diocese, but not to the complete deprivation of Wilfrid: cf. Bright, 320, note 4. Consecration by a single bishop was, in general, against the canon law of the Church, and formed one of the differences between the Roman and the Celtic disciplines; see Plummer II, 49, 75, 178, 324; H.S. I, 155. Yet in his Responsa Gregory the Great had allowed Augustine to consecrate alone, in the lack of other bishops of the Roman obedience (HE I, c. 27, Question 6); Honorius had been consecrated by Paulinus alone (HE II, c. 16; see Dudden, Gregory the Great II, 134; DCA I, 223f.). Colgrave (Eddius, 168) suggests that Theodore was relying here on his position as archbishop.

reminded Wilfrid that Theodore himself owed obedience to the Pope. Thus encouraged, he made ready to start, leaving innumerable monks to lament the necessity of obeying the new bishops while at the same time they prayed for their Father all success in his journey and its end.

There were reasons, more than one, for their prayers. Ebroin, that Frankish "Mayor of the Palace," whom we suspected of slaying Annemund of Lyons, was still master of Neustria, ruling at this time for the boy king, Theodoric III, a sovereign only in name. His ambition had also coveted control, under this same royal pretence, of Austrasia, Neustria's rival state, and here he had already encountered Wilfrid himself. Grimoald, Mayor of Austrasia, had risen in revolt in 656, upon the death of his king, Sigebert, had seized Sigebert's little son, Dagobert II, and lodged him in a monastery in Ireland, where he remained twenty long years. Wilfrid had supported the people of Austrasia in their struggle against Ebroin's ambition, had invited Dagobert, now a grown man, to visit him in England, and had materially helped the Austrasians to place him once more on their throne, only two years before this time of 678. Wilfrid did not lack enemies to send word from England to Ebroin that he was about to sail for France; and naturally the Mayor of Neustria rejoiced that his chance for vengeance had now arrived.[92]

But he caught the wrong prey. Another English bishop was on his way across the Channel, also leaving his diocese because his views did not meet those of Theodore. This was Winfrid, who had succeeded Chad as bishop of Lichfield in Mercia, "a good and temperate man," whom, however, Theodore had deposed for disobedience. We may think that he did not share the Archbishop's eagerness to divide up his holding among the Mercians.[93] A confusion of names saved Wilfrid;

[92] Eddius, c. 28; Bouquet III, 600ff.
[93] HE IV, cc. 3, 6; Bright, 292; Eddius, c. 25.

for the ex-bishop of Lichfield, while peacefully travelling through France, was arrested, stripped of all he had, and forced to see most of his escort murdered before his eyes.

As it happened, Wilfrid did not travel by the usual route to Rome, south to Étaples and onward down through France. He may have been warned; the winds may have been contrary. At any rate, he crossed the North Sea and put to shore in Frisia (Friesland), that part of the Netherlands washed by the Ijssel Meer. The change in his journey not only saved him, but kept him from proceeding on his way. The land was ripe for spiritual harvest, and there was no one to gather it in; Wilfrid's missionary soul was content to tarry awhile. The natives of Frisia, ruled by a king named Aldgils, were entirely pagan, but friendly; they received in peace the bishop's immediate declaration of Christian doctrine and went on with the fishing by which they gained their daily food. But their zeal increased beyond measure when not only sea but also earth yielded them that year a harvest extraordinarily fruitful. Of course, it must be the gift of the new God of whose kindness and generosity this stranger was so eloquently telling; promptly in their hundreds and thousands they came with their tribal chiefs to be baptized as children of this Great Spirit of Heaven.[94]

Accordingly the bishop of York stayed on very happily from month to month in this winter of 678–679. All day long he taught and received the "new people of God," and their gratitude repaid his work. When his enemy Ebroin sent messengers with a letter to King Aldgils, promising rich measure of golden coins if he would only send to him this guest alive or dead, Aldgils invited them to a banquet in his hall among

[94] Eddius, c. 26; *HE* V, c. 19. For previous missionary work in Frisia, during the earlier seventh century (of Amandus, bishop of Maastricht; of Cunibert, bishop of Cologne; of Eligius, bishop of Noyon), see Hauck I, 321ff.; Rettberg, *passim*.

his own men of arms. Suddenly, while all were making merry, he ordered silence, read aloud the letter, tore it up before the whole company and threw the fragments into the fire. Then, turning to the messengers, "Tell your master," he shouted, "so may the Creator of the world tear and destroy the kingdom and the life of that man, so may He burn him to ashes, who shall take the name of his God in vain and forsake his sworn word!" The envoys departed in much embarrassment and Christianity triumphed in its apostle. But it is sad to relate that when some ten years later another Englishman came from Ireland to preach the gospel to these men of Frisia, he worked in vain for two years, "and, finding no fruit of all his toil among his barbarous hearers, returned to that place of dear pilgrimage whence he had come." Of this Witbert and the future missions to Frisia we shall hear later on.

But now the spring had come, and Wilfrid decided he must travel on to Rome. The next stage of his journey found him in Austrasia, at the court of that same Frankish king who so largely owed his throne to Wilfrid's intervention. Dagobert did his utmost to repay his debt. The bishop of Strassburg had lately died; it was the chief see in the realm; would not Wilfrid accept election? When he refused, the king sent him forward with many gifts under escort of Deodatus, bishop of Toul.[95]

Another royal host entertained the two bishops shortly after they entered Italy. He was Perctarit, king of Lombardy, and his life had been a thrilling one. Once, in 661, he had shared the throne of Lombardy with his brother Godepert; Godepert had reigned at Pavia and he himself at Milan. Then a quarrel broke out between the two brother kings, and Godepert sent to ask aid from Grimoald, the powerful Duke of Benevento, never dreaming that Grimoald would be tempted to become

[95] *HE ibid.;* Eddius, cc. 27f.

his deadliest enemy. Egged on by the cunning of Garibaldi, Duke of Turin, Grimoald entered the hall of Godepert at Pavia, murdered the king with his own hand, and declared himself lord of Pavia and Lombardy. News of his brother's death rapidly reached Perctarit in Milan; with horrid apprehension he saw himself the next victim of Grimoald and fled to barbaric refuge, to the chieftain of the Avars in Pannonia. Story tells that here also a bribe of golden coins was offered for the fugitive's surrender, this time by Grimoald to this Avar Khan; the usurper could never feel secure upon the Lombard throne as long as Godepert's brother was alive and free. And here also the protector refused, fearing the wrath of those pagan gods in whose name he had promised Perctarit protection.[96]

The story was told by Perctarit to Wilfrid as they sat together in the palace of Pavia, to which the king had safely arrived after Grimoald's death in 671. He had also been made sole king over all the Lombards and was ruling in the faith of the Church, compelling Jews and heretics to baptism. There was grim reason in the retelling of the tale. At its end Perctarit quietly observed: "Your enemies in Britain, Lord Bishop, have sent me greeting and offer of rich reward if I will hold you now and deliver you into their hands. But I remember the mercy shown me by the king of the Avars long ago and his fear of his gods, heathen as they were. How much more, then, shall I, who know the true God, refuse to deliver my soul to perdition, even for all the gold in the world!" [97]

It was with a mixed sense of thanksgiving for the past and of apprehension for the future that Wilfrid in 679 arrived at Rome. The sight of its streets and churches must have caused him pain as they called up former days, free from care. This

[96] Paul the Deacon, *Hist. Lomb.* IV, c. 51; V, c. 2; Eddius, c. 28; T. Hodgkin VI, 242ff.

[97] *Hist. Lomb.* V, c. 33; Hodgkin VI, 303.

time his errand was far different, and he immediately set to work to obtain a Papal audience.

The Pope of this time was Agatho, elected the year before, "so gentle and kind that he smiled merrily upon all men." [98] He already knew of the trouble between Theodore and Wilfrid, since Theodore had despatched to Rome a monk named Coenwald with a letter describing from his own point of view all that had happened.[99] Doubtless the Pope uttered a sigh; Britain was a very difficult country. But Britain was a precious jewel, nevertheless, and must be carefully guarded. Soon after Wilfrid had pleaded his own cause, Agatho called to formal session for its trial a synod of more than fifty bishops and priests in the church called "the Constantinian," built by Constantine in the fourth century. They sat in its *secretarium,* a room in which bishops met for business, received visitors, and held meetings of their own number or of their clergy; when they assembled, as on this occasion, to consider a case of redress, the petitioner waited outside until decision had been reached.[100]

While, then, Wilfrid sat among sympathizing friends looking upon a closed door, the Pope within presented the matter for debate. His brief words were followed by speeches from the deacon and the sub-deacon of the College of Cardinals, Andrew, bishop of Ostia, and John, bishop of Porto. They declared on behalf of the assembled prelates and clergy that, after reading the letter sent by Theodore and a written statement of his case presented by Wilfrid, and after due appreciation of the fact that many thorny points bristled in this problem of English dioceses, they had found Wilfrid innocent of all crime whatsoever against the canons of the Church.

[98] Duchesne, *Lib. Pont.* I, 350.
[99] Eddius, c. 29; *Gest. Pont.* 222.
[100] Eddius, *ibid.*; Browne, *Theodore,* 144ff. For explanation of so great a number of bishops see p. 165 *infra.*

Moreover, they found that he had done well in avoiding further strife by his prompt referring of the matter to the authority of the Apostolic See.

Upon this, the Pope ordered Wilfrid to be admitted to the council room, that his petition might be heard. It was immediately read aloud by John, secretary to the assembly. As they listened, the bishops and clergy present must have marked its mingling of deliberate respect for authorities in England, for Theodore, Archbishop of Canterbury, for Egfrid and for Ermenburg, king and queen of Northumbria, with a wholly independent claim for the rights of the Church, as distinct from the secular powers, and for the judgment of the Church assembled in synod, as distinct from the aim or desire of any individual prelate, however exalted his degree.

"Certain men have made inroad upon my rights as bishop, though they found me deserving of no punishment for sin against Church law; with unlawful daring against the rules and definitions of the holy canons, in the assemblage of Theodore, most reverend Archbishop of the Church of Canterbury, and of other prelates meeting with him at that time, like robbers they forcibly attacked, filched, and settled themselves in that diocese of mine which for many years I had administered by the merciful grace of God; not only one, but three men advanced themselves as bishops in my church. By no canonical right. How, then, has it come about that Theodore, the most reverend Archbishop, while I am still living, without my consent (of little worth as I am), without the consent of any bishop, by his own authority, ordained three bishops for that diocese which I (albeit unworthy) was administering? Such questions were better left unanswered than pressed, for reverence of that same Theodore; truly I dare not accuse him, a bishop sent from this most Holy and Apostolic See. . . . If then I, who stand convicted of no crime, am adjudged by the dignity of this same See as deprived of these my holdings, with lowly devotion I accept that judgment. If, however, Holy Father, your decision be that I regain my former diocese, may I with all reverence pray that those who have seized by force for their own bishoprics the districts wherein I served you, be cast out by sentence of your synod. And if, moreover, it shall seem good to you to advance men to the office of bishop in that same diocese over which I held rule, at least may it please you to install those with whom I may be able to live in harmony and peace. Let each of us recognize the rights of the Church and watch diligently over those things committed to his care; and if, again, it shall seem good to the Archbishop of Canterbury and my fellow-bishops that the number of bishops in England be increased, at least let them choose such men from the clergy of the English Church as shall be approved in a synod of bishops assembled for the purpose."

The petition was debated at length, and judgment finally pronounced: "That Wilfrid regain rule over his diocese as before constituted; that those suffragan bishops whom he shall choose, with consent of a synod to be assembled for that purpose under his presiding in that same diocese, be men with whom he may live and work in peace; that they be appointed and consecrated to this office by the most reverend Archbishop of Canterbury; that those who in his absence have been irregularly admitted as bishops for his diocese be promptly expelled therefrom."

So ended the first appeal of an English bishop to the See of Rome, with victory for Wilfrid, the petitioner. The very fact that it took place reveals the weakness in the strength of Archbishop Theodore. Admirable as he was, magnificent as was his work of organization of the English Church, his keen conception of his office, joined with a character naturally imperious and an energy that hated obstacle or delay, led at times to arbitrary and high-handed measures. On the other hand, Wilfrid had learned wisdom by this experience. His petition must have cost him intense labour of thought. Both it and the synod's judgment acknowledged that Theodore's principle of division of great dioceses was in itself wise. The nomination, however, of the bishops who should aid him was to lie with Wilfrid himself; those already chosen were to be dismissed. In this his independence was safeguarded. We may perhaps see from this detail some objection on his part to the three men appointed by Theodore; but probably it sprang rather from their appointment to his diocese without his sanction rather than from any hostility to the gentle Eata and to Bosa, "of singular holiness." [101]

The plaintiff, his spirit now calmed and his dignity reassured, would have been more than natural man if he had not for a moment been glad, as he thought back upon the mocking laughter of Egfrid's court. But relief was greater than gladness. Now once more he could pray freely without care at the shrines of Rome which he knew so well; he could gather many relics of the saints for the devout gaze of pilgrims in the crypts of Hexham and Ripon, many works of art and craft for the adorning of his churches.

In this new happiness he scarcely took heed of time; soon it was Eastertide, in March of the following year, 680. The height of his joy was reached on the Tuesday of Easter week when he made one of a synod of a hundred and twenty-five bishops, called in Rome to prepare delegates for the impending Sixth Oecumenical Council of the Church, and to witness, each bishop individually and in his turn, by the words of his mouth and the signature of his pen, to the true and catholic faith on behalf of himself and his province and city. There, in his restored calling of bishop of York, free from any stain of

[101] *HE* IV, c. 23; V, cc. 3, 20.

accusation, Wilfrid declared adherence to this faith "for all the north of Britain and of Ireland, and for the islands wherein dwell the English and the Britons, the Picts and the Scots." [102]

It was now his business to return home, and he set out, bearing, besides relics and adornments for his altars, the decisions of the Holy See duly written, signed and sealed. The journey was uneventful until he came again to Austrasia, where he found his protégé King Dagobert lately dead at the hand of murderers who had opposed his return to power, and himself in danger as Dagobert's friend. It was said that even bishops had helped to plot the killing, and that one of them, attended by an army, met the traveller and threatened him with imprisonment or death, heaping insults upon him and demanding to know why he had aided Dagobert, author of many evils, to return to his throne. To all this tirade Wilfrid made such quiet and courteous answer that the Frankish bishop fell silent, in shame. "Forgive me," he said, "for I have done wrongly toward you, a far more righteous man than I. The Lord and Saint Peter His apostle be with you for your protecting." The story may well be true; for Wilfrid knew his Bible and practised its lessons. [103]

There was much delight among his friends as they welcomed him back, safe and in all honourable standing. True, Bosa in 678, upon Wilfrid's departure, had been established as bishop of York. True, his monastery of Hexham was no longer securely his; Hexham had been offered to Eata as seat of his new bishopric of Bernicia, should he prefer this to a seat in Lindisfarne. Apparently, however, Wilfrid had brought from Rome not only the official decision of its synod, but also a Papal decree confirming to him and his tenure the monasteries both of Hexham and of Ripon.

[102] *HE* V, c. 19. This collective witness was to be presented at Constantinople as part of the general condemnation of Monothelitism.
[103] Eddius, c. 33.

During his absence war had flamed up between Northumbria and Mercia, enemies of old. King Wulfhere of Mercia had died some time before, in 675, leaving a boy, Cenred, who had been passed over, during debate on a successor, in favour of Wulfhere's brother, Ethelred. Then the year 679, which saw Wilfrid on the continent of Europe, had found the armies of these provinces again at each other's throats, this time on the banks of the river Trent. Here another of Wilfrid's friends had died, Aelfwine, that younger brother of Egfrid who had been present at the dedication of Ripon Abbey. Aelfwine had been greatly loved by the people; Wilfrid could well imagine what was now told of the uncontrolled lamenting as his coffin was carried through the streets of York.[104]

Victory had fallen to Ethelred of Mercia, and the disputed province of Lindsey had again come into Mercian hands. Peace, however, had been brought about by the good offices of Theodore as Primate of Canterbury. He was no doubt aided by the fact that Queen Osthryd, wife of Ethelred, was Egfrid's sister, a daughter of King Oswy. Compensation in the form of *wergeld* was paid by Mercia to Egfrid for the shedding of his brother's blood; but Eadhed, the Northumbrian bishop of Lindsey, now found himself without a diocese.[105]

All this was told to their Father by his friends, full of dismay. They took fresh hope when they heard of the letters which he bore from the Holy See. Surely all he had to do was to present them to King Egfrid, his nobles and his bishops; at once he would be triumphantly conducted to his own cathedral in York. The very name of Rome would be enough.

But the name of Rome, enshrined in Wilfrid's deepest

[104] *Ibid.* cc. 17, 24.
[105] *HE* IV, c. 21; III, c. 11; IV, c. 12.

loyalty as head of the Church universal, held no such spell of reverence over the minds of the nobles and clergy of northern England. They had been trained in Celtic tradition from childhood, and their conversion at Whitby, even if more than nominal, was but some sixteen years past. Moreover, their English independence and dislike of intrusion into the affairs of their island, separate in temperament as in distance from the continent of Europe, turned instinctively from a command levied in a foreign land, even a command that had right of their allegiance. [106] Lastly, the personal feeling of Egfrid and his queen against their bishop had by no means abated; the immense wealth and influence of Wilfrid still kept them constantly in fear.

When, therefore, in 680 Wilfrid brought the decision of Pope Agatho and his council before Egfrid and his *Witanagemot,* their reception of it aroused in his fighting spirit no less surprise than wrath. As members of a Church that had submitted to the obedience of Rome, they did not, indeed, question his right of appeal to the Pope. But they rejected this particular judgment of the Holy See; they accused Wilfrid of having bought it with a bribe; and they made no attempt to communicate with Rome on the matter. The king, with the passive acquiescence of nobles and bishops present, including Bosa and Eata, neither of whom apparently lifted his voice in disapproval, gladdened the heart of his wife Ermenburg by ordering that the petitioner, bishop though he was, should be deprived of all his possessions, thrown into prison, and left there with none to aid and comfort him by visit or ministry. All his followers were disgraced and banished from office; everything was taken from him, except only the clothes he wore. The queen, it was said, seized in this moment of triumph a little case containing relics of the saints which Wilfrid

[106] Bright, 336f.

always carried with him. She was his enemy because she hated his power and glory as bishop; but as a devout Christian she believed in the saints and she hoped for blessing from the near presence of the sacred fragments. She hung the case in her own room at the palace and took it in her carriage when she drove through town or country.

It was a crushing blow. But Wilfrid held his head high. Rome had spoken; it was all that really mattered. A word of exhortation to his friends was allowed him, and then he was handed over for safe keeping to an officer in the king's service, governor of Broninis, a northern stronghold now unidentified. Here his days passed slowly in the dark mouldy dungeon of the city's Castle; it was seldom visited by a ray of sunlight, and never cheered by a lamp from the guards who kept watch outside. Even they, however, were struck with awe when they heard their captive chanting the psalms of his monastic offices night and day; these he knew by heart. There was even talk of a mysterious radiance that shone in the prison during the night hours and brought terror to those who saw it.

Temptation was not lacking to Wilfrid in these dark days. The king promised him part of his former see and rich gifts with it if he would only admit that he had obtained the decision of the synod in Rome by fraud and cunning. To which he answered that he would rather lose his head.

Wilfrid's biographer now enters on the marvellous. One day, he writes, the governor's wife fell ill, grew rapidly worse, and seemed likely to die. The governor, like his fellow-countrymen, was a Christian; in his despair he remembered that Wilfrid had been renowned throughout the country both as bishop of York and as a mighty man. He hurried down to the depths of his castle, flung himself on his knees before his prisoner and implored him for God's sake to help him and his wife, lying at the point of death in her room upstairs. Wilfrid at once went with him, prayed over the sick woman, and poured holy water drop by drop upon her face. Miraculously she recovered consciousness in a few minutes, and in due time her health. Her husband in his gratitude plucked up courage and sent messengers to Egfrid: "By my life and your salvation," he begged, "do not force me to punish any longer to my own damnation this holy and blameless bishop, for I would rather die than scourge him for no cause."

The king himself was beginning to be uneasy in his conscience. His pride and his queen took the other side, and in this discomfort he flew into a temper. "Send him to Dunbar's Castle," he shouted, "to its governor Tydlin. He is more the kind of man to handle prisoners; and see that he keep this bishop alone, fettered hand and foot in chains." [107]

Again solitude and long hours for meditation. Wilfrid was now past his forty-fifth year. As he endured with what patience he could, chanted his Hours and listened in his Scottish prison to the North Sea he knew so well, beating upon the rocks below, his mind must often have turned back to memories of the past. Ethelthryd, abbess of Ely, was now dead, since June of 679 or 680. He had heard of her holy life. Men told of her strict and humble abstinence: that she would never wear linen, but only coarse wool; that she would only break her rule of fasting and bathe in warm water when high Feasts of the Church came round; that she prayed from deep in the night until the rising of the sun, and was given by God the gift of prophecy.[108]

The sound of the stormy sea brought also to his mind another abbess newly laid to rest, Hild of Whitby on the Yorkshire cliffs. His memory of her was not unmingled with a touch of wryness; she had opposed him at the synod held in 664 in

[107] Eddius, cc. 34ff. Bede omits these stories of Wilfrid's imprisonment.
[108] *HE* IV, c. 19. For the date of Ethelthryd's death see Plummer II, 239.

her own abbey, and she had even sent witness against him to Pope Agatho fifteen years later, when he was on trial for his good fame as bishop. That was a hard thing to forget. Yet she, too, had been high in saintliness. He remembered the old story of her mother's dream, that she had found under her dress a necklace of great price, so lustrous that it filled all the lands of Britain with its splendour. He was glad to think that Hild had accepted the rulings of Rome against the Celtic tradition; but she had always clung to bare simplicity of worship and had strictly refused the wrought gold and divers colours with which he rejoiced to adorn the churches of his ministry. It was strange to link her with Queen Ermenburg against him for his episcopal magnificence. Had he perhaps loved the outward show too much? He heard that the abbess of Whitby had been brave in her dying; for six years she had suffered torment of disease and had never ceased to teach her monks and nuns and to be glad in the Lord.[109]

He thought back, too, upon his early years in Lindisfarne and tried to picture to himself his fellow-monk Cuthbert, now some five years in retreat in the islet of Farne for the work of prayer, severed from his brethren in Lindisfarne and from the mainland by miles of deep sea, with no sight of its coast to distract his soul. It was told that the ravens brought him food and that the sea was his friend in need when its tide came to his hut upon the shore.[110]

At length nine months of imprisonment with its suffering and its memories had gone, and King Egfrid with the queen set out on a ceremonial progress through Northumbria. On their way they stayed for a night in the monastery of Coldingham upon the Scottish coast south of Dunbar, still under the rule of Ebba, the King's aunt. In the middle of the night

---

[109] *Ibid.* IV, c. 23; Plummer II, 189f.; Eddius, c. 54.
[110] Bede, *Vita Cuth.* (prose), cc. 20f.; *Vita Cuth. Anon.* III, cc. 4f.

Ermenburg was seized with dreadful pain and paralysis; at dawn next morning she, too, like the lady of Broninis Castle, seemed to be departing this life.

The Abbess Ebba was a devout woman. Saint Cuthbert was her friend and had visited her in Coldingham Abbey to the great edification of her monks and nuns. They declared that once, as he was walking up and down upon the sands in the darkness long before dawn, an inquisitive cleric of this "double cloister" sallied out to see just what the holy man was doing down there.[111] Cuthbert fled from him into the sea itself, and when he came out two little seals came out with him, following him to rub his feet with their furry hides and warm them with their breath. It was in the abbey of Coldingham, also, that Wilfrid had given the monastic veil to Ethelthryd, once called queen of Northumbria. That had been a great ceremony. The abbess remembered these things.

Unlike her nephew, Ebba admired Bishop Wilfrid in the extreme, and, when the distracted king implored her help in this crisis, she was not slow to declare that it had come in punishment for his grievous offence against that bishop "dear to God." Tradition declares that this time Egfrid dared not resist; that he ordered Wilfrid to be released and his friends and holy relics to be promptly restored. It states, also, that Ermenburg then regained her health.

However much we doubt the truth of these stories of ladies seized in succession by providential illnesses unto death for the aiding of an imprisoned bishop, in 681 Wilfrid was certainly free.[112] The king had been compelled by persuasion and by his own conscience to release the prisoner; he would do no

[111] See Crawford, *Antiquity* VIII, 1934, 202f., and plate facing p. 129.
[112] The story of Ermenburg's recovery (Eddius, c. 39) is also omitted by Bede. Wells, 545 (see p. 143 *supra*, note 65) suggests that the Abbess Ebba herself "was responsible for the nocturnal chastisement of the queen at Coldingham, which she used to secure Wilfrid's release."

more. None of the chief clergy had come forward in Wilfrid's defence, and clearly there was now neither office nor work open to him in Northumbria. He might have been forgiven some bitter feeling when he thought of the council of bishops, the second in English history, that had been called by Theodore at Hatfield in 680 to witness for England's holding of the Faith. It was hard to have been absent; harder that no word had been spoken for him in all its conference.[113]

His energy, then, had to find work outside, and his first chance came once more from Mercia. It was a nephew of King Ethelred, Bertwald, noble or underking of Mercia and friend of Aldhelm, who in 681 invited him to minister in that land. The homeless bishop accepted the offer, and with a few companions, chosen from those who had been monks under him at Ripon, journeyed south to make in Mercia a new cloister for this little congregation. From there he hoped he might act as bishop and abbot among monastic and lay souls far and wide; lands and religious houses within its borders already were his, by legacy from his days of high power.[114]

But the peace lately made and the kinship between the thrones of Northumbria and Mercia brought dire result. Egfrid's sister, Queen Osthryd, and her husband, Ethelred, would not allow this man, an exile from Northumbria, to find hospitality within their kingdom; they were content with their recent victory and had no desire to upset the present calm. Bertwald received orders to send his guest away at a day's notice. In this perplexity Wilfrid decided to cast himself upon the hope of Wessex, now ruled by King Centwine.

Here, again, a woman's enmity pursued him. The wife of Centwine, sister of Queen Ermenburg of Northumbria, promptly urged her royal relatives to forbid his stay in their

[113] For the date 679 see Poole, *Studies,* 44; Stenton, 137.
[114] See Eddius, c. 40.

land. Finally, defeated wherever he went by this hostility of his home in the north, Wilfrid fled to that shore on which long before as a newly consecrated bishop he had been attacked by heathen robbers, the country of the South Saxons in Sussex. Ever since that experience his missionary zeal must have made him eager to return to this corner of England that still remained pagan, shut off from Christian and civilizing influences on the inland side by its dense forests and marshes, on the seaward front by its dangerous coast. Within these natural barriers its people were living almost unnoticed in the history of the time, still following the primitive and savage manners of their forefathers.

Christianity had touched their race when their king, Ethelwalh, had been baptized at the bidding of his overlord, King Wulfhere of Mercia. Tradition also tells that his queen had been a Christian convert when she came to Sussex from her own country of the Hwicce, the region extending from the southern bank of the Severn's mouth northward beyond Worcester. Moreover, in this same year—still 681, for Wilfrid's stay in Mercia and in Wessex had been very brief—a monk from Ireland was saying his office with five or six brethren in a lonely little monastery amid the Sussex woods. His story in many ways resembles that of Maelduib of Malmesbury; they make together the two Irish pilgrims who ventured into southern England in this seventh century with the hope of converting some of the Saxons that remained heathen. His name was Dicul, and he had built his house of prayer for himself and his companions by the sea at Bosanhamm, now known as Bosham near Chichester. "But none of the dwellers round about cared either to follow their way of life or to listen to their preaching." [115] We hear nothing of any sharing of labour between

---

[115] Cf., however, G. R. Stephens and W. D. Stephens, "Cuthman: A neglected Saint," *Speculum* XIII, 1938, 451.

Dicul and Wilfrid. Possibly Dicul in his retreat was still observing Celtic ritual; possibly distance and difficulty of travel hindered fellowship.

The baptism of their king and queen had in no way affected the South Saxons. Yet some memory still living of his conversion many years ago now stirred in the king, and he allowed this bishop from the north to aid and teach his people, the more willingly because they were in desperate need at the moment. Several seasons of extremely dry weather had befallen their land; their simple harvest had utterly failed them and famine had resulted. So terrible was the hunger of the poor peasants that in their misery, we are told, forty or fifty men at a time would go to the cliffs above the sea and hand in hand would throw themselves down together that they might find a merciful death upon the rocks below.

Wilfrid's practical energy soon found kinder relief. If there was no rain, there was always the sea, and there were rivers; of course, there were fish abounding in both. So backward were his new charges that hitherto only eels had been caught in nets. Four of his priests had followed him into this strange wilderness. We know their names: Eappa, Padda, Burghelm, and Oiddi. Now he sent them off to gather these eel nets wherever they could find them; then they cast them into the sea before an excited crowd of spectators. Again the Lord rewarded the faith of fishermen. Before long three hundred fish of different kinds were being carefully divided into equal shares: a hundred for the poor, a hundred for those who had supplied the nets, and a hundred for Wilfrid and his monks.

Satisfaction of bodies paved the road to souls; the brethren had hearers in plenty. Soon, after due instruction, Wilfrid was baptizing the chief men of this people, and his priests were bringing their humbler folk to the font. The distinction is not without its meaning; the bishop and the abbot in Wilfrid were always bishop and abbot, however gladly he shared in the work at hand. The work was strenuous, but was rewarded by one of those coincidences that so often lay in his path. On the very day when a vast crowd received baptism upon confession of faith, "some of their own will, others urged by royal command," rain began to fall gently but continually; then the corn sprang green again in the fields and abundance crowned the year.[116]

For a home King Ethelwalh gave the missionaries one of his own estates, and added to it many acres, on Seolesia, Seal Island, now Selsey, a headland almost entirely surrounded by the sea.[117] All the peasants and serfs that lived upon it were also handed over to the bishop, who set them free to work upon the soil. There he and his community observed the regular hours of prayer; in token that the house should stand as a monastery for the years to come, he appointed the priest Eappa as its abbot, under himself as warden.[118]

His own active mind could not imagine itself permanently outside the swirl of life in public places. He even dared to appeal again to the bishop elected about 683 as Pope Benedict II.[119] So far as we know, the appeal brought no result at the time. Benedict died in 685 and no doubt the letter was lost. Nevertheless Wilfrid's instinct proved true, for a change was soon to come in his lot.

It came at first from a strange direction. We have already seen in Aldhelm's Wessex a young prince of its royal house,

[116] Eddius, cc. 40ff.; *HE* IV, c. 13; V, c. 19. The story of the conversion by Wilfrid of St. Lewinna (Lewina) may be held as legend; cf. W. R. W. Stephens, *Diocesan Histories, Selsey-Chichester*, 1881, 13f.

[117] Cf. Rudyard Kipling, *Rewards and Fairies: The Conversion of St. Wilfrid.*

[118] See the theory of H. P. Wyndham (*Archaeologia* V, 1779, 362f.) on Wilfrid's work in building between 679 and 685.

[119] Eddius, cc. 43, 46, 51ff. Benedict II was not consecrated until 684: Mann I, ii, 54.

named Caedwalla, driven by the power of Centwine to hide in the lonely place of the Chiltern hills and the Weald. Through the forest he made his way, from Kent into Sussex. Deliberately or by chance he found Wilfrid, who was much edified at the respect paid him by this lawless and even unbaptized prince who came from Wessex, province of Birinus. He gave the exile hospitality and aided him in many ways, hoping, no doubt, that in Caedwalla would soon be found a strong and Christian king of Wessex who would put an end to the conflicts that had raged around its government.

The relation of Wilfrid to this, his "son in the Lord," is rather difficult to understand. When Caedwalla suddenly rose up with his warriors, murdered Wilfrid's benefactor, King Ethelwalh, and laid waste Sussex in havoc and death, when two of Wilfrid's own converts, the Sussex chieftains Berthun and Andhun, fought for their people's defence and drove out the invader, no protest, as far as we know, came to Caedwalla from this bishop and Father of Sussex land and people. Caedwalla was seeking aid to capture Wessex from Centwine, and perhaps Wilfrid had no great love for the ruler of Wessex whose wife had driven him out; moreover, one who had himself lately fled from Wessex could well lend Caedwalla his sympathy. But such friendship need not involve sympathy for robbery and slaughter. In 685 Caedwalla realized his aim, marched upon Wessex and won its throne. Then he called Wilfrid into his realm, and the bishop accepted the invitation, about the year 686.

Probably, like Clovis of the Franks long before him, the new king of Wessex, although himself still unregenerate, declared his intention to conquer bodies that he might make Christian souls, and probably Wilfrid hoped for much good from this promise. Caedwalla at once honoured him with gifts of land and looked to him as his counsellor in all spiritual matters; [120] what Haeddi, then bishop of Wessex in the see of Winchester, thought of this we do not know. Certainly Caedwalla continued his work of blood with much vigour. He took his revenge upon Sussex, killed its chieftain Berthun, and oppressed its people with merciless tyranny. He wrested also from that same kingdom the Isle of Wight, gift of Mercia to Ethelwalh; he vowed to murder its inhabitants and to replace them by Christian men of Wessex. Another vow offered, however, a fourth part of the island, people and all, to the Lord in hope of victory, and caused him, when victory was his, to present this portion to Wilfrid "for the Lord's service." Wilfrid accepted the gift, transferred it to his nephew Berwin and gave him a priest named Hiddila for the teaching and baptizing of its pagans. So good, finally, came out of evil, and whatever may have been Wilfrid's somewhat equivocal position in the midst of his disciple's reign of terror, to him eventually not only Sussex but the Isle of Wight owed their vision of the Faith.

From 680, then, until 686, Wilfrid had now been some six years in exile from Northumbria. During this time Archbishop Theodore had not been idle. As a consequence of Wilfrid's exile he had placed Eadhed, that bishop driven from Lindsey by Mercia's conquest of 679, "in charge of the church of Ripon." These words of historical tradition probably mean that a see of Ripon was created, with Eadhed as its bishop, in order that Deira might be divided into two dioceses, that of York, where Bosa was ruling, and that of Ripon. The year

[120] See, for a charter of gift, Kemble I, No. 18 (holds it spurious); cf. Birch, No. 50; Ehwald, 510f. (holds it genuine). This charter declares Aldhelm as its promoter; *ut beato viro Vuilfrido liberum remaneret arbitrium in vita sua de hac ruris possessiuncula* . . . For Wilfrid and Caedwalla see *HE* IV, cc. 15f.; Eddius, c. 42. Eddius conveniently omits much perplexing detail and paints a most edifying picture of the relation between Caedwalla and Wilfrid. See Wells, *EHR* VI, 1891, 546; Bright, 392; Plummer II, 326.

seems to have been 681.[121] In that year, the see of Hexham, allowed in 678 as alternate choice with Lindisfarne to Eata, was definitely given to Tunbert, who had been abbot of the monastery founded at Gilling in Yorkshire by King Oswy's queen Eanfled in expiation for her husband's sin. Eata is henceforth bishop of Lindisfarne, and we find Theodore's zeal for increase of pastors among the faithful and the ignorant shown once again in a new bishopric, ruled by one Trumwine from the monastery of Aebbercurnig, Abercorn on the Firth of Forth; it was doubtless placed as a missionary centre near the land of the Picts, then under the power of the Northumbrian king.

During these years Cuthbert had been living his lonely life of prayer upon Farne Island, visited from time to time by his brethren monks of Lindisfarne. An exceedingly rare interruption in his days of retreat was brought about at the petition of the woman who had followed Hild as abbess of Whitby. Her name was Elfled, and she had once been that baby girl whom her father Oswy of Northumbria had promised to a convent if he should defeat Penda of Mercia on the river Winwaed. Upon his victory he had faithfully kept his word, and Elfled was trained for the nun's life under Hild at Hartlepool and at Whitby. She was about twenty-six years old when in 680 she was elected abbess upon Hild's death.[122]

We are told that she begged Cuthbert to leave his solitude and to meet her at a well-known monastery on Coquet Island, off the coast between Farne and Whitby; she needed, she said, counsel very badly. Since Cuthbert could not find it in him to refuse a soul in trouble, he journeyed there in a sailing boat.

[121] HE IV, c. 12; III, c. 28; Eddius, c. 45; Plummer II, 224; H. S. II, 6; III, 165; Searle, 174f.; Flor. Worc. MHB I, 536, 625.
[122] Her mother, Queen Eanfled, shared for some time with her the office of abbess, having retired to Whitby after King Oswy's death: HE IV, c. 26; Plummer II, 262f.

Her questions were very numerous, largely concerning her own community of monks and nuns. But only three are revealed to us. "In the name of our Lord Jesus Christ," she implored, "by the nine orders of angels and by all the saints, tell me how long my brother Egfrid has to live." The answer came indirectly: "O handmaid of God, is it not a little while, even if a man live twelve months?" She understood at once that Cuthbert was foretelling the king's death, and asked him to tell her who would be the next king of Northumbria. Again, it is said, he revealed to her the truth: that another son of Oswy, Aldfrid, at the moment studying under Irish monks on the island of Iona, would soon succeed his father and hers upon the throne. Lastly, she asked Cuthbert of himself: would he refuse to leave his island, supposing he were called to the office of bishop in the church? To which he replied that there was no escaping the will of Heaven; if, however, the Lord had determined to lay so heavy a burden on him, his fear was mingled with hope that he would bear it for only two years, at the most.[123]

There was good reason for Cuthbert's fear. While these two, abbot and abbess, were thus conferring on the little monastic island, Archbishop Theodore had already, in 684, deposed Tunbert from his see of Hexham, for some cause unknown to us.[124] Elfled had already heard that her brother, King Egfrid, had Cuthbert in mind as his successor, and in the autumn of the same year a synod of clergy and layfolk decided the matter. It assembled at a place called "Twyford," "Double Ford," near the river Aln in Northumberland; Theodore himself presided, and Egfrid was present.[125] All unani-

---

[123] Bede, *Vita Cuth.* (prose), c. 24; *Vita Cuth. Anon.* III, c. 6; ed. Colgrave, 328.
[124] *HE* IV, c. 28; Plummer II, 268.
[125] *HE ibid.* Possibly this was Alnmouth: Bright, 373; Mawer, *Northumberland,* 4, note 1; Ekwall, *ERN* 5.

mously declared their desire that Cuthbert should be bishop over Bernicia in the see of Hexham, and messengers were sent to Farne to bear the news. They had no effect, nor had the letters they carried. At last, we read, Egfrid himself, with Bishop Trumwine of Abercorn and other leading priests and nobles, crossed the water to plead in person; most unselfishly Cuthbert's own monks came from Lindisfarne to unite their prayers "in the Name of the Lord." He could hold out no more. Sorely against his will he left the dear solitude of Farne and at another meeting of the same synod was acclaimed bishop, not of Hexham, but of Lindisfarne. This one thing he had required, for Lindisfarne had once been his dwelling-place and still held the monks of his community. He was consecrated at Easter of the following year, 685, in the cathedral of York; seven bishops attended the ceremony. Theodore thus attained another step in his purpose of dividing dioceses; with Cuthbert ruling over part of Bernicia from Lindisfarne, Eata, "the most gentle and sincere of men," willingly relinquished Lindisfarne to rule the other part as bishop of Hexham.[126]

Two months later the prophecy of Cuthbert concerning Egfrid was fulfilled. The king's last years were visited by a fierce lust of conquest, which drove him in 684 to send a raiding army into Ireland, "piteously mauling that innocent people which had always been most friendly to the English, not even sparing churches and monasteries." In 685 he followed this up by leading out another host across the English borders to ravage Scottish land held by the Picts. His friends, and among them his newly consecrated bishop Cuthbert begged him to change his mind. No one of them prevailed, and he marched to his death, caught by his enemies among their mountains at Nechtansmere, "tarn of Nechtan." Men of the time believed that Heaven, upon hearing the voices of the

[126] *HE* IV, cc. 27f.

Irish crying for redress, had brought his doom upon him. A strange story, told afterward far and wide, declared that at this same hour Wilfrid was saying Mass in Sussex; that at the *Habemus ad Dominum* he saw in a vision Egfrid, struck on the head, fall in death; and that immediately afterward, as he was saying the words of the Preface, *Per Christum Dominum nostrum,* a still more dreadful scene suddenly rose before him, of two evil spirits carrying the king's soul wailing and crying into the bondage of hell. Another tradition described Cuthbert in Carlisle, warning Egfrid's queen Ermenburg that she depart with all possible speed for the royal city of Bamburgh in Yorkshire; "for it may be that the king has been slain." [127] The prince who now became king of Northumbria was that Aldfrid, called "the Learned," friend of Aldhelm from his youth, and by this time a man of middle age.[128]

Such was the story of Northumbria while Wilfrid was an exile in Sussex. When Wessex welcomed him, his return home to the north was already being prepared.

Archbishop Theodore was now an old man, drawing near the close of his busy years in England. As he reviewed them, one thing troubled him constantly, this long discord with a priest who had worked faithfully for the northern Province. At last he decided upon action. He called Wilfrid to meet him in London and called also Earconwald, bishop in London of the East Saxons, as witness of the meeting. In it the Archbishop declared himself ready to forget, even to regret the hurt to body and mind which Wilfrid had borne with courage and patience. As proof of this, he would restore him to a bishop's seat; record, which may or may not be true, even affirms that

[127] *HE* IV, c. 26; Bede, *Vita Cuth.* (prose), cc. 24, 27; Eadmer, *Vita Wilfridi,* c. 43 (Raine, *HY* I, 206). So long as Egfrid behaved respectfully to Wilfrid, Eddius represented him as successful, and *vice versa: cf.* Colgrave, *Eddius,* xi.
[128] Pp. 47ff. *supra.*

he asked Wilfrid to accept from him, now nearing death, appointment as Metropolitan of England in his own see of Canterbury. "For truly in all wisdom and in the law of the Church of Rome I have found you the most learned of your people." [129]

We may probably find in these last words some part of Theodore's desire for reconciliation. Egfrid was now dead; the old trouble might be conveniently forgotten if some bishopric should be found for Wilfrid. He was undoubtedly the most brilliant priest in the English Church of the day, and Theodore felt it the part of wisdom to recognize this while he could.[130]

On his own side, Wilfrid was longing to administer once more a see of his own, and his character, however impatient of injustice, did not harbour resentment for its own sake. Let there be peace. He only requested that the reconciliation be made known by Theodore throughout England, and that "some part of his former rights be restored to him by command of the Archbishop in accordance with the decisions of the Holy See."

His desire was granted. Among those to whom Theodore sent official letters telling of this making of peace by him and urging that Wilfrid be received in all honour were King Aldfrid of Northumbria, King Ethelred of Mercia, and Abbess Elfled of Whitby. The two kings were willing to do all in their power; Ethelred's previous hostility had, indeed, been due to his wife, King Egfrid's sister. We may imagine that Abbess Elfled, trained as she had been by Hild, infinitely preferred the sanctity of her adviser, the ascetic Cuthbert, to all she had heard of Wilfrid in his high estates since the synod of Whitby more than twenty years before.[131]

Accordingly in the year 686 Wilfrid returned to Northum-

[129] Eddius, c. 43; *Gest. Pont.* 233.
[130] *Cf.* Browne, *Theodore,* 169f.; Wells, *EHR* VI, 1891, 547.
[131] Bright, 395.

bria, to find such portion of his former rule and office as was not now held by other men. The decision of the Holy See seven years before had declared that he should be restored to his dignity as supreme bishop in Northumbria, and that, as such, he should preside over a council for the electing of bishops to aid him. In actual fact, when he arrived, Bosa was still at York, Cuthbert at Lindisfarne.

Yet here again, by an extraordinary succession of events, the wheel of spiritual fortune turned once more round. Shortly before, in 685 or 686, Eata had died after a brief rule. Wilfrid was now restored by King Aldfrid to his monastery of Hexham; it may be that he was asked to undertake a temporary charge of the bishopric of Hexham also, until a permanent occupant should be appointed. The humbler office in a minor see would be attractive, in that its centre was his abbey, if he now became abbot and bishop together over his brethren of former days. Ethelred of Mercia received him with glad affection, restored to him in permanence monasteries and lands which had been his, and held friendship with him unbroken till death. Shortly afterward in some mysterious manner Bosa left his seat at York and Eadhed his government at Ripon; record of the time attributes both departures to King Aldfrid, acting "in obedience to the decree of Pope Agatho and his holy synod." [132] The "bishopric" of Ripon, if such had ever existed, now lapsed, and Wilfrid became once more abbot of its monastery; in joy, moreover, he again found himself entering as ruler his former cathedral of York.[133] Lastly, in March, 687, Cuthbert died in his isle of Farne. He had already

[132] Eddius, c. 44. The matter of the bishopric of Hexham is subject of discussion. After Eata's death, it may have been administered by Wilfrid as bishop until 687; see H.S. III, 171; Plummer II, 326; Bright, 396f.; DCB IV, 1183 (Raine); Colgrave, Eddius, 178; Colgrave, Cuthbert, 9. Another view, based on HE V, c. 2, holds that John succeeded Eata directly; see Stenton, 139; cf. Plummer II, 274.

[133] HE V, c. 19.

retired there shortly before his death, worn out with his labours as bishop and longing to spend the little time that remained in preparation for his departure; perhaps, also, he had wanted to make the road easier for Wilfrid. The administration of the see of Lindisfarne was given to Wilfrid; but, as in the case of Hexham, only until a permanent election should be made. He was now for the moment again dominant in the church of Northumbria. He was bishop of York; ruler *pro tempore* of Hexham and of Lindisfarne; abbot of Ripon; a man in his early fifties, in the prime of his skill and experience. Once more he could look forward to new enterprises for the glory of the Church, in gratitude to the Holy See that had won for him this return.

Some months of this happiness were given him. Then that dormant little clause "for the time being," which perhaps he had chosen to forget as he went again on his busy round, awoke into real meaning. In the first place, five months later —the exact date was the twenty-fifth of August, 687—John of Beverley was consecrated as permanent bishop of Hexham.[134] No better man could have been chosen to succeed him; nevertheless, Wilfrid found it difficult to lose supreme control once more of the abbey he had so lately regained. Secondly, in the following year, 688, the see of Lindisfarne passed in permanent charge to a priest named Eadbert, one recognized for his learning in sacred studies, but still more for his charity, who "every year, as Biblical law bade, gave to the poor not only the tenth part of his live stock, but also of all his harvest of fruit and grain, with part of his clothes." [135]

Perhaps, as it turned out, Wilfrid was not altogether sorry to transfer the bishopric of Lindisfarne into other keeping. The year of his own administration had been full of trouble

<hr />

[134] Bright, 397; Plummer II, 273.
[135] *HE* IV, c. 29; *cf*. III, c. 25.

on its island; after Cuthbert's death, we are told, "so great
a storm of trial rocked the church of Lindisfarne that many
of its brethren chose rather to depart than to stay in the midst
of such perils." It seems probable that here Wilfrid had seized
his chance and had brought to bear all his Roman enthusiasm
upon this home of his early training, so steeped in Celtic tradition. We may well think that he tried to introduce the Benedictine Rule. The older monks would have disapproved this
interference with their long custom; and they may have feared
dismissal at this Superior's hand for lack of willing cooperation. On the other hand, we have seen that Cuthbert himself
had suffered resentment as prior of Lindisfarne; the difficulty
had not disappeared when he had been appointed its bishop.
As he lay dying in a corner of his little chapel on Farne island,
he said to Herefrid, whom he had appointed abbot of the
monks on Lindisfarne: "I know that some have despised me
and my way of life; yet after my death you will see what kind
of man I have been and that my teaching is not to be scorned."
The beautiful and moving story of Cuthbert's last hours as told
by Herefrid leads one to imagine that it must have been difficult for Herefrid to dwell happily under one so different in
experience and temperament as Wilfrid was from Cuthbert.[136]

Other trouble arose gradually through undoubted difference
of outlook between Wilfrid and his king. Aldfrid had cordially
received the returning exile, through reverence for the authority of the Holy See, to which his father had submitted in 664
and which he also acknowledged. Yet he himself had received
a thorough training in Celtic ecclesiastical tradition, both during his childhood at home and during his long exile among the
brethren of Iona. He respected the Roman teachings of his
spiritual father, Aldhelm; but even this respect had a strong
intellectual bias for one called Aldfrid "the Learned." There

[136] Bede, *Vita Cuth.* (prose), cc. 37ff., 40; ed. Colgrave, 9.

was difficulty, too, on Wilfrid's side. He had been denied the decision of Rome; he was obliged to share his plans as bishop with his colleagues, John and Eadbert, who were neither of his appointing nor owned allegiance to him.

Five years passed, of increasing friction. The crisis came in the year 691–692, brought to ripeness by three grievances: First, certain lands and possessions were being withheld from the abbey of Saint Peter at Ripon, so near to Wilfrid's heart. Secondly, King Aldfrid was eager to make this abbey of Ripon once more into a cathedral see, presumably with Eadhed again as its bishop. Thus Wilfrid would lose for the second time that house which he had built and adorned with loving labour and had dedicated at last so proudly in the presence of another king of Northumbria, Egfrid, son of Aldfrid's own father Oswy. The prospect was unbearable.

But it was the third demand that once more caused him to despair. Theodore had died in 690, and the see of Canterbury was vacant. Wilfrid's enemies in the north now managed to require of him that he should obey the orders and decrees of Archbishop Theodore; that he should acknowledge that Theodore had done rightly when in 678 he had summarily divided Wilfrid's diocese among four bishops. This was exactly what had driven him at that time from Northumbria, against which he had obtained decision and redress in Rome. It was the final stroke; there was nothing, he decided, but to leave again for exile, in Mercia. His enemies took quick advantage of his departure. Bosa, it would seem, returned as bishop of York; the attempt, however, to establish a permanent episcopal see at Ripon failed of achievement, to rise again with success long after Wilfrid had departed this earth.[137]

In Mercia King Ethelred welcomed him now as friend. His

[137] Bright, 412ff.; Eddius, c. 45; cf. Colgrave, *Eddius,* 178f.; Plummer II, 327, 384.

lands and monasteries were awaiting him, and their oversight kept him sufficiently busy until an even more important charge came into his hands. Under Theodore's enthusiasm for dividing of dioceses Mercia, too, had been partitioned into several sees. Tradition relates that one of these was now given for a while to Wilfrid's episcopal care; he governed it either from Leicester or from Lichfield, and Leicester is generally preferred by those authorities that decide between the two.[138]

We know a little of his work as bishop of the "Middle English" in this Mercian land. Since Canterbury had for the time no occupant, he was asked in 692 to consecrate as bishop of Worcester in the Hwiccian region that Oftfor who had been monk under Hild at Whitby and student with Aldhelm at Canterbury under Hadrian.[139] The next year, when Bertwald, Archbishop-elect of Canterbury, had gone for his consecration to Lyons in Gaul, Wilfrid again officiated, in consecrating Swidbert as missionary bishop for those Frisian people among whom he himself had laboured fifteen years before. In August, 693, Bertwald was again in England and was solemnly enthroned.[140] Soon after this time Wilfrid's name and title of bishop followed his and that of Bishop Oftfor in witness of a grant of land by Oshere, underking over the Hwiccians, to a convent of nuns at Penitanham in Worcestershire.[141]

About two years later, probably in 695, a great happiness brightened this second time of exile.[142] Sixteen years had passed since Ethelthryd, abbess of Ely, had been laid to rest in a simple wooden coffin at the centre of her own cloister. It was now decided by her sister Sexburg, who had succeeded

[138] Flor. Worc. in Appendix, *MHB* 623; H.S. III, 127ff.; Eddius, c. 45, and Colgrave, 179. This does not mean that Wilfrid was officially bishop of Leicester; *cf.* Bright, 415; Stenton, 134; A. S. Cook, *Speculum* II, 1927, 257.

[139] *HE* IV, c. 23.   [140] *Ibid.* V, cc. 8, 11.

[141] Kemble I, No. 36; Birch, No. 85; H.S. III, 232.

[142] *HE* IV, c. 19; Plummer II, 239; Colgrave, *Eddius*, 179.

her in office, that her relics should be placed in a new coffin of
stone and carried for permanent burial to the monastery
church. But since the fens and marshes of Cambridgeshire
yielded no large blocks of stone and in many places were
covered with wide lakes of water, some of the monks of Ely
—we have noted that it was a "double" foundation—crossed
in a boat to a little Roman town then lying in ruins, Grant-
chester, that delightful village to which one now walks from
Cambridge across the meadows by the river's bank. As they
searched among its fallen pillars and fragments, they came
upon a coffin of white marble, beautifully wrought and covered with a lid of the same. Quickly they brought it back to
their abbess, who then sent out invitations to bishops and
abbots and many people who had known the saint, that they
attend the feast of her transferring.

Wilfrid was naturally one of these. The company gathered
around the old tomb, the brethren monks on one side and the
sister nuns on the other. Over the grave a tent was spread;
the sacred relics were raised from the earth, and the abbess
with a few others went inside the tent to receive and wash
them. Suddenly Sexburg was heard by all in a loud cry:
"Glory be to the Name of the Lord," and a physician was
called within, one Cynifrid, who had attended Ethelthryd
when she was dying. He tells the story: that her body was
found whole and fresh, as though she were asleep. Then there
was great excitement and rejoicing, which increased immeas-
urably when he described the saint's last days: how she had
been troubled by a tumour in her neck, and how he had
lanced it, but only for temporary relief; the pain had soon
returned, to be ended by death on the third day. Now, however, the wound of this surgery was seen completely healed;
nothing but the faintest scar remained. He went on to tell of
Ethelthryd's courage in her suffering. "She used to say," he

declared, as all the monks and nuns pressed round to hear the words of their first abbess, "that she delighted to bear this burden of her neck, red and swollen, which once she had proudly encircled with foolish chains of gold and pearls."

For some seven years Wilfrid now disappears from the records of history. He doubtless spent them quietly in Mercia, homesick for his own work and brethren in Northumbria, waiting in hope of recall with a patience that increased as he grew older. Once again, we may believe, he sent a petition to Rome, this time to Pope Sergius, and received in return an answer supporting the decree made in his favour by Pope Agatho in 679.[143] He heard with horror of the murder by her own Mercian nobles of Mercia's queen Osthryd, wife of the King Ethelred whose power was now protecting him in exile.[144] As he said requiem for her soul so swiftly departed from this life, he thought for a moment, yet without bitterness, how she, sharing her brother Egfrid's hostility, had refused him shelter in Mercia sixteen years before. In greater content he may have visited the hermit Guthlac, whose fame was now spreading throughout Mercia.

Guthlac had been one of a community of monks and nuns ruled by Abbess Elfrida in Repton, Derbyshire. He had left it not long before in search of a more lonely life, and had found his way, through the marshes which stretched from the river Granta to the North Sea, into the fens of Lincolnshire. There he had built himself a hut on Crowland, one of the islands of tangled reeds that rose from the waste of waters, and was spending his nights and days in watchings and in prayer. After the sun had set, he took his one meal of barley bread and muddy water; often, it is said, he struggled with Satan

[143] Eddius (cc. 43, 46, 51) states that the decree of Agatho was confirmed by Benedict and by Sergius I. See H.S. III, 254, note a; Colgrave, *Eddius*, 178.
[144] *HE* V, c. 24.

and his angels, as Saint Anthony had done in the sands of
Egypt. Guthlac was twenty-six when he reached Crowland;
Wilfrid must have reverenced in him another young Cuthbert,
whose call to solitude differed so widely from his own vocation.[145] Nor was Cuthbert himself forgotten in Wilfrid's
prayers. In March, 698, the exile offered Mass of thanksgiving for this saint of Farne, whose tomb was now opened
and his body, like that of Ethelthryd, "found whole, as though
he were not dead but sleeping, and his burial shroud marvellous in new and dazzling sheen," eleven years after his death.
It was transferred to a new tomb above the ground which
might be seen and revered by all who came on pilgrimage to
Lindisfarne.[146]

A few weeks later news came of the death of Eadbert, who
as bishop of Lindisfarne had allowed this transferring. He
himself was laid to rest beneath Cuthbert's tomb. His bishopric
fell to Eadfrid, who restored Cuthbert's chapel on Farne
Island and who is more widely known as the writer of the
Lindisfarne Gospels. Another death followed in 701, that
of Pope Sergius; Wilfrid may well have felt anxious in this loss
of one who had defended his cause.[147]

So we come to the year 702. Wilfrid was now an old man,
nearly seventy, and his second exile had lasted ten years.
Again he longed to see his people and his brethren, in York,
in Hexham, and in Ripon. He waited, more and more anxious,
as winter after winter passed to spring, for news of a change

---

[145] Felix, *Vita S. Guthlaci*, Mabillon III (1940) 263ff.; W. de G.
Birch, *Memorials of St. Guthlac*, 1881 (with reproductions of pictures in
the Harley Roll Y6. Brit. Mus.); Paul Gonser, *Das angelsächsiche Prosa-
Leben des hl. Guthlac* (with Latin text): *Angl. Forsch.* XXVII, 1909;
Felix, *Life of St. Guthlac*, A.S. text with Eng. trans. by C. W. Goodwin,
1848; B. P. Kurtz, "From St. Anthony to St. Guthlac," *Univ. of Calif.
Publ. in Modern Philology* XII, 1926, 103ff.
[146] Bede, *Vita Cuth.* (prose), c. 42; *Vita Cuth. Anon.* IV, c. 14;
Raine, *St. Cuthbert*, 37f.
[147] Bede, *ibid.* c. 46.

of feeling in the mind of Aldfrid, of his bishops and the nobles of his court. Yet nothing came to cheer him. Others, too, were worried at his long unhappiness. Succeeding Popes of Rome pondered how best they could bring Britain to an understanding of her duty in the communion of churches; King Aldfrid at times thought uncomfortably of Wilfrid's years spent in exile from his see and his abbeys; their occupants sat uneasily now and again in their seats.

The trouble was that things were proceeding very peacefully at the moment. Here, we may think, lies one clue to the silence of Wilfrid's fellow-bishops. They did not lift their voices in his behalf because they feared for Northumbria. Wilfrid's return would bring conflict between men of different temperaments; he was always the petrel bringing storm in his wake. Thus they allowed the ruling of Rome to remain forgotten, excusing their lack of action on the ground of the good of the Northumbrian Church.

At last, however, this ruling could no longer lie unheeded; king and clergy felt that some decisive action must be taken, if only to settle the matter in their minds. In 703 a great council of the English Church gathered in Yorkshire at a place called in contemporary record by two names, Ouestraefelda or Eostrefeld, and Aetswinapathe; most probably it was Austerfield near Bawtry. The importance of the assembly is shown by the presence of Bertwald, Archbishop of Canterbury, of nearly all the bishops of Britain, of King Aldfrid and the nobles who attended his court.[148] A request, its cogency veiled in courteous words, was sent to Wilfrid that he appear. The assembly, he was told, would debate upon the canonical statutes concerning his former complaints, if he did not refuse to be present.[149]

---

[148] Cf. the letter of Sergius to Ceolfrid, abbot of Wearmouth: *exortis quibusdam ecclesiasticarum causarum capitulis*: H.S. III, 249.

[149] Our informant here is Eddius, cc. 46ff., 60; Bede omits the council altogether. See Colgrave's notes, 179ff.; Bright, 439ff.

When, however, he arrived with some abbots and clergy who were his friends, he found the council hostile to him on every side. From strife and questionings of those who differed from one another there arose one general decision: that he must abide by the judgment meted out long before in 678 and in 691. This now meant that he would share episcopal rule over Northumbria with Bosa, bishop of York since 691, with John of Beverley, bishop of Hexham since 687, and with Eadfrid, bishop of Lindisfarne since 698. In other words, he was still where he was before; he must again accept the conditions which he had consistently opposed.

Wilfrid in his answer made it again clear that he was willing to submit to partition of the Northumbrian diocese. But once again he repeated his firm stand: that this must be carried out in accordance with the rulings laid down in 679–680 by Agatho and the synod at Rome, rulings since that time twice reaffirmed by Popes of later years.[150]

To Wilfrid it was not now a matter of that ambition which had played its part in his youth; it was not even a matter of his former joy in building, in adorning, in administering the congregations under his rule. In old age these things seemed less important. Life had treated him roughly and he was weary; these things might well be entrusted to other and younger hands. He himself was entirely sure of the holiness of men like ʻBosa and John of Beverley. It was his loyalty alone which now forbade him to yield. He, who had preached the authority of the Church of Rome in youth and in the prime of his years, could not now acquiesce in anything which might seem to contradict her word, whether it concerned himself or some other man. "The case is ended, let only error also end,"

[150] According to Eddius, c. 32, Wilfrid was permitted by the Papal synod of 679–680 to choose his own assistant bishops, under approval in England: *quos cum consensu concilii ibidem* (i.e., in England) *congregandi elegerit ibi adiutores episcopos, cum quibus debeat pacifice conversari.* Wilfrid's choice might well disagree with that of an English council in the north; *cf.* Stenton, 143.

are words as true of Wilfrid in the eighth as they were of Augustine in the fifth century.[151] A clue to his treatment by his opponents may perhaps be found in the fact that the bishops Bosa and John had both received their early training under Hild of Whitby. It may be that, like Cuthbert and Guthlac, they wanted for their monks and their people a simpler, more austere example than Wilfrid had shown in Northumbria. They did not know him as the missionary who had suffered with his disciples in Frisia and in Sussex.

Finally, no doubt many of those present at this synod resented the "many hard words" of this exile who stood there boldly to rebuke them. "Have ye not feared," he demanded in the face of all, Archbishop, king, bishops and abbots, monks and clergy of England, "to resist thus obstinately these two and twenty years the Apostolic authority? With what audacious front did ye dare to prefer the decrees of Archbishop Theodore before the Apostolic judgments, delivered by holy Popes, Agatho and Benedict-elect and Sergius, to Britain for the salvation of men's souls?"

One friend, however, tried to help him. In an interval between the sessions of the council one of Aldfrid's nobles, whom Wilfrid had known and loved as a son from the cradle, came to him in disguise, with the warning that its leaders were hoping to get him to sign his assent beforehand to whatever they should decide, in such manner that nothing could be changed, once their decision had been made. "And I know, too," the young man went on, "what they want to make you sign away—all your possessions in Northumbria, bishopric and abbeys and the rest, and all that King Ethelred has given you in Mercia; all these holdings and dignities, once yielded, the Archbishop will give to whomsoever he shall choose. Then, last of all, you yourself will be held to have condemned your-

[151] Augustine, *Sermon* 131, *ad fin.*: *PL* XXXVIII, col. 734.

self to loss of all your estate as bishop, by the fact of this signature of yours."

The warning came in time. Soon afterward one of the bishops of the council arrived at Wilfrid's quarters with a message from Aldfrid and Bertwald. Would he submit to Archbishop Bertwald alone, swear to carry out faithfully whatever Bertwald should decide? Naturally enough, Wilfrid answered that he would have to know what this decision was before he agreed to accept it. The bishop replied that he himself did not know what Bertwald might decide and that neither Wilfrid nor any of his friends were to know; his orders were simply to request Wilfred to sign his name in pledge of faithful compliance with conditions unknown, reserved for the single judgment of the Archbishop. At this Wilfrid burst out that he had never heard of an agreement which bound a man to observe its conditions before he even knew what they were. The messenger returned to report that he had failed.

The old hostility of Aldfrid now flamed up again. Of Bertwald we have already seen that he was learned in the Bible, and in discipline ecclesiastic and monastic; yet in no way was he to be compared with Theodore.[152] He seems at this time to have been eager to maintain the authority of this predecessor of his at Canterbury, even to excess; probably he was also under the influence of the forceful king of Northumbria. To both men the English Church and her Archbishop meant more, in reality, if not in profession, than the edicts of distant Rome, and their wrath at a shadow of doubt cast upon English spiritual justice was great. At the next session of the council Wilfrid was solemnly asked whether he would submit then and there to the judgment of the Archbishop of Canterbury, duly confirmed by its members, before such judgment had been pronounced. His answer was direct. "First I will hear the

[152] P. 82 *supra.*

judgment of the Archbishop; then, if it is in accord with the rules laid down by the Fathers of the Church, then with all my mind I will submit."

This was defiance and brought speedy retort. Bertwald, supported by Aldfrid, declared it his judgment that Wilfrid be deprived of his possessions and tenure in both Northumbria and Mercia, down to "the least tiny part of one cottage." The ruthlessness of the sentence shocked even Wilfrid's enemies, and a murmur ran round the assembly. "It was wrong," men whispered to their neighbours, "to deprive a man so famed among all nations, on no capital charge, of all his goods and belongings."

The leaders realized that they had gone too far, and a slight amendment was introduced. Wilfrid might keep the monastery of Saint Peter which he had built at Ripon and might exercise there the office of abbot over the brethren as had been allowed by Pope Agatho. But he must take oath and witness by writing in his own hand that he would not leave the abbey grounds without permission from the king and that he would in no way exercise his office of bishop.

Not for this, thought Wilfrid, had the twelve Frankish prelates laid their hands upon his head so long ago at Compiègne. As he stood facing the congregation, some of those present must have remembered what great honour he had added to the church in Northumbria by his monasteries at Hexham and at Ripon, by his renewing of the cathedral at York. One wonders what John of Hexham and Bosa of York felt at this moment. But Wilfrid himself said nothing of these things. When his voice rose, clear and steady, in spite of his years, it told, once again, in no measured terms, of his own conception of right.

"Wherefore do you drive me to turn upon myself the sword of dire ruin, to sing my own condemnation? Am I, innocent as I am, to cause offence of stumbling to all who hear my name, I who have been called bishop, unworthy as I am, for nearly forty years? Was I not the first, after the leaders sent by holy Gregory, to uproot the noxious growth of Scottish planting? Did I not convert all the Northumbrian people to the true Easter and the tonsure of the crown, following the custom of the Apostolic See? Was it not I who taught their monks to sing psalms, as did the primitive Church, in response and antiphon of twofold choir, who trained them in the Rule of Saint Benedict which none before had brought into Northumbria? And now—how shall I pass sudden sentence of guilt against myself, I, who am unconscious of any guilt? No! You have brought accusation against me, trying to dishonour my sacred office; concerning this accusation in all confidence I appeal to the Apostolic See. Whosoever among you presumes to degrade me from my standing as bishop, him today do I call to go with me to that judgment-seat. Let the wise men of Rome debate well for what crime you desire to depose me, before I yield to your will alone!"

At this, we are told, Archbishop Bertwald and King Aldfrid declared: "Now indeed he is guilty; let us brand and condemn him, because he has chosen their judgment rather than ours." And the king added that, if Bertwald willed, he would order his soldiers to wring submission from Wilfrid by physical force. The bishops of the council, however, reminded him that the accused had accepted their call under promise of safe-conduct, and Wilfrid was allowed to depart unmolested.

Thereupon this "useless assembly" was dispersed, and all, cleric and lay, went home with their various opinions and thoughts. Wilfrid returned at once to Mercia to tell its story to his friend Ethelred. "What, Lord King, have you in mind to do," he asked as he ended, "concerning those lands and properties you have given me here in your country?" "Nothing," Ethelred replied; "I would not add to your trouble. But I will send my messengers to Rome with you when you go, that I, too, may know what I ought to do in this grievous case."

Wilfrid's enemies were naturally delighted at the council's decision. He was declared no true member of the Church, and order was given, we do not know where or by whom, that no one of the faithful laity might eat of food blessed by one of his abbots or priests. Such food was to be thrown away, as if offered in pagan sacrifice; even the cups and plates used by his monks were to be purified in special washing before they could be placed before any decent Christian.

In time, therefore, the influence of the council made itself felt. The king's word was of supreme importance; joined with the condemnation meted out by the Archbishop of Canterbury, it was final for most men, monastic or lay. Even the abbots of monasteries under Wilfrid's rule began to waver and seriously to consider transferring their allegiance to another Father in God. If their abbot were prohibited from exercising his ministry as bishop, must they not place themselves and their novices under the care of one who would be at hand to install, to ordain and to bless?

At this moment, it seems, a fellow-abbot from the south of England came forward in Wilfrid's cause. A letter was written to these doubtful monks by Aldhelm of Malmesbury. We know little about his connection with Wilfrid, but we may perhaps think that he had made friends with him when Wilfrid as exile was invited by Caedwalla into Wessex about 686.[153] Aldhelm was held in universal respect. A letter pleading with monks that they remain faithful to their Founder and Father was not likely to destroy this respect in the case of Bertwald, who knew the abbot of Malmesbury as one of his

---

[153] The date of Aldhelm's letter is not certain. For its text and various arguments see Ehwald, 500ff.; *Gest. Pont.* 338f.; Bright, 446; Bönhoff, 79ff.; Hahn, *Bon. und Lul,* 26; Browne, *Aldhelm,* 84ff.; H.S. III, 254ff.

most faithful and most learned priests. If, as a fellow-abbot, Aldhelm felt that his sympathy for Wilfrid called for a letter at this time, we know enough of his character to be sure that he would write it at any cost.

"As you yourselves know by experience," he began, "a raging storm has lately struck the Church to its foundations. And so I beg and implore you as brethren of one body with me, that your loyalty weaken not nor die away, even although this crisis drive your head, deposed from his bishop's estate, as an exile into foreign lands. How could you forsake him who has nurtured, taught, rebuked, and led you forward as sons of his love, from your first steps in your holy calling to the full flower of its profession? Take a lesson from the world of Nature, whose children act, not by reason as you, but by instinct given them of God. Do not the bees in ordered squadrons follow their king from the hive when spring has come? Do they not fly back again with him if sudden wind or rain bid him return to safe retreat? If these children unguided by human law thus follow their leader, what dreadful fault shall you incur, you to whom has been given the sevenfold grace of the Holy Spirit, if you break the curb of devout obedience? What? even laymen who know nothing of Divine law are held in open scorn when in times of trouble they abandon the lord they have owned in his happy days. What, then, of you, if you send away alone and deserted the bishop who has fed and reared you?"

We can forgive Aldhelm his many tiresome meanderings in prose and verse when we read this letter!

And so Wilfrid took again the road to Rome. At least his monks of Ripon were faithful. As he left its monastery, they knelt to receive his blessing, and their prayers held him before God day by day as he retraced his former passage over sea and land. Some of his brethren went with him; of these the most interesting is Acca, who was to take up his work after his death.[154] Acca had been taught and trained as a boy in the clergy-house of Bosa at York, after Bosa had assumed rule of that see. When, however, it returned once more into Wilfrid's hands in 686–687, Acca, it seems, stayed, to become priest-chaplain. Now as they travelled together, once again by way of Frisia, they broke their journey to rest awhile in the house of Willibrord, Archbishop of the Frisians in this year, 704.[155]

Contemporary record describes Wilfrid and his friends as "marching on foot" through the lands.[156] It probably allows us to picture them sometimes riding on horseback, sometimes for short distances walking as pilgrims. In either case, it was a heavy task for a man nearing his seventieth birthday.

At last—also in 704—they reached Rome. Here Acca must have given keen delight to his bishop, for he equalled Wilfrid in his desire to discover relics of apostles and martyrs for the church of Northumbria, to collect with patient search records of the lives of these saints and other sacred writings, to buy vessels and lamps and all things which could add to its beauty. He was skilled in music, also, and knew both his Bible and the history and law of the Church; as Wilfrid had done on his first visit so long ago, he asked and learned the meaning of many things which had been problems to him in England.[157]

But the first errand was to Pope John VI, who had succeeded Sergius in 701. He is remembered in history as a man of Greek birth who used his power for the quelling of disturbance and disorder.[158] Audience was speedily granted, both to Wilfrid with his supporters and to messengers from Archbishop Bertwald who arrived at the same time with a written letter of accusation.[159]

[154] For Acca see Cook, *op. cit.* (p. 151, *supra,* note 77).
[155] *HE* III, c. 13. On Willibrord see pp. 345ff. *infra.*
[156] Eddius, c. 50, with Colgrave's note.
[157] *HE* V, c. 20.   [158] Duchesne, *Lib. Pont.* I: *Vita Ioh. VI,* 383.
[159] Eddius, cc. 50, 52.

For the second time, then, a council of prelates, "assembled from all quarters" and presided over by the Pope, met to try this appellant bishop from Britain. Once again Wilfrid pleaded his cause before them from a document delivered in writing, praying "that decision might be made by the Holy See between him and his accusers, present for judgment; that, for his part, the decrees previously passed in his favour by the Popes Agatho, Benedict the elect, and Sergius might be confirmed by this, their successor, and that bidding be made to King Aldfrid to observe diligently the same; that, if he should be acquitted of all charge by John, as by his predecessors, the Pope would then confirm for him possession of the monasteries and lands granted him by the kings Wulfhere and Ethelred in Mercia, and of his own monasteries of Ripon and Hexham in Northumbria. As for the bishopric of York and the many other monasteries formerly ruled by the petitioner, let the Holy See do as it deemed best. Indeed, in all things he again submitted himself right humbly to its will."

For four months and in seventy sittings the council debated these matters; both sides were heard; the bishops spoke in Latin for the ears of the contending parties and in Greek when their Greek Pope was conferring with them. At last, when the long, weary trial had already turned in Wilfrid's favour, their ears suddenly caught from the recital of evidence an interesting detail: that a bishop of Wilfrid's name had been one among a hundred and twenty-five holders of sees of the Church who at Eastertide, 680, in the presence of Pope Agatho had witnessed to the Faith on behalf of their various peoples, and that this man had declared the loyalty of northern Britain and Ireland and the adjacent isles.[160]

The clerk paused in his formal reading of records, and those

[160] This evidence was, no doubt, introduced by admirers of Wilfrid; it was irrelevant to the main issue. See Stenton, 144, and the brief account of Bede, *HE* V, c. 19.

who were listening began to ask one another, "Who was this bishop Wilfrid?" "The same who now is standing before you accused by his own countrymen," the answer told; "the same whom Pope Agatho, having acquitted of offence and having restored to his rightful bishopric, commanded to sit and bear witness to the Faith among his peers."

It was enough. The synod agreed that all the evidence had been negative. Surely a man of so great authority, for nearly forty years a bishop, was now in no way deserving of condemnation. Thus Pope John declared, with general approval, and prepared to write to Bertwald, to Ethelred of Mercia, and to Aldfrid of Northumbria, declaring the same.

So far all was comparatively easy. But the question still remained: What was the Holy See to order in regard to this dethroned bishop? John knew well that the kings of Northumbria had always held a spirit of independence behind their formal submission to the Church of Rome. Moreover, in this case King Aldfrid was on the side of the Archbishop of Canterbury, of the bishops of York, Lindisfarne, and Hexham, and of a host of monks, nobles, and clergy. On the other hand, Wilfrid had always been devoted to "his mother, the most glorious See," and the authority of this See over distant lands must be firmly upheld.[161]

The Pope decided that cautious tact was in order in his letter to the kings of Mercia and Northumbria. Theodore, he reminded them, as Archbishop of Canterbury, had acknowledged the innocence of Wilfrid, declared by Pope Agatho. Now let Archbishop Bertwald, "our most reverend brother," hold another council of the British clergy, and call to it in especial Wilfrid and the bishops Bosa of York and John of Hexham; if possible, let this council after due debate reach a satisfactory solution of the problem. If this should prove fruit-

[161] Bright, 453.

less, the contending clerical parties are commanded under pain of deprivation and excommunication to present themselves at Rome for the thorough discussion and deciding of this matter in peace by a greater synod of the Church. If any one of these should delay or—God forbid!—should refuse to come to Rome, deprivation and expulsion from his place among the clergy and the faithful would be his punishment as a rebel against the Lord of all. And so, the letter ends, "May Divine grace keep and guard you both in your high estate." [162]

The difficult question of Wilfrid's destiny is here left undecided by the Pope. Bertwald is not affronted by an order to dismiss Bosa from York and to place Wilfrid once again as bishop there; on the other hand, the innocence of Wilfrid is expressly declared, and Bertwald is bidden to resume responsibility for his honourable standing in England. No doubt Pope John, always a diplomatic ruler, was hoping that in the course of time some circumstance, now only clear to Heaven, might decide these vexed matters of the British Church, before it should again become necessary to call in the authority of Rome. The burden of immediate action was placed squarely upon the shoulders of Wilfrid's superior in English ecclesiastical order; the kings, as civil powers, were required to aid and abet the same.[163]

With a heavy heart Wilfrid said goodbye to Rome. His whole spirit longed to quit the world of strife and care, to live once more under that monastic discipline which his youth had known, in the centre of all that his faith cherished on earth. It was not to be. The Pope directed him to go forth to witness to his innocence and the Church's highest authority among friends and enemies alike in Britain. For the last time he knelt at the shrines of the saints, gathered here and there precious relics, bought costly purple vestments for his priests and altars,

[162] Eddius, c. 54; HE ibid.   [163] Browne, Theodore, 210f.

and with the Papal blessing set out for home. He carried, of course, the letters written to his Archbishop and his kings. He may have carried also another from this same Pope, bidding the English clergy to change their "full-gathered lay habit" for the long straight cassock worn by the Roman priests, as the English clerics residing in Rome had lately done.[164]

No longer, as on the outward journey, could he travel on foot. Even the effort of riding a horse was too much for a body that had awaited the judgment of those seventy sessions in Rome. He struggled on resolutely, broke down altogether not far from Paris, and was carried by his friends into Meaux on a rude bier, unconscious and to all appearance already gone from earth. Four days he lay in a coma; at dawn on the fifth he awoke and called for Acca, his faithful chaplain. A wonderful dream, he declared, had visited him. Michael, "messenger of God Most High," had stood by his side and declared that the prayers of his brethren, aided by the intercession of the holy Mother of God, had called him back from death. Once again he would see England and would enjoy possession of those places he loved best; four years still remained to him before Michael would again return to call him hence. But of one thing let him be careful. He had built churches in honour of the apostles Peter and Andrew; he had raised nothing to the glory of holy Mary, ever-Virgin, for her who pleaded for him in Heaven. For this fault he must make speedy amends.[165]

So, in gladness, like Hezekiah of old, Wilfrid took up his life once more. After a few days he was strong enough to cross the Channel and land in Kent. It was now 705. He sent off immediately messengers to Bertwald with the letter from Pope John; it moved the Archbishop, we are told, to such an extent that he then and there offered his peace and promised

[164] H.S. III, 264.
[165] Eddius, c. 56; *HE* V, c. 19. The story seems to fit Wilfrid exactly; *cf.* Bright, 455.

to relax the sentence of the Northumbrian council. With this hope in mind Wilfrid and his monks made their way into Mercia, bent on rejoicing in the sympathy of their friend Ethelred.

The history of Mercia, however, had changed again in Wilfrid's absence. In 704 its ruler, like so many Anglo-Saxon kings and nobles, had forsaken his throne for the monastic life.[166] Many of these went to Rome; Ethelred, however, chose retirement to the cloister which he and his wife Osthryd had loved so well and often visited, the "double" monastery of Bardney in Lincolnshire. There Osthryd had laid to rest the relics of her uncle, Oswald, king of Northumbria, and there in consequence many miracles were said to have taken place.[167] There Ethelred was already installed as abbot when Wilfrid arrived in Mercia; in his place as king he had left his nephew Cenred, son of his brother, King Wulfhere.

The company then turned toward Bardney, and there the two friends kissed each other as brethren in holy rule. The royal abbot bent low in reverence before the Pope's letter and vowed to do all within his power. Messengers departed at once to bring King Cenred to the monastery and to advise most earnestly that he heed well the bidding of Rome.

Cenred willingly gave his word. Not so, however, the king of Northumbria, Aldfrid, who refused to withdraw in any way from the judgment passed at Eostrefeld. To Wilfrid's request that he might present before him the Papal letter, Aldfrid sent back a defiant answer: "That which my predecessor on this throne and Archbishop Theodore with his advisers once decided, that to which I, also, and Bertwald, lawful Metropolitan of Canterbury, and almost all the bishops of Britain did assent, that ruling, I say, never as long as I live will I

---

[166] *ASC ann.* 704; *HE* V, c. 24; *Gest. Reg.* I, 54, 78.
[167] *HE* III, cc. 11f.

change for any writings sent, so you affirm, from the Apostolic See!"

Shortly afterward Aldfrid fell sick. Tradition tells that in this he recognized the wrath of Heaven and declared to God and Saint Peter that he would repent and obey, should he recover. "But if by God's will I die, in His Name I direct my successor, whoever he shall be, that he enter into peace with Wilfrid the bishop for the healing of my soul and his own." Several people declared that they had themselves heard these words of the king, among them the abbess of Whitby, Aldfrid's half-sister.

The Lord willed that he should depart this life in this same year, 705. With him passed the glory of Northumbria, already marred by the tragic defeat and death of his half-brother Egfrid twenty years before. Now Eadwulf, possibly a kinsman of Aldfrid, seized the Northumbrian throne and held it for two months. His words were even rougher than those of the late king. By this time Wilfrid had sought refuge in his abbey of Ripon, which even the hostile council of Eostrefeld had yielded to him, and from this, his only home in England, he sent messengers to Eadwulf in friendly greeting. The answer came in no uncertain terms, suggested, it was said, by Wilfrid's enemies among Northumbria's nobles. "By my salvation I swear," Eadwulf declared, "that unless he leaves my kingdom within six days, all of his companions whom I shall find shall die." But the usurper did not hold his power for long. A rebellion drove him from the throne, and the eight-year-old son of Aldfrid gained his father's kingdom. His name was Osred, and no power or renown were to come to Northumbria through his brief and wayward life.[168]

The sudden sickness and death of Aldfrid and the expulsion of Eadwulf made no little impression on men's minds. Had not

[168] Eddius, cc. 57ff.; *HE ibid.; Gest. Pont.* 241f.

these rulers rebelled against the head of the Church in disallowing the Papal judgment? Now the throne of Northumbria was held by a mere child; its enemies were many; surely it were folly to incur the anger of Heaven. Moreover, had not Aldfrid himself on his deathbed declared his submission to the will of Rome?

Archbishop Bertwald, then, found the north already prepared when he for his own part made good his declared intention and called together its leading dignitaries in church and state. They gathered in the first year of Osred's reign, 706, near the river Nidd in Yorkshire, perhaps in the village of that name.[169] Secular rule was represented by Osred, the boy king, by Bertfrid, for many years his leading minister, and by many nobles; the Church of the north sent her bishops and her abbots, also Elfled, abbess of Whitby, herself kin to Osred, her half-brother's son.

Once more the judgment of the Holy See was read; next, upon Bertfrid's request, its involved and difficult language was carefully explained by Bertwald of Canterbury. The prelates remained unconvinced. "Who," they protested, "can alter the decisions of Theodore and of Egfrid, of you yourself, most excellent Archbishop, and of almost all the bishops of Britain, confirmed at Eostrefeld in the presence of King Aldfrid?"

Then a woman entered the debate, in itself a strong witness to the power and influence of nuns in Anglo-Saxon days. Abbess Elfled of Whitby affirmed the repentance of her brother and his last command, that his heir fulfil for Wilfrid the Papal bidding. Her words were supported by Bertfrid, who told how Eadwulf, the usurper, had laid siege to Northumbria's royal city of Bamburgh: "While, then, we were beset on every side by the enemy and lay concealed in a narrow cleft

169 Raine, HT I, 89; Ekwall, ERN 302. For varied dating of this council (705 or 706), see Plummer II, 306, 320; Bright, 457f.; Colgrave, Eddius, 129; Poole, Studies, 79f.; Stenton, 144.

of rock, we promised the Lord that, if He should grant to the boy Osred his father's kingdom, we would fulfil the Apostolic will concerning Wilfrid the bishop. At once the minds of our opponents were changed and turned to friendship with us; the gates of our city were opened and we were freed; Eadwulf was put to flight and Osred received his throne. This, therefore, is our desire, that we obey the authority of the Apostolic See and of Aldfrid our king."

The bishops talked for some time in private; they examined Elfled on her statement and listened to Bertwald's counsels of peace. Finally, another compromise was made. Wilfrid was to hold in permanence his monasteries of Ripon and Hexham with all their revenues, to which was added a promise of some jurisdiction in the north as bishop of the see of Hexham. The decision was accepted by all. Wilfrid and the bishops who had sat in judgment upon him knelt at one Mass, shared the Bread of communion, gave in brotherly greeting the kiss of charity, and with thanks to God went each to his home in peace.[170]

*　*　*　*　*

This was the story that Wilfrid, bishop of Hexham and abbot of Ripon, told to his friend and chaplain-priest Tatbert as they rode through the English Midland country not long before his death. Perhaps, because he was old and weary and had learned much wisdom since his hot-headed youth, he did not tell that in this compromise the bidding of successive Popes —Agatho, Benedict, Sergius—had again been unfulfilled. In 680 Pope Agatho had ordered that he be restored to his northern diocese, aided by such auxiliary bishops as he should himself deem congenial for fellowship of ministry; instead, after a long period of imprisonment and exile, on his return in 686–687 he had received for permanent holding as bishop

[170] Eddius, c. 60.

a limited see of York. Now, although again judged innocent at Rome of all evil, the English Church, taking advantage of the freedom permitted by Pope John VI, had left him with the promise of the humbler see of Hexham. This actually came to him when, after the death of Bosa, John of Beverley was transferred to York and Hexham was vacant. The exact year is not certain.[171]

He had been too tired, too frail in health, to think much about his position in the Church. It had been good to hold again his monastery of Ripon, to rule his see from Hexham. Besides, his time was short, and there had been still many things to arrange before Michael should return to call him hence. That church of Mary ever-Virgin was still waiting.

Into this work at Hexham Wilfrid no doubt built his memory of Italian architecture; its centre was almost round in shape, rising like a tower, and there were four apses or small chapels running out from this at the four points, north, south, east and west.[172] When it was finished, gratitude called for another church at Hexham in honour of the Archangel Michael himself, as a remembrance of the years granted at Meaux, and for a second church of Saint Peter, also at Hexham, in memory of the freedom and respect he had found in Rome.

Thus he had continued to the end his joy in creation of the beautiful. Most of his time, however, had been spent in the monastic life of Ripon, in the pastorate of Hexham, in teaching and preaching in its churches, in journeying from place to place about its diocese, in guiding those many communities

[171] Neither the date (704 or 705?) of the death of Bosa nor that of the consequent translation of John of Beverley to York (705?) and of the accession of Wilfrid to Hexham (705 or 706?) is certain; see Plummer II, 275; Stubbs, *DCB* I, 331.
[172] Prior Richard, *Hist. of the Church of Hexham, SS* 44, 1864, 14ff.; Baldwin Brown II, 1925, 181f. *Cf.* Clapham, *ERA* 46: "This is the earliest instance in this country of the centrally planned church"; see also his pages 144f.

of monks who knew him as their Founder and Father in rule and discipline. Three of the four allotted years had been given to active labour, too heavy for his strength. He had been on his way to Hexham, probably in 708, when the sickness that had attacked him at Meaux had struck again, far more severely. At the news "all his abbots and his anchorites had come hurrying from their monasteries." [173]

Once more, however, he rallied. The months that now remained he used in thought concerning his possessions and his various ministries. At Ripon he called a meeting of two abbots and six monks whom he trusted above all; in their presence he asked his treasurer to take out from its secret place his store of gold and silver and precious stones and to divide all into four parts. Then, as they stood in wonder, he spoke his last wishes: "You, my brethren so dear to me, should know that long since I hoped to visit again the See of holy Peter where I have been so often set free from care, that there by God's will I might end my life. There I would have offered the best of these four shares of treasure in gifts at the churches of the saints, and especially at the church of holy Mary, Mother of God, and of holy Paul the Apostle, for my soul's relief. But if God provide otherwise, as often happens to the old, and the day of my death come suddenly upon me, I bid you, my faithful friends, in the Name of Jesus Christ, to send these offerings of mine by messengers to those same churches. Of the other three portions, give the first to the poor among my people for the redeeming of my soul; let the abbots of those two monasteries so often in my mind, of Ripon and of Hexham, divide between them the second, that with gifts they may win the friendship of kings and of bishops; the third you must divide among those who have endured long toil and hardship with me in

[173] The story of Wilfrid's last months and of his death is told by Eddius, cc. 62–65.

exile, to whom I have given no lands or holdings—divide it according to each man's measure of need, that they may have means of living when I am no longer here."

For a while there was silence, and then he spoke again: "Brethren, lay my words to heart, that I appoint this Tatbert, the priest, my kinsman and constant fellow-worker, as head of this abbey of Ripon, to share with me its rule as long as I shall live and to possess it without hindrance after my death. And these decrees I declare, that when Michael the Archangel shall come he may find all ready; for signs of death are coming fast about me."

The little conference then broke up. At Wilfrid's word a bell was rung and the whole community of Ripon filed into the chapter-house and took their accustomed places. Last of all he himself walked to his chair, sat down, and began his farewell words: "Our brother Caelin, now for some time Prior among us, wishes to return to his former manner of life, serving God in contemplation amid wild and lonely places. This no longer will I refuse him. But do you all keep faithfully your accustomed Rule until, if God will, I come again to you. For our two abbots, Tibba and Eabba, have come from Ceol-red, king of Mercia. They earnestly desire that I go with them to talk with the king, as he asks, concerning our monasteries in his land, and I have consented to their request, since he promises obedience to my counsel. And when I return to you, I will bring with me him whom I have found worthy to preside over your community. But if God will it otherwise through my many infirmities, do you accept and install as your abbot him whom these witnesses now sitting here by my side—the abbots Tibba and Eabba, the priests Tatbert and Hadufrid, the teacher Alnfrid—shall declare to you when they come. And that obedience which you did promise and render to God and to me, do you yield to him according to my command."

In such words Wilfrid entrusted his abbey of Ripon to Tatbert, and blessed his monks for the last time as they knelt around him. Then he went on his way to Mercia, and they heard his voice no more.[174]

In Mercia King Cenred at this time had followed the example of his uncle Ethelred and had resigned his throne for the monastic life. Unlike Ethelred, however, he had retired from the secular world to a monastery in Rome and remained there till he died. His successor, Ceolred, was his cousin, Ethelred's son; of him, as of Osred, king of Northumbria, we shall hear dire details later in this story.

But Wilfrid did not reach the Mercian court. Many of his religious houses lay between him and his destination; all must be visited, cheered by gift of land or money, as heirs of the wealth that he knew was his no longer. He had come to the monastery and church of Saint Andrew at Oundle, founded by him on land given by King Wulfhere of Mercia, when he realized that his work was over. The brethren gathered for his blessing around the bed where he lay in peace, dimly conscious of the psalms which monks of the choir sang in intercession night and day for his body and his soul. Suddenly at the words, "Send forth Thy Spirit and they shall be created, and Thou shalt renew the face of the earth," [175] there came a sound as of the flying of birds, and he was gone. The day has been held in tradition as the twelfth of October, in the year 709.[176]

With every care his body was prepared for burial, clothed in the robes of his calling, and carried by the monks in solemn procession and continual chanting along the road to his home

---

[174] For the later history of Wilfrid's monasteries of Hexham and Ripon see Thompson, 95ff.

[175] Psalm (Vulgate) CIII, verse 30.

[176] The date is not certain; Levison, *Scr. rer. Merov.* VI, 178f., defends April 24, 710; *cf.* Poole, *Studies,* 80f.; Plummer II, 328; Colgrave, *Eddius,* 186.

at Ripon. As they arrived, the words of the Office of the Dead came to meet them, and the community fell into place, each according to his rank, to escort the Founder's relics to their resting-place near the altar, on the south side of his church of Saint Peter. There they lay till late in the tenth century, when they were transferred to the north side by Oswald, Archbishop of York, who ordered that April 24th, the day of this translation, be observed as a Feast yearly in the calendar of York.[177]

* * * * *

Forty-five years Wilfrid was bishop among men, a very great prelate, a very real man. His human failings bring him nearer to us, perhaps, than would the unmarred pages of a less stormy life. For him the beginning and the end in the Lord he loved so well was the Church founded upon the rock that was Christ. For her he drew from every source, far and near, the magnificence which should make her shrines all glorious within and without; for her he used to the full that sense of loveliness in art and design which was especially his own, and left his mark on buildings and monuments of northern and middle England. From her he caught that conception of reasoned law and discipline after the mind of Saint Benedict which he introduced into his many religious houses. In none of these things could the Celtic Church satisfy his need. He knew her in the noble life of Aidan, devoted, selfless, learned and austere. He himself was not of that stern simplicity which could utterly forego the world and its ways; unlike Aidan, he held lavish entertaining, gifts of land and money lawful means toward his ends as priest and monk. Unlike the Celtic brethren of his youth, he sought a faith articulate in complex organism of grand proportion and nice detail, visi-

[177] Prior Richard (*op. cit.*, p. 209 *supra*, note 172), 30; *HE* V, c. 19. On the controversy regarding the resting-place of the relics see Raine, *HT* I, xliiiff.; Colgrave, *ibid.* 186f.; Plummer II, 328.

ble in form and in colour, in ritual and in rule throughout the world. The Church of Rome offered him this in measure running over, and he in his turn gave to England of what he had received. He looked back upon the labours of Gregory the Great and saw in Rome the mainspring of God's society on earth, ordering, nourishing, healing, by the outward and visible sign of the inward, spiritual grace.

So rapt was he in this vision that he was impatient of everyone and everything that seemed incapable of receiving its light; like Jerome long before him, the friends of Rome were his, her enemies targets for his bold attack. And, like Jerome, the humblest were his children and his friends, if only he might bring them within her fold; no suffering, no disgrace mattered, if he might keep her creed and hold out her words to those still heathen. Many, and with cause, feared his stubborn will, his intractable mind, the power of his wealth; true sons of Rome, even John of Beverley, so holy that miracles were laid to his prayers, would not have acquiesced in Wilfrid's years of exile and deprivation had they not seen in him omens of storm and strife for religion in Northumbria, had they found in him the frugal living of a simple pastor of his sheep. If he had trusted less in his own powers and with a humbler sympathy had willed to share his possessions with his fellows, England would perhaps have owed him more. But in many of her churches she inscribed his name as patron and saint, as one who gave all that was his for the splendour and the increase of the worship of God.

Chapter III

BEDE OF JARROW

Shrines of St Cuthbert
and Venerable Bede,
Durham.

CHAPTER III

BEDE OF JARROW

THE STORY now goes back thirty years, to the time of 679–680. King Egfrid is ruling in Northumbria; Wilfrid of York at the age of forty-five, is in Rome, making his appeal against Archbishop Theodore; Cuthbert, at about the same age, is in retreat upon the islet of Farne; holy Ethelthryd has lately died of the plague in her cloister at Ely. In the south, King Centwine of Wessex is driving back the British to the mountains and the sea; Aldhelm, now a man of forty, has been already some six years abbot of Malmesbury in Wiltshire.

In the church of the monastery of Saint Peter at Uiurae-muda, "Wearmouth" in Bernicia, modern Monkwearmouth in the county of Durham, the brethren are all assembled. A ceremony is in progress, centering around a little boy of seven, who with his kinsfolk is standing in front of the altar. As the monks watch, one of these strangers from without, evidently the child's guardian, takes his hand under the abbot's direction and wraps it, together with gifts of bread, wine, money, and a paper covered with writing, in a cloth of fine linen; then he solemnly raises it as high as the child's arm can reach, in the manner of the priest when he offers oblation.[1] The paper is a petition for the receiving of this little boy of seven for permanent membership in the monastery, as long as his life shall last. His name is Baeda, or Bede, since honoured as "the Venerable," and the abbot who thus receives him under his care is already known to us as Benedict Biscop.

[1] *Rule of St. Benedict,* c. 59.

217

We last saw Biscop in 653, a youth of twenty-five, arriving in Canterbury, talking with young Wilfrid, travelling with him as far as Lyons and leaving him there while he himself hurried on to Rome, an ardent pilgrim. There he studied several years before he returned to his home in Northumbria to pour out all the wonders he had seen into the ears of Alchfrid, King Oswy's son.[2] Again, about 665, Biscop made ready to cross the Channel.[3] Arrived in Rome, he once more plunged into learning here and there to his mind's content.

After some months, however, it seemed well to add to his growing store of knowledge experience gained from some other centre renowned for monastic discipline. The place chosen after due deliberation was the monastery of Lérins, built upon an island off the southern coast of France near Cannes. There he stayed two years, received the tonsure and made his vows as monk.[4] A third time a longing to see Rome came upon him. A merchant vessel was just sailing, and he reached Italy in 667.

His arrival in Rome was well-timed. In the next year Pope Vitalian consecrated Theodore as Archbishop of Canterbury and then tried to find for him and his company of priests, monks and teachers some escort who could act as interpreter and guide for a Greek prelate on his way to England. Biscop was exactly the right man. Naturally, as the Pope remarked, it was disappointing for him to have to give up the rest of his stay in the city. But, then, he was an Englishman, and England was in great need of a chief Pastor, since the see of Canterbury had been vacant more than three years.

In gratitude to Biscop for his service, in reverence for his learning, and for the words with which Pope Vitalian had

[2] Pp. 121ff. *supra; VA* cc. 2f.
[3] Flor. Worc. *ann.* 665: *secundo Romam adiit;* but *cf.* Plummer II, 357.
[4] For Lérins see Bury, *St. Patrick*, 38ff.; Duchesne, *Early History of the Christian Church* III, 190.

described him, "a man wise, hard-working, devout and of goodly rank," the Archbishop requested that he remain in Canterbury as abbot of the monastery of Saint Peter and Saint Paul outside the city's wall. He accepted the honour and held it for two years, until his work awoke again in him the desire of travel to the continent. English churches, he reasoned, so badly needed adorning; English monasteries had so few books for their students. Moreover, by this time Abbot Hadrian had arrived in Canterbury, and the headship of monastery and school would properly pass into his hands. Biscop could leave with an easy conscience and in great content.[5]

This fourth visit, in 671–672, was rich in result. He brought back, by purchase or by gift, many books dealing with Biblical and theological learning, collected in Rome and in France, especially at Vienne on the Rhône. When he again landed in England, he planned to visit that notable Catholic convert, King Cenwalh of Wessex. Cenwalh was a good friend of Northumbrian nobles; he knew Prince Alchfrid well, and he had done Biscop kindly service. But news now came in this year 672 that Cenwalh had just died, and the traveller, keen once more to tell his people of all he had seen and heard in Italy, hurried straight on to his Northumbrian land.

Here, again, was a change of ruling. King Oswy had died in February of 671, and his son Egfrid at the age of twenty-five had succeeded him. Biscop, however, was naturally well-known to Egfrid and his father's court. Audience was promptly granted, and the monk and scholar used it to good purpose. He described all the details of Church law and monastic discipline which he had gathered in his travels through Italy and France; he displayed all the books and relics of the saints which he had brought back with him. Egfrid was deeply im-

<hr />

[5] *VA* cc. 3ff.

pressed, as was his queen, Ethelthryd. She was at the time much attached to Wilfrid, at the height of his glory as bishop of York, and in this year, 672, was planning both to leave Egfrid for the monastic life and to bestow upon Wilfrid land for his abbey at Hexham. Doubtless she used her influence with the king on behalf of Biscop also.[6]

For Egfrid gave him from his own private estate a grant of land for the building of a monastery in honour of Saint Peter. In 674 its foundation was laid, and for a year Biscop watched its buildings rise on the north bank of the river Wear, near its mouth. There were a number of these buildings, formed roughly of stone to serve the brethren in common: one or more as dormitory; another as refectory; another as general living-room for study, talk, and instruction; others as work-rooms for the varied occupations of the monks; another, per-haps, as infirmary for the sick.[7]

Then Biscop, the founder, lifted his ambition to its highest point. There must be a church, standing in the centre of all and surpassing all in form and content. Beauty must mark it as distinct from the secular houses that should look up to it; but, like them, it must be solid, to resist the cold of long winters and the damp of continual rains. In his enthusiasm Biscop again travelled to France, and, as Wilfrid did before him, brought back masons skilled to work in stone after the "Roman" style, inherited from the old classical temples which he had admired in southern lands.

By this time men had already come to be trained for the monastic life under Biscop's authority; already he had thought out long and carefully the Rule which should govern his cloister. Into its details he had gathered, it is true, the best of all that he had observed and held in mind in no fewer than

[6] Eddius, cc. 19, 22; HE IV, c. 19; V, c. 19.
[7] Peers, in Thompson, 109. See also Mabillon II (1936) 1001ff.

seventeen monasteries in which he had stayed during his travels. His was no work of one man, himself or another. Yet, above all, the Rule imposed by this Biscop "Benedict" was that of the saint whose name he had probably taken at the time of his own entry upon monastic life. He did not, it is true, inaugurate Benedictine discipline in England; the abbey of Ripon had known it, at least in some degree, ten years before under Wilfrid. Even Wilfrid had passed some of his most impressionable years under Celtic monastic governing on Lindisfarne; Biscop, on the other hand, had gained all his own formal experience as monk under Roman discipline, in Italy, in Lérins, in Canterbury. In his time, unlike that of young Wilfrid, the Roman Church had practically conquered the Celtic tradition of Iona in Britain, while on the continent of Europe the Benedictine Rule was steadily replacing the code of the Irish Columban. Undoubtedly the path was open for a monastery essentially Benedictine, and Biscop followed this direction in an obedience none the less commendable because it took account of other religious constitutions.[8]

The sixty-fifth chapter of the Rule of Saint Benedict prescribed that, "if the needs of the monastery required it," a prior, or "second" Father, might be appointed by the abbot, to aid him in administering large communities and to rule in case of his absence from home or of sickness befallen him. Now Biscop deeply desired to be free to travel for the good of his house. He, therefore, used the permission he had found in this rule and appointed a prior as his deputy—Ceolfrid, who was to be one of his most valued monks.[9]

Ceolfrid had been born of parents noble in rank and devoted

[8] *VA* c. 11; *VAA* c. 6; Laistner, *Thought and Letters,* 118, note 1; Knowles, 23; Thompson, 84.
[9] *VAA* cc. 5ff. The appointment seems to date from 674 (*VA* cc. 19, 22; Plummer II, 369f.). Ceolfrid must therefore be regarded as a co-founder of Wearmouth with Biscop.

to religion. It was told of his father, one of Oswy's thanes, that once he had prepared a splendid banquet for the king but that unhappily an unexpected crisis of impending war had kept Oswy from enjoying it. At once the host had called to his table all the poor, strangers, and sick he could find in the neighbourhood; in his own castle he had served to the men and his wife to the women those many dishes prepared for royalty, "humbly waiting upon them as upon the King of all." [10] At the age of eighteen his son entered the monastery of Gilling in Yorkshire, where an elder brother, Cynefrid, had lately been abbot. Another kinsman, Tunbert, was holding the office at the time, and under his direction Ceolfrid worked and studied. But the Great Plague of 664 brought death to many of the brethren, and two years later Tunbert felt it the part of wisdom to accept the invitation given him by Wilfrid, then in retirement as abbot of Ripon, that he and his monks make their home in Ripon Abbey. The community of Ripon, as we have seen, had been transferred from the rule of Eata to that of Wilfrid some five years before; and this change, together with the decision of the synod of Whitby in favour of the Roman tradition, had caused a number of the Celtic monks of Ripon to withdraw. Wilfrid was glad to fill the cells of his monastery. Ceolfrid stayed there till 669, when Wilfrid ordained him priest; he was then about twenty-seven years old. [11]

Upon him, as upon so many others, Wilfrid exercised the charm of his enthusiasm. Soon the young man was longing to go south to Canterbury that he, too, might learn in this new school of Theodore and of Hadrian to which so many of his friends were hurrying. His desire was granted and led to further ambition. Before returning home, would it not be

[10] *VAA* c. 34.
[11] *Ibid.*, cc. 3f.; Plummer II, 372.

well to find out more by practical experience about the Rule of Saint Benedict, so glowingly described by Wilfrid? The most renowned teacher of this Rule in eastern England at this time was one named Botolph. He had lived under its training on the continent of Europe and had lately founded a monastery amid the fens of Lincolnshire, in "the most dismal district of all England, on a mound covered with trees, girdled with rushes, surrounded by a vast stagnant morass, the haunt of wild fowl." The name of the place was Icanhoe, where, as it is generally thought, Boston, "Botolph's town," now stands; its church is dedicated to the saint.[12] The year of Ceolfrid's visit was 670; and after gathering much instruction in the little time he could stay, he hastened back to Ripon.

A cheerful picture is given us of his life there. By this time he was one of the most learned monks in the abbey; yet he took his part in all the manual labour which its Rule required. His special duty was to bake the community's bread, and he attended to the whole business himself, sifting the flour, cleaning and lighting the oven. But, at the abbot's command, he would go from the kitchen to say Mass and fulfil all his part as priest, to study his Bible and the writings of the Church Fathers.

When, therefore, Biscop had looked about him in search of one who should help him in his new foundation, his eyes had rested on this promising Benedictine scholar. Wilfrid had set him free, and Ceolfrid had received the call eagerly. He had arrived at Wearmouth in time to give his aid in the building of both house and church and in the admitting of aspirants into its life. He was left in charge when Biscop

[12] Bond, *Dedications and Patron Saints of English Churches,* 1914, p. 312, gives sixty-four ancient churches of St. Botolph; *cf.* Arnold-Forster, *Church Dedications* II, 52ff.; III, 343f. For Botolph see his *Life* by Focard, *saec.* xi: Hardy, *Cat.* I, i, 373f.; Mabillon III, i (1939) 3ff.; *ASC* ann. 654; *DNB* V, 446.

journeyed in 675 to France in search of masons, and on other occasions when the abbot was away on the business of his monks.[13]

Biscop, perhaps, left too much to his prior, for Ceolfrid's peace in prayer and study was constantly interrupted by the problems and needs of the young community. Moreover, some of its novices who had come from rich and noble families found this Benedictine house very uncomfortable, its routine monotonous; and they were very rude indeed about it. At last Ceolfrid's homesickness for the quiet days at Ripon became unbearable; he took his staff and sandals and plodded on foot back to Yorkshire. His abbot promptly went after him, however, and by his pleading induced him to return. And yet Biscop hastened to profit by the lesson. Now, as the outward structure of his church drew near completion and his mind turned to its inward furnishing, a journey to France seemed again necessary. But this time he did not go himself. He sent messengers instead, bidding them bring to him makers of glass, still rare in England but familiar to him from his travels, and many other things needed for Mass and for the various duties of the brethren.

France, however, could not satisfy his desire, and once more, in 678, he set out for Rome, careful this time to take Ceolfrid with him. Surely his prior must learn, as he himself had done, the details of monastic and ecclesiastical law in Rome itself. During their absence the monastery was ruled by one of its monks called Eosterwine. All kinds of treasures were in their bales and packages when they returned.[14]

It was just after their home-coming that Bede was brought to the monastery of Wearmouth. We know little about his

---

[13] *VA* c. 5; Plummer II, 358.
[14] *VAA* cc. 7–10. Among the MSS. brought back by Ceolfrid was a text of the *codex grandior* of Cassiodorus; see *Inst.* ed. Mynors, p. 40; *VA* c. 15; *cf.* also p. 316 *infra,* note 237.

earliest years. He was born in 672 or 673 on the land which King Egfrid gave about this time to Biscop for his abbey. Tradition places his birth at Monkton near Jarrow, although there is some evidence suggesting Sunderland.[15] His parents are entirely hidden from us; he himself tells that his "kinsmen" delivered him to the care of Biscop when he was seven years old.[16] In his name they promised that he would spend his life in Wearmouth's monastery, unless sent elsewhere by his abbot; that he would always endeavour diligently to obey its Rule as administered by those placed in charge of him; and that he would have no property of his own. He would owe reverence to every older member of the brethren, would be treated firmly but kindly, and would share so far as he could in the general life of the house.

He slept with the other "oblate boys" of his cloister in a dormitory shared by them with older monks; each one was assigned to the charge of a special "senior" brother. Night and day he wore the same dress, a long tunic of coarse woollen material, fastened by a girdle. In the winter he rose between two and three in the morning at his master's touch, or, if he were unusually sleepy, at a light stroke of the rod; then he took his place in the solemn procession as all, each with his lantern in hand, went toward the church. He waited outside while his elders entered for the preliminary prayers; when these were said, he walked in with the other children, placed his lantern where it might cast its light on all he did, and recited in high treble chant the opening invocations. He attended as well as he could while the Night Offices, known to us as Matins and Lauds, were said in all their length, went to rest again until day dawned, and then rose once more for Prime. After Prime he sat quietly among the other boys, all intent, or seemingly intent, upon their hornbooks under the

[15] Plummer I, ix; Whiting, in Thompson, 4.
[16] HE V, c. 24, end.

eye of some "senior." Presently it was time to return to the dormitory to wash and make oneself generally tidy for the rest of the day. This was done by all, and all met afterwards in the church for Terce. The monks then assembled in chapter for conference with their abbot and for individual confession of faults committed against the Rule; the children had their breakfast of bread and milk or light ale.

About ten o'clock the morning's task would be given to each boy. Sometimes he would help in a corner of the kitchen, preparing vegetables or cleaning pots and pans; sometimes in the bakery or in the wash-house, laundering clothes and laying them outside on the grass to dry; sometimes in the garden, pulling up weeds or sweeping the barn and granary, where the grain was threshed and stored, or hunting eggs in the hen-house. As he grew older, he was promoted to churning the milk in the dairy for curds and whey, for butter and cheese, to tending the cows and sheep and horses; sometimes, to his great joy, he would be allowed to go with the monks who fished for their dinner from the stream near by. Now and again he would run errands for the brother who was sowing seed or ploughing in the monastery fields or beating out iron with a hammer in the forge.[17]

But to Bede his lessons were far more interesting than any other duty, even than fishing in the stream. As soon as he arrived, he began to learn his Latin, in the *Paternoster* and *credo;* next, to understand and even to memorize the psalms, the hymns and the chants, the antiphons and the responses, which were used in the daily Offices of the Rule. He and his classmates were drilled well in reading these aloud, and they worked hard; for slips and mistakes in chanting or in reading were held grievous faults, even in a grown-up brother. Their

[17] See the *Rule of St. Benedict*, cc. 30, 37, 39, 45, 63, 70; Knowles, 450ff.; Coulton I, c. xiv; *Aelfric's Colloquy*, ed. G. N. Garmonsway, 1939, 11ff., 43ff.; S. H. Gem, *An Anglo-Saxon Abbot*, 1912, 193ff.

Latin gradually became a second language, added to their native Anglo-Saxon. Presently they began to read different parts of the Latin Bible in the Vulgate or in the Old Italian text, with Latin stories of saints told in simple language. They learned, also, Latin names for things of daily life, of the monastery, of the church, of the farm and fields and of the various callings of men. Every day their store of words grew, and every day they practised their hands and minds in writing Latin sentences, even, as time went on, Latin narratives. It helped much that they were forbidden to talk in their own Anglo-Saxon except on special occasions, such as great Feasts of the Church.

Sometimes, again, they watched the monks writing in the *scriptorium,* where manuscripts were copied and adorned with illumination. Those among them who showed enough interest and skill were trained little by little in these arts. Bede learned to use his pen well. He enjoyed, too, his lessons in singing, given by a monk named John the Chanter, whom, by special permission of Pope Agatho, Benedict Biscop had brought back with him on his last return from Italy.[18] John was very skilful, as became one who in Rome had been Arch-chanter of Saint Peter's; he had also ruled his own monks there as abbot of Saint Martin's monastery. In Wearmouth he wrote down the proper order and form in which the music of the monastery was to be sung on Feast-days throughout the year, according to the practice of his choir at Saint Peter's; many monks who were interested in chant came from all over Northumbria to hear him and begged him to come and teach their brethren also. Bede never forgot how wonderful the music at Wearmouth had seemed. All his life he was to love sacred songs and hymns, whether written in his own Anglo-Saxon language or in the Latin of the Church, from

[18] *HE* IV, c. 18; *VA* c. 6.

Ambrose and Prudentius in the fourth century down to Aldhelm of his own time.[19]

He was a thoughtful child, not given to the whispering and laughter of the more mischievous among his companions. As the years went on, he felt more and more at home in this monastery. Especially he loved the church of Saint Peter [20]— at night when the lamps of glass threw light from its chapels, lost in the darkness of the walls rising high above his head, and in the day when he watched from his place at Mass the altar adorned with jewelled vessels and tapestry of gold, the priests in their vestments of deep, rich colouring. Often, too, he would ask permission to stay awhile in the church alone, when all the monks were occupied elsewhere. Then he would walk around and look long at all the things it held. There were the strange animals carved in stone upon the archway; the relics of saints and martyrs in their reliquaries, which reflected the sun as it fell through the glass windows upon their jewels, red and blue and green; the pictures which stood on boards, on both sides and across from wall to wall. Wherever you looked, you saw either the Lord or one of His saints; it made you feel very, very much in their presence, almost afraid. As you walked across the church, you saw first the Mother of God, and then all the twelve Apostles, one after another; when you reached the south side, you found the stories of the Gospels, the life of the Lord Christ from His birth to His ascending into Heaven; on the opposite, the north side, were the sights of which Saint John had told in his *Apocalypse*.[21] That was a Greek word, and little Bede had not yet begun his Greek, but he knew well that the pictures told of what

---

[19] *De obitu Baedae:* Plummer I, clxi.

[20] For a most interesting description of the remaining parts of the churches of Wearmouth and Jarrow "which we may suppose that Bede himself must have seen" see Peers, in Thompson, 107ff.; *cf.* Clapham, *ERA*, 38f.; Baldwin Brown II, 1925, 120ff., 470ff.

[21] *VA* c. 6.

happened to good and to wicked people after they died. He would linger a long time on this north side and think about the Last Judgment of which his teacher Trumbert had told him and the other boys. Trumbert now and then would bring them all into the church and give them their Bible lessons while they looked at the pictures. Sometimes, too, he would tell them of the saints whose images were standing there; sometimes he talked about holy men whom he himself had known, especially of Bishop Chad, under whom he had been trained as monk in Lichfield, in the province of the Mercians to the south.[22]

There was one story which Bede heard his teacher tell again and again, for it was one of Trumbert's favourites. Sometimes, when Chad was reading or busy in some other way, the wind would rise and sweep around his monastery; as soon as he heard it, he would look up from his work and pray the Lord for mercy for mankind. If the wind blew stronger in a gathering storm, he would shut his book and fall on his face to pray more earnestly. But if, as sometimes happened, the storm lasted long and thunder and lightning filled earth and air with terror, then he would go into the church and stay there, lost to everything but prayers and psalms, until all was over and the sky was clear again. His brother monks were curious and asked him why he always did this. "Have you not read," he answered, "that 'the Lord thundered from heaven and the Most High gave His voice; He sent His arrows and scattered them, He multiplied lightnings and discomfited them'?[23] Why, then, does He this? Surely that He may rouse mortal men to fear Him, that He may banish their pride and confuse their boldness in bringing again to their minds that dread time when the heavens and the earth shall flame with fire and when He Himself shall come in power and majesty

[22] *HE* IV, c. 3.   [23] *Ps.* XVIII, 13f.

to judge both the living and the dead. And so," Chad went on, "we must respond with fear and love to His warning from heaven. As often as the air is shaken and He puts forth His hand as though threatening to strike, and yet for the time withholds the stroke, let us implore His mercy and search thoroughly the innermost places of our hearts; let us cast out the garbage of our sins and take care that we never deserve to be stricken." [24]

The story, in Bede's mind, seemed to belong to the pictures of the Last Judgment. Life was certainly a very serious business, he thought; perhaps one day, like Trumbert, he might teach people how to escape such punishment for wickedness.

There was another church in the monastery, one which Benedict Biscop had built in honour of the blessed Mother of God; sometimes Mass was said there as well as in Saint Peter's. The monks, too, had in their dormitory a little chapel of Saint Laurence the Martyr, where they prayed their own private prayers.[25] But both of these were still very bare, without interesting things to look at.

At noontide Sext was said in the church of Saint Peter and shortly afterward None; then all had dinner in the refectory about two o'clock, the first meal of the day for the brethren who were not sick or old. Some, who were sufficiently skilled, read aloud while the others sat at tables; others served the dishes from the kitchen. These duties were assigned in turn, week by week, to each brother. The food was varied, fish, eggs, cheese, butter, green vegetables, porridge; the children were allowed some meat, forbidden to the adult monk, unless prescribed in illness by the brother in charge of the infirmary. The rude cups were filled with beer or mead, milk or water.

After dinner there were lessons, held in the afternoon as

[24] *HE* IV, c. 3. *Cf*. Bede's own teaching in *On Ezra*: Giles VIII, 456f.; Plummer II, 209.
[25] *VA* c. 17; *VAA* c. 25.

well as in the morning; when the sun had set, all gathered in church for Vespers. After Vespers the children had their supper in the refectory and returned to church for a short reading by one of the monks, followed by Compline, the last Office of the day. In the winter-time all the community went to bed about seven in the early darkness; in summer, when the days were longer, dinner was served at midday and all were allowed to sleep a while afterward. Vespers, supper and Compline then came in the daylight, and long before dark the Great Silence had settled on the house.

It was a hard life; but, of course, there were compensations. No doubt the children were often set free to play and talk with one another and were sent to rest when they were tired. On the other hand, discipline was firmly maintained, and wilful or careless faults were frequently visited by the rod of chastisement.

Thus a year or two passed after Bede had come to Wearmouth. When he was about nine years old, there was rejoicing in Saint Peter's monastery over the announcement by the founder, Benedict Biscop, that King Egfrid was so delighted at the result of his former gift that he had decided to give yet another piece of land for the building of a second monastery. This was at In Gyruum, Jarrow, where the rivers Don and Tyne meet. Here, then, Biscop built houses of stone, as at Jarrow, with a church, dedicated by Egfrid's wish to Saint Paul. Although the two monasteries were about five miles apart, they were always held as one, and the brethren of both belonged to the same community. It took three years to make ready this second group of buildings; the church of Saint Paul was dedicated, it would seem, on April 23, 685. Egfrid watched with all interest the progress of Jarrow's monastery and himself chose the place where its high altar should stand.[26]

Long before this, however, and shortly after this second

26 *HE* V, c. 21; *VA* c. 7; *VAA* cc. 11f.; Plummer II, 361.

house was planned, Biscop had called a chapter of his monks
and with their consent had appointed for it its own abbot,
Ceolfrid, his prior at Wearmouth. As soon as the necessary
rooms were ready, Ceolfrid, now thirty-nine years old and
increasingly diligent in his profession, had moved to Jarrow,
taking with him about seventeen monks, some of them ton-
sured, or professed, brothers, others yet untonsured. Among
the latter very probably was the child Bede, who certainly
spent nearly all his life at Jarrow. In this case he must have
watched the gradual rising of the church and must have taken
part in the constant practise of chanting of hymns and psalms
which Ceolfrid ordered for his new little household. Some of
its brethren were not at all skilled in music, yet Ceolfrid was
extremely eager that Jarrow should sing to the Lord as well
as Wearmouth did.

Another change was made at the same time. Biscop of
Wearmouth had passed his fiftieth year; a younger man, he
decided, would better cope with the problems of its household. Moreover, and this was to him of even greater importance, his monastery needed more books and the new
church of Saint Paul the adorning that had enriched the
church of Saint Peter. Italy, as always, was the land of
treasure. And so, that he might be free to journey abroad,
Biscop now formally entrusted the care of Wearmouth to
the Eosterwine who had ruled it during the absence of
Ceolfrid and himself in 678.

Eosterwine was of noble birth and a cousin of Biscop. He
was known for his humble simplicity; as abbot *pro tempore*
of Wearmouth he had gladly forgotten his aristocratic origin
and had worked with his companions of the monastery in all
its different labours, even the most menial. The same spirit
lay behind all his acts as its permanent ruler; he tried hard,
it was said, to warn those who were tempted to sin against

the discipline of the Rule, rather than mete out punishment after they had offended. He ate of the common food and in the common refectory; he slept in the same dormitory with his monks; when he went into workshops, or garden or fields, to inspect their doings, he would take a hand himself, driving the plough or wielding the hammer or shaking the fan that winnowed the grain. After his appointing, all responded willingly to his rule, for he was strong and good-looking, cheerful and generous of mind; he was gentle, too, in manner, except when discipline demanded sternness. Like Ceolfrid, he was a priest, but of Wearmouth's training.[27]

Over both his abbots Biscop retained the right of chief ruler and director. He was now happy and at rest regarding his spiritual sons. Moreover, he trusted that their future was secure. When he had last returned from Rome, he had brought with him from Pope Agatho a "privilege" like that which Aldhelm was to win from Pope Sergius some twelve years later for his abbeys at Malmesbury and at Frome; it granted to the monastery of Wearmouth-Jarrow liberty of election. This had been wholeheartedly endorsed by King Egfrid; after the deaths of their present abbots the monks of the united congregation of the two houses would be free to choose from their number him whom they should desire as their head.[28]

In 684, therefore, while the church of Saint Paul was steadily rising at Jarrow under Ceolfrid's eye, the Father Biscop again left England to search in Rome after proper array for its walls, its altars, and its priests. He was away until 686, and tragedy fell upon his monastery in his absence. In 685 there came upon England one of those terrible visitations of the "Yellow Plague" which were frequent during this seventh century. As might be expected, it vented its most

[27] *VA* c. 8.
[28] *HE* IV, c. 18; *VA* c. 6; *VAA* c. 20.

fatal fury upon communities of monks and nuns, who lived night and day in crowded rooms and who took no account of segregation or of measures of hygiene. Nor did they at best busy themselves very much with healing; to depart this life and to dwell with the Lord was to them a far better lot, whether for the one or the many. Many, indeed, of the brethren of Wearmouth now died, among them Eosterwine himself. For two days he lay sick upon his bed in the common dormitory; five days before his death he allowed his monks to carry him into a more private place. In his last hours he bade them bear him outside into the open; sitting in a chair, he gave to each one in turn the farewell kiss of peace as they filed before him, weeping for their Father whom they were to see no more. He passed away in the darkness before dawn on the seventh of March of this same year, while the monks were singing Matins, and was buried in the entrance porch of Saint Peter's. He was only thirty-five years old.[29]

Even more heavy was the mortality at Jarrow. At length all who could read or chant the music of the Offices were dead, except Abbot Ceolfrid and one boy, about thirteen. Tradition has commonly held that this was Bede himself. The abbot ordered that all the Hours except Matins and Vespers should be recited without music. After a week, however, his sense of form and ritual could bear this no longer; he decided that he and this boy would chant the psalms together, each in turn, verse by verse, until he had trained the novices who were ignorant of music or had found brethren from without who could take part.[30]

Still further news awaited Biscop's return. The monks of Wearmouth had elected one of their number as their head and ruler, a young man in deacon's orders called Sigfrid, and

[29] VA cc. 8, 10; VAA c. 13; Whiting, in Thompson, 7.
[30] VAA c. 14.

Ceolfrid had accepted him as fellow-abbot. Probably Sigfrid had been chosen for his knowledge of the Bible and his marked asceticism in fasting. His practice of religion was made difficult because he was suffering gravely from advanced tuberculosis; we may presume either that the monks of Wearmouth did not regard good health as essential for their abbot or that the ravages of the plague had left Sigfrid as the outstanding choice. Nevertheless Biscop confirmed his election willingly, for this brother was loved and respected by all.[31]

Both houses, although sadly depleted, were exceedingly glad in the Father's return and in the treasures he had brought. There were many books to add to the store of those he had brought back from previous visits to France and Italy. For the church of Saint Paul there were pictures of a new kind, painted in pairs, one picture from the Old Testament, explained and illustrated by another from the New. Bede never tired of looking on these and thinking out their meaning. There were two pairs he liked especially. One showed Isaac, a boy like himself, carrying wood for the sacrifice of his own death, and, just above, the Lord Christ carrying the Cross on which He, too, was willing to die. The other was more puzzling. There was a great wilderness, dark and lonely, and people in dreadful suffering, like the brothers he had seen dying from the plague; in the middle Moses had just lifted up an enormous snake, so bright that it seemed to be burning with fire, upon a pole for all the people to see, and they were stretching out their hands. You saw the snake already twined about the pole, and then you looked above and saw in the other picture the Lord lifted up upon the Cross. Bede decided that he must ask Trumbert about this explaining of the Old Testament by the New; perhaps there were many other comparisons like these. Then there were many pictures

[31] Raine, *DCB* IV, 666; Plummer II, 363.

which told of the life of the Lord. These were to make beautiful the Wearmouth church of Saint Mary; and Bede studied
them all in order when, as often, he walked over from Jarrow.
And, lastly, he looked with much interest at two altar-cloths
of silk, embroidered in wonderful designs and colours.[32]

The world outside the monastery, also, had changed for
Father Biscop. While he had been away, King Egfrid had
died; now Aldfrid, "the Learned," was on the throne of
Northumbria. But Aldfrid, too, was friendly toward the monks
of Saints Peter and Paul; Biscop sent him the two altar-
cloths in exchange for another piece of land near the mouth of
the river Wear, on its south bank.

Not long after his return the monks of his community
noticed that their Father Founder was failing in health. Soon
paralysis attacked him, creeping slowly on until he could no
longer walk or stand, although his hands still held his books
and his mind was clear. This lasted for three years of patient
endurance and increasing helplessness. He was living in the
house at Wearmouth, where Abbot Sigfrid was also fast approaching his release from sickness on earth. Both of them
constantly spoke to the brethren of the twin monasteries, and
Bede must often have thought afterwards of their words,
especially of Biscop's last counsels. The library which he had
assembled with so great care was to be kept safe and whole,
he said, injured neither by neglect nor by selling nor by giving
away of its books. Above all, the monks were to be very
cautious in their choice of the Father who should preside over
them in the future. Let no thought of rank or family kinship
count in this matter, he warned; better that the monastery
be laid waste than that even Biscop's own brother after the
flesh should be chosen, should he lead it into evil ways. Let
them always be mindful of Saint Benedict of Nursia, from

[32] *VA* c. 9.

whom in chief measure their Rule had come; let them remember also their own freedom of election, granted by Pope
Agatho. And so in all liberty and wise consent let them
choose from their own number him whom they should judge
in life and learning and discretion to be best fitted to rule them;
then let them ask of their bishop that he confirm their choice
and install this brother in the abbot's chair with his blessing.
For thus the Rule of Saint Benedict had decreed.

Wearmouth lost both abbot and Founder within one year;
Sigfrid died on August 22, 688, and Biscop four months later,
on January 12, 689.[33] Bede was then a little over sixteen. In
after days he remembered vividly the story of that time. The
monks of Wearmouth told how night after night Biscop could
not sleep and would call to his bedside one of them to read to
him some passage from the Bible that would comfort and
encourage him, especially from the Book of Job. As long as
he was able, he insisted upon joining with the monks in their
Offices of night and of day, carried to the church on his bed;
toward the end some of them sang the psalms appointed for
each Office by his bedside, their voices carrying the words he
tried to say.

Then the hour came when Biscop and Sigfrid said good-bye
to each other, when Sigfrid was carried into the Father's room
and they lay side by side upon one bed, so that, with the help
of the monks who were caring for them, they might manage
to give each other the last kiss of peace. There was a little
conference with the senior monks of Wearmouth; finally, with
the consent of all, Biscop sent to summon Ceolfrid from
Jarrow and solemnly appointed him Father Abbot of both
Wearmouth and Jarrow combined, that these might truly be
one house under one head.

The last night of Biscop's life in Wearmouth was another

[33] *VA* cc. 11ff. *Cf.* Whiting, in Thompson, 9; Poole, *Studies,* 46f.

of Bede's memories. He received his communion for good speed on his journey; then, as the words of the battle psalm, *Deus quis similis,* "Lord, who is like unto Thee?" were sung by the monks in choir, he found release from his pain. He was buried near the altar of Saint Peter, his own especially beloved saint.[34]

Meanwhile, Bede's studies had long passed from those of the child to higher things.[35] His education resembled that of Aldhelm. He learned the mathematics and the astronomy by which men calculated the Feast days of the Church; he read the literature which had dealt with this. He pored over his Bible in the Old Latin and in the Vulgate version, over the writings of the Latin theologians of the West: Cyprian, Ambrose, Jerome, Augustine, and Gregory the Great. The Greek writers on theology he read very largely in Latin, translated by Rufinus or by Eustathius. His own knowledge of Greek, even if not very thorough, is proved beyond doubt;[36] he shared in the learning of his century and wrote his books long after Theodore and Hadrian had made Greek scholars of many of his contemporaries. We know, in particular, that he used a Greek copy of Acts in commenting on this book; whether he possessed the whole of the New Testament in Greek, or the Septuagint version of the Old, is not certain. Of lesser commentators he knew well his Cassiodorus on the Psalms. Lives of holy men he had read in Athanasius, Paulinus, and Possidius, teachings on monastic discipline in the *Conferences* of

---

[34] *VA* c. 14; *Psalm* 82.

[35] No student of Bede's knowledge and use of his sources can move a step without consulting Werner, and Plummer *passim,* and the various writings of Laistner. Of these see especially here "The Library of the Venerable Bede," in Thompson, c. ix, and "Bede as a classical and patristic scholar," *TRHS* Fourth Series XVI, 1933, 69ff. See also here Ruby Davis, "Bede's Early Reading," *Speculum* VIII, 1933, 179ff.

[36] *Cf.* Werner, 98, note 2; Thompson, 36 (Whiting), 157ff. (Jenkins); Laistner, *Thought and Letters,* 125, 192; *TRHS ibid.,* 90ff.; *History* IX, 1924, 178.

Cassian, history in the Latin version of Josephus made under
Cassiodorus, in Marcellinus Comes, in Eutropius, in Orosius
and in Gregory of Tours. Grammar and metrical science came
to him from abundant sources—Audax, Donatus, Servius,
Victorinus and Charisius, to give only a few of the authors
whom he shared with Aldhelm. Like Aldhelm, too, he read
long and deeply in books that gave comprehensive knowledge
of nature and natural law, of geography, of man and man's
arts and crafts; such were the tomes of Pliny, of Macrobius
and of Isidore. Like Aldhelm, he knew his Christian poets,
Prudentius and Juvencus of Spain, Paulinus of Nola, born in
France, Sedulius and Fortunatus and Arator of Italy. In
pagan poetry he was more ignorant than Aldhelm; his reminiscences may well have been culled from Pliny or from
Isidore. But he knew his Vergil, though not so well as did the
abbot of Malmesbury.

The great difference between Aldhelm and Bede as writers
springs from their different aim. Aldhelm loved words and the
manipulating of words for their own sake; hence the swollen
periods and bizarre decoration of his Hisperic compositions.
Bede has no trace of the Hisperic; his Latin is clear, easy to
read. He had no temptation to dally on his path with words
as words, for his aim was to teach facts, to drive home lessons
of moral truth, and to do both as simply as possible. Even
when he was writing the numerous narratives of miracle, descriptions of character, and allegorical interpretations which
fill his books, he wrote without any more insistence on words
than would convey his meaning. Unlike Aldhelm, he strove
to attract and to teach by the power of his story or his argument itself, not by the colour in which he clothed it.

Thus the time passed until he had reached his nineteenth
year, in 691 or 692, when his monastery, in common with all
Northumbria, was pondering the news that Wilfrid had once

again been driven from his see of York. The age prescribed by
canon law of the Church for entry upon deacon's orders was
twenty-five, and we can imagine how far Bede must have out-
stripped the average when he was accepted in this same year
by his bishop, upon Abbot Ceolfrid's request. The teaching of
Trumbert, trained in Irish-Scottish discipline under Chad, and
of Biscop Benedict, student of England, France, and Italy, at
Canterbury, Lérins, and Rome; opportunity of learning from
the many scholars who visited Jarrow upon their travels;
access to a library almost unrivalled in the England of his
time—all these, working upon a very gifted and a very serious
student, had brought him early to ripeness of knowledge. His
character was as delightful as his understanding was deep.
His writings give full witness of his humility; of his devoted
love and praise of good men and women in every class, balanced by a passion for truth which drove him to reveal and to
castigate evil for the sake of good; of his loyalty toward his
Church, his country, his colleagues, his students, and his
friends. He loved best to pray and to read; and therein he
wrought a splendid harmony.

The bishop who ordained Bede deacon was that John of
Beverley who was just then causing Wilfrid anguish of spirit
in holding the see of Hexham; the same John advanced him
to the priesthood in his thirtieth year.[37]

Shortly after he entered the diaconate we may imagine him
as not only teaching in Jarrow but also as writing manuals
that would aid his instruction. His first efforts would naturally
be concerned with text-books, and of these we have three from
this earlier time. One of them describes itself as *On Orthography;* [38] but its matter scarcely deserves the name. It is simply
a list of words arranged alphabetically, with notes on grammar

[37] *HE* V, c. 24.
[38] Ed. Keil VII, 261ff.; Giles VI, 1ff.

applied to each: details such as derivations from the Greek, correct spellings, conjugations and usages with verbs, whether of case or of preposition, declensions and genders of nouns. In fact, it resembles notes which a modern teacher might use in quizzing his Latin class. The whole is very informally put together and seems to be a number of jottings used by Bede in drilling his students at Jarrow, written down more or less at random as they occurred to him. He did not take the trouble, for instance, to arrange words in alphabetical order within the selection allotted to each letter. There are many sentences for purposes of illustration, taken from both pagan and Christian sources. As has been indicated, examples from Cicero, Plautus, Terence, and so on, probably came from the Latin grammarians and from Isidore, the compilers upon whom Bede drew so freely here and elsewhere. Vergil is much in evidence, also the Bible and the Latin Fathers. The standard is not high; evidently the book was used for pupils at an elementary stage. Occasionally a more interesting example strikes the reader:

Stranger: often followed by a noun in the dative case, as saints are said to be strangers "to this world."

Nouns in *-ius* have vocative in *-i;* so the Latin Bible has "Corneli," spoken by the angel to the centurion Cornelius in Acts X, 3.

It is correct to say "I drank half *a* glass," not "half *the* glass." For you don't drink the glass, but what is in it.[39]

The little book had the distinction of being used by Alcuin and by William of Malmesbury in their treatises on orthography; William maintained "that Alcuin simply plucked Bede's material, adding nothing of his own." [40] This is not literally true, for Alcuin's work is of a rather more advanced type.

---

[39] Keil, *ibid.,* 269, 278, 286.
[40] *Gest. Reg.* I, cxli. For the light which the *De Orthographia* throws upon the MSS. of Bede see Laistner, *AHR* XLVI, 1941, 380.

The two other text-books, *On the Art of Metre* and *On the Figures and Tropes of Holy Scripture*, were dedicated to "Cuthbert, my fellow-deacon," from which it appears that they were written before 702, or perhaps 703; in one or the other year we know that Bede was ordained priest.[41] They, also, contain instruction for his students in Jarrow, among whom Cuthbert seems to have been numbered. Here Bede has diligently gathered from the same sources passages and paragraphs and examples for the explaining of form in poetry and in prose. The discussion on metric starts with the letters of the Latin alphabet, goes on to deal with scansion of syllables, then with the various kinds of feet and of feet combined to make the different varieties of line, with a section on verse that, although rhythmic, is bound by no exact rule. Examples of this last form, we are told by Bede, occur in the well-known volume of the poet Porphyry which won for him from the Emperor Constantine his return from exile. "But since his verses are pagan I did not care to touch them." Bede was not drawn, as was Aldhelm, by the beauty of classical Latin verse; he used it only to further his direct Christian aim. On the other hand, the far inferior Christian poetry of the earliest Middle Ages was freely represented in his work.[42]

In these treatises he wanted, above all, to show that the charm of rhythm and of metre abounded in Biblical literature long before Greek classical days. His aim was practical, and he did not linger by the way to indulge in the curiosities of acrostics and strange shapes in verse. Some have said, he

[41] Ed. Keil, *ibid.*, 227ff.; Halm, *Rhet. lat. min.* 607ff.; Giles VI, 40ff., 8off.

[42] See Laistner, *TRHS* 72ff.; *Thought and Letters,* 122f.; also in Thompson, 241f. He points out that quotations from ancient authors in Bede may have been borrowed from grammarians or from Isidore, *Etymologies. Cf.* E. F. Sutcliffe, "The Venerable Bede's Knowledge of Hebrew," *Biblica* XVI, 1935, 300ff.: "a few scraps . . . from the writings of St. Jerome."

affirms, that the song of Moses in the thirty-second chapter of
Deuteronomy and the alphabetical Psalms 118 and 144 were
written in elegiacs, and that the Book of Job was written in
hexameter verse.[43]

For him, likewise, all pagan classical figures of rhetoric had
their prototype in the Bible, with the reasoning that holy
Scripture is older, is of Divine inspiration and, hence, of paramount utility as guide of mortal men toward eternal life.
Away, then, with the vain boastings of the Greeks! And, therefore, as he describes these figures one after another, he explains them by Biblical illustrations.[44] The fact that he wrote
Hebrew words in one passage of his *On the Figures,* in explaining *paronomasia,* yields no proof that he could read Hebrew;
he could easily have quoted the words from Jerome, his
source.[45]

To the period of Bede's diaconate belong the twin questions: Did he visit Rome? Was he invited by the Pope to do
so? These are complicated matters, depending on the evidence
of uncertain manuscript readings and the equally uncertain
interpreting of human psychology.[46] The answer to the first
may be given in the words of a modern authority: "As far as
we know, Bede never left his native shores." [47] For the second,
it is possible, but not proved, that he received an invitation
from Pope Sergius and that he did not use it, perhaps because
the Pope died in 701. In this year, shortly before his death,
Sergius certainly wrote to Abbot Ceolfrid requesting that he

[43] Keil VII, 243, 252.
[44] See J. W. H. Atkins, *English Literary Criticism: The Medieval
Phase,* 1943, 46ff. He points out that here is the first reference of an
English scholar to the literary "kinds" (i.e., dramatic, narrative, and
mixed); that Bede "is the first to attempt an appreciation of Biblical
literature"; that he "enlisted grammar in the service of religion."
[45] Jenkins, in Thompson, 163.
[46] Stubbs, *DCB* I, 300f.; Hunt, *DNB* IV, 98f.; H.S. III, 248ff.;
Whiting, in Thompson, 11ff.
[47] Whiting, 13.

send one of his monks to confer with him on important business of the Church; we cannot now be sure whether he actually mentioned Bede in this letter or left the choice to Ceolfrid's discretion. We do know that some monks from Wearmouth Abbey were in Rome in 701 and that they brought back with them from Pope Sergius a privilege for the protection of their monastic freedom similar in content to that granted Benedict Biscop by Pope Agatho. As Egfrid had done for Biscop, so King Aldfrid, also, by assent confirmed this second charter. Bede, however, was not of their company.[48]

His own evidence concerning himself, written toward the end of his life, shows that he was no traveller from home:

"I, Bede, servant of Christ and priest of the monastery of the blessed apostles Peter and Paul at Wearmouth and Jarrow, born on the estate of this same monastery, was given by my relatives when I was seven years old to the care of the most reverend abbot Benedict, and afterward of Ceolfrid. From that time I have spent my entire life in the dwelling of this same monastery, devoting myself wholly to study of the Scriptures, to following the regular discipline and the round of daily chant within the church. I have always held it my joy to learn, to teach, and to write." He tells us, also, that for nearly thirty years, from the time he received the priesthood until he was approaching old age, he devoted his time and energy to gathering material, mostly upon the Bible, from the Fathers of the Church in preparation of commentaries upon the same, "for the need of me and mine."[49]

Bede might be called a Christian Cicero in his intense desire to hand on knowledge. Although he does show originality, in criticism, in selection, in adaptation, this was not his primary aim. He wanted, above all, to teach, whether by his own

[48] *VA* c. 15; *De temp. rat.* c. 47; Jones, *ODT* 267.
[49] *HE* V, c. 24.

thought or, primarily, in his humility and reverence, by that which he so freely borrowed and made available for less well-provided readers.[50] The words of Seneca the philosopher might have been written by him:

Gaudeo discere, ut doceam. Nec me ulla res delectabit, licet sit eximia et salutaris, quam mihi uni sciturus sum; [51]
"I rejoice to learn, that I may teach. Nor will anything delight me, no matter how excellent, how good for me, if I am to know it for myself alone."

As priest, then, Bede continued to teach and to write. From work on the rules of prose and poetry, belonging to the elementary course of liberal arts, the *trivium,* he now turned to write for his students a little manual, *De Temporibus, On Times,* based on the study of one of the subjects of the more advanced *quadrivium,* that of chronology.[52] The primary reason for this was the perennial dispute concerning the date of Easter. Although in practice this had been settled for Northumbria, home of Bede and his monastery, some forty years before this time by the synod held at Whitby in 664, yet many of the Celts still persevered in their own way of dating. It was, therefore, of great concern to Bede that the young monks of Wearmouth should fully understand the true doctrine on this matter. It may be of interest to note here Bede's use in this work of the word *sacramentum,* "sacrament," for the mystical meaning lying behind external facts. As the Feast of Easter moves from day to day, year by year, in the calendar, so the soul of man must move, year by year, from death to life.

---

[50] Jenkins, in Thompson, 170; *cf.* Jones, "Bede and Vegetius," *CR* XLVI, 1932, 249: "It is dangerous to assert that any words in Bede's works were his own; it is less dangerous to say that, if we had all the materials with which Bede worked, we should find very few statements originating with him."

[51] *Epp. Morales* I, 6.

[52] Jones, *ODT* 130f., 295ff.; Manitius, *Gesch.,* 77.

The progress of the book leads from the consideration of
smaller divisions of time and of their names to the greater,
from minutes and hours to days and nights, weeks, months,
and years. Weeks are ascribed to Divine ruling, months to
human custom, years to natural order. Bede's sources here
were, of course, the various writings on the Paschal calculation
then current in England and Ireland; [53] he borrowed also from
Pliny, from Macrobius, and from Isidore, that bishop of
Seville in Spain from about 600 to 636, whose compilations
contained vast learning and were of immense influence in the
Middle Ages.[54] Throughout his literary life he used Isidore
so much, albeit with scholarly independence, that it is no
marvel to note that Dante placed the two side by side among
the scholars who dwell in the sun of Paradise, radiant with a
light no words can describe.[55] From Isidore, supported by the
teaching of Augustine,[56] he derived the chronology on which
he loved to dwell, of the six ages of the world; it recurs again
and again in his books. The six ages run:

1. From the Creation to Noah and the Flood:
2. From Noah to Abraham:
3. From Abraham to David:
4. From David to the Captivity of the Jews:
5. From the Captivity to the Birth of Christ:
6. From the Birth of Christ to an indeterminate date, the end
   of the world, known to God alone.[57]

The time already passed is reckoned here as far as the fifth
year of the rule of Tiberius III, Emperor of the East in Constantinople; and this gives the date of 703 for Bede's writing

[53] Jones, *ODT* 105ff.
[54] *Etymologiae,* ed. Lindsay V, 38f.; *De nat. rerum, PL* LXXXIII,
coll. 963ff.; *Chronicon, PL ibid.,* coll. 1017ff.
[55] *Paradiso* X, 130f. For Bede's independence see Laistner, in Thompson, 256; Jones, *ODT* 131.
[56] *De civ. Dei* XXII, 30.
[57] *De temp.* 16: Jones, *ODT* 303.

of his book.[58] To these six ages of the world correspond in mystical interpretation the six periods of the life of each individual man: infancy, boyhood, youth, middle age, old age, last years, which are destined to end, like our present world, by death.

Five years later Bede heard that this little book had brought on him an unspeakable charge. A messenger arrived one day at Jarrow, bearing friendly greetings from Plegwin, a monk of the same diocese of Hexham in which Jarrow lay. Less welcome words followed. Certain "rustics" at a feast, so Plegwin was informed, had drunkenly shouted that Bede was a heretic, and this, too, in the presence of his and their bishop, Wilfrid, who held the see of Hexham from 706 to 709. It seems that those who thus jeered at Bede's views on theology must have been monks; we shall find other evidence of looseness of monastic living in this age. On the other hand, that monks commonly read and discussed such books as this is to the credit of the time.

Bede turned pale with horror and asked what could the heresy be? "According to them," was the answer, "you denied that the Lord came in the flesh during the sixth age of the world."

For two days he pondered. Then he poured out his indignation in a long letter to Plegwin.[59] As a priest of the Church of Christ, he wrote, he could not possibly have denied His Incarnation; as a student of the Bible, he could not deny that the Lord had come as very Man in the sixth age of the world. This most false slander had arisen from a misunderstanding of his description of the successive eras in the *De Temporibus*. It was, he said, purely a question of the number of years assigned to each of the five ages preceding the sixth. In his calculating Bede had considered the authority of the Vulgate,

[58] Plummer I, cxlvi. [59] Ed. Jones, *ODT* 132ff., 307ff.

translated from the Hebrew, to be better than that of the Greek Septuagint, followed by Isidore and the writers, including Jerome, from whom Isidore had drawn. Thus, although he had certainly placed the Incarnation in what he himself held to be the sixth age according to the Hebrew-Vulgate calculation, yet he had dated it at a considerably earlier time after the Creation than the Septuagint reckoning had done, the reckoning followed by Isidore and his sources; in fact, Bede's date for it lay within their fifth age of the world. Hence all the trouble. We may note that Bede showed scholarly independence of judgment in differing thus from Isidore and Jerome.[60]

While he was on the subject, it would be good, he decided, to warn Plegwin not to let himself be deceived, like so many people, by the idea that this present age of the world was to last six thousand years, or, "as I remember reading in some heretic's book when I was a boy," that the year of the Last Judgment could be foretold by men. No, indeed! When the Lord said, "But of that day and hour knoweth no man," He did not mean that we could tell the year. "I get really sad and even more angry than sad when the country people round here ask me how many years still remain to this world. The Lord never has told us whether His coming is near or far off; He only bids us watch and wait with loins girded and with lamps burning until He shall come."

His letter ended with an admonition that it be read in the presence of "our reverend Lord and Father, Wilfrid, our bishop, in order that, since in his presence and his hearing I was stupidly insulted, he may now hear and know how wrongly I have been used."

The relation of Bede toward Wilfrid is of interest. He met and talked with him, and he wrote of him at a later time with

[60] Levison, in Thompson, 116f.

that courtesy which was his unfailing characteristic. He praised
Wilfrid's work among the people of Sussex, a work that had
rescued them "not only from the bitterness of everlasting
damnation, but also from the unspeakable disaster of temporal
death." He called him "a man most learned," "a man most
reverend, who first among the bishops that were of the English
people learned to pass on the Catholic manner of living to the
churches of the English," a statement which was certainly in
error. He repeatedly referred to him after his death as "of
blessed memory." [61] Yet "it is evident that there was but little
sympathy between Wilfrid and the great scholar." [62] In writing of the Church history of his time Bede deliberately omitted
much that was of importance in Wilfrid's life. He himself was
devoted to John of Hexham, the bishop who ordained him
deacon and priest, and to Cuthbert of Lindisfarne; yet both
of these held their sees contrary to Wilfrid's will. He admired
greatly Egfrid and Aldfrid, those kings of Northumbria who
were Wilfrid's enemies. Finally and chiefly, we may reasonably surmise that Bede wholly sympathized with Archbishop
Theodore's desire to divide responsibility in the greater English dioceses, and that Bede, the monk of simple life and intellectual interests, found little to attract him in the relatively
worldly ambitions of this bishop of York.

With his *On Times* Bede on three occasions couples another
treatise of his, *On the Nature of Things*.[63] As he does not give
us its date, we only know that it was written before 725.[64] But
as it also seems to have been intended for the use of his stu-

[61] *HE* IV, c. 19; III, c. 25; IV, c. 2; Plummer II, 206.
[62] Raine *HY* I, xxxiv; W. Bright, *Waymarks in Church History*, 1894,
285: "In fact, if one could be angry with Bede, it would be for his leaving
us so much to depend on Eddi for information about Wilfrid." On Bede's
account of Wilfrid see Plummer II, 315ff., 325, 327; Colgrave, *Eddius*,
xiif.
[63] Giles VI, 99ff.
[64] *Ibid.*, 139; *HE* V, 24. The mention of the *De nat. rerum* in the *De
temp. rat.*, written in 725, shows its earlier date.

dents in elementary science, there is some ground for supposing its date to have been near that of *On Times,* in or about the year 703. Here he deals with cosmography, teaching his monks what Pliny in his *Natural History* and Isidore in his *Etymologies* had told concerning Nature.[65] They read of the heavens and the waters above the firmament; of the sun and the moon and the stars of heaven; of showers and winds, of hail and snow, of lightnings and clouds; of why the sea is salt and why the Red Sea is red; of the earth and its shape, its inner fires and quakings, its divisions and their placing.

We come now to the maturity of Bede as writer. In the thirty years which followed he steadily pursued the aim of his literary life: the teaching of men, both by the history of the Church and of her saints and by the interpretation of the various books included in her Scriptures.

With regard to the former we shall notice here two biographies and a martyrology, all of which we shall only date with certainty as written before 731.[66] *The Life and Martyrdom of Saint Felix of Nola,* as Bede himself tells us, was a translation into prose of the *Life* composed in verse by Paulinus, a native of Gaul, for twenty years in the earlier fifth century bishop of the Italian city of Nola. Paulinus had a special reverence for his patron, Saint Felix, priest of Nola in the third century, whose shrine in that city was visited by a multitude of pilgrims. Every year he made known his reverence in verses which rise here and there to real poetry in an age of artificial borrowings from pagan writers. In his Preface to his *Life of Felix* Bede observes that Paulinus wrote "most beautifully and fully"; that he himself, however, "is explaining the same matter in plainer words of prose for the benefit of many simpler people." [67]

[65] On Bede's sources here see K. Werner, 107ff.; Manitius, *Gesch.,* 77f.
[66] They are mentioned in *HE* (V, 24, dated 731).
[67] Giles IV, 173ff. (Latin text and Eng. trans.)

Bede's *Life and Martyrdom of Saint Anastasius* is now lost. It told of the Persian convert to Christianity put to death under King Chosroes of Persia in 628 and still venerated in the church of Saints Vincent and Anastasius on the outskirts of Rome. Bede had found a *Life* of the saint "badly translated from the Greek and altered for the worse by some one who did not know his business"; he made the best sense he could from its jumbled text.[68]

More ambitious was the Martyrology, of which he wrote in later days: "I have tried to note all the martyrs I could find, and not only on what day, but also in what kind of conflict and under what judge they overcame the world." [69] His work, then, was of considerable importance here, in that he enlarged upon the bare notices which previous martyrologies had given. The best known of these notices was that which was falsely ascribed to Saint Jerome, since its Latin text, translated from the Greek, dated from the fifth century. Bede wanted something more interesting. In consequence, this *Book of Martyrs,* which he composed by gathering details from many Lives of saints and much ecclesiastical literature, became the model for what are called the "historical martyrologies" of the ninth century; they in their turn formed the basis of the present Roman Martyrology.[70]

From these brief details we pass to the Lives written by Bede of those whom he knew and loved as friends and fellow-monks. As a little boy in Wearmouth and Jarrow, he had heard of Cuthbert, Father of the brethren of Lindisfarne. Later, he had thought of this same Cuthbert when the solitary had left his island to undertake the active life of a bishop; as a lad of about sixteen, he had been present with all his com-

---

[68] *Cf.* Mommsen, *Chron. min., Auct. Ant.* XIII, 310f.; H. Quentin, *Les Martyrologes historiques du moyen âge,* 105f.
[69] *HE* V, 24.
[70] Quentin, *ibid.,* 683; Leclercq, *DACL* X, ii, coll. 2603f.; Giles X, 95.

munity when Jarrow sang requiem for the holy man in 687. And so, as he grew more skilled with his pen, he longed to write the marvels that had answered Cuthbert's prayers during his life, the miracles wrought on Lindisfarne at his tomb, the wonders that accompanied things he had worn or known. Paulinus and Fortunatus [71] of Gaul had written in verse the Life of Saint Martin of their country; perhaps Bede felt inspired to follow their example.

He had, however, a model from his own country, a *Life of Cuthbert* written by some unknown monk of Lindisfarne in simple Latin prose between 699 and 705. This had told in vivid picturing and detail the story of the Founder as his community remembered and treasured it, a story composed at the desire of Eadfrid, bishop of Lindisfarne. The writer, whoever he was, had taken care to record the names of men from whom he had heard the various incidents which he described, and those of the places where they happened. [72] With this, then, to guide him and with information gleaned from monks who had known Cuthbert as abbot, Bede wrote at their petition nearly a thousand lines of hexameter verse in his honour. [73] Naturally, as the author of a treatise on Latin metre, he knew its rules. But he deviated at times from classical usage in imitation of Christian mediaeval poets, Juvencus, Sedulius, and, especially, Arator. On the whole, here and elsewhere, Bede is no poet, although his verse is crystal clear compared with the artificial lines of Aldhelm, and occasionally he shows a sense of the poetical. It has been well said that he is composing here a story of miracles rather than a Life of Cuthbert. The whole was offered to a certain priest named John as a relaxation and comfort on the long journey which he was about to make to Rome. The time of writing is shown by a mention of the

[71] Paulinus, ed. Petschenig, *CSEL* XVI, i, 17ff.; Fortunatus, ed. Leo, *MGH Auct. Ant.* IV, i, 295ff.; K. Werner, 104.
[72] Colgrave, *Cuthbert*, 11ff., 59ff.
[73] Ed. Werner Jaager, *Palaestra*, No. 198, 1935, 58ff.

ruling of Osred as king of Northumbria, who as "a young Josiah" has come to its throne. Both Osred and Josiah, it is true, began their reigns at eight years of age; but Osred in his later years did not do that which was right in the sight of the Lord. He was king from 705 until 716; here, therefore, we have the limits of date for Bede's composing of his poem,[74] which brought its own reward to its writer. For in the preface Bede declares that he cannot tell all the wonders wrought by Cuthbert; new ones are being shown daily; even he himself, while he has been telling of them in these verses, has found relief from some canker on the tongue! [75]

Some time afterward the community of Lindisfarne and their bishop Eadfrid requested a more definite, detailed, and formal Life in prose, and Bede set to work again. With scrupulous care, while relying in the main upon the same sources, written and oral, he investigated facts anew, searched here and there to discover further material of reliable authority, and submitted his work to examination by Abbot Herefrid and the senior monks of Lindisfarne. During two days they read and debated, then pronounced it to be truly worthy of its subject. It was finished before the end of 721, as the preface of the completed work was written to Eadfrid, who died in that year.[76]

This Life of Cuthbert in prose of Bede is more interesting than the metrical one, although in spite of all his care it cannot compete with that graphic sketch written by the unknown monk.[77] He omits here many names of persons and places, follows the anonymous Life so closely that often he seems only

[74] *Ibid.*, 4, 100; Manitius, *Gesch.*, 84.
[75] Jaager, 57.
[76] Colgrave, *Cuthbert*, 142ff. The date cannot be much earlier than 721, as the *De temp. rat.* (725 A.D.) states that it was composed "lately" (*nuper*): Plummer I, cxlviii; Colgrave, *ibid.*, 16. See also *HE, preface* and IV, cc. 27ff.
[77] Kurtz (p. 191 *supra*, note 145), 137ff.; Colgrave, 15ff. (*cf.* his remarks in Thompson, 227): Plummer I, xlvi; Manitius, *Gesch.*, 85.

to have changed its wording, and when he does introduce his own contribution, supplies frequently unnecessary thought rather than biographical detail. Moreover, he has hardly improved upon his source by exchanging its simplicity for a somewhat ornate and coloured style. Yet we may be grateful that he has given us this time a real Life of the saint rather than merely a description of spiritual wonders.

From time to time we come upon some story or detail here which we could not spare: how while travelling Cuthbert refused to break his fast on a Friday but begged for food for his horse, and how the horse, inspired of God, found bread for its master in the evening, when fasting hours were over; how, when he was sick of the plague, the brethren of Melrose prayed for him all night, and when he heard of this, he cried, "And why do I stay in bed? God certainly has not despised the prayers of so many men such as you! Hand me my staff and my shoes!"; how Boisil, prior of Melrose, read with him the Gospel of Saint John in the seven days before Boisil died, that he might teach him all he could in the time still left, and how they read right to the end because they talked only of the simple "faith which worketh by love" and left out all the knotty problems; how an eagle brought a fish for Cuthbert and his boy to eat when they were on a journey, and Cuthbert scolded the boy because he did not give the eagle half of the fish for its share; how on Lindisfarne "he wore ordinary clothes, and was conspicuous neither for elegance nor for shabbiness," so that his monks did not wear a habit of any striking or expensive colour but merely of natural wool; how, when he was alone on Farne and his brethren of Lindisfarne came to visit him, he gave them a goose to cook and to eat before they went home, and how they forgot, because they were not hungry, and were punished for their disobedience by a raging storm which kept them on Farne for seven days and would not abate until the goose was sizzling in the pot; how he spent his last hours on Farne, as Herefrid told, who tended him and gave him communion of the Lord's Body and Blood just before he died.[78]

In another book Bede showed that he could write the histories of men as men, holy and learned, but unadorned by the working of miracles. This was his *Lives of the Abbots of the Monastery in Wearmouth and Jarrow,* in which he gave the details set forward in all modern pictures of his own abbey and the years he spent there.[79] It is refreshing to read so early a narrative, one of our first historical descriptions of an English monastery, which tells of men and their workings, spiritual, intellectual, physical, in a purely human and natural way. Here, also, another account lies before us, a story of the Lives of the same abbots written by a monk of their monastery; his name and date are unknown to us.[80] Both his book and that of Bede must have been written after 716, as both describe the death of Ceolfrid in that year. We do not know which was written first; priority has been suggested for each.[81] The chief difference between the two works is that the unknown monk gives more interesting detail about Ceolfrid's life before he settled down permanently in Jarrow—the story of his father, of his flight from Ripon and of his chanting Offices with his small boy disciple in the choir—while Bede paints more vividly the journeys of Benedict Biscop, their fruit of treasures for the abbey, and the charm of Abbot Eosterwine.[82]

[78] Colgrave, 168ff., 180ff., 194ff., 212, 266ff., 272ff. The narratives of Boisil, of the goose, and of the death of Cuthbert are not found in the anonymous *Life*: Colgrave, 15f.
[79] Ed. Plummer I, 364ff.
[80] *Ibid.,* 388ff.
[81] For Bede as the earlier writer see Whiting, in Thompson, 22f.; for the anonymous author's priority see Plummer II, 358, *cf.* I, cxlviii; Levison, in Thompson, 129ff. Levison points out that Bede used the anonymous work, not his own *Lives,* in his chronicle at the end of his *De temporum ratione,* which seems to date his *Lives* between 725 and 731; *cf.* Laistner, *Hand-List,* 112.
[82] *Cf.* Bede's sermon for the anniversary of Biscop: Giles V, 182ff.

Yet it was to the second part of his aim as teacher, to the passing on for other men the learning of the Church Fathers and theologians in their interpretation of the Bible so far as his age knew it, judiciously selected and mixed with a few comments of his own, that Bede gave most of his time for study.

One of his first books of interpretation of holy Scripture was his *Explanation of the Revelation of Saint John.*[83] Its early date is shown by Bede's especially close adherence to his sources; [84] very much of his matter was taken word for word from former writers. We know that he composed it before 716, as it was prefaced by a letter to "Brother Eusebius," whose Saxon name was Hwaetbert and who was one of the monks sent on the mission to Pope Sergius in 701. We know that in 716 Hwaetbert was elected to the office of abbot; the simple epithet of "Brother" shows that this election had not yet happened.[85]

As so much in this work was not original, it will be in place to consider briefly Bede's sources and their influence upon it. Chief among them was Saint Augustine, whom Bede followed closely in his preface. In his work *On Christian Doctrine* Augustine had stated and had carefully examined seven Rules, laid down as keys for the unlocking of secrets of holy Scripture by Tyconius, an African who flourished about 370 A.D.[86] Tyconius had unhappily separated himself from the Catholic Church by joining the Donatists, those schismatics who believed the doctrine of the Church but refused to ac-

[83] Ed. Giles XII, 337ff.

[84] See K. Werner, 186ff.

[85] Laistner, *Hand-List,* 25, dates it between 703 and 709, before the *Acts.*

[86] The *Rules of Tyconius,* "the first book in western Christendom which attempts to treat of the meaning and inspiration of the Bible as a whole," have been edited by F. C. Burkitt, *Texts and Studies* III, i, 1894 (see his Preface). For Augustine see *De doct. Christ.* III, cc. 30–37: *PL* XXXIV, coll. 81ff.; *cf. Epp.* XLI, *CSEL* XXXIV, ii. 83.

knowledge as valid the ministry of such of her priests as led unworthy lives, and even rejected communion with those who did acknowledge such ministry. He had not, however, been willing to go the whole way with these separatists; rather, he had vacillated between them and the Church in a manner which Augustine found both sinful and illogical. The Rules of Tyconius, therefore, so Augustine declared, must be treated with great caution. Nevertheless, they were of value for the understanding of Biblical writings and as such merited serious consideration by Biblical scholars.

Tyconius also wrote a *Commentary on the Revelation of Saint John* and in it applied the seven Rules or keys which he had previously formulated. Bede's monastery possessed a copy of this *Commentary*, and, as he mentioned Tyconius ten times in his own work, we may think that he used it freely. It was still in existence in the ninth century, but is now lost to us; and our knowledge of what it contained comes only through reconstruction by modern scholars from fragments quoted by those later Latin writers who knew and used it.

As Bede used Tyconius on the Revelation, so naturally he would study his Rules.[87] This he was able to do through the medium of his trusted guide, Augustine, in the *Christian Doctrine;* and such part of the Rules of Tyconius as Bede repeated in his preface to his commentary on the Revelation he drew from Tyconius as amended by Augustine. Since he did follow Augustine in holding these Rules of value to students of the Bible, and since he undoubtedly bore them in mind and applied them while he was writing his own commentaries on Biblical literature, it may be worth while to summarize them here, according to Tyconius-Augustine-Bede.

They declare, severally, in substance:

[87] Traugott Hahn, *Tyconius-Studien* (1900) 4; Thompson, 154f. (Jenkins), 266 (Laistner).

Rule One: That Christ and His Church are one whole, of which He is the Head and the Church is the Body. In statements, therefore, dealing with the whole, care must be taken to distinguish what properly refers, on the one hand, to the Head, Christ, and, on the other, to the Body, the Church.

Rule Two: That the Body of Christ, the Church, consists of true members, who will be His through all eternity, and of false or seeming members, who will be revealed as hypocrites on the Day of Judgment. This must be borne in mind when the Bible speaks of the Church.

Rule Three: That the Divine grace which alone enables us to carry out the works of the law is the gift of God alone. [Here Augustine amended Tyconius through the knowledge he had won in refuting the Pelagians, declarers of man's natural ability to obey Divine law].

Rule Four: That the student of the Bible must distinguish statements which are general, and apply to the whole, from those which refer to the individual part. This is difficult, because in Biblical statements the transition is made at times from the general to the particular, or from the particular to the general, without the reader's understanding what has happened. For example, a statement may begin by referring to Solomon and may pass on to tell of that which is not properly applicable to Solomon alone, but to Christ and His Church, that whole of which Solomon is but part.

Rule Five: That, if the student would understand the meaning of times and numbers in the Bible, he must explore the method of reckoning used in the sacred text, also the thought of its writer, especially when times and numbers are used by him in a mystical sense. Thus: "Seven times in the day will I praise Thee" really means to its writer, "His praise shall continually be in my mouth."

Rule Six: This deals with "Recapitulation," and requires the student to eliminate repetition in Biblical narrative and to think of events in their proper or logical order, not necessarily that which they seem to possess. He must place the process before its result in his own mind, although the Biblical narrative may describe the result before it describes the events that led to it. Moreover, several series of descriptions, given in differing varieties of symbolic language, do not necessarily tell of different events.

Rule Seven: This is similar to *Rule One,* only it requires care in distinguishing between statements made regarding the devil and those regarding the wicked, who in a manner may be held to be his Body.

Having, then, briefly given his readers these Rules as meet for his and their guidance, Bede ends his preface by stating that he has divided his *Explanation of the Revelation* into three short books for their relief; for, as blessed Augustine remarked, the reader's energy is refreshed by the pause at the end of a book just as a traveller breaks his hard journey at an inn. He has, moreover, tried to write in a manner clear, concise, and brief, because his nation, the English people, is lazy of mind and has been decidedly lacking in enthusiasm for intellectual study of that Faith received not long ago under blessed Gregory. Words few and clear, declares Bede, stay in the memory better than lengthy discussions.

He now began the commentary. We shall glance at his sources in their chronological order: [88]

Victorinus, bishop of Pettau in Upper Pannonia (modern Austria) and martyr, probably under Diocletian in 304 A.D., had written in addition to other works, now lost, a *Commentary on the Apocalypse.*[89] In this he revealed three details concerning himself as a student of this book of the Bible: First, he interpreted it, in part at least, according to what is called the Contemporary-Historical method, which explained the events described in figurative language as actual ones, known to the writer in his own life time. Thus in his explanation of chapter 17 he dated the Revelation in the time of

---

[88] R. H. Charles: *Revelation of Saint John, ICC* I, 1920, clxxxiiif.; *Studies in the Apocalypse,* 1913, 10f.; *Lectures on the Apocalypse,* 1923, 1ff.; Laistner, in Thompson, 252ff.

[89] J. Haussleiter, ed. *Victorini episc. Petav. Opera, CSEL* XLIX, 16ff.

Domitian;[90] the agonies which were besetting the Church under Domitian's reign were described in the vision of evil appearing to the seer. Likewise, in chapter 13, the beast rising out of the sea was the Emperor Nero, who had so persecuted the Christians that, when the Revelation was written under Domitian, many people were still expecting Nero to return again, to war against the saints until he should be conquered by God. Secondly, Victorinus introduced the theory of "Recapitulation" into his commentary, declaring that the three series of plagues—of the seven seals, of the seven trumpets, of the seven golden vials—described one and the same course of events. Thirdly, Victorinus was a Chiliast; that is, he believed from Revelation XX that, after the end of this world, the righteous would literally reign a thousand years in rest and blessedness with Christ before the Final Judgment should come to all. The millennium to him was the "first resurrection" in this sense.

Tyconius in his commentary, written in the latter half of this same fourth century, turned toward allegorical and spiritual interpretation of the visions recorded in the Revelation, without, however, wholly forsaking the Contemporary-Historical method. Allegory had attracted him through the Greek Alexandrian school of interpretation in the writings of its exponents of the third century, Clement of Alexandria and Origen. He followed Victorinus in his theory of "Recapitulation," but he rejected Chiliasm. With him the millennium, the "thousand years of the first resurrection," meant the Christian era between the coming of Christ Incarnate to this world and the end of time in His second coming to judge the world.

Saint Jerome, who died in 420, also partook of both the historical and the allegorizing methods. He made a thorough revision of the commentary of Victorinus, deleted all his Chili-

[90] *Ibid.*, 118, lines 9f.

astic doctrine, and inserted much which he took from the commentary of Tyconius.[91]

Saint Augustine wrote his *City of God* between 413 and 426. We have seen that he was indebted to Tyconius for the seven Rules which govern Biblical interpretation. He owed much, also, to the commentary of Tyconius. From it he drew inspiration for his teaching on the Two Cities, of God and of the devil, although Tyconius used the figure in explaining the vision of the Revelation, whereas Augustine extended it in a meaning far more wide and deep. It was Augustine who established as the tradition of centuries the allegorical explanation of the book as distinct from the Contemporary-Historical. For him, as for Tyconius, the "thousand years" meant our Christian era; it was for him a purely symbolic number. During this indefinite era the "first resurrection" was and is proceeding; it means the saving of elect souls by Divine grace from the "second death," of the soul, at the Day of Judgment. So, he taught, shall the "second resurrection" at this Last Day end the "first death," of the body in this world. To Augustine Chiliasm was a heresy.

In the sixth century, Primasius, bishop of Hadrumetum in northern Africa, who died about 560 A.D., wrote another commentary on the Apocalypse.[92] In this work he followed the allegorical method of Tyconius and of Augustine, their rejection of Chiliasm, and the theory of "Recapitulation" of Victorinus and of Tyconius.

We come now to the position of Bede. The commentary of Victorinus-Jerome was later revised in two more versions, to which the names Ø and S have been assigned. Bede read Victorinus in one of these latter versions and borrowed its very wording for his own book; he laid its scene of John's exile under Domitian; the theory of "Recapitulation" was also

[91] *Ibid.*, 14ff.   [92] *PL* LXVIII, coll. 793ff.

his.[93] He not only drew in his work upon the Rules of Tyconius, but he also used the Tyconius commentary freely; he followed Augustine in using the allegorical method of explaining the Revelation and owed much to the eschatological doctrine expressed in Augustine's *City of God*. Finally, he often copied passages *verbatim* from the commentary of Primasius and occasionally used, at second hand, matter drawn from this, originally derived from Victorinus-Jerome.[94]

As an example of the allegorical interpretation put forward here by Bede, we may take the meaning of the twelve precious stones which garnish the wall of the City of God.[95] The jasper here typifies the fresh green of unfading faith; the sapphire's blue raises men's thoughts to heavenly things; the chalcedon, that gives out its brilliance under the open sky, resembles holy souls bidden by God to let their light shine before men; the emerald, whose lustre sheds its green on all that it reaches, tells of that living faith which vivifies dormant souls; the sardonyx, shining red and white at different angles, symbolizes the red glow of bodily passion conquered by Christian purity; the sardis is blood-red with the glory of martyrs; the chrysolite reflects the golden radiance of true wisdom; the beryl, sparkling as water in sunlight, shows human intellect illumined by spiritual grace; the topaz loses its yellow fire if it be rubbed, as Christian souls lose their beauty in the attrition of this busy world; the chrysoprase, of green shot with gold, dwells under the sun of India as Christians under the Sun of righteousness; the hyacinth is dull on cloudy days but shines in the sun, like him who weeps or rejoices in sympathy with sorrow or glad-

---

[93] *Cf.* Giles XII, 344, 373. Bede held the traditional view that the writer of the Revelation, of the Fourth Gospel, and of the Johannine Epistles, was one and the same John. For modern theories see Charles, *ICC op. cit.* (p. 259 *supra*, note 88) ; Ernest Findlay Scott, *The Literature of the New Testament*, 1932, 230ff.

[94] *Cf.* Laistner, in Thompson, 253.

[95] Rev. XXI, 19f.; Giles XII, 437ff.

ness; the amethyst unites the royal purple of the King of kings with the violet of His humility.

And truly this last symbolic amethyst might be thought to reflect Bede himself. In this book he confesses how little he has done, how lightly he has touched a theme so deep. He begs his readers to give thanks to God if he has led them aright; if he has done otherwise than he would, may they add their prayers to his own for his forgiveness from the Lord. May they reward his toil by their remembrance of him before Heaven, and may they win by their merit the substance of that Tree of life, the shadow of which he has tried to show them from afar.[96]

It was probably after writing on the Apocalypse that Bede began his *Expositio in Acta Apostolorum*,[97] although we cannot determine relatively the dates of his many commentaries. We do know that this, too, was written before 716, as Eusebius was still a simple "brother" in its preface. This preface was a letter addressed to Acca as bishop, and Acca, whom Wilfrid just before his death in 709 had chosen as abbot of Hexham, succeeded Wilfrid that same year as bishop of Hexham, and thus as Bede's own diocesan. We reach, therefore, a date between 709 and 716 for the completion of this commentary. There is reason, however, for believing that Bede had been making notes for some years on the text of Acts and that he put these together to make his book.

He thanks his bishop in the preface for many letters written to encourage his pursuit of Biblical study, says that he has sent him the commentary on the Apocalypse to be copied for the bishop's use, and that he is tremendously keen to work on

[96] Giles, *ibid.*, 446, 452.
[97] We have here the text edited by Laistner, 1939; see bibliography *infra*. To his introduction of that edition the reader is referred for information regarding manuscripts, editions, date, sources, place-names; also for various indices.

the Gospel of Saint Luke. But various hindrances have stood in the way, the appalling labour involved and other obstreperous worries which Acca knows well enough. Exactly what had been troubling him is uncertain; very probably it was the charge of heresy mentioned in his letter to Plegwin.[98] As an apology, Bede continues, for delay in writing a more considerable work, he is now sending Acca something, at least, from Saint Luke—a little book on the Acts of the Apostles which he has just put together and finished as quickly as he could, not to disappoint his bishop. In it he has tried to bring out allegorical meaning from the narrative and to explain its obscurities. In the mystical teaching he has found Arator very helpful.

This Arator was a subdeacon of the Church in Rome who wrote about 544 an exceedingly bad poem on this same book of Acts; he then made a vast reputation by reading part of it in the church of Saint Peter *ad Vincula* to Pope Vigilius himself and a company of bishops and priests. His importance to Bede lay in the fact that his poem, which we still possess, was full of allegory.[99] And Bede was steadily falling deep in love with allegory. Other sources on which he drew were those he had read so well: Jerome, Rufinus, Augustine, Gregory the Great, and Isidore of Seville.

The manuscripts of the Acts of the Apostles used by him in writing this book are of much interest.[100] Abbot Ceolfrid

[98] Laistner, ed. *Acts*, xvi.
[99] For Arator see Manitius, *Gesch.*, 162ff.; for Bede's use of Arator see Laistner, *ibid.*, xxxviii, 3, 13, 27, 36f., 55, 64, 71, 73, 76.
[100] Laistner, *ibid.*, xxxixf., also in *HTR* XXX, 1937, 37ff.; Kenyon, *Our Bible and the Ancient Manuscripts*, 1939, 175f., 148; H. J. White, *Studia Biblica* II, 1890, 273ff.; Leclercq, *DACL* s.v. Ceolfrid, coll. 3262ff.; Lowe, *CLA* II, Nos. 177, 251, 150, 260; III, No. 299, and in *Speculum* III, 1928, 13; Souter, *The Text and Canon of the New Testament*, 1913, 91f. On the *Codex Laudianus* Lowe (*CLA* II, 37) remarks that "Bede, in his commentary on Acts, uses a text in remarkable agreement with this unique MS., but it should be noted that no marginalia in Anglo-Saxon script occur"; *cf.* Laistner, *Acts*, xl.

was as keen a lover of books as Benedict Biscop had been; through the energetic labours of the two, one after another, the library of Wearmouth-Jarrow had constantly been enlarged. We have noted, moreover, that some of the monks were occupied in copying manuscripts. Thus it had come about that under Ceolfrid three copies were made, at either Wearmouth or Jarrow, of a text of the Bible brought back by Ceolfrid or by Biscop from Italy. This text was very probably that of the Vulgate of Saint Jerome, revised by the Roman noble, Cassiodorus, in the monastery which he founded about 540 A.D. at Vivarium in southern Italy.[101] These three copies and their original were available for Bede, since they were finished by 716. One of them is now in the Laurentian Library at Florence, known to all the student world as the *Codex Amiatinus* because it lay in the abbey of Monte Amiata near Siena from the ninth century until the eighteenth. It is written on large leaves of 19½ by 13½ inches in beautifully clear uncials with decoration in gold and vivid colours. As satisfactory as the preservation of this marvellous work of art, made in England between 690 and 716, is the finding of eleven leaves of one of its two sister manuscripts, dating from the same place and time; one was discovered in 1909 and the others within very recent years. They show passages from the two books of Kings. The fact that these three copies were written in uncial letters points to an Italian original; it is possible, though not inevitable, that they were made in Bede's monastery by an Italian scribe brought to England by Biscop or by Ceolfrid for the purpose.

The most important Old Latin text used by Bede in this commentary was the Latin half of the bilingual *Codex Laudi-*

---

[101] See Dom J. Chapman, *Early History of the Vulgate Gospels*, 3f., 20, 23. But *cf.* the same author in *RB* XXXVIII, 1926, 139ff.; XXXIX, 1927, 12ff.; XL, 1928, 130ff., and A. van de Vyver, *Speculum* VI, 1931, 266.

anus, so called because it was given to the Bodleian by Archbishop Laud; it is still in Oxford. The Latin script (e) is in the left column and the Greek (E) in the right; it seems to have been written in Sardinia during the seventh century and brought to England either by Archbishop Theodore when he arrived in 669 or, more probably, by Biscop or by Ceolfrid on their return from the continent.[102]

When we come to study Bede's writing on Acts, we shall do well to remember that "there are seventy-seven extant manuscripts, no less than fourteen of these having been copied before A.D. 900."[103] Further proof is not needed of the eagerness with which students read his notes upon the Bible. Here, as elsewhere, he discusses variations of texts; he compares Greek with Latin, not always felicitously; he gives details of geography, chronology, and mythology; he borrows, at times too trustfully, a meaning for words from Jerome and other authority;[104] he imparts Scriptural tradition. The more we read, the more we realize how extraordinarily wide for that time was his knowledge of the books useful in his task. He treats of theology; for example, the question "so often asked," whether persons baptized in ignorance but in good faith by those who themselves are not baptized require re-baptism, is answered by Acts XIX, 1–5.[105] He inveighs sturdily against heretics and explains the meaning of the word "heresy" itself. He points out the errors of copyists. Nor is good counsel forgotten; on the "sharp contention" between Paul and Barnabas he observes, "Do not think this was a sin. It is not wrong to be angry, but to be angry without strong and just cause."

[102] *Cf.* E. A. Lowe, *Speculum* III, 1928, 12ff. Possibly Bede may also have known the Codex F *(Fuldensis:* see p. 454 *infra,* note 251; *cf.* Laistner, *HTR* XXX, 1937, 43. It may also have been brought to England by Biscop: Chapman, *Early Hist.* 188.

[103] Laistner, *TRHS* 93.

[104] Jerome, *Liber de nominibus Hebraicis; Liber de situ et nominibus locorum Hebraicorum: PL* XXIII, coll. 815–976.

[105] Laistner, *Acts,* 70; *cf. Homilies:* Giles V, 110.

Great energy is given, of course, to drawing out the meaning of words either in a literal or an allegorical sense:

The former treatise have I made, O Theophilus, of all that Jesus began both to do and teach:
The book of Acts was written by Luke the physician for the healing of every lover of God. And note, that "doing" comes here before "teaching." [106]

And a cloud received Him out of their sight:
All creation pays homage in the Bible to its Creator. The stars of night revealed His birth, night hid his sufferings, clouds received Him ascending into heaven, and shall bring Him once again to judge the world.

Others mocking said, These men are full of new wine:
Despite their mocking they spoke truly. For here was not the old wine, now drained, of the marriage of the Law with the Church, but the new wine of spiritual grace, poured into new vessels.

That at least the shadow of Peter passing by might overshadow some of them:
So the Church of God, founded on the rock that is Peter, marches on its way, casting its shadow of healing on those who lie sick and helpless by the wayside.

A great sheet knit at the four corners, and let down to the earth; wherein were all manner of four-footed beasts of the earth, and creeping things, and fowls of the air. This was done thrice:
Herein lie types of divers kinds of men, gathered from the four quarters of the earth, cleansed by baptism in the Name of God, Three in One. So unclean men in Holy Writ are likened to the beasts that perish: Herod to a fox, the Pharisees to vipers, shameless men to dogs, the lustful to swine, the proud to birds comfortable in their nests.

Gird thyself and bind on thy sandals:
The prison floor was very hard and Peter's cell was very cold. So he had taken off his sandals and tucked his robe snugly around

[106] *Cf. In Lucam:* Giles X, 376.

his bare feet to rest and warm them. So, also, we may relax our "rule of life" sometimes, when we are sick or in trouble.[107]

In the preface to this work on Acts Bede told his bishop Acca that he was also sending him a commentary on the Epistle of Saint John.[108] Presumably, therefore, this work was written at about the same time as that on Acts. It is also probable that Bede produced his commentaries on the rest of the General or "Catholic" Epistles within the same period, between the years 709 and 716.[109]

He finds explanation for the placing first of the Letter of James, "the Lord's brother," in that he was leader of the Church in Jerusalem.[110] This James Bede describes elsewhere, in accordance with Jerome, as the apostle who was son of Alphaeus, as "cousin" (not literally "brother") of the Lord, as born of Mary, sister of the Blessed Virgin. He goes on to narrate, also from Jerome, details of the life of this apostle and bishop: that he was surnamed "the Just," that he abstained from all meat, wine and strong drink, was never shaved, never entered the public baths, never wore woollen but always linen clothing, and prayed alone in the Temple so long that his knees became hard as a camel's, that he was a bishop for thirty years after the Lord's Passion and then himself was martyred.[111]

In general, these commentaries of Bede on the Epistles are in marked contrast to those on the Revelation and on Acts; they enlarge on spiritual and practical progress in the good life rather than on allegorical conceptions and scientific en-

---

[107] Laistner, *ibid.*, 6, 8, 17, 28, 47, 54.
[108] Giles XII, 269ff.   [109] Plummer I, cxlvii.
[110] That Bede's commentary on the Epistle of St. James was written at a different time from that on the Epistles of St. John is shown by Laistner, *TRHS* 85, note 2. Text in Giles XII, 158ff.
[111] Giles XII, 157; Jerome, *De vir. ill.* c. 2: *PL* XXIII, coll. 639ff.; Bede, *In Lucam*: Giles XI, 12f.; Ropes, *ICC St. James*, 1916, 57ff.; Dimont, in *A New Commentary on Holy Scripture*, ed. Gore-Goudge-Guillaume, 1928, II, 628f.

quiries.[112] Thus, in this interpretation of the words of James, Bede sets forward the three ways in which temptation may catch the unwary: by suggesting, by delighting, finally by winning consent.[113] He paints the folly of talking, the merit of silence: "It is safer to hear the truth than to preach it. For the hearer saves his humility; scarcely will the preacher escape, be it but a little boastfulness." Naturally, the tongue receives special treatment. All beasts, declares Bede, may be conquered. Here illustration is drawn, from the Elder Pliny, of an asp, most terrible of serpents, that was tamed in Egypt by the father of a household and came day by day from its hole to receive its daily "allowance" from the family table.[114] Yet the poisonous tongue is more dreadful, he warns, for no mortal man may conquer it. Life really shall begin for the just man when he shall attain true knowledge in the eternity to come;[115] the man of malicious tongue shall be carried away as smoke upon the air. So, too, they who are rich only for themselves shall not only be forever tormented by real, visible fire of hell, but by the inner pain of memory, as they think back upon lost opportunities of cleansing their souls in charity. No! with the tongue let a man believe God, that His words are true; let him believe in God, that He is very God; let him believe through God, which is truly to love Him. With the tongue, therefore, let him praise the Lord, and pray for himself and his fellows, for time and for eternity; let him confess his little daily sins to his fellow-Christians, that by intercession of his friends day by day he may be forgiven; let him tell his foul and leprous offences to the priest, according to the Church's ordinance, and find purifying by ghostly prescription and command.

[112] K. Werner, 200.
[113] Plummer points out (II, 54f.) Bede's following here of Gregory, *Moralia* IV, c. 27, par. 49: *PL* LXXV, col. 661.
[114] *Hist. Nat.* X, c. 74, par. 96.   [115] *Cf. Homilies:* Giles V, 74.

Bede, therefore, prescribes the sacrament of Penance for grievous offenders. He prescribes it also for those who are sick in body because of the sins of their souls. "If," he writes, "the sick are guilty of sins and shall confess these to the priests of the Church and shall truly endeavour to forsake them and amend their lives, their sins shall be forgiven them. For sins cannot be forgiven without the confession of amendment."

The sacrament of holy Unction, bidden for the sick by Saint James, was well-known in Bede's eighth century. "The custom of the Church still prevails," he writes, "that the sick be anointed with consecrated oil by the priests, that with the prayer that attends this unction they may find healing for their ills. And not only priests," he continues, "but, as Pope Innocent declared" (in a letter written in 416), "all Christians may use the oil of anointing in their own need or that of those belonging to them; but the oil must be blessed by bishops." [116]

In regard to the First Epistle of Saint Peter, Bede adheres to the tradition of the early Christian Church that it was written by Peter at Rome, described by the name of Babylon, in the time of Claudius Caesar (41–54 A.D.).[117] Modern theory either accepts Peter as author and dates the Epistle in Nero's reign (54–68 A.D.), or rejects Petrine authorship and assigns it to the time of Domitian (81–96 A.D.).[118] Now and again Bede is concerned here with various readings of the text. Thus we find the Old Latin "Visitor of your souls," standing in his work side by side with the Vulgate "Bishop." We find the Old Latin, "He preached unto those imprisoned in the flesh," *in carne* (meaning that the Lord through Noah and other

[116] Giles XII, 164, 167, 175, 184, 194ff., 201; *cf.* V. 198f., 420f.; X, 26; Puller, *The Anointing of the Sick in Scripture and Tradition,* 1910, 48ff.; Maclean, *s.v. Unction*: Hastings, *ERE* 512, note 9, and 513.

[117] Giles XII, 242; I St. Peter V, 13; Jerome, *De vir. ill.* c. 8: *PL* XXIII, col. 654.

[118] See Bigg, *ICC St. Peter and St. Jude,* 1901, 87; Kirsopp Lake and Silva Lake, *Introduction to the New Testament,* 1937, 165ff.; Scott, *op. cit.* (p. 262 *supra,* note 93) 219ff.

holy men warned the sinners alive here on earth before the Flood), standing side by side with the Vulgate reading *in carcere* (explained as referring to those imprisoned in Hades for their disobedience in the days of Noah, to whom the Lord descended after His death to offer the preaching of repentance). Bede rejects this view, declaring that the Lord descended into Hades for the sake of His faithful alone, and that repentance of sins is preached in this life, not to the spirits of the departed. Instead of the reading, "have fervent charity," he uses the Vulgate *continuam,* in the sense of "continual." For "think it not strange concerning the fiery trial which is to try you," he gives the Old Latin *mirari,* to wonder; he also quotes the Vulgate *peregrinari,* explaining this in its literal sense: "do not deem yourselves strangers to Christ in your fiery trial." Instead of "the Church which is in Babylon, co-elect with you," as the Vulgate has it, he writes "the Church collected at Babylon," and explains the phrase as describing the City of God mingled in this world with the City of the devil.[119] His authorities here, besides the four greater Latin Fathers, include Cyprian, and, from the Greek, Athanasius and John Chrysostom, whose treatise on the doctrine "that no one can be harmed by any save himself" he advises his students to read.[120]

The detailed comment, albeit so largely borrowed, shows once again Bede as both a teacher of practical virtue and of spiritual mystery. Like Aldhelm, he warns cloistered women against luxury of dress; they, he tells them, can plead no husbands in excuse. He warns the intellectually-minded that to know of God is far different from knowing Him. Truly a man must first learn with his mind through reading or listening to others; yet shall he never progress toward contemplation of

[119] I St. Peter II, 25; III, 19; IV, 8, 12; V, 13; Giles XII, 223, 229, 235ff., 242; Bigg, 150, 162f., 172.
[120] Laistner, *TRHS* 87, 91, *cf.* 92; Giles XII, 211, 222, 226, 228.

the Divine Majesty save he be reborn and fed by the sacraments of the Church. Then the more he gazes in contemplation, the more shall he hunger anew for the same, even as the
angels in heaven, never content; he alone who knows not has
no care to know. Thus the faithful raise in mystic building
God's Sanctuary on earth. The Lord is the foundation; the
first stones rest their weight on Him, and then each stone, supported by its fellow immediately beneath, adds its part to the
rising whole. Only those dead in heresy, or in evil life, are
cast aside as of no profit to the work; of these none shall be
saved.[121]

Doubt cast upon Saint Peter's authorship of the Second
Epistle had reached Bede's eye from the writings of Jerome;
he followed Jerome in holding it genuine, and he cited the
account of the Transfiguration as proof of this.[122] Modern
scholarship holds it written long after Peter's time.[123] In this
Second Epistle the words, "No prophecy of the Scripture is of
any private interpretation," draw from him much emphasis, as
was natural in one who so seldom allowed his own thoughts to
find place among those of patristic authority.[124] "How foolish," he exclaims, "to compare to the varied sounds made by
man's breath playing upon a flute the inspiring of the prophets
by the Divine Spirit! Can the lifeless flute understand the
sound which it gives forth? Let the learned interpret as the
Spirit shall guide them, and let the simple listen in humility."
"All heretics pervert the Scriptures," and Bede gives here a
most formidable list of these "false prophets," with a description of the particular untruth characterizing each sect.[125] To
the six ages of this present world, of which he treated in his

[121] Giles XII, 209, 212ff., 224.
[122] Ibid., 158, 250; Jerome, Epist. 120: CSEL LV, 508; Epist. 53:
ibid., LIV, 463; Bigg, 199f.
[123] Lake and Lake, 167f.; Scott, 228f.; cf. Bigg, 242ff.
[124] Giles XII, 251f., 267.
[125] Ibid., 258.

On Times, he adds here, from Augustine, first the seventh which is the Sabbath of the saints, in which they rest in peace until the Day of Judgment, then the eighth, the age of eternity for both soul and body, both of the saved and of the lost.[126]

Much of Bede's comment on the First Epistle of Saint John,[127] as he himself tells us, was taken from the *Tractates* of Augustine [128] dealing with that same Epistle; he used also Augustine's *De videndo Deo,* the commentary of Ambrose on Saint Luke's Gospel, and Jerome, *Against Jovinian.*[129] The work is assigned to the Apostle John, and its twofold aim is described: the glory of the true Christian life in the unity of the Church, and the wickedness of heresy. Here, again, is found stout polemic. He inveighs against Cerinthus and Marcion, against "the insanity of the Manichaeans," against Apelles, against Nestor, against the Arians and the Donatists, and, especially, against the Pelagians who believe that a man's natural grace *might* enable him to live without sin. Bede had read the *Lament* of Gildas on his England; he had read, too, the *Life of Saint Germanus,* which told how this "foul pestilence" had brought the bishops Germanus and Lupus from Gaul in the fifth century to Britain for the confuting of its lies.[130]

Concerning the authorship of the second and third of the Johannine Epistles, Bede records the doubt of earlier times, but continues: "They are now accounted the work of the Apostle John by general consent of the Church, since they are so like in word and faith to the First Epistle and since they

---

[126] Augustine, *De civ. Dei* XXII, 30. *Cf.* Giles V (*Homilies*), 128ff., 161.
[127] Giles XII, 269ff.   [128] *Ibid.,* 4.
[129] *Ibid.,* 304, 313, 319. He also borrowed *verbatim* a long passage from Augustine, *De Sermone Domini in Monte,* c. 73: PL XXXIV, coll. 1265f.
[130] Plummer I, li; II, 31f.

abjure heretics with equal zeal." [131] He thinks it worth while to emphasize holy John's detestation of heresy by telling two stories of Polycarp, "John's disciple": how Polycarp rushed from the baths at Ephesus the minute he saw the heretic Cerinthus in the building, terrified lest it might fall down through the presence of such an enemy of truth; how also Polycarp met Marcion by chance one day, and, in answer to his request for an introduction, called him "the eldest son of Satan." [132] The "Gaius" of the Third Epistle, contrary to modern scholarship, which leaves him unknown,[133] Bede identifies with the citizen of that name with whom Saint Paul stayed at Corinth.

Lastly, the Epistle of Jude must be held genuine, he declares, again following Jerome.[134] He did not know, we may think, the commentary on these Catholic Epistles, written by Didymus the Blind, although this had been translated into Latin in the sixth century by Epiphanius, friend of Cassiodorus of Vivarium.[135]

For a long time now he had wanted to write on the Gospel of Saint Luke, but he had not yet dared. It was one thing to comment on the words of apostles, another to try to interpret the words of the Lord Himself. Luke, however, especially attracted him because he saw an affinity between the physician, the healer of the body, and the teacher, the healer of the

---

[131] Giles XII, 321f.; Jerome, *De vir. ill.* c. 9: *PL* XXIII, col. 655. For modern views see Brooke, *ICC The Johannine Epistles,* 1912, lxxiii ff.; Lake and Lake, 168ff.

[132] Giles XII, 324. See K. Werner, 203, on Bede's dating of heretics.

[133] Giles, *ibid.;* Romans XVI, 23; Brooke, lxxxi, 181f.

[134] Jerome, *De vir. ill.* c. 4: *PL* XXIII, col. 646. On the modern question as to its authorship see Bigg, 317ff.

[135] Cassiodorus, *Inst.* ed. Mynors, 1937, 22, 29f. For the tradition of Jude, verse 9, of which Bede owns ignorance (Giles XII, 330) see Charles, *The Assumption of Moses,* 1897; Burkitt, *HDB* III, 450. On Bede's extracts from Augustine's comments discussing the Pauline Epistles (still extant but unpublished), see Dom André Wilmart, *RB* XXXVIII, 1926, 16ff., and Laistner, *Hand-List,* 37f.

soul,[136] and, perhaps, because Bede himself greatly longed to
heal and to teach by his own labours. It was therefore a joy
when he received a letter from his bishop Acca, chiding him
because he had failed to write on Saint Luke.[137]

"I have often suggested," Acca wrote, "both by letter and
in our conversations that you should follow your work on
Acts by another on Saint Luke's Gospel. But you always make
two excuses—that the undertaking is so formidable, and that
it has already been done by no less a writer than Saint Ambrose. What else, you say, would you do but merely repeat his
words or write others less worth reading?

"To all of this I answer in the saying of the comic poet,
'There is nothing said that has not been said before';[138] that,
as charity upholds all things, it becomes no man to envy or to
provoke another, but each man to offer all that lies within
him for the glory of the house of the Lord. The Catholic Faith
remains the same for each writer, but each treats of it in his
own particular style. In this way very many persons may be
taught, each in the way that suits him best.

"It is quite true that parts of the commentary of Ambrose
on Saint Luke are very subtle, very deep; only scholars can
understand them. Yet Augustine when he wrote *On the Vision
of God* for the nun Paulina dealt very largely with this same
commentary, explaining its matter in simple language. I think
that was very wise. So will you please write your book on Saint
Luke and publish this letter of mine as a preface to it, in order
that all may understand that I asked you to write in clear and
plain words for those of plain education?

"Besides all this, there are matters which Saint Ambrose
did not discuss; he was so learned that he did not see their

[136] Giles XII, 2.
[137] X, 265ff. The letter of Acca and Bede's reply are summarized in
my description.
[138] Terence, *Eunuchus*, Prologue, line 41.

difficulty. Would you please explain these, too, either by the words of other Fathers or by your own? I am sure that the Author of light will aid a student who works as hard as you do, night and day. And again, surely it is proper that you, so free from worldly business, should follow without ceasing after true wisdom and attain a clearer understanding; so shall you at last with pure heart behold the King in His beauty.

"I think, too, that I ought to tell you that some people are worried because in that part of Revelation which deals with the four animals you gave a new interpretation—of Matthew as a lion and of Mark as a man. It has been the other way round: Matthew pictured as a man because he wrote of the Manhood of the Lord, Mark as a lion because he wrote of 'the voice roaring in the desert.' Would you tell in your work what you think on this question?

"The God of love and peace keep you and give you light, my revered brother."

To these words of encouragement Bede speedily replied:

"Your trust in me, holy Father, in actually sending me a preface to put in front of a book not yet even begun, would make me ashamed not to start at once.[139] Indeed, I did begin this labour—a very difficult one, since, to say nothing of innumerable duties in the monastery, I have to make my own shorthand notes while reading my sources, to copy out the passages I take from these, and to write my books themselves with my own hand. And there are so many sources, so important and so impressive! I must diligently examine what blessed Ambrose, what Augustine, what Gregory, the apostle of our race (so well called Gregory, the Vigilant!), what Jerome, what other Fathers have said in their works about the words of Saint Luke. Then, since there is so much that is theirs for me to include and since I do not want to be thought a thief in

[139] Bede wrote his *St. Luke* between 709 and 716.

putting down as mine what is really theirs, I have decided to
place the first letter of the name of each authority in the
margin, against each passage taken from his writings. I beg
and pray that these marks be copied from my original if at
some future time my works shall be judged worthy of repro-
duction. There *are* some things of my own which I have
thought good to add here and there, revealed to me, as you
said, by the Author of light. I don't really work 'night and
day'; but it is quite true that I do toil hard to reach a right
judgment on all that I read.

"As to the 'new interpretation' of Matthew and Mark in
the Apocalypse, those critics of mine, whoever they are, ought
to have known that I took it from ancient patristic sources,
especially from Saint Augustine's book, *The Harmony of the
Evangelists*.[140] There he explains Matthew under symbol of a
lion, since Matthew emphasized the royal Christ, the Lion of
the tribe of Juda, worshipped by rulers from the East, feared
by Herod the king. Luke, symbolized by a calf, tells of the
Victim of priestly sacrifice, of His consecration to priesthood
from infancy; Mark tells of the Lord as very Man and of His
life on earth; John as an eagle rises above the clouds of our
human unknowing.

"This explanation, holy Father, I am putting in the preface
to my *Saint Luke* as witness against the aspersions of those
who have complained. Pray for me, and may the Aid from on
high keep and strengthen you for the defence of His holy
Church." It is obvious from such a letter as this that Bede was
very sensitive concerning his work, as one who left no stone
unturned lest he be found by error to lead astray those whom
he longed to enlighten.

The information he gives here of the signs which mark the

[140] *De cons. evang.* I, c. 6: *CSEL* XLIII, 9; Bede quotes here exten-
sively from this. *Cf.* Jerome, *Commentary on St. Matthew*, Preface: *PL*
XXVI, col. 19.

extent of his individual borrowings is of much importance. At
present it is impossible to distinguish in many of his works
between the innumerable passages inserted by him in verbal
copying from very many Latin works or Latin translations of
Greek works, and the comparatively small amount of his own
original contribution. Repeatedly the need has been urged of
an editing of his commentaries and other treatises which shall
rescue them from their present state of neglect. In the meantime every student of his work is grateful to those scholars who
have given us excellent editions of his texts or have fulfilled
research on them.[141]

This commentary of Bede does, indeed, view the Gospel of
Luke as emphasizing the Priesthood of our Lord.[142] It begins
with the priesthood of Zacharias; it tells of the Christ as
priestly Intercessor for His enemies, as Priest and Victim upon
the Cross; it ends with the apostles offering praise to God in
His Temple, as priests of the new order to come. So, Bede
comments, the Lord still stands at the altar as Priest by the
side of His ministers, and woe to that one whose hand betrays
Him at the table.[143] As Zacharias was alone, free from natural
ties, during the days of his ministry before God, so must the
Catholic priest always serve the altar in the freedom of chastity. Not only, however, must he watch before the Lord without cease. He must care for the flock committed to him, teaching each one according to individual need; and for his aid the
grace of the Lord shall shine in greater measure round about
him. But let not those dare to preach and teach the gospel who
lack due ability, or learning, or experience; let them sit still

[141] In regard to Bede's commentary on St. Luke such research has
been done by Laistner, in pointing out extant MSS. of this work which
show the marginalia copied from the original: see *JTS* XXXIV, 1933,
350ff., and Thompson, 237f. *Cf.* Souter (see p. 264 *supra,* note 100), viii;
Plummer I, xxiii, note 3.
[142] K. Werner, 197f.
[143] Giles XI, 392, 364, 366, 334.

until they be endued with power from on high.[144] Did not the Lord Himself wait thirty years before He began His ministry? And does not Holy Scripture impress upon us that God never hurries, but always abides the fulfillment of time? So with holy Elizabeth, so with blessed Mary; so Solomon "finished all his house" and Abraham died "full of years"; so the Lord who came to enfold all mankind in His reign of peace and order was born just when all the world was being ordered anew under the peace of Augustus. On the other hand, let none who shall be bidden to office in the Church refuse or answer slothfully by excuse, as a wicked servant laying up his talent in a napkin.[145]

All men are called to serve God: first, in Himself, by adoration; secondly, in His creatures, by charity of service. Within the Church are three classes of human beings, each giving of its will and knowledge to the whole. In the night of this world's sorrow her priests live as men in the field; her monks and nuns as those in the bed of tranquillity, asleep to worldly distractions; her laity as women busy in the mill of secular duties, grinding their minds in restless thought. Of these, some shall be welcomed at the last as faithful servants; the others shall be left to the reward of their neglect.[146]

Yet the monastic state is the safer, the state of one bound by the vow of poverty not only to refuse to cleave to the things of this world, for that is the duty of every Christian, but to abandon them altogether. This state is for the few and the perfect in Christ, for those to whom poverty in act means nothing without poverty in will. Nevertheless, there are many who surrender their wealth, yet cleave to their own desire. Those do not follow the Lord who enter the cloister for praise of men, or buy and sell office in their congregation, as thieves

---

[144] X, 283, 312, 339, 355; XI, 173, 390; cf. Homilies, V, 189, 348.
[145] X, 298; XI, 280f.   [146] X, 370; XI, 255ff.

in the house of prayer; who run from their cells to visit kinsmen they have left behind in the world and thus neglect their
vocation to stability; who presume to question why one
aspirant is chosen and another dismissed, as though it were
theirs already to rule.[147] But the joy of the monastic life out-
weighs its trials and temptations: the joy of brotherhood in
the unity of the Three Counsels. And all is not hard work.
"Pray without ceasing" bids the monk to try always to serve
God; it does not mean he must always be hungry and thirsty,
always chanting Office, always praying or studying or teaching
or keeping silence or working in the garden. Sometimes the
community must relax for the sake of guarding these very
obligations.[148]

Of patristic teaching Bede gives much in these many pages.
The Christ, very God and very Man, is preached again and
again.[149] The Virgin Birth is stressed in many ways. Mary's
question to the angel Gabriel reveals that she had already
dedicated herself to the virgin life. We must not believe with
Helvidius, the target of Jerome's attack, that other sons were
born afterward to her; nor with Photinus, another of Jerome's
heretics of the fourth century, that Joseph was father of the
Lord. Joseph is indeed named "father" by Saint Luke, but
only in the sense of the most intimate guardian of the Christ-
Child.[150]

Heaven, in Bede's words, is the soul's rest in the Beatific
Vision, the glory of light, the refreshment of eternal peace.
There the angels stand always, as Gabriel, in the presence of
God; even although their outer selves appear to men on earth,
yet their inner selves, in the Spirit Who is God, are ever con-

[147] XI, 207, 265, 364, 293, 114, 123, 267ff.; cf. V, 409.
[148] XI, 258, 339f.; cf. V, 68f.
[149] X, 354, 290; cf. V, 71: *rogabit Patrem per humanitatem qui dabit
cum Patre per divinitatem.*
[150] X, 310, 292; cf. V, 26, 338, 364, 385f., 405.

templating Him. Death brings to every man his own particular
judgment and knocks upon his door by illness in warning.
He who loves Death as the messenger of God opens the door
quickly; he who has despised God, the Judge, dreads to see
Him.

Few, indeed, Bede teaches from Augustine, will be saved in
comparison with the multitude of the damned. The souls elect
have merit of good works done on this earth; they look
forward with joy and assurance to the Last Judgment when
their bliss shall be made perfect by the union once again of
body with soul. Mingled with their ineffable happiness shall
be the comfort of beholding the souls of the lost, through the
vision of God in Whom they can see all creation; [151] their
love and pity, so needful on earth, are now swallowed up in
sympathy with the just wrath of the Lord and in gratitude to
Him for their own rescue from such fate. The lost, like the
saved, know their destiny immediately after death; the pain
of awaiting the Last Day is enhanced for them, not only by
the knowledge that their bodies will then be joined in suffering with their souls, but also by the sight of those who rejoice
expectantly in Paradise and by the thought of those still on
earth, surely coming to this same misery. After the Last Judgment the vision of Heaven is forever lost to the damned; but
the saints will still look upon the denizens of Hell, sweating
in the anguish of unbearable heat, their teeth chattering
through icy cold. So declared blessed Job: *They shall pass to
exceeding heat from the waters of the snows.*[152]

To this Gospel of Priesthood also belongs Bede's comment
on the sacrifice made for the prodigal son. "This feast," he
writes, "is still held throughout all the earth. Its calf is still
seen in the Body and Blood of the Lord; it is offered to the

---

[151] XI, 170; *cf.* 235: *quia qui Creatorem sui claritatem vident, nihil in
creatura agitur quod videre non possint.*
[152] X, 350ff.; XI, 158f., 234ff., 253, 191; Job XXIV, 19 (Old Latin).

Father and feeds all His house." [153] The Church covers her altars with fair white linen, symbol of purity, even as the Lord's Body was wrapped therein. As the angels stood by the Body of the Lord in the tomb, so we must believe they stand by our altars at the time of consecration. "With Angels añd Archangels" descending from Heaven, we share our offering on earth; in reverence women veil their heads as they approach. So ought we all, Bede warns, as often as we enter the church, to draw near with humility and with awe, both of the holy oblation upon the altar and of the angels who stand there to guard it. Moreover, he observes, as the women of the Resurrection "bowed down their faces to the earth," so the custom obtains that "on all Sundays and throughout the fifty days of Paschaltide we do not kneel to pray but bend low." This order of ritual, emphasized by Bede, had been prescribed for general practice by the Council of Nicaea in 325; kneeling was held a token of penitence, and standing a token of freedom won through the Resurrection of the Lord.[154] We fast, Bede also reminds us, throughout the Church before Communion "in honour of so great and so dreadful a sacrament." Only the disciples received their communion after supper, because it was needful that the Passover of the Type be ended before it pass to the sacrament of the true Paschal Feast.[155]

Once again Bede returns in this work to the subject of Penance. "Public guilt," he teaches here, "requires public remedy, but venial sins can be blotted out by lighter and secret penitence." From the *Penitential of Theodore*, describing, we may think, the discipline in practice under this Archbishop of Canterbury, we learn that public penance was not enacted in his time "in this Province." As he died in 690, and this

[153] XI, 218.
[154] XI, 374ff.; Hefele-Leclercq I, 618 ff. *Cf. Giles* V, 65, 67, 410, 428.
[155] XI, 333.

Penitential which bears his name was addressed "to all Catholics of the English" and edited by a writer who calls himself "a disciple of the Northumbrians," [156] we may presume that its statements were true of Bede's own experience of the north, as well as in the south of England. His remark on public penance, then, is of a general nature, in agreement with Augustine and Ambrose, true of his time so far as life within a monastery went, but not extending to the Church as a whole. The excommunicate is restored "through the decree of priestly judgment"; "holy doctors instruct us in confession of our sin, healing with the tongue, as it were, the wound of our mind." The greater the sin, the greater need lies upon the penitent of bearing penance fruitful in good works. Bede here "gives his opinion" that a man "sins unto death" when he deliberately breaks the bond which binds him to the brotherhood of the Christian Church; when, not in fear or through other weakness, but resolutely, against the grace and knowledge which the Church has given him, he becomes the enemy of his fellow-Christians. Such a sin does not admit of intercession on the part of others; it is, without question, the betrayal wrought by Judas Iscariot himself.[157]

Again and again the word of warning is written. Upon one passage Bede remarks, "This is terrible, beyond the reach of comment." He is writing of the unclean spirit: *I will return unto my house whence I came out.* Once or twice he refers directly to the loose living of his own time: "Men without number are now given up to eating and drinking, buying and selling, to other things of this world; clearly they are provoking the wrath of the stern Judge. No wise man but looks on this with deep sorrow; even now we dread worse things to come. . . . Why are they not afraid to be overcome by such deadly

---

[156] XI, 88; Watkins II, 648ff.; McNeill and Gamer, 180ff.
[157] XI, 215, 44, 236, 23f. (*cf.* XII, 318f.); X, 345.

poisons? Because, I believe, they scorn to give the Lord the faith they place in the words of their medical adviser. . . . And so they prink it in fine clothes, crave to be distinguished from their fellows by unusual garments, particularly good or particularly austere, build splendid houses, erect costly tombs. It is not wrong to be rich; [158] but it *is* wrong to love riches and to use them selfishly." [159]

Exorcism of those afflicted by evil spirits, Bede declares, cannot be effectual unless the patients confess all that they have done or borne under such influence. Such doctrine the priests of his time commonly taught. He tells in illustration a story related to him by one who lived near Jarrow Monastery. A woman through possession by an evil spirit had contracted hideous ulcers. As long as she remained silent, nothing could be done for her; but when she had told all that had happened, she was cured by prayers and by application of holy salt, together with the doctor's medical aid. Only one stubborn ulcer remained, against which no remedies prevailed. At last, by her own suggestion, based on previous experience, oil blessed for the sick was applied, whereupon the ulcer immediately responded to treatment by priest and doctor.[160]

The life of prayer is described by Bede in its two aspects, of activity and of contemplation, with special emphasis upon the mingling of both. We ought not to consider the one more acceptable than the other. As the Lord wrought miracles in the city and retired to the desert or the mountain for prayer, so the Christian must neither neglect his neighbour's worries nor cease his own striving after the ascent to Heaven. He will learn to pray on the mountain by climbing above earthly cares, to pray in the desert by retiring from the tumult of

[158] So, in the *Homilies* (V, 51), the faithful are allowed to pray for health, good harvests, and good weather.
[159] XI, 20, 142, 253, 323f., 231, 166, 328, 371, 47, 76.
[160] XI, 76f. *Cf.* X, 88; Plummer II, 156f.

active things to the inner silence of the Presence of God. The shepherds of the flock, especially, will at one time watch and pray while others sleep the sleep of secular occupations; they will now visit the faithful, now teach and minister in open church, thus giving to their people the fruits of their lonely vigils in this world's night. But to attain to the prayer of contemplation is a long and slow business. For not in crowds do men ascend the mountain of transfiguration, but one by one, gradually extinguishing the flame of desire in the dawn of goodly knowledge. Finally, the life of active prayer belongs to this earth alone and ends with this body's death; the prayer of contemplation merely begins here, to find its permanence and perfection in the country of Heaven.[161]

Never begin any work of charity without prayer, Bede counsels, and remember that selfish prayer is sin. Zacharias was not foolishly praying for a son as he stood within the Temple. "Your prayer is heard," referred to his intercession for his people; the promise of a son was entirely separate. Remember, also, that prayer is difficult. Images and memories crowd our minds when we try to pray, confuse us with their noise and overwhelm the voice of supplication. Never mind; the harder this crowd of distractions tries to silence us, the louder it shouts, the faster fleshly thoughts press upon us, so much the more decidedly must we step out in the way prescribed.[162]

Above all, however, this commentary on Saint Luke is crowded to overflowing with allegorical interpretation. It would be impossible to describe here Bede's mystical explaining of names, of numbers, of details of every sort, inherited from patristic method, especially from that of Gregory the Great. The numbers three, four, six, seven, ten, and a hun-

---

[161] X, 329f., 398, 318; XI, 64, 15, 129f.; cf. V, 262ff.
[162] X, 279; XI, 7f., 270f. Cf. V, 248 and 22, where unworthy thoughts are compared to pestering flies.

dred, in particular, illustrate virtue rising to perfection, and the more so when one number is multiplied by another.[163]

Two or three examples must be taken as representing others innumerable: The woman who had ten pieces of silver is symbolic of the Lord and His Wisdom; the coin which is lost to Him is the impression of His own image stamped upon the soul of man, lost by the Fall. That this may be recovered He lights the Light that came into the world, the Wisdom of God Incarnate, and sweeps diligently through the soul until in man's shaken conscience the Divine image again is found. The image of God is also stamped, however, on all His higher creation; therefore, the nine coins which were not lost represent the nine orders of Angels who never sin.[164]

Or take the grain of mustard seed, in Saint Luke, chapter 13. It tells of the lowliness of God Incarnate, for it was planted in a garden as the Crucified Lord was buried in the garden of Joseph. As it grew and waxed a great tree, so the Lord rose and ascended into Heaven. And now His great tree, the Church, born of Him, spreads over the earth her branches, the priests and preachers of the Word, and birds—that is, the faithful laity—find rest and support in their ministering. Of the other parable, that of Saint Luke, chapter 17: *If ye had faith as a grain of mustard seed,* Bede's interpretation is less elevated. Mustard, he remarks, is good for a cold in the head. If you pound a little of it very fine and mix it with honey, then use it as a gargle in the hot sun or in a steaming bath before breaking your fast, it will clear all the congestion away. Even so your faith must be pounded in the mortar of temptation, cleansed by the sieve of discretion from all frivolous thoughts, sweetened by the honey of perfect charity—then it

[163] See Jenkins, in Thompson, 173ff.; Plummer I, lxf.; V. F. Hopper, *Medieval Number Symbolism,* Columbia Univ. Studies in Eng. and Comp. Lit. CXXXII, 1938.
[164] Giles XI, 210ff.

will drive out for ever the foul matter of sins congested in your heart.[165]

The lingering eye of Bede dwells thus over each text, carefully scrutinizing each for what it may yield. The beggar is called Lazarus, the rich man is nameless; contrary to the custom of this world, the friends whom God calls by name are found among the poor and lowly. The angel Gabriel needs no name in heaven, for in heaven there is perfect knowledge; but for ignorant men on earth his name describes his special virtue, the "strength of God." He addresses blessed Mary by her name as an intimate friend, that she may not be afraid.[166] Notice is constantly taken by Bede of differences between the Hebrew version and the Septuagint, differences culled undoubtedly from his sources. Here, again, we need not assume that he knew Hebrew.[167] He dismisses very often differences among the Evangelists, although his treatment of these problems would not at all satisfy modern scholarship.[168] His trust in Biblical and patristic statements allows him to leave matters as he finds them, explaining each passage for its own individual merit and moral. Again and again he inserts in his explanations the words *puto, credo, ut opinor, ni fallor, reor, arbitror;* as one to whom "the key of knowledge is the humility of Christ." [169]

His spirit as student of holy Scripture is summed up in the prayer he offered before beginning the fourth part of this work on Saint Luke:

"Grant me, O Christ, I beseech Thee, of Thy grace that Thy good Spirit may lead me in the right way, and may make far from me him who cometh from the North to destroy: that, casting away all malice of evil, I may search into the commandments of my God, and with the eyes of my mind

[165] XI, 188, 241. [166] XI, 231; X, 286; *cf.* V, 362.
[167] Jenkins, *ibid.,* 163. [168] *Ibid.,* 193f.
[169] Giles X, 322; XI, 32, 34, 43, 45, 123.

awakened may go forward faithfully to read and to weigh the marvels of Thy holy Law." [170]

From the New Testament Bede now passed to the Old and studied with deep care the First Book of Samuel. The attraction he had always felt toward mystical comment now reached its zenith, and he deliberately called his commentary *Allegorica Expositio*.[171] This extremely mystical bent was unfortunate; for many of the interpretations spring from a mind in some ways over-busy in imagining, and their continuance without end soon tires a reader who was not born to enjoy them for his soul's edification in the Middle Ages. We need only note here that he chose this particular book for its meaning to those of his own vocation, priests and monks. As Elkanah had two wives, allegorical lessons were obviously in order: "For if we take heed to bring forth from the treasure of Holy Scripture only its literal forms and figures after the Jewish manner, how shall we, whose life is ordained by the Church for celibacy, far removed from wife's embrace, as we read or listen to the story of Elkanah and his two wives, how shall we, priests and monks, find therein rebuke for our daily sins, or comfort amid the increasing troubles of our time, or spiritual lessons amid the countless errors of this life, if we do not understand how to chisel out from such narratives an allegorical meaning which shall give our souls new life?" Of the two wives, the elder, called Phenenna in the Vulgate version, represents to Bede the Jewish synagogue; the younger, Anna, more familiar as Hannah, is symbolic of the Christian Church. The aim of the commentary in general is to follow that scribe of Saint Matthew's Gospel, "instructed into the kingdom of heaven," and to bring forth from treasure "things both new and old"— in other words, to trace the progress from the Jewish rule of Law to the reign of Christ in His Church by the contrasted

[170] XI, 137.   [171] VII, 368ff.; VIII, 1ff.

lives of Eli and Samuel, of Saul and David. Bede was drawing here, for his history, from Josephus, either in Latin translation or, perhaps, in the original; for his allegorical matter, from Isidore of Seville and from Augustine; from Jerome, as usual, for interpretation of names.[172]

While he was thus engaged, there came from Acca, his bishop, requests for enlightenment on two problems of holy Scripture. He at once put away his *Samuel* and turned to new study. The first concerned the itinerary and encampments of the Israelites on their way from Egypt to the plains of Moab and the river Jordan.[173] This problem of history did not trouble Bede's mind, sensitive as he was to the danger of putting forward untrue statements on the Faith. The second problem did make him hesitate: the meaning of the words of Isaiah XXIV, 22 : *And they shall be shut up in the prison and after many days shall they be visited.* He carefully consulted Jerome's *Commentary on Isaiah* [174] and wrote to Acca that he hoped he was saying nothing against Catholic doctrine in interpreting these words as pertaining to the souls of wicked men and angels who wait long in prison for the Last Judgment and then shall be assessed in their final doom. At any rate, he warned, let no one take the passage as meaning that those whom God has once condemned to Hell will ever again be visited by His mercy. Then, having done his best for Acca, with a sigh of relief he turned back to less perplexing matters in Samuel.[175]

During all these years of literary work Bede faithfully fulfilled his whole daily round. Very probably he was excused

---

[172] See Isidore, *PL* LXXXIII, coll. 391ff.; Augustine, *De civ. Dei* XVII, 4; *cf.* Giles VII, 382; *CSEL* XL, ii, 212; K. Werner, 168ff.; Laistner, *TRHS* 78.
[173] Numbers, c. 33.
[174] *PL* XXIV, coll. 296f.   [175] Giles I, 198ff., 203ff.

from manual tasks in house and garden on account of the many hours he spent each day in the library and in his cell, poring over a multitude of manuscripts hard to decipher, often written in obscure and dim characters; taking roll after roll from their cases, examining, comparing, replacing them, at last patiently inscribing, page after page; and doing all with none of the comforts so necessary to a modern scholar. Much time, also, was given to teaching the younger brethren of the monastery.

Yet these occupations, beloved as they were, stood only as the lower part of his life. As priest he gave his time to administering the sacraments, to preaching in Saint Peter's Church; every day he prayed alone; at the appointed Hours of night and day he sang the monastic Offices with his brethren. There is a pleasant passage in praise of Bede as priest and monk in a letter written long afterward to the monks of Jarrow by Alcuin, once of York, from his abbey of Tours in France. Alcuin was now about seventy years of age. He had been born just when Bede reached his end on earth, and he had inherited in England the legacy of Bede's learning. Now as he wrote to these monks of Jarrow he thought back upon his own life as student and as teacher in England and upon the reverence he bore to the monastery where Bede had lived:

"Your house was truly dear to my heart; even though work abroad took me from you, I loved you none the less. All things which I saw among you, either in your dwellings or in your monastic life, I found right good; may your loyal obedience and humility and steadfast keeping of your Rule be ever pleasing to God.

"This is your praise among men, that you remain constant, both in your habit and in all details of the discipline which your fathers taught you, men loved by God and honoured by their fellows. They who first founded your community, surely very often they visit the places where you dwell, and whomsoever they find living righteously and keeping their decrees, with them they rejoice, for them they never cease to pray in the presence of the just and merciful Judge. But, of a truth, angels often visit your holy places. Once, so men tell, blessed Bede, my master and your patron, said during his life at Jarrow: 'I know that the angels are present when our monks chant their Office and meet in chapter. What if they did not find me among them? Would they have to say, "Where is Bede? Why comes he not to the appointed prayers with his brethren?" ' " [176]

Nor did Bede the historian lack concern for the happenings of the world outside his monastery. He had heard with regret of the death of Aldhelm, whom he revered as "a man of widest knowledge, a writer of polished style and of admirable learning in both secular and sacred literature." Aldhelm's verses were well-known to him, and he was especially interested in his discourses on the virgin life and on the dating of Easter.[177] The death of his bishop Wilfrid in the same year of 709 had led to the joy of Acca's appointment to Hexham, Acca, "dearest and best beloved of all bishops on this earth," to whom he looked for inspiration in all his study, who constantly encouraged him to write commentaries on the Bible for the instruction of the Northumbrian people of his diocese.[178]

Acca was, indeed, a gifted and energetic administrator. He had learned much about architecture in Italy and in France during his travels, especially as a chaplain and companion of Wilfrid; and as his successor at Hexham it fell to him to complete Wilfrid's work. He enlarged the abbey church of Hexham, adorned it with vessels and lamps of gold and silver, sparkling with precious stones, vested its altars in richly-

[176] *Mon. Alc. BRG* VI, 843f.; *MGH Epp.* IV, No. 284, p. 443.
[177] *HE* V, c. 18.
[178] Giles I, 169f., 196; Plummer II, 329f.

coloured silken frontals, and solemnly dedicated the whole in honour of Saint Andrew. In side chapels, which he made especially for the purpose, he placed the relics of saints which he had brought from Rome, and he was constantly on the alert to procure more, wherever they could be found. He also finished the building of the other churches erected by Wilfrid at Hexham, of Saint Mary ever-Virgin, of Saint Peter, and of Saint Michael.[179]

To do further reverence to the saints whose relics lay at Hexham and to enlighten his people concerning them, Acca eagerly gathered rolls describing their lives. Thus, with other writings on sacred subjects, he made, as Bede called it, "a very large and admirable library." He was himself expert in Biblical knowledge and exegesis of that time, in theology, in canon law and in music, as one who had lived under the shadow of York cathedral during childhood and youth. Probably the music in the churches of Hexham diocese had not progressed under Wilfrid as far as other arts had done; at any rate, Acca imported from Canterbury a skilled precentor to teach him and his clergy how to sing. The name of this master of Hexham's music was Maban, and he stayed twelve years, drilling priests, monks, and laity in hymns, chants, and psalms, introducing much that was new, and restoring to proper tune and time much that had slipped into careless rendering.

Five years after the death of Wilfrid, Bede heard of the passing of the hermit priest Guthlac in his retreat of Crowland among the fens on the southern border of Lincolnshire.[180] He had been born about the same time as Bede himself, and the monk of Jarrow must often have remembered in his prayers

---

[179] *HE* V, c. 20; Eddius, c. 22; Raine, *Hexham* I, 1864: *SS* 44, xxxii; W. G. Collingwood, *Antiquity* VI, 1932, 37f.

[180] P. 191 *supra*, note 145. See H. C. Darby, "The Fenland Frontier in Anglo-Saxon England": *Antiquity* VIII, 1934, 185ff.

this solitary of the marshes. Visitors to Jarrow brought many stories of his strange life. Sometimes, they had heard, a whole army of evil fiends would sweep around him at night, horrible with their huge heads, long necks, foul beards, teeth like tusks, and mouths belching flame. They tore him with briars and beat him with whips and carried him high in the cold air; they bore him down to hell and terrified him with the sight of the lost spirits undergoing punishment. But it was all to no avail! Even the devils wept because their power was broken on this valiant soldier of Christ. Another time they swept down at cock-crow, speaking in the British language, and vanished like smoke when he hurled back a Latin psalm!

But the birds and the fish in the mere and the wild beasts prowling around, all came at his call to be fed; the swallows settled on his head and shoulders, crying that spring had come. Another monk called Wilfred, who was visiting him, could not understand why they did so, and Guthlac answered him readily: "Did you never read, Wilfred, in the holy writings that he who has lived according to God's will, him the wild beasts and birds hold as their friend? And the angels, too, draw nearer the man who would spend his days apart from worldly things. But he who longs for worldly talk knows not how to speak with angels." [181]

As time went on, it became known that Guthlac possessed the gift of healing, of body and of mind. Soon people of every degree and kind sought him out in the waste lands, bishops, abbots, secular nobles and rich men, with the humble and the poor. He welcomed and aided all. Sometimes, too, visitors would come to talk with him of the things he and they loved. Among these was a bishop, named Haedda, who was so filled with reverent wonder at Guthlac's knowledge and wisdom that he begged the hermit to receive from him holy ordering

[181] *Vita Guthlaci,* cc. 15ff., 25.

to the priesthood that he might henceforth say Mass in the little church which he had built. Guthlac yielded, and Haedda not only laid his hands upon him but also blessed all his tiny isle of Crowland. It was then harvest-tide, just before the Feast of Saint Bartholomew, Guthlac's special patron and guardian.

Fifteen years had passed, so Bede heard the story, since Guthlac came to the fens, when on Wednesday of Holy Week, 714, as he was praying in his church, he was suddenly attacked by sickness and knew his days on earth were over. He was about forty years old. A young man whom he was teaching, named Beccel, was with him at the time. On Easter morning Guthlac offered the Holy Sacrifice for them both; the third day afterward he gave his last messages. "When my soul has left my body," he said to Beccel, "go to my sister, Pege, and tell her that for this reason I would not see her here on earth, that we might meet in heaven before the face of God. Tell her, too, that she wrap my body in linen, which I never wore while I lived; but now let her bury me in the linen shroud which the handmaid of Christ, Egburg, sent me for gift." [182] On the morrow he died and was buried as he had asked, in the church upon the island. In after years a monastery was built upon the place and the abbey of Crowland became famous in history.

From further afield there came to Bede's cell news of a gradual conversion of the Celts to the Roman obedience in regard to Easter and the tonsure. About 710, Nechtan, king of the Picts of Scotland, decided upon this conversion for himself and his subjects. In order that he might obtain not only instruction on the exact manner of tonsure for his monks but also arguments for the refuting of those who clung to the old ways, he despatched messengers to Abbot Ceolfrid of

[182] *Ibid.*, c. 35.

Wearmouth-Jarrow, asking that letters providing such aid
should be given them and that skilled master-masons might
also be sent him for the building of a stone church in the
Roman style. For himself and all his realm he promised
adherence to the discipline of Rome, so far as he and his
people in their remote land might learn of this.[183]

Ceolfrid sent Nechtan the architects whom he desired. He
also sent him a letter, written in his name but generally held
to be the work of Bede, a long and learned discussion of
Paschal reckonings, relieved with mystical interpretation, entirely in Bede's manner. Naturally, as Nechtan had already
professed himself converted, its tone was very different from
that of the letter addressed by Aldhelm to the British chieftain
Geraint in southwestern England five years before. Toward
its close, Ceolfrid, or Bede for him, stated that he had re-
proached Adamnan, abbot of Iona, when Adamnan was visiting Jarrow, for adherence to Celtic schismatic practice, and
that Adamnan had not only admitted the error but on his
return to Scotland had converted many others to the Roman
way. He had not, however, been able to convince his own
monks, who still continued as before in their Celtic reckoning.

It must have given the community of Jarrow special happiness some years later to hear that Iona had at length submitted, in 716, one hundred and fifty years after its foundation by Columba. Their abbot at the time was Dunchad,
eleventh in succession; but the change was due to the preaching of an Englishman named Egbert who had lived many
years in Ireland, and, as it seems, had been ordained bishop.[184]

When Bede turned his mind from the ecclesiastical to the

---

[183] *HE* V, 21; Plummer II, 331. Nechtan drove out from his kingdom
the clergy who would not submit: *Annals of Tigernach*, ed. Whitley
Stokes, *RC* XVII, 1896, 225.

[184] *Cf.* pp. 343ff *infra*; *HE* V, 22; *ASC ann.* 716. *HE* III, 4, gives the
date 715; see Plummer II, 335f. Some of the monks refused to submit
and schism lasted until 772 (Skene, *Celtic Scotland* II, 288).

secular happenings of these years, he found great cause for anxiety. Osred, the boy king of Northumbria, whom we last saw in 706 at the age of eight in his royal chair at the council of the Nidd, assembled for trial of Bishop Wilfrid, had grown up into a vicious youth. So had Ceolred, king of Mercia, whom we left promising obedience to Wilfrid in 709. Of them both these fearsome words were afterward written: "Inspired by devils they sinned accursedly in England; in the midst of their crimes, raping nuns and destroying monasteries, they were condemned by the just judgment of God, cast down from the height of their kingship in early and dreadful death, shut out for ever from light, sunk in the depths of hell." [185]

Another source tells that in Northumbria Osred killed many of his nobles and drove others into monasteries. After eleven years of evil doing he met his doom, either slain in battle, or murdered by two of his kinsmen who reigned after him. One of these was Cenred, who ruled only two years; the other was Osric, who ruled eleven, from 718 until 729. Tradition declared that neither did they die peacefully in their beds: "This only was to be remembered concerning them, that they atoned by their own blood for the death of their lord . . . and polluted the air by their foul end." [186]

Of Ceolred of Mercia we hear that he fought a fierce battle in 715 against King Ine of Wessex at Woodborough in Wiltshire and was driven back from his invasion, although he showed "marvellous courage." In the next year he was suddenly struck down as he sat feasting with his courtiers, and died in convulsions of madness. His crown came to a distant relative, Ethelbald, of whom it was said that Ceolred had

----

[185] Pp. 207, 211 *supra; HE* V, cc. 18f., 22, 24; Boniface, *Epp.* ed. Dümmler, 73; Ethelwulf, *De abbatibus,* in Simeon of Durham, *RS* LXXV, i, 268.
[186] *ASC ann.* 716; *Gest. Reg.* I, 58; Henry of Huntingdon, *MHB* I, 724; Plummer II, 336.

driven him into exile and that he had come to the hermit Guthlac for comfort in his trouble. Guthlac had prophesied that Ceolred would fall, that Ethelbald would reign in his place, and that he would gain the throne, not by robbery and rape, but by the Lord's aid. In his gratitude Ethelbald enriched Crowland with buildings and endowment. It is this king whom we have seen suggested, without convincing evidence, as the young correspondent who sent to Aldhelm verses for his criticism. He reigned long, from 716 until 757, and gradually increased his power; before Bede died, he was supreme over all the kings of southern England and as far north as the Humber river.[187]

Sacrilege, murder, and madness among kings of their own North and the adjacent Midlands must, then, have weighed very heavily on the hearts of this community of Jarrow. Perhaps they did even more to the tired mind of its abbot. For one day, Tuesday, the second of June, 716, when Bede was just ending the third book of his *Samuel*, Abbot Ceolfrid called the monks of Jarrow, Bede among them, into their church to announce to them that after much thought he had decided to resign his office. He was now an old man, he said, weary with years, and the community needed another Father for its better keeping of the Rule. For himself, he longed before he died for a little time to spend in peace with his own soul, free from the onerous cares of the world and of his time. Once, many years ago, he had been in Rome with the Founder, Benedict Biscop; to Rome he would now return, to await calmly his last days. His brother Cynefrid, once abbot of Gilling in Yorkshire, had retired to Ireland in the same desire.[188]

Ceolfrid was now, indeed, seventy-four. Bede was about

---

[187] *ASC* ann. 715; *HE* V, 23; *Gest. Reg.* I, 79; R. Hodgkin, 332ff.; *Vita Guthlaci*, c. 34; pp. 446 *infra*, 74 *supra*.
[188] *VA* cc. 15ff.; *VAA* cc. 19ff.

forty-three, and had known him all his life. Under Ceolfrid he had grown from a little boy to manhood, had been ordained deacon and priest, had begun his years of study and writing. The Father Abbot had been devoted in his own life of prayer, fasting and poverty, to an extent, as Bede remarked, "unusual for rulers"; he had governed his congregation with energy, charity, and discretion; he had gained from Pope Sergius a deed of privilege for its independence. He had also extended its territory. In exchange for a manuscript of writings on geography he had gained from King Aldfrid, "the Learned," who loved such rare possessions, a piece of land near the river Fresca, now unidentified; later on, under King Osred, by paying money to make up the price, he had exchanged this land for a much larger tract at a township called Sambuce, nearer the monastery. In his time, also, a certain Witmer, a scholar of advanced years, had been attracted toward Wearmouth-Jarrow through its life of devotion combined with learning. Not only had he become a monk there, but he had given to the abbey in permanent possession the estate which King Aldfrid had given him at Dalton in Durham. Not less important had been the encouragement which the Father had given to his monks in the copying of manuscripts. One of these, the famous *Codex Amiatinus,* Ceolfrid decided to take with him to Rome as a gift to the Pope; the other two he left in the churches of his monastery in order that any monk who desired might be able to read from both Old and New Testament.[189]

All had been planned by Ceolfrid before he spoke of his departure; he had been afraid lest his monks might constrain him to wait awhile. He had even thought to leave that very same day. The shock and evident grief, however, which his words caused everyone induced him to remain a few more hours. His cell was in the house of Jarrow. The next morning

[189] *VA* c. 15; pp. 244, 265 *supra.*

with many of its brethren he set out for Wearmouth; there he spoke the same words to the monks of that house, bidding all to keep the Rule, to let him go without hindrance, and to remember him as he would remember them for evermore. He looked so frail as he spoke that they feared he would not live to see Rome. Death, however, in itself was nothing to be feared by these men; they quietly asked his prayers in either land, in the sanctuary of the saints here on earth or in their presence across the unknown.

On the morrow, Thursday before Pentecost, Mass was sung in both the churches of Wearmouth, of Saint Mary and of Saint Peter; all those present made their communion. Afterward all gathered in Saint Peter's, where the departing abbot kindled the incense and said the *Itinerarium,* the prayer for travellers, at its altar; then, turning round, while the smoke from the censer he was holding rose by his side, he bade them good-bye with his blessing. After he ended, he moved, censer in hand, toward the little chapel of Saint Laurence in the dormitory, and they followed him in procession, chanting the antiphon:

> *Via iustorum recta facta est, et iter sanctorum praeparatum est:*
> *Ambulantes de virtute ad virtutem;*

> *The way of the just is uprightness, and the path of the saints is made ready:*
> *Walking from strength to strength;*

and the sixty-sixth psalm:

> *Deus misereatur nobis, et benedicat nos;*
> *Inluminet vultum suum super nos, et misereatur nobis . . .*

> *God be merciful unto us and bless us;*
> *And cause His face to shine upon us, and be merciful unto us . . .*

In the chapel he stayed a moment, begging all, for none was free from human weakness, to live in charity, without quarrels, backbitings and offence, always bearing in mind that the two monasteries, which in this same year numbered more than six hundred monks, novices, and oblates,[190] were in reality one, to be ruled by one and the same Father.

Now they walked to the bank of their river, the Wear, still chanting their verses. A boat was waiting there. After Ceolfrid had given the kiss of peace to those nearest him, he went on board with several monks, especially chosen. He sat down in the prow; two of his deacons, acting as escort, sat near him, one holding a cross wrought of gold, the other lighted candles. The oarsmen rowed from the north to the south bank, while the brethren he was leaving watched him pass. He heard from the other side the sound of their chanting, broken by their sorrow; again and again he himself cried in prayer to God that He in His mercy and infinite power would keep safe this company: "for none better and more prompt to obey have I ever known." The boat grounded. He knelt in reverence of the cross, mounted the horse which stood ready, and rode on his way.

Those who had gone with him to the river now returned. After Terce a chapter of both houses, Wearmouth and Jarrow, now assembled for conference, decided to elect with prayer and fasting one of the brethren as their abbot. Ceolfrid had asked them specially not to fast on the day of his going from them, but rather to hold it as a Feast Day. They kept strict fast, therefore, on Friday, and on Saturday until the Office of None in the afternoon, which marked the beginning of Pentecost and the end of lawful fasting. All were bidden to continue their prayer, "that on the day on which the Mercy on high deigned to consecrate through the coming

[190] *VAA* c. 33.

of His Holy Spirit the beginnings of His Church, may be given to us, a portion of that Church, a worthy ruler through the grace of that same Spirit." [191]

On June 7, the Feast of Pentecost, unanimous election fell on Hwaetbert, Bede's friend, also called Eusebius. Like Bede, he had been brought to the monastery as a little boy, had been trained in the same education, and had been ordained priest. He was well-read, an experienced teacher, skilled in writing and in chant, and, like Aldhelm, given to riddling in his leisure time.[192]

One of his first acts as abbot was to draw up a letter commending his predecessor to the Pope of the time, Gregory II.[193] With this and with gifts, which he wanted to offer at Rome in his new dignity, he hastened after Ceolfrid, knowing that he had planned to embark at the mouth of the Humber. He overtook him at the monastery of Aelbert, in a place called Cornu Vallis, now unknown, but presumably near the Humber's mouth, since Ceolfrid was already waiting for a ship. Hwaetbert told of his election, and was answered by "Thanks be to God." He presented his letter and said good-bye a second time to the Father. On his return to Wearmouth-Jarrow he requested the Visitor of the monastery, Bishop Acca of Hexham, to come for the customary installation and blessing of the new ruler.[194] Hwaetbert was abbot during the rest of Bede's life, and Bede with his brother monks felt the new tide of energy, the new prosperity, which came from this younger administrator. His early days of office were marked by a great ceremony, when on the twenty-second of August in this

[191] *Ibid.*, c. 28.
[192] *VA* c. 18. This Eusebius is "almost certainly identical" with the Eusebius who followed Aldhelm in writing Latin riddles: M. R. James, *CHEL* I, 86f. For his riddles see Giles, *Anecdota Bedae, Lanfranci et aliorum*, Caxton Society, No. 7, 1851, 54ff.
[193] Pope 715–731.
[194] *Cf. The Pontifical of Egbert, SS* 27, 1853, 105f.

same year of 716 the relics of Abbots Eosterwine and Sigfrid were translated and buried anew, with those of the monk Witmer, in Saint Peter's church beside the grave of Benedict Biscop.[195]

In the meantime Ceolfrid was still on his journey. On Saturday, July 4, he embarked; three times during his voyage to France his ship put into harbour, and at each place of stopping he was welcomed with marked respect. On August 12 he landed at last on the French coast; soon the king of Neustria, Chilperic II,[196] received him with equal courtesy and gave him letters of commendation to the various provinces of his own kingdom as well as to Liutprand, king of the Lombards.[197] Every day, except once on board ship and three times when his increasing frailty would not allow it, he offered to God the Sacrifice of the *salutaris hostia;* twice daily, in addition to the monastic Hours of prayer, he and his monks recited the Psalter from beginning to end. At last he could no longer ride, but had to be borne in a carriage drawn by horses. In this way, escorted by more than eighty Englishmen who had joined his company, he reached Langres, a town standing high above the valley of the Upper Marne. It was now the twenty-fifth of September, and he knew that only a few hours of life remained to him. He died toward evening of the same day in the fields skirting the city and was buried on the morrow in the monastery of the Holy Twin Martyrs, two miles outside, honoured at the last by the presence of many people—the monks of this monastery, the pilgrims who had come with him, and the clergy and laity of Langres.[198]

The departure of Ceolfrid was deeply felt by Bede. When the abbey resumed its usual routine, he took up again the

[195] *VA* cc. 19f.; *VAA* cc. 29f.   [196] 715–720.
[197] 712–744; *cf.* pp. 367, 414 *infra.*   [198] *VA* c. 21; *VAA* cc. 31ff.

commentary on Samuel and prepared to write its fourth book. At the beginning he told of a little rest he had hoped to take on ending Book Three and of the "unexpected and acute trouble" that had scattered this thought. But now that tranquillity had been restored, he could once more give his whole mind to his task.[199] This work on Samuel seems to have aroused the interest of Nothelm, a priest of London; for about this time he wrote to Bede, asking him to explain thirty passages from the books of Samuel and Kings. With his usual readiness Bede dealt with them all, adding a petition that his "brother Nothelm would, like himself, constantly read, mark, learn, and inwardly digest the Holy Scriptures." [200]

A commentary on the Gospel of Saint Mark followed next, with much repetition of material from the previous work on Saint Luke. The *Saint Mark,* also dedicated to Acca, contained in its margins the same indications of the sources from which Bede had borrowed.[201] He vigorously defends the writer of this Gospel from criticism. If Mark attributed to Isaiah words found in Malachi, what did it matter? All the prophets drew their substance in common from the one Holy Spirit; and to the evangelists the prophetic meaning of passages in the Old Testament was more important than their actual wording. Once again there is lament over the evil state of his present world. On Mark III, 20,

And the multitude cometh together again, so that they (i.e., the Lord and His disciples) *could not so much as eat bread,*

he writes: "Lord, that Thou wouldst give also in our days such grace to Thy faithful that in their eagerness to learn they would keep their teachers, not only from pleasures of

[199] Giles VIII, 162f.; *cf.* VI, 331.
[200] Before 731: *HE* V, c. 24; Giles VIII, 232ff.
[201] Giles X, 2f.; Sutcliffe, *Biblica* VII, 1926, 428ff.; Laistner, in Thompson, 237, 240f.; *cf.* pp. 277f. *supra.*

the flesh, but even from time to eat their daily bread!" It is better, therefore, to be diligent than to be brilliant: "In general we may be sure that the able student who is lazy loses what the slow but persevering gains by his toil." [202]

On the cleansing of the Temple Bede comments: "The Temple of God is the mind and conscience of the faithful, the house of prayer; it becomes a den of thieves when evil thoughts dwell therein for the harm of others." [203] There is also a comment on the words, *And Jesus entered into Jerusalem and into the Temple,* which shows us Bede himself. "Whenever," he writes, "we enter a village or a town or any other place in which there is a house of prayer consecrated to God, let us first go aside within it; and so, after we have commended ourselves to Him, then let us pass on to the business for which we have come." [204]

In describing the tomb of the Lord he draws on a description given by "those who came from Jerusalem to Britain in our time." This is a reference to Arculf, a bishop from Gaul, who, somewhere about 670, had travelled on pilgrimage to the Holy Land. He stayed nine months in Jerusalem with an old monk, Peter, as guide and interpreter. As he was returning to Gaul, contrary winds carried his ship to the west coast of Britain; and, after some hazardous adventures, he reached Iona, where Adamnan was abbot. When he had told the story of his pilgrimage, Adamnan in his enthusiasm wrote "a most beautiful and most profitable" description of its details and presented it to Aldfrid of Northumbria when he was visiting that kingdom. We know that Adamnan made two visits to Aldfrid, one, it would seem, in 686, and the second two years afterward, in 688. It was probably at the time of this second stay that he went to Wearmouth-Jarrow and talked

[202] Giles X, 5ff., 49, 64, 80, 93.
[203] St. Mark XI, 15ff.; Giles X, 179.
[204] St. Mark XI, 11; Giles X, 173.

with its abbot Ceolfrid about the dating of Easter.[205] Bede,
who would have been about fifteen then, no doubt saw so distinguished a guest.

He, also, read the book of Adamnan, for by the generosity
of Aldfrid a copy was sent to Jarrow, and he was so impressed by it that some time before 731—we do not know
exactly when—he himself composed a work *On the Holy
Places*.[206] This, however, was a compilation of extracts, not
only from Adamnan's text, but also from a Latin version of
the *Jewish Wars* of Josephus, made by Hegesippus about the
year 400, and from a book on the city of Jerusalem which is
extant under the authorship, probably incorrect, of Eucherius,
bishop of Lyons in the fifth century. Naturally, students would
fare much better in reading the narrative of Adamnan, taken
from an eye-witness, than a mere collection of borrowings.

Probably in 720 Bede was writing his commentary on
Genesis, carried only as far as chapter XXI, verse 10.[207] Its
reader will be especially interested in its many comparisons of
texts: Old Latin (*antiqua translatio; quidam codices*); Vulgate (*nostri codices ex Hebraeo fonte transfusi; Hebraica
veritas*); Septuagint. The last he mentions so frequently and
firmly that it would seem he must have had it before him
rather than always drawing indirectly from Jerome or some
other Latin authority. For the Hebrew he depended on
Jerome. The borrowings, as usual, are numerous and varied:
from the *Hexaemeron* of Basil of Caesarea in the Latin version
of Eustathius; from the *Hexaemeron* of Ambrose; from
Jerome, *Quaestiones Hebraicae* and *Liber de nominibus*

[205] See Reeves, *Adamnan*, cli f.
[206] Giles X, 251f.; IV, 402ff.; *CSEL* XXXIX, ed. Geyer, xxxiii, 123ff.,
221, 296f.; Reeves, *ibid.*, pp. clii, 77, 191; *HE* V, 15ff.; Plummer II,
303f.; Laistner, *Thought and Letters*, 113f. and, in Thompson, 246; T.
Wright, *Early Travels in Palestine*, 1848, 1ff. Cf. *Homilies*, Giles V, 430.
For a date before 709 (possibly 702–703) see Laistner, *Hand-List*, 83.
[207] Giles VII, 1ff.; Plummer I, cxlix. See Laistner, *ibid.*, 41, for an
earlier version, explaining only Genesis, chs. 1–3.

Hebraicis; from Augustine, *De Genesi ad Litteram, De Genesi contra Manichaeos, Contra adversarium legis et prophetarum* and the *Confessions*; from Josephus and from Isidore. Perhaps, too, Bede had seen the works of one or more of the Biblical poets who had written during the fifth century on Paradise and the Fall of Man in Adam and Eve: Claudius Marius Victor and Alcimus Avitus in Gaul, Dracontius in Africa.[208] He tells us in his preface, again addressed to Acca, that the books which must be used in studying Genesis are so many that only the rich could buy them, so deep that only the learned could study them. "And so, Holy Father, you have desired me to pluck sufficient instruction for the necessity of weaker brethren from all the sources available to me, as though from the most pleasant fields of Paradise." Here then, he modestly observes, is a beginning from which the student may advance to higher ground.

To the modern scholar it is this comparison of texts, this drawing from earlier sources, which makes the study of Bede full of interest and value. On the other hand, in our time, when Biblical scholars have made documents J, E, and P and the saga of Abraham comprehensible to our ignorance, it is rather difficult to sympathize with the mediaeval's conception of the narrative of the Old Testament. Not even E, as against J, defended Abraham so stoutly as did Bede, seeing in this character of the Old Testament a holy patriarch of firm, historical substance. Abraham, of course, told no lie *at all* (*nihil mentitus*) when he declared to Pharaoh of Egypt that Sara was his sister. "He hid the fact that she was his wife, commending to God's protection his wife's honour and guarding against human snares in a human way; if he had not taken every possible precaution against peril, he would rather

---

[208] Giles VII, Preface, p. 1; Claudius Marius Victor, ed. Schenkl, *CSEL* XVI, i, 359ff.; Avitus, ed. Peiper, *MGH Auct. Ant.* VI, 2, 203ff.; Dracontius, ed. Vollmer, *ibid.,* XIV, 21ff.

have been presuming on God's aid than hoping in Him."
Thus all ended well, except for Pharaoh, who had dared to be
horrified at Abraham's behaviour. The story of Lot's wife,
Bede declares, "must literally be believed; and Josephus tells
that in his time that same pillar of salt was standing at the
gates of the city." This is the Bede of miraculous stories.[209]

Allegory in this commentary on Genesis is found everywhere. The ark in especial gave wonderful opportunity. In the
thought of Bede, as of so many others since he wrote, this is
the Church, crowded with many passengers, united in one
faith and one baptism. It is pitched within and without by
faith that never yields; its form is that of a human body,
typifying the Body of Christ in Whom all shall dwell who
will come to the stature of a perfect man; its window, giving
light after the flood to the dwellers within, reminds us of
the spiritual learning known only to those who have passed
through the water of regeneration. The dove, the spirit of
Christian man, soars upward through the window of contemplation; the "olive leaf pluckt off" which she brings back
tells of converts, brought into the refuge of the Church at long
last by the labours of pious souls.[210]

There is also much instruction of a plainer kind. God first
created His work, and then "saw that it was good"; in man
faith thus must be the forerunner of knowledge: *Tanto enim
quisque facilius aliquid proficiendo cognoscit, quanto re-
ligiosius antequam cognosceret Deo credidit.* Man was originally made without fear of death, without pain of hard labour,
without need of food; for his happiness he was to dwell among
the beasts and birds, erect above all in his human dignity,
to eat of the herbs of the field and the fruit of the trees of

---

[209] Giles VII, 161f., 209. On Bede as recorder of miracles see Colgrave, in Thompson, 201ff.

[210] Giles, *ibid.,* 96ff., 114; Augustine, *De civ. Dei* XV, 26 (verbal
borrowing by Bede: *cf. CSEL* XL, ii, 117, and Giles, 98).

Paradise. The Fall brought to man toil, ended only by death's relief; to earth, the thorns wherewith to prick him in memory of his sin; to beasts and birds, their terror of this being who henceforth must hunt them in his necessity. Now man must journey through the wilderness, protected, as Japheth in the tents of Shem, by constant study of the deeds and works of the Fathers of the Church; ready and fervent of spirit, as Abraham at the door of his tent in the heat of the day, to recognize at once the vision of the Lord and to depart in haste for the joy of the life to come.[211]

Now and again we seem to come once more upon Bede in his own thought. As Vergil in the *Georgics,* so Bede from the Vulgate reading of Genesis I, 11, *Germinet terra herbam virentem et facientem semen,* thinks that the days of creation must have been in spring-time, made lovely in new life by green fields and trees of the forest suddenly bursting into flower.[212] The words of I, 14, *Let there be lights in the firmament of the heaven to divide the day from the night,* seem to have reminded him of the dark hours before dawn when the brethren hastened to their prayers in Jarrow Church, their lanterns in their hands. So often in those hours all the earth was hidden in dense fog, through which floated wraiths of mist; yet far above they knew the stars were always aglow in the heavens. Another time he asks how there could have been light on the earth before the creation of sun and moon and stars, and answers his own question by picturing the gray light of early morning before sunrise, "which we see every day." He describes, too, the drops of dew upon the grass in the morning and the rainbow in the sky; its blue brought back to him the comfort of God's promised protection; the red he saw in its depths portended the fire of judgment upon the

---

[211] Giles, *ibid.,* 18, 24, 26ff., 48, 62, 72, 121, 128, 194; Augustine, *De Gen. contra Manich.* I, cc. 17f.: *PL* XXXIV, coll. 186f.
[212] Giles, *ibid.,* 13; Jenkins, in Thompson, 171f.

world at the end of time.[213] Incidentally, Bede's scathing denunciation of "all such as handle the harp and organ" and of "every artificer in brass and iron," save those who work directly in the Lord's service, seems to point to a monk differing in temperament from both Wilfrid and Aldhelm. Not that Wilfrid and Aldhelm would have condoned frivolity in the least, but they surely would have written more respectfully about music of any kind.[214]

Bede now reverted to his first love, that of chronology. For many years the monks of Wearmouth-Jarrow had been complaining, as well they might, that the little work which Bede had written in 703, *On Times*, was not detailed enough. In 725, therefore, more than twenty years later, he wrote another treatise, far more elaborate, on the same subject. It has come down to us under the name of *De temporum ratione, On the Reckoning of Times;* Bede himself called it his "longer book on times." [215] In the preface he dedicated it to his abbot, Hwaetbert, and declared once more his preference for the *Hebraica veritas,* the Hebrew scriptures from which he drew through intermediaries such as Eusebius, Jerome, and Augustine.

This longer work begins with a description of the reckoning on the fingers practised in ancient and in mediaeval times; and the account given here by Bede is the earliest still existing.[216] The symbolic meaning, of course, seen in the various positions of the fingers was that which especially attracted him. Again and again he inserted in his commentaries what he borrowed

---

[213] Giles, *ibid.,* 14, 16, 19, 125.

[214] Genesis IV, 21f.; Giles VII, 8of. The *Interpretatio psalterii artis cantilenae,* included in *PL* (XCIII, col. 1102C) among the *Bedae dubia et spuria,* contains a short description of a pipe-organ, written by Cassiodorus: Laistner, *Speculum* V, 1930, 218f.; *PL* LXX, coll. 1052D–1053A.

[215] *HE* V, 24; Jones, *ODT* 135ff., 173ff.

[216] Jones, *ibid.,* 329f.; D. E. Smith, *History of Mathematics* I, 1923, 184f.; II, 1925, 200; L. J. Richardson, "Digital Reckoning among the Ancients," *American Mathematical Monthly* XXIII, 1916, 7ff.

here from Jerome.[217] The thumb and index finger of the left hand meet in a circle to represent thirty; this symbolizes the union of marriage. The same finger of the left hand is bowed down over the thumb, bent against the palm, to represent sixty; this pictures the sorrows of widowhood. To form a hundred (the symbol, in general, of perfection, and, to Jerome, of virginity) the sign of ten, made by placing the tip of the index finger of the left hand upon the middle joint of its thumb, is multiplied tenfold by being made by the right hand. Thus one passes from the left side, that of the imperfect, to form a circle or crown upon the right side, that of highest attainment.

Occasionally, in the discussion of times and seasons, of moon and sun and the laws which govern them, which was to make Bede once more the pilot light of the Middle Ages, we come again upon a bit of digression reminiscent of his life. He rejoices that the rites offered to the spirits of the dead in February of pagan times have been replaced by the solemn procession in honour of blessed Mary at Candlemas, when priests and people, bearing each a lighted candle, walk through church and streets with chant of hymns. He tells of the months, Hebrew, Egyptian, Greek and Roman,[218] and then decides that it would be unfitting to leave out their names according to the tradition of his own country. This decision was of some importance; for Bede has thus left us the earliest list still extant of the names as used in England by heathen Saxons. Of special interest is the name of May, *Thrimilchi*, the month of three milkings a day; for August, *Weodmonath*, the month of weeds; for September, *Haligmonath*, the month of sacred rites in honour of idols; for October, *Winterfilleth*,

[217] *Adv. Iovin.* I, c. 3: *PL* XXIII, coll. 223f., described in Mayor's learned note on Juvenal X, 249, as "much allegorical trifling."

[218] Jones, *ibid.*, 203ff., 346ff.; *cf.* his "Polemius Silvius, Bede, and the Names of the Months," *Speculum* IX, 1934, 50ff.

the winter's full moon, the moon which marks the beginning
of winter; for November, *Blotmonath,* the month of animal
sacrifices offered to pagan gods. The month of March, in
Anglo-Saxon, *Hredmonath,* is explained here as the month
of the goddess Rheda, to whom the Saxons made offerings in
March; she may have been a deity of beauty, or of renown
(A.S. *hreð*: victory, glory). So, also, Bede interprets the old
pagan name of April, *Eastermonath, Eosturmonath,* as the
month of the goddess "of the growing light of spring." The
Anglo-Saxon name for both June and July, Liða, he explains
by the calm weather which is good for sailors; that for December and January, Giuli (*geola* or *iula*), is generally explained by the Old Norse *jol,* a festival, although Bede interprets the name as coming "from the turning of the sun to
the increase of daylight." [219] February, *Solmonath,* has caused
much trouble to scholars, because of Bede's note that "it may
be called the month of cakes (*mensis placentarum*), offered
at this time to the Saxon gods." The only support for this has
been seen in the Épinal Glossary, where the gloss is read,

panib: *sol*

and where *sol* has been explained as meaning cakes shaped in
the form of the sun. [220] At the end of the list Bede piously gives
thanks to God that "such emptinesses have been turned to
the Divine Praises."

Occasionally, a vivid and interesting illustration appears in
the midst of the lore of reckoning, as in the picture of a

[219] Jones, *ibid.,* 211ff., 350f.; the Old English *Menologium,* ed. Grein-
Wülker, *Bibliothek der angelsächsischen Poesie* II, i, 1888, 282ff.; Earle
and Plummer I, Appendix A, 273ff.; R. Imelmann, *Das altenglische
Menologium,* 1902, 56ff.; G. Herzfeld, *An Old English Martyrology,*
EETS CXVI, 1900, *passim; Kalendarium Anglicanum, PL* LXII, coll.
621ff.; R. Hodgkin I, 241f.; Jakob Grimm, *Teutonic Mythology* (Eng.
trans.) I, 1880, 289; II, 1883, 885.
[220] The *Épinal Glossary,* ed. Sweet, *EETS* LXXIXb (1883), 21, line
11; ed. Schlutter, 1912, *ibid.*; F. Kluge, *Englische Studien* VIII,
1885, 479.

church at night, illuminated throughout on some martyr's Feast by innumerable candles and by two lamps hanging from the roof. Bede lectures here at length on what he himself must have imagined of optical phenomena by his reading.[221] The proper time to cut trees for building war-galleys provides another glimpse of his curious speculation. He learned it, he says, from a manual on military science. Surely we must imagine him handling every manuscript, of whatsoever nature, that came into his monastery.[222] A diagram shows the movements of the moon for those unskilled in astronomy, and there are careful directions for its use; scientific observation on tidal waters is also provided, and tables give the dating of Easter from the year 532 to the year 1063.[223]

In addition, three smaller works by Bede on chronology may be mentioned here, as two of them are found with this work. The first, which is incorporated with it as chapters 38 and 39, was written as a letter to one called Helmwald, of whom we know nothing except that, while on a journey abroad, perhaps to Rome, he had sent a letter to Bede, asking for an explanation of the intercalary day inserted every fourth year in the calendar.[224] The second was also in the form of a letter, written to a priest named Wicthede, likewise unknown, though Bede recalls with pleasure the hospitality which Wicthede had once shown him. The subject discussed here is the spring equinox in its connection with the dating of Easter; it all turns about the Paschal canon, attributed to Anatolius, bishop of Laodicea in 270 A.D., which had played

---

[221] Jones, *ODT* 127, 229f.
[222] *Ibid.*, 231, 362. For the source of this passage see his "Bede and Vegetius," (p. 245 *supra*, note 50) ; *cf.* M. Deanesly, *EHR* LVIII, 1943, 138f.
[223] *ODT* 218ff., 354, 126, 232ff., 362f., 105f.; Levison, in Thompson, 119. On the contempt of both Aldhelm and Bede for astrology see Laistner, "The Western Church and Astrology during the Early Middle Ages," *HTR* XXXIV, 1941, 269.
[224] *ODT* 250ff., 371ff.

so important a part in the synod of Whitby in 664.[225] The
third was really a separate work, but, like the first, was included
in the *De temporum ratione,* of which it forms chapters 66
to 71, entitled the "Chronicle" and dealing with the six ages of
this world. Bede had already described these in his previous
work *De temporibus.* He now enlarged upon them with material drawn from a multitude of sources; Gildas, especially,
afforded him much description of events and people connected
with Britain during the sixth age.[226] We find here that method
of dating from the Incarnation of our Lord which Bede had
found in the work of Dionysius "the Humble" on the reckoning of Easter. This Christian method he had already mentioned in his *De temporibus* and used in his *Lives of the Abbots
of Wearmouth-Jarrow.* It is his constant application of it in
his *Ecclesiastical History,* written in 731, that has made him
renowned for its use in historiography.[227]

And now once more back to the Bible. From time to time
more commentaries came from Bede's ceaseless industry. Of
these we can date *On Ezra and on Nehemiah* between 725
and 731, since Bede mentioned it in his *Ecclesiastical History*
as finished, and referred in its preface to his *De temporum
ratione,* written in 725. He had already been planning his
work on Ezra some years before, when he was dedicating his
Genesis to Bishop Acca.[228]

Jerome was again here his master and his source as drawing
"the pith of allegory from the outer bark of historical narrative." In the decree of Cyrus, by which after the conquest of
Babylon in 538 B.C. the Jews of the Captivity were set free
for their return to Jerusalem, is seen the Lord, freeing His
people from the bondage of sin and everlasting death and

[225] *ODT* 138ff., 168f., 319ff.
[226] Ed. Mommsen, *Chron. min.,* 247ff.
[227] *VA* cc. 4, 23 (cf. *VAA* c. 7); Levison, *ibid.,* 130ff., 147ff.
[228] Giles VIII, 36off.; VII, 2; Jones, *ODT* 175; *HE* V, c. 24.

sending them in joy upon their way to Jerusalem which is both on earth and in heaven, the dwelling of eternal peace.

Then rose up the chief of the fathers of Judah and Benjamin, and the priests, and the Levites, with all them whose spirit God had raised, to go up to build the house of the Lord which is in Jerusalem. And all they that were about them strengthened their hands with vessels of silver, with gold, with goods, and with beasts, and with precious things, beside all that was willingly offered.[229]

All human souls have fallen, writes Bede, and must be rescued. In the new life of deliverance the priests and the preachers build the Temple of God for the faithful who support them with their offerings, sharing after their individual measure in the work. The kingship of Zerubbabel and the priesthood of Joshua portray in mystic meaning the authority of the Christ, leader of the marching Church; the servants and the maids represent layfolk who walk in its ranks; the singing men and the singing women on the long return to Jerusalem are monks and nuns who teach by their life and by their words; even the horses and mules and asses form part of the great procession of the redeemed from Babylon to Jerusalem, souls that must be drawn on by the power of their companions lest they stray and stop along the road! Enemies beat upon the host from without; peril threatens it from within, through those who take to themselves strange wives from the heathen, those who are enticed away from the fellowship of the Church by the charm of heretics and false philosophers.[230]

Nor does Bede neglect to point lessons in the midst of his allegory. Do not dare, he warns, to trust your human frailty to its work by day or its sleep by night before you

[229] Giles VIII, 360; Ezra I, 5f.
[230] Giles VIII, 370ff., 374f., 377ff.

have commended it to God; once again do not try to lead others in the spiritual life before you yourself have learned to walk therein; let layfolk receive freely of the fruits of sacred study from their guides on the march, the Fathers who shall answer for their safe arrival in the Holy City; let kings aid the Church by the arm of secular power, but let none be compelled to enter its ranks; let monks be missionaries in heart, not seekers of their own comfort in the beauty of their cloister. Remember, however, that even the evil of sin may be turned to good; lazy Christians have often been shaken from their sloth by the penitence that follows the mortal sin into which their unpreparedness has betrayed them. Thus sincere penitence has served God better than careless innocence.[231]

Finally, it is pleasant to note that the date of the Artaxerxes of this book, a point of discussion and of disagreement among modern students, did not leave Bede himself untouched. He was obviously no believer in the soul unaided by the intellect![232]

In the part of the work assigned to Nehemiah he repeatedly laments the lack of care and the selfishness rampant in the Church of his own eighth century. "Would that in our days," he exclaims, "some Nehemiah would come from God to stay our wrong-doings, to turn our hands from indulging our own desires toward the building of the City of Christ! This is the work of him who is set over the people of God, rather than the seeking of worldly profit and wealth from those to whom he preaches. Woe to those bishops and ministers of holy rites who delight in living upon their flocks and care nothing to toil for the souls of men by word or by deed![233]

[231] *Ibid.,* 388, 394, 445, 419, 436, 426, 401.
[232] *Ibid.,* 421.
[233] IX, 21, 23, 46f.; Plummer II, 381f.

Other writings on the Old Testament told of sacred properties and their ritual. The commentary *On the Tabernacle and Its Vessels and the Vestments of the Priests,* which explains in the same allegorical manner and in three books some six chapters of Exodus, XXIV, 12, to XXX, 21, finds one limit of date from the fact that Bede mentioned it when writing his book on St. Mark.[234] Another later work of similarly mystical interpretation, called *On the Temple of Solomon,* of I Kings V–VII and II Chronicles II–V,[235] must have been composed shortly before 731, for he wrote of it as "recently published" in a letter to his friend Albinus, abbot of the monastery of Saints Peter and Paul in Canterbury, when he sent to Albinus his *Ecclesiastical History* in that year.[236] Both commentaries draw upon the Latin version of the *Antiquities* of Josephus made in the monastery of Cassiodorus.[237] The preface to the work *On the Temple*[238] speaks with much feeling of "the present anguish of our times, the persecutions wrought by the unjust upon the just." Here, doubtless, we may see a reference to the political tragedies that were still visiting Bede's own land of Northumbria.

In 729 King Osric died. As we have seen, report affirmed that he had been murdered in revenge for his share in the slaying of that Osred who had reigned some years before.[239] He himself had named for the throne Ceolwulf, brother of King Cenred, his immediate predecessor, and Ceolwulf now entered upon his rule. In the year 731 Bede wrote at the end of his *Ecclesiastical History:* "Both the beginning and the

---

[234] VII, 225ff.; X, 37.
[235] VIII, 262ff.; 357.   [236] Plummer I, 3.
[237] Laistner, in Thompson, 246. In *De Tab.* (Giles VII, 307) and *De Templo* (VIII, 314), Bede tells of pictures he has seen in the *codex grandior* (or a copy of it), made by Cassiodorus at Vivarium: Mynors, ed. *Inst.* 23; *PL* LXX, col. 109; Chapman, *Early Hist. of the Vulgate Gospels,* 4f. For influence of his *De Templo* at a later time see Owst, *Literature and Pulpit in Medieval England,* 1933, 141f.
[238] VIII, 263   [239] P. 296 *supra.*

following years of King Ceolwulf's reign have abounded in so great disturbance of contrary happenings that one cannot yet know how to write of them or what end each of them will have." [240]

As in pagan days of Rome, so now in Christian England men's hearts failed them for fear, as comets of evil omen shot through the darkness of their night. Ceolwulf was a convinced Christian, and Bede had hoped for much, but in vain. Two years after the king's crowning, his chieftains rose against him, seized him bodily and mocked his devotion to the Church by tonsuring his head.[241] In 731 or 732, Acca, bishop of Hexham, Visitor of Wearmouth-Jarrow and Bede's special friend, was also driven by violence from his seat. Acca, it would seem, never returned, and the brethren were without a bishop almost, if not entirely, all the remaining days of Bede's life.[242]

On the other hand, King Ceolwulf was soon restored to his throne, and held it till after the death of Bede. The tonsure, however much it had been intended by his enemies for ridicule, was, indeed, the secret longing of his heart. Soon after this time, in 737, he was to resign his crown of his own will and begin the passing of the twenty years or so that still remained to him on this earth as one of the brethren of Lindisfarne. Some of these were, perhaps, well content at his reception, if the story is true that through his influence wine and cider appeared upon their refectory table; hitherto, as we saw in the experience of Wilfrid, only milk or water had been allowed. The royal brother, moreover, was to serve his profession well; at his death his renown of holy living was to earn him burial near the grave of Saint Cuthbert.[243]

---

[240] V, 23.

[241] Plummer I, 361 (*Baedae Cont. ann. DCCXXXI*); II, 340.

[242] Plummer I, *ibid.*; II, 330; Sim. Durh. II, *RS* LXXV, ii, 30, *ann.* 732. Frithbert, his successor, was not consecrated bishop of Hexham until 734 (S. D. 31), or 735 (*Baedae Cont.*)

[243] Sim. Durh. II, 102; *Gest. Reg.* I, 67.

But this was still six years in the future. He was still king of Northumbria when in 731 Bede dedicated to him that familiar book, written amid dark shadows upon politics and religion alike, the *History of the Church of the English People*. Ceolwulf had wanted to possess for himself and to circulate among his subjects the narrative of the coming, the spreading, and the ripening of the knowledge of the Faith throughout the different parts of Britain, north, south, east and west. He must have been grateful for the list of sources now described, for Bede had done all he could in seeking material for the truth and fullness of his record.[244]

Of conversion in the earliest days at Canterbury he had learned from Abbot Albinus, who had both encouraged him to undertake this work and had been his chief aid in carrying it through. Most valuable details had been obtained from letters of Pope Gregory the Great, which Nothelm, priest of London, soon to become Archbishop of Canterbury, had found among the Papal archives in Rome. From Daniel, bishop of Winchester, he had received information with regard to Wessex, Sussex, and the Isle of Wight; the brethren of Lastingham, monastery of Chad, had sent him answers to his questions on Mercia and Essex, and an abbot Esi, of whom we know nothing, had informed him concerning East Anglia; the writings of Cynibert, bishop of Lindsey, had given him details concerning Paulinus and other priests who had worked and preached in that province. Of the life of Cuthbert, a most important subject, the monks of Lindisfarne had told him in abundance. Here, however, as in all other parts of this work, Bede had endeavoured to find confirming of individual witness in other "most sure affirmation of trustworthy men." His knowledge of Northumbria was his own, supported and enlarged by more authorities than he could count.[245]

[244] For the sources, the achievement, and the influence of this work see Levison, "Bede as Historian," in Thompson, 132ff.
[245] *HE*, preface.

The narrative extends from the time of Caesar's invasion
of Britain in 55 B.C. until the year 731 A.D. So many have
described its vivid pictures that it would be waste of time and
space to retell the story. Kings and queens, bishops and simple
priests, abbots and abbesses, with their communities of monks
and nuns in these days of double monasteries, hermits and
missionaries, nobles and peasants, walk in the procession of its
pages along the highways and byways of this earth toward
their destiny of joy or pain in the life to come. The narrative
is never monotonous. Now it glows with vision and miracle,
with the learning and the charity of those called to be
saints;[246] now it lowers dark with battle and murder, plague
and famine, death and descent to the torment of hell. As we
pass from one to another of its five books, we gather innumerable details concerning life in England, ecclesiastical, monastic, secular:[247] of the ritual and usages of the Church; of
the daily life and rule of religious communities and solitaries;
of the manners, the doings, and the sufferings of ordinary men
and women in this eighth century of Bede. All reminds us of
that *History of the Franks* which Gregory of Tours wrote in
sixth century France. There is the same wealth of story, the
same leisurely pace, the same impartial description of saint
and sinner, in high places as in low, the same devotion to the
honour of Holy Church.

Yet there are many differences[248] between the English and
the French work. The *History* of Bede was written by one who
had lived his years in peace from external enemies—*felix
opportunitate vitae,* even if storm-clouds were gathering within
his land, who gave God thanks for Saxon settlements of
Christian rulers and knew not of the destruction and devasta-
tion to be wrought by the "kings from the north." Gregory,

[246] On Bede as hagiographer see Colgrave, in Thompson, 226ff.
[247] Bright, *Waymarks* (*op. cit.,* p. 249 *supra,* note 62), 285ff.
[248] *Cf.* F. J. Foakes-Jackson, *A History of Church History,* 1939,
pp. 119ff.

on the other hand, lived and wrote amid the tumult of the France he bravely tried to aid. His prose reflects his part in the confusion of battle on every side, as Bede's Latin mirrors the tranquillity of years given to prayer and study within the cloister. Not that Bede turned from the tragedies of his time; rather, he was still able to recollect his feeling in the quiet shelter of his cell. It is our gain that he lived to write of the widening life of the Church in England at a time when the teachings of Mahomet and the hordes of the Saracens were threatening the Church across the seas. And since he wrote with a scholarship and passion for accurate knowledge to which Gregory could not pretend, he is still to us the "Father of English History."

His legacy to his land was far greater even than this. To Bede we owe the first conception of the English as one people, gathered from different tribes and different origins; as one nation, welded, by one faith and one civilized organizing, from the various invaders, Angles, Saxons, and Jutes, who had settled from time to time within its shores.[249] In this sense, the *History* of Bede is an *Aeneid* of England.[250]

Gregory's *History of the Franks* was known to Bede, but he quoted it only once, in his revised edition of the Commentary on Acts: *Liber retractationis in Actus Apostolorum*. It might well seem that he had brought his writing to a splendid climax in his *History*. But his was the mind of a scholar and a saint. He could not bear to leave his work any shorter of perfection than was inevitable; and he felt strongly that his *Acts,* written "many years before," needed further effort. The second edition is not mentioned in the list of his books which, like Gregory

---

[249] R. W. Chambers, *PBA* XXII, 1936, 27f.; *cf.* his *Man's Unconquerable Mind,* 1939, 23ff. See also A. L. Maycock, "Bede and Alcuin": *HJ* XXXIII, 1934–1935, 402ff.
[250] For the readers of this work in England and on the continent during the eighth century see E. A. Lowe, *EHR* XLI, 1926, 246.

of Tours, he gave at the end of his *History,* and scholars have, therefore, generally concluded that it was written after 731.[251]

If this be so, it is the more noteworthy that in spite of the political strife within the land he loved so well, and in spite, too, of the increasing weakness of his own hard-driven body, Bede's scholarship reached its maturity in this book. He was already an old man, in health if not in years, when he ended the *History.*[252] His poring over dim and difficult manuscripts had ruined his eyes, his bending over their sheets had stiffened his limbs, the eternal mists and fogs of England, sending their damp cold into cell and dormitory and church, had brought rheumatism and bronchitis as familiar visitors. Nevertheless, he girded himself with all the energy of his younger days to follow Augustine in this reconsidering of earlier toil. His knowledge of Greek was now considerably enlarged, his textual criticisms therefore more frequent; his questioning of historical data was more searching, his chronological science more profound, his reading wider, his independence of thought and judgment more free and bold. It is, in fact, in this revised work that Bede stands out as now grown from the diffident recorder of excerpts into the scholar of full stature, ready for shrewd investigation and questioning as well as for following in paths he has tried and proved by his own research.[253]

It remains to consider briefly a few works which we cannot date with any precision. Four of them were certainly written before 731, since Bede mentions them in the list appended to

[251] See, however, the suggestion of Laistner, in ed. *Acts,* xiiiff. (*cf.* *HTR* XXXI, 1938, 269, and *Hand-List,* 20) that since Bede includes in his list of his works (*HE* V, 24: date 731) one entitled *In Actus Apostolorum libros II,* and since there is no evidence of the division of the first commentary (see pp. 263ff. *supra*) into two books, we might well date the second commentary, also, before 731 as the second book of the *In Actus.*

[252] He was in his 59th or 60th year; see Whiting, in Thompson, 4.

[253] Laistner, *TRHS* 86f.

his *History*. They are allegorical interpretations of the usual type: *On Proverbs;* [254] *On the Song of Songs; On the Song of Habakkuk; On the Book of Blessed Tobit*. The *Song of Songs* had been discussed before by Origen, by Jerome, by Isidore, and by Julian, bishop of Aeclanum in Italy in the fifth century. Bede, indeed, devotes some space to attacking the Pelagian views of this Julian, against whom Augustine of Hippo had once thundered.[255] He wrote *On the Song of Habakkuk* for some "beloved sister in Christ," a nun, now nameless, who had asked Bede to interpret this book for her.[256] All four treatises were well thumbed by scholars during the Middle Ages.[257]

There are three writings, however, which are of a different kind, each of interest in its own way. The first consists of sermons, *Homilies,* composed by Bede at various times, delivered by him at Mass in person, and read in monastic chapels after his death.[258] They are discourses on the Gospel for the day, composed in a Latin which, though simple and clear, overflows without stop into sentences of great length, packed full of detail, earnest in encouragement and in warning. Doubtless their foreign sounds were almost as if native to these sons of the cloister who listened. Their content marks them as intended for hearers well versed in the doctrine of the Church. It repeats Bede's teaching of the commentaries on the Bible, and we need notice here only a few words.

---

[254] Giles IX, 53ff.
[255] *Ibid.*, 186ff.; K. Werner, 179f.; Jenkins, in Thompson, 184ff.; Laistner, *ibid.*, 247.
[256] Giles IX, 405ff. For the book on Tobit see *ibid.* 427ff.
[257] For other works listed by Bede or assigned to him, known to us only by title, and for works possibly or certainly spurious, see Laistner, *Hand-List*, 154ff. For the "Psalterium Bedae" see *BRG Mon. Alc.* 748f.; Dümmler, *MGH Epp.* IV, 417.
[258] On the *Homilies* of Bede see Dom Germain Morin (*RB* IX, 1892, 316ff.), who has established a list of 50 genuine sermons. See also H. Quentin, *DACL* II, coll. 633f.

On Holy Mass:

He washes us day by day from our sins in His own Blood
when the memory of this same blessed Passion is unfolded anew
at the altar; when things created, bread and wine, are transferred
into the sacrament of His Body and Blood by the ineffable sanc-
tifying of the Spirit;

And each one of us is first cleansed by the water of Baptism
from all his sins, as it were by true circumcision, and thus with
the grace of new light working in him comes forward to be consecrated at the holy altar by the saving Victim of the Body and
Blood of the Lord.

On our Lady:

Let us ever keep in memory the example of blessed Mary,
Mother of God, so that, being found humble of spirit in His sight
and subject with due reverence to those about us, we, together
with her, may be worthy to dwell on high for evermore . . . And
so this good and wholesome practice has become customary in
holy Church, that her hymn be sung every day by all at the
chanting of Vespers for the kindling of our devotion by the
memory of the Lord Incarnate and the buttressing of our will to
virtue by the remembrance of His Mother. Fitly, too, was this
prescribed for the hour of Vespers, in order that the mind, tired
by labours and distracted by divers problems, in dwelling awhile
on the *Magnificat* might be lifted from the day's passing busi-
nesses and hurts to face the night in the reality of penitence and
new resolve.

On Prayer:

It may be that our intercessions for others cannot be granted;
yet the love which we give to them will find elsewhere its answer
from God;

The souls who dwell in the light of Heaven's eternal peace, in
the glory of blessed spirits, pour forth their prayers for us who
still tread our dark and dangerous path in a strange land;

The souls who walk toward their eternal hope amid the

redeeming pain of Purgatory may surely be furthered in their way by our prayers and our penitence, by the repeated oblation of the Holy Sacrifice at the hands of their loyal friends on earth.[259]

Naturally such observations were the direct fruit of Bede's reading in the Church Fathers. Their interest for us lies in the fact that he gathered and handed down this fruit for his own people of England, for the peoples of Europe, abbots and priests, monks and layfolk, in his own time and in the centuries to come.

One last passage should be quoted, as true of him in all his work of preaching and teaching. It comes from his sermon for the Sunday within the octave of the Epiphany, on Christ among the doctors in the Temple: *Descendit cum eis et venit Nazareth, et erat subditus illis.* "Let us think for a moment," Bede comments here, "how different from His subjection is our pride. Through the aid of the Lord we learn to under-stand difficult intellectual matters, not for eternity, but for passing time, and we are at once puffed up with conceit because simpler brethren cannot follow when we talk about such things. We therefore look down upon them from the height of our singular and vast erudition; nay, we even make fun of them, we, who would not want to be scorned by scholars more learned than ourselves, of whom there are plenty and to spare. We never think that the door of the Kingdom of Heaven lies open, *not* to those who only know in their learned minds the mysteries of faith and the commandments of their Creator, but to those who have progressed far enough to live by them." [260]

The second writing consists of some fourteen hymns which have come down to us under Bede's name, although we can-not now be certain how many were actually his work.[261] The

[259] Giles V, 272, 175 (*cf.* 429), 305f., 16, 18f., 381.
[260] *Ibid.*, 121f.

matter is not very important. We have already noted that Bede was no poet, however learned he was in the metrical science of his day. The chief interest of such composition as his lies in the development from classical to mediaeval verse. Here, however, we learn little, since he uses classical forms, hexameters, elegiacs, iambic dimeters. These last, indeed, show the mediaeval rhythm already known in the hymns of Ambrose, and taught by Bede, with acknowledgment to this master, in the treatise *On metrical art*.[262]

In this hymning we meet once more with the reckoning of days and of seasons, with the six ages of the world, with the Day of Judgment. The hymn on this last subject has been ascribed also to Alcuin; it was translated long after Bede's death into an Anglo-Saxon version, still extant.[263] It is summer-time in England, and the poet is sitting in a meadow full of flowers, under the shade of a great tree. As the wind awakes music among its branches, he, too, sings, of the life hereafter, the old familiar story he has told so often. Other hymns celebrate various Feast Days of the Church, of the Ascension, of the Holy Innocents, of the Blessed Virgin, of St. John the Baptist. One on Ethelthryd, abbess of Ely, is certainly by Bede, for he placed it at the end of his story of her life and death, as part of his *History of the Church of England*. It is written in elegiacs, with the tedious repetition known as epanalepsis:

A spouse betrothed to God, she reigned on earth for twice
    six years,
    Then in a cell she dwelt, a spouse betrothed to God.[264]

[261] Fourteen are printed by Giles (I, 54ff.), sixteen by Dreves (*Anal. Hymn.* L, 98ff.). See also Laistner, *Hand-List,* 122ff.; Julian, *Dict. Hymn.* 2nd ed. 1907, 124f.; Plummer I, cliii f.; Raby, *CLP* 147ff.; *SLP* I, 174f.; also in *DHGE* VII, 401f.; Whitney, in Thompson, 25f.

[262] *De art. metr.* c. XXIV.

[263] Ed. J. Rawson Lumby, *EETS* LXV, 1876, 2ff. For the Latin see Sim. Durh. *Hist. Reg.* 26: *RS* LXXV, ii, 23ff., and for criticism, Manitius, *Gesch.*, 86, Laistner, *Hand-List,* 126f.

[264] *HE* IV, 20.

The authorship of the third work, the "Penitential of Bede," is in doubt, and it is probably not his. A Penitential was a list of penances, primarily intended as an aid to a priest in prescribing due token of contrition to his penitent after confession of sin; as such, it placed against each of the offences which the author's learning and experience had led him to expect in confession the penance he believed best suited for the help and healing of the sinner. Such documents are familiar to all students of Church history in Britain and in continental Europe, especially during the earlier Middle Ages.[265]

It would be pleasant to record that Bede's last years passed in peace as he looked out from his beloved cell and tried to do all he knew lay still unfinished for Church and State while time still was his. But it was not to be. The kingdom of Northumbria had never ceased to stand uneasily since Ceolwulf had been restored to "its quivering throne"; and it had been gradually eclipsed in power and glory by Ethelbald of Mercia.[266] Its Church, too, had fallen on evil days; so evil, indeed, that on the fifth of November, 734, six months before he died, Bede sent from Jarrow a letter full of their story and their warning to his friend Egbert, bishop of York.[267]

We last saw John of Beverley placed in rule of this see of York upon the death of Bosa in 704 or 705.[268] In 721 John died in the peace of his monastery at Derewood, afterward

[265] For probable authorship of Bede see Wasserschleben, 37ff.; H.S. III, 326; K. Werner, 93; for possible authorship, McNeill in McNeill and Gamer, *Medieval Handbooks of Penance,* 217ff., and in RC XXXIX, 1922, 296f.; against Bede as author, Laistner, HTR XXXI, 1938, 263ff.; Schmitz I, 550ff.; II, 645ff. For full discussion and bibliography see Laistner, *op. cit.;* T. P. Oakley, *English Penitential Discipline,* 117ff.; McNeill and Gamer, *supra;* Le Bras, *s.v.* Pénitentiels, DTC XII, 1168ff. Text in H. S. III, 326ff.; Schmitz, II, 654ff.; translation in McNeill and Gamer, 221f.
[266] *Gest. Reg.* I, 58; HE V, c. 23.
[267] Plummer I, 405ff.   [268] P. 209 *supra,* note 171.

called Beverley, in Yorkshire. Three years before his death he had consecrated Wilfrid, one of his priests and abbot of the monastery at York, to assist and to succeed in office there as bishop, which he did under the name of Wilfrid II. This second Wilfrid, like his more famous predecessor, also added splendour in material offerings to his cathedral and other churches; he, too, was generous in aid for mind and body to a multitude of folk within his diocese. At length, in 732, he resigned, to yield his see to Egbert.[269]

This prelate was of the royal blood of Northumbria, cousin of its present King Ceolwulf and brother of the Eadbert who was to succeed Ceolwulf in 737. Later on, Egbert did much for the Church in the north. But at the moment he was still untried, and Bede poured out his soul in hope of new and better things under the new ruler. He had already met Egbert in the monastery at York, in a journey from home exceedingly rare in his life of stability at Jarrow, and he had looked forward to a second visit; but increasing sickness had made this impossible. Nothing remained, therefore, but to write the new bishop a letter.

It opens with a personal exhortation to Egbert as bishop: "Neither may a man live aright and neglect the duty of teaching, nor may the bishop who teaches well refuse to carry out his own instructions." As guide in the way of right living, let Egbert read the Epistles of Saint Paul to Timothy and to Titus, with the *Pastoral Rule* and the *Homilies on the Gospel* of Pope Gregory. "For as it is not meet that the vessels of the altar should ever be profaned by common and unworthy use, so it is altogether wicked and deplorable that he who has been ordained to consecrate upon the altar the Lord's sacrament and who stands there to speak and act in His Name, should

[269] Raine, *DCB* III, 377f.; *HE* V, cc. 2, 6; Flor. Worc. *ann.* 721; Plummer II, 273, 278. On Wilfrid II and on Egbert see Alcuin, *De sanct. Ebor. eccles.*, lines 1215ff., 1247ff.

offend his Lord by empty and silly behaviour directly he leaves the church."

From counsel Bede passes to condemnation of the evils rampant within the Church in Northumbria of the year 734:

First, the diocese of York is far too large for its proper administration by one bishop. Here we may easily see that Bede, in spite of all his reverence for authority and his own kindly nature, must have deeply disapproved of Wilfrid as diocesan of this same see. "Indeed, we have heard," he writes, "and it is common talk, that many hamlets and farms in remote mountain districts or in tangled ravines have not seen a bishop for many years; not only have souls, already baptized, no one to confirm them by the laying on of hands, but no teacher reaches the ignorant to instruct them in matters of faith or to explain the difference between right and wrong." Equally grievous is the state of things regarding Holy Mass and Communion. "Remember how healthful to Christians of every race is the daily reception of the Body and Blood of the Lord; this, as you know, is the constant practice of the Church of Christ throughout Italy, Gaul, Africa, Greece, and the whole of the East. Here, however, this form of devotion and of dedication to God is so lacking to the laity through the carelessness of their teachers that in nearly every part of our province it is almost foreign to them; even those who seem to be more devout do not venture to communicate except at Christmas and Epiphany and Easter. Yet there are numberless boys and girls of innocent and pure lives, as well as men and women both young and old, who without any shadow of doubt might make their communions every Sunday and on the Feast Days of the Apostles and Martyrs, as you yourself have seen them in the holy and apostolic church of Rome. Even married people, if some one would teach them due measure of continence and purity, might freely do the same to their heart's content." In spite of this lamentable situation, Bede continues in wrath, all, even the folk of remote farms and villages, are obliged to pay tribute to the bishop: "And when a bishop through love of money has assumed the right of episcopacy over more people than he can possibly visit or preach to in the whole year, then without doubt he is bringing deadly peril both upon himself and upon those given by false assumption to his charge."[270]

With the help, then, of his kinsman, King Ceolwulf, from whom much may be hoped, let Egbert endeavour to carry out the original intention of Pope Gregory: that twelve bishops be consecrated for the northern Province of England; that among these the holder of the see of York be appointed Archbishop by the receiving of the pall of authority from Rome. Let him, moreover, ordain priests and appoint teachers to help him in each village, by preaching the gospel, by consecrating the Holy Mysteries, and, especially, by administering the rite of baptism wherever needed. Thus will all the souls under Egbert's charge learn the Catholic faith as contained in the Apostles' Creed and the Lord's Prayer. These are, indeed, known to those who can read Latin; let translations into the Anglo-Saxon vernacular be given to those who cannot.

It is interesting to note that Bede includes among these "ignorant people, who only know their native language," both clergy and monks; he admits that he himself has often given Anglo-Saxon versions to priests of no Latin training.

Of further interest are the words "in each village," for they point to the growth of the parochial system. The parishes of Saxon England came gradually into being during the seventh, eighth, and following centuries. Many of them clustered around the greater monasteries and their daughter-houses;

---

[270] The amount of this *tributum* is unknown. In the *Laws* of Ine, King of Wessex (688–725), we find (c. 4) mention of necessary payment of Church dues at Martinmas: Attenborough, 36f.; Plummer II, 382.

the dwellers upon the wide lands belonging to these monastic endowments would naturally be sought out, converted, taught, and placed within reach of the sacraments of the Church by the monks to whom they also looked for succour in things of the body.

Again, sacred "places of prayer" were set apart in memory of deeds wrought by the power of the Lord, such as at Heavenfield, where Oswald under the sign of the holy Cross had conquered Cadwallon, king of the British. At such a place missionary priests, as they journeyed, would gather the people of the district for Mass and other ministrations, in a chapel or around a cross erected on the site.[271] Moreover, the growth of secular parishes had been encouraged by the determination of Archbishop Theodore in creating new bishoprics, whose occupants ruled and invigorated secular clergy as well as monastic. Under the influence of their bishops rich noblemen founded on their lands churches in which the tenants of townships owned by them might worship. Here was a salutary check upon unrestrained monasticism.[272]

Neglect of the laity, Bede writes to Egbert, was error by omission. But there was evil, crying for rebuke, in open sins committed, and this, too, in regard to monasteries. To monks England had owed her conversion, her learning, and the reclaiming of much of the vast tracts of forest, swamp, and wasteland that lay in her various kingdoms. But the tide was now bearing things bad as well as good in its course. So much territory had been donated for monasteries by kings and nobles, hoping for a safe passage to the life beyond, that many

[271] Cf. W. Page, *Archaeologia* LXVI, 1915, 64ff.; Stenton, 150f.
[272] *HE* V, cc. 4f.; V, c. 12; A. Hamilton Thompson, *Parish History and Records (Helps for Students of History* XV), 1919, 6ff.; *CMH* II, 531 (Whitney); G. M. Trevelyan, *History of England*, 1926, 64f.; J. H. Maude, in Traill and Mann, *Social England* I, 1901, 234; T. Hodgkin, *History of England*, 1906, 243ff.; E. L. Cutts, *Parish Priests and their People in the Middle Ages in England*, 1898, 46ff.

parts of the country had been bereft of secular protection against invaders, such as the Picts. Land was also lacking for the proper settlement of young nobles and soldiers who had deserved well of the Crown in war and who must be encouraged in loyalty. Nothing now remained to many of these but to leave their own shores, so grievously in need of their strong arm in these days of peril from without, or to give themselves up in careless poverty to a life of shameful indulgence. Were these monasteries true houses of God, the problem would be different. But so many of them utterly belied their name.

Bede had worse still to tell Bishop Egbert. Many men of noble rank were buying grants of land from the king and building monasteries upon them for their own comfort and ease. There they installed themselves as "abbots," although they neither knew nor desired to know anything of religious rule and discipline; indeed, one of their chief objects was to escape by this means from military service. Within these houses they lived in lust and vice unspeakable, assembling as their "monks" those as evil as themselves, especially men who had been expelled from true monasteries or had wandered from such of their own wayward will. These houses they gained as hereditary possession by edict of the king, that their sons and kinsfolk might enter upon an equally comfortable existence.[273] Some even founded like houses for their wives, who as "abbesses" presided over the "handmaids of Christ" who gladly flocked to luxurious and merry company. Worst of all, the bishops themselves were not only shutting their eyes to these blasphemies but even aiding them by their signatures on charters of grant. Here, then, Bede urged, was further work to do. Let Egbert and his king get instantly to it! Let them revoke charters, seize ill-gotten estates, dissolve unworthy com-

---

[273] Hereditary succession was known in monasteries of good report: Plummer II, 262f.

munities, and use the lands thus gained for the creation of the
new bishoprics so earnestly to be desired.

The effect of this letter was only partial. Yet in 735 Egbert
did obtain the pallium, sign of his investiture as Archbishop;
he did promote learning throughout the north of England;
and in founding the Cathedral School of York he sowed seed
of rich harvest for Europe.

And now the work of Bede was nearly over. The story of
his last days in the spring of 735 has been told again and again
from a letter sent by Cuthbert, afterwards abbot of Wearmouth-Jarrow,[274] to Cuthwin, at the time of its writing his
fellow-lector (in minor orders) and fellow-student in the
monastery. The Father and teacher, wrote Cuthbert, so beloved by all his community, had been rapidly failing. For
about two weeks before Easter he had suffered from marked
weakness and shortness of breath, though with very little real
pain. Then he had rallied, and from Easter to Rogationtide he
was serene and happy, constantly given, as ever, to secret
prayer and study, save when he joined the brethren, so far as
he could, in their chanting of the Hours, or slept for a short
while at night. Every day, also, he taught in the monastery
school and spoke to his yet unlearned novices in their Anglo-
Saxon tongue; more and more these last words turned upon
the soul's journey from this earth to the judgment-seat of
God.[275] He was also translating into Anglo-Saxon the Gospel
of Saint John and some passages from the works of
Isidore.

But on the Tuesday before Ascension Day his breathing

---

[274] See, on the doubtful suggestion that he was the Cuthbert to whom
as "fellow deacon" Bede dedicated his *On the Art of Metre* and *On the
Figures and Tropes of Holy Scripture,* Plummer I, cxlv; Whiting, in
Thompson, 34f. For the text of the letter and a beautiful translation see
Plummer I, lxxiiff., clxff.
[275] For Bede's "Death Song" see A. H. Smith, *Three Northumbrian
Poems,* 1933, 4ff., 15ff., 23ff., 42f.

became much more laboured and a swelling was noticed in his feet. He continued to teach, however, and to dictate his translation; from time to time he urged his young men to be quick to learn, "for I do not know how long I have to live— whether my Creator may soon take me hence." Very early the next morning he bade them take up once more their writing and went on dictating to them until the third hour of the day, when the community marched out in the Rogation ritual, carrying the relics of saints as they walked and sang the litany of prayer for God's blessing on their fields. One of the novices remained behind, a boy named Wilbert. "There is still one chapter left to translate," he said, "and it is hard for you to answer any more questions." "No, it is easy," Bede answered: "put your pen in the ink and write fast." At the ninth hour in the afternoon Cuthbert was with him. Suddenly he made a request: Would Cuthbert call together the priests of the monastery? In fear the young man ran to gather them together. Bede then said good-bye as he gave to each something of the little possessions that were lying in his box, gifts sent him by friends, pepper, used for seasoning, napkins, and incense. "Long have I lived," he ended, "and the gracious Judge has wisely ordered my life. The time of my departure is at hand, for my soul longs to behold the Christ, my King, in His beauty."

Once more he was alone with the boy Wilbert as it drew slowly toward evening and as he still worked on. At last Wilbert spoke again: "Dear master, there remains yet one sentence to write." He answered, "Good! Write it." For a moment the pen went on. Then the boy said, "Now all is written," and Bede replied, "It is well, you have spoken the truth; for 'it is finished.' Take my head into your hands; I would sit over against the place in which I used to pray, that there I may call upon my Father." So, sitting on the floor of his cell, his head resting on the boy's arm, he chanted the *Gloria* and with its end ended his life on earth.

"And none could doubt," wrote Cuthbert, "so faithfully had he laboured in the service of God, that his soul was borne by the angels to the gladness of desire in heaven." Already the Church at Vespers had entered upon the Feast of the Ascension, May 26, 735; the secular world marked the hour as before midnight, May 25.[276]

His relics lay at Jarrow until the eleventh century. Then they were secretly carried away to Durham Cathedral by its sacrist, Ælfred Westou, who believed it to be his special mission to gather the bones of holy men from their burial-places for the adorning of his own church. There they lay in honour, with those of Saint Cuthbert, till the time of Hugh de Puiset, bishop of Durham in the reign of Henry II, who enclosed them in a shrine of gold and silver. The same bishop built the Galilee of the cathedral; later on the shrine was placed in this at the request of one Richard of Barnard Castle. Under Henry VIII, during the despoiling of so many monasteries, this tomb of Bede was broken, and his relics, so report declared, were buried beneath the ground in the same spot. Examination in 1831 revealed the presence of a number of bones interred in a coffin. We would gladly think that they are his, still lying there; above them rests a great stone of blue marble, on which has been reproduced the old legendary inscription:

> *Hac sunt in fossa*
> *Bede venerabilis ossa.*[277]

Its jingle is hallowed by the legend of the monk of Durham who was told to write an epitaph for Bede but who, try as he

[276] Whiting, in Thompson, 35.
[277] Sim. Durh. I, *RS* LXXV, i, 88f.; *Rites of Durham*, II, ed. Fowler, *SS* 107, 1903, 44f., 136, 233ff.; *Historiae Dunelmensis scriptores tres*, ed. Raine, *SS* 9, 1839, 11; Appendix, cccxli.

would, could not get the necessary dactyl in the fifth foot of the hexameter verse. He went to sleep on his problem, and found next morning that an angel had filled up the line with *venerabilis*.[278]

The description of "Venerable," however, has a more natural origin in history. It was the usual title for a man of holy life who was not included in the calendar of saints; and it would easily be given to one so renowned for learning. In the Middle Ages Bede's figure, clad in a blue habit, looked down from the windows of Durham Cathedral; his name was given to one of its Nine Altars in the chapel at the east end.[279] As "Saint Bede" his Feast was recorded in a goodly number of churches and monasteries of England, especially in the north, during the Middle Ages and afterward. But for the most part he was known rather through his writings than through the fame of prayer, fasting, and miracle which called Cuthbert or John of Beverley to saintship; and writings were not so evident a certifying of holiness.[280] Moreover, the year's memory of Bede on May the twenty-sixth was for long overshadowed by that of Augustine of Canterbury, kept on the same day, until the former was permanently transferred to the twenty-seventh. In 1661 the name of Bede was added to the calendar of the English Prayer-Book; in 1899 Pope Leo XIII decreed that the Feast of the Venerable Bede, as Doctor of the Church, should be observed on the twenty-seventh throughout the world.

[278] Giles I, ciii f.; Plummer I, xlviii f.
[279] *Rites of Durham*, II, 109, 114, 117f.
[280] His name was found in the York calendars, but not in those of Sarum (except for the years 1530 and 1546). See the *York Breviary*, I, ed. Lawley, *SS* 71, 1880, *Calendarium*, 7; II, *SS* 75, 1883, col. 286; the *York Missal*, I, ed. Henderson, *SS* 59, 1874, xxii, xxxiv; *English Kalendars before A.D. 1100*, I, ed. Wormald, *HBS* LXXII, 1934, 34, 118, 132, 160, 188, 202, 230; *English Benedictine Kalendars after A.D. 1100*, I, ed. Wormald, *HBS* LXXVII, 1939, 6, 23, 55, 88; *Brevarium ad usum insignis eccles. Sarum*, I, ed. Procter and Wordsworth, 1882, Kalendar for May. Bede's works were used for the Lessons in monastic Offices in England and on the continent: *York Breviary*, II, 286ff.; *Second Recension of the Quignon Breviary*, I, ed. J. Wickham Legg, *HBS* XXXV, 1908, 88, 301.

Increasingly in modern days churches are dedicated in his name.

It were well that the manifold gifts of this early English saint should be more widely recognized today. His devoted toil, seeking no end but the enlightenment of men in the ways of God, bequeathed to students of future centuries in England and on the continent of Europe his knowledge of the history, the science, the faith, of his country, his day, his Church, a knowledge imparted in all honesty, expressed in all simplicity, and with a beauty all his own.[281] His pupil, friend, and bishop, Egbert, was to train in the Cathedral School of York the man, Alcuin, to whom Europe was to owe renewed radiance of learning—learning to shine afar into a naughty world from this monk of Jarrow, this "candle of the Church, kindled by the Holy Spirit in the English land." [282]

[281] S. Gaselee, *An Anthology of Medieval Latin,* 1925, 24f.

[282] Boniface, *Epp.* ed. Dümmler, 91; *cf.* 75f. As in the case of the Latin Vergil, so Bede was held in mediaeval days long after his death to be the author of "prophecies"; see Kittredge, 58 and 226. This doubtless was due to his fame in astronomical calculation; *cf.* Lynn Thorndike, 676f., 688f.

Chapter IV

BONIFACE OF DEVON

BONIFACE OF DEVON

IT WAS the year 716, a year notable for many happenings in England. That evil youth, King Osred of Northumbria, was slain by his kinsmen, and Cenred received his throne; Ceolred, the lustful king of Mercia, died in raving madness and was succeeded by Ethelbald, friend of Saint Guthlac, the hermit. Abbot Ceolfrid bade farewell to his monks of Wearmouth-Jarrow, and Hwaetbert was elected in his place; the monks of Iona, taught by Egbert, at last yielded submission to Rome. The south of England had come under the rule of two men renowned for their codifying of laws, Wihtred of Kent and Ine of Wessex.[1]

Once again we return to this land of Aldhelm in the south-west. Things had been going well within it since he had died in 709. The very next year King Ine had driven from Somerset that British chieftain whom Aldhelm had rebuked for his Celtic practices, Geraint of Devon and Cornwall; in 715 he had also beaten back the Mercians, who had invaded under Ceolred. By occupation of British holdings, by wise and generous ordering for Saxon and Briton alike, by whole-hearted loyalty to the Church, Ine was already paving the road to the Wessex of the ninth century, of Kings Egbert and Alfred.

One day of this year of 716, within the cloister of Nursling near Romsey in Hampshire,[2] a monk was pacing up and down as he struggled in the grip of two powerful forces, each contending for his body, soul, and mind. Many months now had

---

[1] Attenborough, 24ff.; 34ff.   [2] Knowles, 22.

passed since first he had felt this crisis coming upon him, this parting of the ways; today, he knew, must see his decision affirmed and openly acknowledged. The rushing of the little river Test, swollen by the tidal wave from Southampton Water, seemed to reflect his stormy mood, and he threw himself at last in weariness upon an old stone bench that stood upon its bank. Once more he would think the whole matter through before he went within to tell Father Abbot Winbert what his best judgment had bidden him decide.

He had been born about 675 in Devonshire to a family of noble blood and wide estates; his name was Winfrid.[3] As a very little boy he had loved to hear the stories of the saints told him in his nursery; and his father's decision to send him for schooling to a monastery in the neighbourhood had naturally fostered a child's religious bent. Tradition places this monastery in the modern Exeter, then known as Adescancastre. The abbot of its congregation, Wulfhard, was a kindly ruler; under him Winfrid passed through the same training as Bede, himself at this time a child oblate in his northern monastery on the bank of the Wear.

But Wulfhard was no Benedict Biscop. As Winfrid grew into manhood, he had found within himself that longing for wider reading which had possessed the mind of young Aldhelm, now famous throughout Wessex as the learned abbot of Malmesbury in Wiltshire. Many students from Wessex had followed Aldhelm to the school of Canterbury, and a wave of enthusiasm for knowledge, promoted by his influence, was still in flood among the monasteries of southwestern England. Adescancastre held neither the books nor the teachers which could satisfy the hunger of Winfrid's mind, and he had left it for the monastery of Nursling, at that time under the rule of the scholarly Winbert.

[3] Hauck, 449f.

Long afterward, when Winbert was dead and Winfrid had passed his sixtieth year, he looked back upon this Father Abbot with reverence and affection, remembering with delight the copy of six books of the Prophets which Winbert had written "in bold and separate letters, clearly formed." [4] At Nursling he had gained also that knowledge of the Bible and its interpretation, intellectual and mystical, of classical and Christian literature in poetry and in prose, of sacred chronology, history and canon law, of composition in Latin paragraphs and in lines of rhythm, which we have seen bearing fruit in the works of Aldhelm and of Bede. As time went on he, too, like Bede, had progressed from student to teacher in his monastery; like him, he had turned to writing for the use of his classroom. We have a Latin grammar of his, and poems and riddles, full of that artifice of acrostic and metric contrivance which Aldhelm loved.[5] To Winfrid Aldhelm must have been as master and ideal in the study of words and their composing; no doubt, the two met again and again during these years in Wessex. There is also witness, in letters written during Winfrid's later years, of the respect in which he himself, like Aldhelm, was held as a teacher and a critic of Latin verse.[6]

[4] *Bonif. Epp.* No. 63 (the numbering of the *Letters* of Boniface throughout this chapter follows the edition of Michael Tangl, 1916, unless another editor is named). Hahn, *Bon. und Lul,* 27, and Ehwald, ed. Aldhelm (502f.), identify him with the Winbert who was clerk at the courts of Kings Caedwalla and Ine of Wessex (*Gest. Pont.* 355; Kemble I, No. 48). He may also have been the Winbert to whom Aldhelm wrote a letter asking for his intervention with Caedwalla for the recovery of land for Malmesbury Abbey (*Gest. Pont.* 355f.; Ehwald, *ibid.*).

[5] For the grammar see Manitius, *Gesch.,* 149f.; Mai, *Auctores classici* VII, 1835, 475ff.; C. Bursian, *Sitzungsber. Akad. d. Wiss. phil. hist. Cl.,* Munich, 1873, 457ff.; P. Lehmann, *Die Grammatik aus Aldhelms Kreise: Hist. Vierteljahrschrift* XXVII, 1932, 758ff.; G. J. Gebauer, *Prolegomena to the Ars Grammatica Bonifatii,* 1942. For the metric, see A. Wilmanns, *RM* XXIII, 1868, 403f.; for the poems, written in Germany, see Dümmler, ed. *Poet. lat. aevi Karol.* I, *MGH* 1881, 1ff.; for the so-called Penitential of Boniface, "probably a product of the ninth century," see McNeill and Gamer, 427f.

[6] *Bonif. Epp.* Nos. 98 and 103; Willibald, c. 2.

Thus at Nursling he had laid step by step the foundation of renown both intellectual and spiritual. Many came now from outside to consult him on their reading of sacred texts; women, too, as to Jerome centuries before, poured out their longing for enlightenment in letters addressed to his cell. Long ago he had passed from novice to professed brother in the monastic life; at the proper age he had been ordained priest, and soon caught the minds and souls of his own community and of its many visitors by his power and vividness as preacher. Nursling was proud of this Aldhelm of its own and keenly hoped that it might gain from him a work such as Aldhelm had wrought at Malmesbury.

And all the more because he had proved himself able in practical affairs. A synod of bishops and priests of Wessex had met some time before 712, under the presidency of King Ine, to debate measures for quelling disturbance in the kingdom. At length it was decided to refer the matter to Bertwald, Archbishop of Canterbury. When nominations for the office of envoy upon this important errand were in order, three abbots, Winbert of Nursling, Wintra of Tisbury in Wiltshire, and Beorwald of Glastonbury in Somerset, had promptly declared the name of Winfrid. The nomination had been accepted, and the young monk had fulfilled his mission so well that he was rapidly becoming much in demand at assemblies of the Church in the West.[7]

All this was struggling for remembrance in his mind as he sat now near his river in the year 716. As monk, he knew himself honoured by his community, valued by his abbot; as priest, he was on terms of warm friendship with his bishop, Daniel of Winchester; he had proved his worth to the Primate of his province. The way lay open, if he wanted to follow

[7] Willibald, c. 4, ed. Levison, 14. On the date of the synod see J. Armitage Robinson, *Somerset Historical Essays*, 31.

Aldhelm, whether as bishop in Wessex, as participant in its councils, as abbot of one of its religious houses, as teacher and, joyful thought, as writer and student in its peace. Moreover, he loved his country passionately. He had been born on the border that had kept back Saxon conquest from the forests and moors where Geraint still ruled his British people; perhaps, indeed, some of their Celtic blood ran in his own veins and bound him to the soil of their land.

If so, this very Celtic strain was now dividing him against himself, as he turned to confront the other side of his thought and saw as in a vision those same Celts, daring all in their journeyings over land and sea: Patrick of Britain; Columba and Columban of "that race of the Irish, for whom pilgrimage is second nature." [8] England was now Christian, through the labours of those who had crossed the sea. But what of the heathen who still sat in darkness on the continent of Europe? [9]

Above all, his mind turned to that mysterious region where Wilfrid of York had harvested souls nearly forty years before —Frisia, the territory lying toward the northeast of Holland, on the shore of the Ijssel Meer. Much had been attempted for the conversion of its heathen people since Wilfrid had preached among them in the winter of 678–679. Some five or six years afterward, that Englishman named Egbert, exile with so many others from his native country for the sake of study in Ireland, home of sanctity and scholarship, had been seized by a desire to preach the gospel among the German tribes beyond the sea. Egbert was a priest, or a bishop, and devoted to the prayer and fasting which were his work in his Irish monastery of Rathmelsigi, now of unknown location. There he had gathered a small company of good and muscular clergy

[8] *Vita S. Galli:* Pertz, *Script.* II, 30; *cf.* Plummer II, 170.
[9] Kinship between Anglo-Saxon and Teuton must have called forth Anglo-Saxon missionaries only less strongly than their Christian zeal; *cf.* S. J. Crawford, 36.

and laymen, as enthusiastic for this new project as he himself.
He had been just on the point of starting out when early one
morning a brother monk had come to him with discouraging
news. This monk had had a vision in the darkness before the
dawn: the Lord had decided that Egbert should teach His
ways, not to the German tribes, but to the monks of Iona,
still obdurate in their refusal of the Roman Easter.

A vision was all-important, the brother had been very sure,
and Egbert had been made exceedingly uncomfortable. But
his heart had not allowed him to abandon those costly prepara-
tions. Alas! a few days later the conscientious brother had re-
appeared on the same errand. There had been another vision,
and he had been rebuked for speaking to Egbert so mildly.
"Tell him"—so the Voice had warned—"to get him to Columba's monks, whether he likes it or not, for the ploughs of their
souls do not drive straight." A second time Egbert had refused
to hear. Was not all ready in the ship lying off the Irish shore,
waiting to sail for the German or the Dutch coast? But the
Lord had been determined. A terrible storm had swept down
and thrown all into disorder. The would-be missionary had at
last recognized with Jonah that "for his sake this tempest
came about"; and he had resolved to start for Scotland. As
we have seen, he brought about the conversion of Iona in this
same year of 716.[10]

He had done his best, however, to encourage others to take
his place. One of his brethren, Witbert, also an Englishman
who had lived long in Ireland, had actually set sail and had
arrived in Frisia. He had found the friendly King Aldgils dead,
and the throne in possession of his son, Radbod, a chieftain at
this time entirely happy in his pagan gods and in no way disposed to help a Christian intruder. For two years Witbert had

[10] *HE* III, c. 27; V, cc. 9, 22; Plummer II, 197, 285; Hauck, 432f.;
p. 295 *supra*.

struggled with disappointment, only to return in hopeless resignation to his Irish monastery.

The third adventurer had been the great Willibrord, born in Yorkshire about 658, some eighteen years before Winfrid's birth in Wessex.[11] Shortly afterward the prevailing thirst for monastic life had driven Willibrord's father, whose name was Wilgils, away from their home to found a community of monks under the protection of Saint Andrew, on the headland that looks down upon the Humber rushing to the sea. He had not gone forth without thought for his small son. As Benedictine ordinance allowed, he had entrusted him to the care of the monks of Ripon, lately brought under rule of Wilfrid by gift of his friend Alchfrid of Deira.

Here the child had grown up in devotion to the Catholic discipline of Rome, had watched the walls of Wilfrid's beautiful church slowly rise, had seen around him the richness which magnified all that Wilfrid did as abbot and bishop. Here he had delighted in the regular recital of the Benedictine Office, by night and by day, until his delight had been sealed in the tonsure and the vows that made him himself a Benedictine monk. Thus the years had passed until his twentieth, when he, too, had decided to travel on pilgrimage to Ireland.

No one cause can be given for this resolve. Doubtless he had felt the enthusiasm of Egbert, of Witbert, of so many other travellers. Perhaps, as a son of the North, like Aidan and Cuthbert, he had caught from its lonely moors and hills a warning to flee the comfort of this transient world; perhaps the troubles attending the expulsion of Wilfrid in 678 had

---

[11] Alcuin, *Life of Willibrord* (prose), ed. Levison, *MGH Script. rer. Merov.* VII, 81ff. A. Grieve (*Willibrord*, 1923) gives full details, with a translation of Alcuin's *Life* and a bibliography. See also especially Albert Poncelet, *Acta SS.* Nov. III, 1910, 414ff., and Verbist, *Saint Willibrord*, 1939.

made him restless and unhappy. Ireland would give him a deeper knowledge of his calling, and peace withal.[12]

In Ireland he had stayed with Egbert twelve years, constantly conferring with missionary adventurers, until he, too, was longing to pass on to the ignorant the things he had learned to know. To him, also, Frisia had called; the harvest there was waiting, the labourers unknown. At last in 690 he had sailed with eleven companions, to land at the mouth of the Rhine and to travel from there to Utrecht, the old Roman city of Trajectum. Soon, like Witbert, he had found Radbod an impassable barrier. This time, however, the pilgrim had come prepared. He had simply turned south, to ask aid of Pepin of Heristal, Mayor and acting ruler for the Frankish king, now Clovis II.

Most fortunately Pepin had lately defeated Radbod in battle, and so severely that the Franks at this moment were the chief power over that part of Frisia which bordered on the Frankish territory proper, even although Radbod still had Utrecht. His defeat at the hands of the Christian power would naturally confirm him in adherence to his pagan gods. On the other hand, Pepin, avowed son of the Church, would be glad to find in Willibrord one who would advance Christian practice in the newly acquired territory, for Pepin knew the material value of adherence to his faith.

So things had seemed well begun. But not in vain had this new missionary priest been trained in Ripon Abbey under Wilfrid. Pepin's authorizing was, it is true, a practical matter. But far more important to the mind of Willibrord had been the spiritual blessing of Rome upon his enterprise. He must promptly, he had felt, place all in order by a journey to Rome, where he would tell the Holy Father all about his plans and obtain proper sanction as a basis for his work. The Pope in

[12] Hauck, 435; Grieve, 23f.

690–691 was Sergius I, to whom Wilfrid had appealed from England and Aldhelm had made so happy a visit at Rome. The same joy awaited Willibrord; and he had returned to Utrecht in 691, definitely appointed by the Pope to labour under authority of the Church for the conversion of the Frisians.

Meanwhile that labour was eagerly calling for the ministrations of a bishop, and the Anglo-Saxon missionaries as eagerly wanted one of their own blood and speech. With characteristic courage they had taken action. Either during Willibrord's absence or, more probably, soon after his return, they had chosen from their number the monk Swidbert for this office. When we ask why Willibrord was not elected, we find ourselves confronted by a mystery never entirely solved. In the circumstances we might have expected Pope Sergius to consecrate Willibrord as bishop for Frisia; and certainly it would have been natural for his own brethren to desire him as their chief Pastor. The answer to both questions probably lies in Willibrord himself. He was much younger than Swidbert, and, we may think, may modestly have put his friend forward as one more experienced in administration, as better fitted in other ways which we have now no means of understanding. Willibrord may well have hesitated before assuming so responsible a position at the age of thirty-four.[13]

It is interesting, also, that Swidbert, the Anglo-Saxon, did not seek consecration at the hands of any Frankish bishop. Perhaps Pepin, the greatest power among the Franks at this time, objected to his election in place of that Willibrord whom he had already approved for the Christianizing of his subject Frisians. At any rate, Swidbert travelled to England, where, as we have seen, in the absence of Bertwald, Archbishop-elect of Canterbury, he had received the laying on of hands from

[13] *HE* V, c. 11; Hauck, 437, note 1; Poncelet, 427; Grieve, 34ff.

Wilfrid, exile at this time in Mercia. The fact that Wilfrid had once been Willibrord's abbot at Ripon may also suggest that Swidbert was elected with the full consent and desire of Willibrord, his leader in Frisia.

But, whatever the history of his election and consecrating, Swidbert's episcopate among the Frisians had been short. He had soon gone off across the eastern border to convert the Boructuari, a German people living between the rivers Ems and Lippe, in the district where Münster now stands.[14] The reason for his departure is not known; perhaps admirers of Willibrord had made things hard for him. Nor had this second field proved any more fruitful. For a while "he had led many into the way of truth by his preaching"; then his converts had been scattered by a sudden invasion of the pagan "Old Saxons," [15] and he had fled in despair to the refuge of Pepin's court. Apparently he had now decided that his days of public mission were over.

In this time of gloom a woman had brought comfort. If Pepin did not admire Swidbert greatly, the Lady Plectrude, his strong-willed wife, did.[16] At her urging the Mayor had allowed this exiled bishop an island retreat amid the waters of the Rhine, known as *In Litore* and now identified with Kaiserswerth, on the river's bank, some seven miles from Düsseldorf. There he had built a monastery, long since vanished, although pilgrims of modern times have seen and venerated a shrine within its Parish Church, believed to guard the bones of Saint Swidbert.[17]

The work in Frisia meanwhile had been carried on by Willibrord in the best way he could. Some encouragement must have come to him from the arrival of two other priests

---

[14] The Bructeri of Tacitus: *Ann.* I, c. 51; *Germ.* c. 33.
[15] The Saxons of continental Europe.
[16] *HE* V, c. 11 (where she is called Bliththryda).
[17] Plummer II, 291.

bent on the same exciting, if perilous, adventure. They were of his own nation, Englishmen who had received, as he himself, long training in Ireland; they had come, however, to work among the "Old Saxons," those pagans near the Frisian border who had dealt so hardly with Swidbert. Both were called by the same name, Hewald; but as one was fair-haired and the other dark, they were described as "the White" and "the Black." Both were most devout, but Black Hewald knew his Bible better. Only a brief time had been theirs after they entered this barbaric land; its savages, in dread lest they, like their neighbours, be brought under subjection to a Christian God, had promptly murdered them both and thrown their bodies into the Rhine.[18]

At last Willibrord had told Pepin that a bishop must be appointed for his work; and Pepin in return had declared that Willibrord was the man. This time necessity had won the day; doubtless there had been no other so fitted for the office. A second journey to Rome had followed, and in 695 the same Pope Sergius had consecrated Willibrord Archbishop of the Frisians.[19] As a mark of this new life, Sergius had given him another name, Clement, and had sent him back at once to confirm and ordain his new converts.

The title of "Archbishop" had been desired for Willibrord by Pepin himself. By this time Pepin's power had absorbed the Frisian city of Utrecht,[20] and he was dreaming of a widespread province in the Frisian land, ruled by himself as Frankish overseer of State and Church, with Willibrord as his minister in matters spiritual and ecclesiastical. Such had al-

[18] HE V, c. 10.
[19] H. A. Wilson, ed. Calendar of St. Willibrord, HBS LV, 1918, 43. The year 696 given by Bede (HE V, c. 11) would be 695 according to the Bedan Indiction: Poole, Medieval Reckonings of Time, 30; Wallis, English Regnal Years and Titles, 16. The day was November 21: Wilson, ibid., Poncelet, 427.
[20] HE, ibid.

ways been the views of the Frankish kings when they really had been rulers in deed, and Pepin was boldly following in their train.

Utrecht, therefore, had been given by him as seat of rule for his Archbishop in Frisia; money, facilities, and men had been forthcoming in plenty for the work. Soon churches and cloisters were rising among old ruins both in Utrecht and the adjacent country. Most famous among those outside the city in later times was the monastery of Echternach, founded by Willibrord in 698 on land given him along the river Sure near Trèves by Irmina, abbess of a convent in that region.[21] From here, as from Utrecht, the teaching of the truths of the Bible and the Church began to progress, encouraged by a truce between Radbod of Frisia and Pepin; indeed, this truce even led to some kind of alliance, for Radbod's daughter Theutsind became wife of Pepin's son Grimoald.

The rising hope unfortunately had quickly ebbed. Radbod might deem it prudent to be friendly with his conqueror Pepin and even to refrain from open resistance to the labours of Pepin's Catholic Christians. Nothing, however, would induce him to offer active aid, and the mass of his people sat persistently in their darkness, far outside any missionary ray of light. At last Willibrord had decided that he was wasting time at the moment in this barren field, and he had moved further north by boat to preach among the Danes.

Once more disappointment had awaited him. Ongendus, king of this warrior race, is described as "more savage than any wild beast and harder than any stone."[22] He had been no more promising material than Radbod; but he had allowed his unwelcome visitors to depart in safety, even, prob-

[21] Pertz, *Diplom.* I, 93f., 173. The tradition of Irmina is here held false, but *cf.* Hauck, 301, note 2; Levison, *MGH Script. rer. Merov.* VII, 88f. The monastery was fully established in 706: Verbist, 132.

[22] Alcuin, *Vita,* c. 9.

ably with indifferent scorn, to take with them thirty Danish boys for their instructing in Christian doctrine, after the manner of Gregory the Great in his anxiety for the pagan British.

After the Danes, the Frisians had seemed mild; and Willibrord had decided to begin work among them all over again. But new trouble had arisen, and even Nature had joined men for his hindrance; for on the way back a storm had driven his boat ashore upon an island, the modern Heligoland, held sacred to heathen worship by the Frisians. What, however, were pagan gods to Willibrord compared with perishing souls? While he waited in the wind and the rain, the Archbishop had used all his eloquence upon these souls, and not without effect, for three had been brought to Catholic baptism in a spring conveniently near. Unfortunately its waters were hallowed by a custom of reverent silence which not even heathen words might dare to violate. At the sound of Christian prayer the natives naturally had been horrified; and King Radbod, hurriedly informed, had decreed in his wrath that human blood must wash away such insult offered to the island's deity.[23] For three days, three times a day, lots had been cast according to Frisian usage, to decide which of the Christian offenders should die. The old story is here marked by a reticence extraordinarily different from modern realism. Nothing tells us of the feelings of Willibrord and his fellow-captives as they waited those long hours between the castings of lots, or as they welcomed those few minutes thrice a day which should bring a swift death to some one among them! Death was so familiar; to die for the Faith was a sure path to heaven; to many the lack of its seal upon their lives, to pass from earth peacefully in bed, was itself a harder sacrifice. We may feel sure that not only Willibrord, but all his fol-

[23] *Cf.* B. S. Phillpotts, *CMH* II, 490.

lowers envied the one of their company on whom the lot had
finally descended, to confer upon him by immediate martyrdom this honour among Christian men. The king himself was
so impressed by their courage that he sent them on their way
to Utrecht with something approaching courtesy.

In Utrecht the years had now marched bravely on, cheered
by visits to Echternach, which more and more became for
Willibrord his chief source of relaxation and spiritual support.
There had been no more talk of withdrawal, in spite of infinite
discouragement and doubt. Few souls had surrendered to conversion among the denizens of this dour and savage land,
although many friends had given of their generosity to help
on the work. The superficial peace between Franks and
Frisians had been easily broken. In 714 Pepin's son Grimoald,
son-in-law of Radbod, had been murdered as he prayed in the
shrine of Saint Lambert in Liége. Tradition ascribes the deed
to a Frisian, probably resentful of his country's alliance with
its conquerors.[24]

Shortly before, in this same year, the death of Pepin had
thrown into turmoil the country he had governed so long as
Mayor under a succession of worthless Frankish kings. Struggle
for its dominion had at once risen between his widow, Plectrude, and a son, Charles Martel, born to him out of wedlock
by a mistress called Alphaïda. Radbod had been quick to seize
his advantage by marching against the divided rule. Soon he
had regained his lost Frisian territory and joyfully had marked
his triumph by destroying far and wide the buildings raised
there under Pepin for the rites of his Catholic faith. Willibrord's patient achieving had been wrecked, he and his priests
had been forced to take refuge at Echternach, and the cause
of Christianity in Utrecht once again seemed fated to fail.

This, then, was that other side of the picture which was

[24] *Lib. hist. Franc.*, c. 50: *MGH Script. rer. Merov.* II, 324f.

rising at the moment before the mind of young Winfrid in his monastery at Nursling. Was the turning from darkness to light of heathen souls abroad even more important than life in Wessex, as abbot or bishop, as teacher and searcher after truth, as missionary, no doubt, to the pagan British still hidden in its hills and forests? He did not know. But gradually from his perplexity one thing became clear: the vision of Frisia had come to stay so completely within him that never again could he rest happily in this land he loved so well. Perhaps happiness and peace of heart were signposts on the road of decision? At this moment they pointed definitely away from home; and slowly he turned down the path to Abbot Winbert's cell.

The feelings of the community at Nursling were very mixed over Winfrid's decision. Of course, it was a great and splendid thing to send out one of their number to preach to the Gentiles, perhaps to be enrolled in the noble army of martyrs. Yet the glory of God's house in England was not to be forgotten. Scholars were few; abbots of influence and administrative ability were scarce; did the Lord really require Winfrid at their hands?

But Winfrid, once determined, had no thought of yielding to argument. There seemingly remained to his brethren only the care of sending him forth well-equipped with money and supplies. Nevertheless, they did even more; for two or three asked permission to go with him, and were allowed, to his immense satisfaction. Just before the last day, as Abbot Winbert blessed his pilgrims, a special word of farewell arrived from Archbishop Bertwald of Canterbury, promising a bond of communion in prayer between them and their Church at home while they were absent one from the other.[25]

[25] *Bonif. Epp.* No. 33.

Thus fortified, they travelled from their west country to London, already a busy centre for many traders, coming and going to and from its rude docks and markets.[26] There they found a boat leaving for the Dutch coast. With the wind speeding them forward they soon reached haven and proceeded by river to Dorostat, the modern Wijk bij Duurstede, a market town a few miles from Utrecht, standing where the Kromme Rijn ("Crooked Rhine") leaves the broad stream of the Lek.

Nor could they wonder that Willibrord had been driven out. For everything was much worse than they had dreamed. Charles Martel, imprisoned for a while at Cologne by Plectrude, had escaped from her hands, had gathered around him an army of followers, and had openly declared himself Mayor of Austrasia in his father's place. As such he had naturally come into violent conflict with Radbod of the Frisians.[27]

Winfrid did all he could. Determined to seize any opportunity he could find, he even, so tradition tells, sought audience of Radbod at Utrecht. But every door was firmly closed to him. Radbod would have nothing of him or his preaching, and at last, probably in the autumn of this same year 716, he felt himself obliged to return with his companions to England.[28] So far as we know, it had not even been possible for him to meet Willibrord, still impatiently enduring as best he might the shelter of Echternach.

The monks of Nursling were delighted—*sic visum est Deo*—and they offered high thanksgiving for their pilgrim's safe return. Winfrid resumed his old place in the choir, his teaching, his sermons, and his pastoral ministry.[29] Thus the time slipped by until the spring of 718. Very probably it was within

[26] *Cf. HE* II, c. 3.   [27] Willibald, c. 4.
[28] Authorities are divided between the autumn of 716 or of 717: Hauck, 443, note 3; Levison, ed. *Vitae,* 17, note 2.
[29] Fifteen sermons are extant under the name of Boniface (Winfrid): *Opera S. Bonif.* ed. Giles II (*PEA*) 57ff.; *PL* LXXXIX, coll. 843ff. It is not quite certain whether they are by him: *cf.* Hauck, 478, note 4, with A. Ebert, *Gesch. d. christ. lat. Lit.* I, 1874, 614f. and Whitney, *CMH* II, 794; Fischer, 81ff.; Nürnberger, *Neues Archiv* XIV, 1889, 111ff.

these months that he wrote a letter, still full of interest for us, to a nun called Eadburg, then, or afterward, abbess of the famous monastery at Minster upon the Isle of Thanet in Kent.[30]

The history, actual and traditional, of Thanet and its monastery is also filled with interest and meaning. On this island, entirely divided at the time from the mainland by the river Wantsum, a branch of the Stour, Augustine and his companions had been welcomed by King Ethelbert when in 597 they first arrived in Britain. As we have seen, to Ethelbert had succeeded Eadbald, and to Eadbald Erconbert, befriender of Wilfrid, in direct line of descent of the Kentish royal house. Erconbert, however, had an older brother, called Eormenred, passed over for the kingship in favour of Erconbert by will of their father, King Eadbald; and it is with the family of this Eormenred that the story of the monastery upon Thanet is concerned.[31]

Six children were born to him, among them a daughter known by two names in the records of historians, as Eormenburg or as Domneva, and two sons, Ethelred and Ethelbert. The old tradition dwells with great emphasis upon the virtue of these two princes. At an early age they lost both their parents and their uncle, King Erconbert; they were then handed over to the care of his successor on the throne of Kent, their cousin, King Egbert, son of Erconbert.

Now Egbert had an adviser in matters of state, one Thunor, who appears in the story just as wicked as these royal wards were good. He was forever insisting on the danger which both Egbert and Egbert's sons might incur by the presence at court of two members of an older branch of the family. "It were surely well," he whispered in the king's ear, "to take measures

[30] Bonif. Epp. No. 10.
[31] Dugdale I, 447ff.; Gest. Reg. 78; Sim. Durh. II, 4ff.; Flor. Worc. MHB 534, 635; ASC ann. 640; Earle and Plummer II, 21f.; Hardy, Cat. I, 263f., 377f., 382; Horstman, NLA II, 188ff.; Eckenstein, 85ff.

against such dangers. Send the princes far away into exile. Or, instead, be quick," he continued, swinging his hand across his throat, "and hand them over to me!" Egbert in horror at first refused to hear a word; then, as the argument was constantly repeated, he began to think about it. Naturally his temper grew bolder. At last, during the king's absence, Thunor ordered that both the young men be put to death and hidden deep beneath the foundations of the royal house.

But murder would out. To the consternation of the king's household an unearthly radiance shone above the palace roof night after night. The king, disturbed by the foreboding of those within, went outside to see the sight and promptly made his way to the chapel, himself attacked by horrid fear. It must be, he decided, some visitation from heaven, perhaps of God's anger, as the dark sky was broken by this strange path of flame directed straight upon his dwelling. Questionings followed. At last the murderer confessed, and an awe-struck company of nobles and clergy, hastily summoned, watched the uncovering of the mutilated bodies.

The princes were buried with all reverence; Thunor met the vengeance of Heaven; and Eormenburg, their sister, eventually founded this monastery upon Thanet, on land given her by Egbert as token of his penitence, "as much land as her pet hind could run over by divine inspiration within one day." Here she gathered seventy nuns and established them in their Rule. She then recalled from the abbey of Chelles, near Paris, one of the three daughters she had borne to Merewald, ruler of the West Hecani in Herefordshire, and called on the Church to install the girl as abbess of this community at Minster on Thanet. Her name was Mildred, and she had been sent to Chelles by her mother for training in the religious life. Archbishop Theodore of Canterbury himself laid hands upon her now in blessing. So runs her story in old record. After her death this house of religion was called by her name, and her cult spread far and wide through southern England. Many churches were dedicated in her honour, best known among them London's church of Saint Mildred in Bread Street.[32]

Her two sisters, Milgith and Milburg, were also revered by the Church. Saint Milgith was a simple nun, remote from the pages of history; but Saint Milburg, apparently the eldest of the three, was almost as famous as Mildred. About 680 she built a monastery for both men and women at Wimnicas, now Much Wenlock in Shropshire, and was herself its ruler. Miracles were ascribed to the sanctity of both.

It was the successor of Mildred as abbess of Minster in Thanet who was the Eadburg to whom Winfrid wrote. About 717 he described to her in this long letter a vision of mysteries beyond the grave that had been granted to a monk, dead and raised again to life, it was said, in the monastery governed by Abbess Milburg at Much Wenlock. The story had first been told to Winfrid by that Hildilid, abbess of Barking, to whom Aldhelm had written his letter on the duties of nuns. Since then, "thanks be to Almighty God," he had been able to learn more of it from the monk in question, who had lately returned from abroad.[33]

Since Winfrid's narrative is typical of many other tales of visions in these Middle Ages, especially that of Drythelm, given by Bede,[34] we may find it worth while to look at some of its details:

[32] Arnold-Forster II, 362.

[33] Dümmler thinks *de transmarinis partibus* means "from England to Frisia," and that Winfrid was writing from Frisia: ed. *Epp.* p. 252, note 5 (also Tangl, ed. p. 8, note 5; he dates the letter 716). But, to an Englishman, "from abroad" would more naturally mean "from the continent." Dümmler dates the letter c. 717; Hauck (443, note 3, 457) places this stay of Winfrid in England 716–718. *Cf.* Hahn, *Bon. und Lul,* 83, note 4.

[34] *HE* V, c. 12. *Cf.* III, c. 19; Sim. Durh. I, 130ff.; *Bonif. Epp.* No. 115. There is a curious detail in the vision described in this Letter 115 of "a sad and mournful company of very many little children who had died unbaptized, especially under Bishop Daniel" (i.e., of Winchester, bishop of Aldhelm and of Winfrid).

Immediately after death, the monk relates, he was freed from the pain of his sickness. From his eyes there fell, as it were, a thick veil, and for the first time he could see things hitherto hidden and unknown—all the world, with its lands and seas and peoples. As he left this earth, angels of exceeding radiance received his soul, chanting in harmony: "Lord, rebuke me not in Thine anger; neither chastise me in the fury of Thy wrath." As they lifted him in the air, he saw around the world a mighty flame shooting on high to devour all things; yet constantly an angel stayed its rush by making against it the sign of the Cross. So fierce was the light from the angels and the fire together that he was in agony until the angel of the vision placed a hand upon his head and thus protected him from harm.

Even in the moment since he had died, a multitude of souls, more than he could imagine, had followed him in their passing from this life. Then suddenly, in the midst of the bright angels of mercy, there appeared a company of evil spirits, also without number, to convict these souls of many grievous sins. While he listened in terror, from the various devils came the tale of those offences of his own which the Lord had not yet put away—all that he had neglected to confess, or had forgotten, or had committed in ignorance. "I," cried one, "am thy greed, by which thou didst cherish desire against Divine command." "I," joined in another, "am thy vain glory, wherewith thou didst boast thyself among men." "I," cried the third, "am the spirit of lying in which thou didst declare falsely." Then the others continued, one by one: "I am the idle word, spoken in vain." "And I, the eyes that looked on unlawful things." "And I, the stubborn disobedience that would not obey the brethren set over thee." "And I, thy lazy neglect of sacred study." "And I, those wandering thoughts and foolish occupations, within and without

the church." "And I, the sleepiness that brought thee late
to prayer." Thus all the hideous chorus, singly and in unison,
brought to light all the stains, little and great, that still lay
foul upon the pages of his book of years before God.

Then, on the other side, rose from the angels the pleading
of his good deeds, sorry and imperfect as they were: "I am
his obedience." "And I, his fasting." "And I, his prayer,
purely offered." "And I, his kindness to the sick." "And I,
the psalm he said as penance for his idle word." Thus they
took, one by one, his small, sad efforts, and on their lips these
seemed greater and more excellent than ever he had thought
they could be.

After this he heard the wailing of souls lost for ever in the
flames of the bottomless pit of Hell, and turned away quickly
to behold Paradise, land of sweetness and delight, where dwell
the blessed who rejoice in God.

Nor was Purgatory left unseen. Across a boiling, bubbling
river, black as pitch and dreadful to look upon, lay a rude
log as a bridge. Souls were always setting foot upon it, for
they must pass that way to reach the other side. Some crossed
with firm and steady step; others fell into the waters, either
altogether immersed or covered to knee, or middle, or shoulder.
Yet all eventually reached the further bank and, as they
climbed its side, seemed far more pure and lovely than before
they had sunk into that cleansing stream. One of the angels
told of them: "These are the souls that needed of God's grace
chastising for their tiny faults before they could be fitly offered
in His sight."

Evil spirits in the monk's vision were ever busy at their
work of seducing men. Whenever a soul yielded, the tempter
in his joy would rush to proclaim the victory to his fellow-
demons. Never would he wait for sin to follow sin; each fall
was speedily counted, directly it occurred.

There were prophecies, too, in the vision, concerning the fate of souls still on earth. Among these the most dreadful was that declared of King Ceolred of Mercia. To the eyes of our terrified monk he appeared to be attacked, while yet ruling in his English land, by devils who were trying hard to pluck him from beneath the shelter, as it seemed, of some great book whose widely-spread pages an angel was holding over his head. Soon they triumphed. "Alack!" wailed the angel, even more upset than usual at this particular tragedy, "the sinner will not let me defend him any longer; therefore he must go, through his own deserts." And he withdrew the umbrella of the book. Instantly the devils in high festivity gathered from earth and sky and sea to rend the miserable man in tortures beyond imagining.

At last the monk was ordered to return to earth in his own mortal body and make known what he had seen to such inquirers as would listen with reverent and believing minds. One of these had been Winfrid, who now ends his long narrative to Abbess Eadburg in the customary manner of his time: "These things I have carefully written at your request as they were described to me and to three other witnesses, brethren of religious and very venerable life, of whose integrity as guarantee for this letter there is no question. Farewell.

> God grant you, holy maid, to gain the Angels' grace,
> A virgin right revered, in Heaven's realm to reign."

Perhaps it was about this same time that another lady, called Egburg, poured out in a letter to Winfrid all the sorrow and longing of her heart.[35] Although we know nothing of

---

[35] Dümmler (ed. *Epp.* p. 258) dates it 716–720; Tangl (ed. p. 18), 716–718; Hahn (*Bon. und Lul,* p. 101, note 5), 717–722, to Boniface "on the continent." Hauck, (443, note 2) thinks it was written during Winfrid's first stay in Frisia.

her from other sources,[36] she must have been well-read. Her letter is short, and her misery is very great; she manages, however, to bring in four reminiscences of Vergil's *Aeneid,* two of various writings of Aldhelm of Malmesbury, dead now some seven years, two of a letter written by Jerome to the monk Rufinus,[37] together with at least half a dozen quotations from the Bible. Her frank expression of devotion to her Father in God is equally characteristic of Anglo-Saxon women. "The bond of your affection dwells in my inner self, as a taste of honeyed sweetness in the depths of my heart. Only for a moment did I see you, and no more; yet I shall always hold you in a sister's embrace. To me you are both father and brother in the Lord; now that cruel and bitter death has taken away my own brother Oshere, dear to me above all, I have cared for you in my love almost more than any other man. Never a day or a night passes but I think of your counsel to me. . . . .

"And now my dearest sister Wethburg has vanished from my sight. Would that God had rather given it me to die! For a barrier more bitter than of death has divided us. She, doubtless, is happy. How unhappy am I, whom she has left like a castaway thing to serve this present world! She knew how much I loved her. Now, so they tell me, she is shut up in a cell at Rome. Hold me up, most blessed master, I beseech you, upon the rock of your prayers, and of your kindness send me comfort of holy relics, or at least a few words of writing from your Reverence. . . ."

As winter gave way to spring in 718, Winfrid's thoughts turned back more and more to Frisia, in spite of every inducement held out by his brethren to keep him with them. During

[36] See Hahn, *Bon. und Lul,* 101ff. There is no proof that this Egburg was identical with Heaburg-Bugga of *Epp.* No. 14; *cf.* Dümmler, ed. p. 259, note 2; Hahn, *ibid.,* 345.
[37] *CSEL* LIV, pp. 14, 17; Tangl, ed. *Epp.* No. 13, notes.

the winter Abbot Winbert had died; and all the community begged the young monk, now known for his work as priest, as envoy, and as traveller, to become their father and serve the Church in Devon.[38] But he had once tasted the thrill of adventure on a foreign shore. If it were the Lord's desire for him, he could rule an abbey, he could learn and write, wherever he might be. Perhaps, as has been conjectured, he was thinking of Frisia when about this time he wrote to a youth whom he called Nithard, urging him to study well. "If Almighty God allow that I return sometime to those places where you are, as I have resolved to do, I promise you all my aid in your reading of Holy Scripture." This letter, as so many others, holds a poem of good wishes, including in its lines an acrostic that spells the name *Nithardus*.[39]

His bishop, Daniel of Winchester, gladly approved the decision to return to the continent. Not only did he install another abbot in Nursling, a monk named Stephen, but he wrote a letter commending the traveller to all in places of authority whom he should meet upon his way.[40] It was still 718 when Winfrid left his monastery and journeyed first toward Rome. It would be only right, he reasoned, to tell the Holy Father of his hopes and to ask for his blessing upon them, especially if this were to be the beginning of a life work as he already dared to dream.

The Pope of these years was that Gregory II whom Ceolfrid of Jarrow had thought to see when he set out from England as an old man in 716, only to die at Langres in France. Contemporary tradition still tells us of the smile that played upon the Pontiff's face as he now listened to this youthful pilgrim.[41]

---

[38] Willibald, c. 5.

[39] *Bonif. Epp.* No. 9; Hauck, 456, note 2; Hahn, *Bon. und Lul,* 50. Note that the letter reflects Boniface as versed in the learning of his time: "die schwülstige Adresse ganz im Stil Aldhelm," Tangl, ed. p. 4. See also M. R. James, *EHR XXIX,* 1914, 94, and *cf.* Tangl, p. 7, note f.

[40] *Epp.* No. 11; Willibald, c. 5; H. S. III, 302.

[41] Willibald, *ibid.*

Winfrid assuredly reminded him that things had greatly changed for the better across the North Sea since he himself had left Frisia. Charles Martel as lord of Austrasia had marched with his supporters against Neustria, had defeated the Neustrians twice, in 716 at Amblève near Liége and in 717 at Vincy near Cambrai, was openly victor over Queen Plectrude at Cologne, and well on the road to becoming sovereign master of all the Franks. Undoubtedly, therefore, he would control Frisia and its tyrant Radbod and would give all encouragement to Christian work. Was not Charles a devoted Catholic as his father Pepin before him? Willibrord would now certainly be returning to his own see of Utrecht, and he, Winfrid, might aid him in restoring his ravaged Church and scattered converts.

The Pope was himself equally keen to build once more in Germanic lands upon foundations already laid but quickly lapsing. He read carefully the letter from Winfrid's diocesan; he talked long and earnestly with his petitioner. Day after day passed, month after month, until the summer of 719 had set in. Then, fully assured, he laid his hands on Winfrid in blessing, and, as Pope Sergius to Willibrord, gave to him a new name. Henceforth Winfrid disappears, and we follow the adventures of the missionary priest, Boniface.[42]

On May 15, Gregory wrote his official commendation: "Therefore, in the Name of the Indivisible Trinity, by the unshaken authority of blessed Peter, chief of the Apostles, whose ruling and doctrine we administer in the government of his holy See, we bid and command you as priest and monk in due humility to hasten forth to those nations, of whatsoever race, who are held fast in the snare of unbelief. Depart in the grace of God, you who, as I believe, are lighted by that saving fire which the Lord came to send upon earth. Preach the ministry of the kingdom of God in the Name of Christ, de-

[42] Hauck, 458.

claring the truths of either Testament to the ignorant, in the Spirit of virtue and love and soberness. Be mindful, in receiving those who by God's guidance shall be brought to believe in Him, that you dispense holy sacrament according to the prescribed manner and rites of our Holy Apostolic See, already known and familiar from your instructing therein. And whatsoever you shall perceive to be lacking for the fulfilment of your work, that you will make known to us in so far as you are able." [43] Thus was Boniface sent to labour across the sea under the definite mandate of the Church of Rome. There was to be no sharing of effort with the Celtic clergy who had already sown and gathered within this same wide vineyard.

His own particular plot in this vineyard was, indeed, assigned to him before he left Rome. He was destined for Thuringia, a country reaching from the Harz Mountains on the north to the Thuringian Forest on the south. In the sixth century its people had been conquered by the Franks of Austrasia, its far more important neighbour on the west, and had remained under direct Frankish rule until 634, when Dagobert I, king of Austrasia, had given them one Radulf as their own "duke" or ruler. Successive chieftains had presided over the land in this same independence, an independence ended, however, by Charles' father, Pepin, who had brought the Thuringians again under Frankish control and had given them Frankish nobles as governors.[44]

Pepin's action was causing much unrest among the people in this early eighth century, not only in matters of politics, but also of religion. Under the Franks many of the Thuringians had been converted to the Catholic Church, both by Frankish priests and by foreign missionaries. Chief among the latter had been Saint Kilian, of Irish birth, so it was told, and

[43] *Epp.* No. 12; H. S. III, 303.
[44] Fredegarius IV, cc. 77ff.: *MGH Script. rer. Merov.* II, 159ff.; Hauck, 383ff.

of true Irish ardour for work among the heathen of distant lands.[45] He had made Würzburg in Austrasia his base, and from there he had travelled far and wide with his assistant priests. Upon his death—he is said to have been murdered for the courage of his creed in Würzburg about 688—Thuringia was no longer a pagan land. Yet the fact that it had passed from independence into the hands of Catholic Austrasia was itself likely to turn against the Catholic faith those not already firmly rooted in their religion. Moreover, two of these Austrasian governors, Theotbald and Heden, generous as they were toward the Catholic treasury, seem to have laid heavy hands upon their Thuringian subjects for imprisonment, confiscation of property, and even death.[46]

And many Celtic clergy had worked for long, were still working in these regions, clergy who were alien to the See of Peter. Here again, as in Britain, religion suffered through the schism which had divided the Celtic Church from the obedience of Rome, and this schism itself bred hostility between the Thuringian disciples of these Celtic clergy and their Catholic Frankish lords. Here, too, the progress of Celtic conversion had been inhibited by lack of that power of organization in which we have seen the Celts so markedly wanting and the Church of Rome so exceedingly able. Without a central See and its ruler to guide and support, these isolated Celtic units naturally slipped into careless or even heathen ways.

For these various reasons—dissension, instability, ignorance —religion in the eighth century throughout Thuringia and the adjacent countries, the lands of the Rhine and the Danube, was at a very low ebb. Many of their various peoples were unbaptized, unaware of the very name of the Christian God;

---

[45] For Kilian see Hauck, 386; O. Holder-Egger: Pertz, *Script.* XV, i, 46; F. Emmerich, *Der heilige Kilian,* 1896.
[46] Willibald, c. 6; *cf.* Hauck, 386f.

many professing Christians were offering sacrifices to heathen deities and feasting upon the fruits of this evil consecration. Pagan rituals were celebrated in number, at the graves of the dead, in the forests and the fields, at springs, upon sacred stones, before the shadowing of the moon and the growing power of the sun in springtime, by spells and by augury and by casting of lots, by the need-fire, born of rubbing of sticks from "male" and "female" trees, by the blessing of herbs for impious service, by magic which sought to control the forces of nature and the hearts of men. Countless priests of orthodox orders were living in lust and vice unmentionable; the sacraments were often dishonoured by sacrilege; monastic life had fallen into sloth; laymen were living in gross disease of body and of soul alike.[47]

As for the dwellers beyond the Thuringian Forest, they certainly offered a terrific problem to the conscience of the Church. The Pope must well have felt anxious as he dismissed this young priest "to look into the most savage peoples of Germany and to consider whether the wild fields of their hearts, if tilled by the ploughshare of the Gospel, might be made ready to receive the seed of preaching."[48]

Of these matters Gregory and Boniface naturally talked at length during the days in Rome; but, we may think, there was other and deeper discussion. The Pope had followed with ever-increasing concern the rapidly encroaching tide of the Arabs.[49] In the seventh century they had advanced from Arabia into Palestine, conquering Damascus, Jerusalem, and Caesarea, until the Byzantine power had collapsed before their invasion. From there they had gone forward over

[47] *Indiculus superstitionum et paganiarum: MGH Cap. Reg. Franc.* I, 222f.; Hefele-Leclercq III, ii, 836ff.; McNeill and Gamer, 419ff.
[48] Willibald, c. 5.
[49] Moss, *The Birth of the Middle Ages*, 1935, 149ff.; Becker, *CMH* II, 329ff.

Mesopotamia, over Persia, over Egypt, seeking as their goal the capture of the heart of the Byzantine empire, Constantinople itself. The turn of the century had seen North Africa in their hands; in 711 the great Tarik had led them into Spain; in 715, when Gregory had ascended the throne of Saint Peter, Spain was theirs. Just at this time of his meeting with Boniface, they were making ready to enter France.

It was not so much the political menace of these Arab hordes which was deeply troubling the Pontiff's mind, nor even the knowledge that lust of booty was one of their chief characteristics as they marched into the rich treasuries of churches, convents, monasteries, filled with the offerings of the faithful in Spain and in France. It was, rather, the fear of their Muslim faith. As a matter of fact, they did not require those in their power to embrace the creed of Mahomet. They allowed freedom of religion, and in this respect were far milder masters than the Byzantine emperors had been. But they granted this liberty of conscience at the cost of a poll-tax, and many men were choosing Islam in preference to such burden. Furthermore, the Muslim faith encouraged polygamy. The increase of the followers of the Prophet within Europe was causing grave alarm to the Church in these years, and Gregory must have longed for a strong missionary hand and head which could organize Germanic countries against the menace. No realization of the organizing power which lay latent in the youth to whom he was so seriously talking could have gladdened his mind at this moment. But workers were few, the field was certainly in desperate need, and he hoped for the best. At any rate, the new recruit would bring comfort and encouragement to the much harassed Willibrord.

So Boniface set out and travelled first to Pavia, to the court of Liutprand, king of the Lombards in northern Italy, the greatest and most powerful of their rulers. He had been elected in 712 to succeed his father Ansprand and was at this time about thirty-five, known for his issue of laws to his people and for living on good terms with the Papal See.[50] The letter which Boniface carried from Gregory assured the traveller a friendly welcome, and he stayed with Liutprand some days before venturing across the Alps. His baggage, we are told, was augmented by "a multitude of relics collected in Rome." [51]

When at length he arrived in Thuringia, the Frankish chief, Heden, was dead. He had been a good friend of Willibrord, and Boniface doubtless missed his support at this critical moment. No Frankish governor, so far as we know, had been appointed to succeed him, and the new priest-in-charge at once introduced himself to various prominent men in the land, whom he knew to be loyal to the mother Church. The names of some of these have come down to us: Asulf, Godolav, Wilar, Gundhar, Alvold. All were delighted to see a priest direct from Rome. The pagans had been urging them with threats to abandon their faith for the worship of Woden and Thor, ancient gods of heathen Germany; and although they had stoutly resisted, they were hoping for some practical reassurance.

Boniface set to work with all determination to collect again into a congregation some of this scattered flock; he travelled here and there, as much as he could, and did his best to bring about some kind of order. But soon he saw that any such attempt on his part must be supported by civil authority, and the only power to which he could appeal was Charles Martel, by now conqueror of the Neustrians in a third battle, at Soissons, and master of Burgundy as well. It was no time for hesitation; and this year of 719 had not yet ended before he was on his way to the Frankish court.

[50] T. Hodgkin VI, 389ff., 440f.
[51] Willibald, *ibid.*

As he travelled, good news arrived. Radbod, that fierce old king of Frisia, was dead, pagan to the last. A story, which may be true, tells that Saint Wulframn, bishop of Sens in the seventh century, had once visited Frisia for mission work among its heathen and had met with considerable success. From this point the narrative is far more doubtful, albeit entirely characteristic. By the bishop's plain teaching, it goes on, Radbod himself, with many of his people, had been persuaded to approach the baptismal font. He had even dipped one foot in the holy water, when a question suddenly entered his mind: "Where shall be found the larger company of kings and noble chieftains of Frisia—in heaven or in hell?" Wulframn answered that all Radbod's ancestors who had died unbaptized were assuredly damned. The proffered foot was at once withdrawn. He could not possibly live hereafter without his forefathers, the king declared, or sit down with only a few of his own men in the kingdom of heaven. He died unbaptized,[52] and was succeeded by his son, Aldgils II, a devout Catholic, who welcomed Archbishop Willibrord once again to his city and cathedral of Utrecht. Aldgils also sought peace with the Franks, and soon all was ready for the restoration of Christian life in Frisia.

This news inevitably had its effect upon Boniface. Had he not always hoped to convert the Frisians? No doubt this possible turn of events had been discussed by him in Rome with Gregory, for he at once changed his plans, journeyed down the Rhine to Utrecht, and offered his services to its Archbishop.[53] Willibrord was overjoyed. He was now past sixty; his enormous diocese was a tangled mass of wreckage, misery, and confusion after the havoc wrought in it by Rad-

[52] *Annal. Xant.*: Pertz, *Script.* II, 221; H. S. III, 225; *DCB* IV, 1195; Rettberg II, 514ff.
[53] Doubtless he also sought the aid of Willibrord for his own new mission to Thuringia: see Fischer, 35.

bod; all his work, so carefully planned and fulfilled since his consecration to Utrecht in 695, over twenty years ago, had somehow to be restored. The young energy of Boniface would do wonders under his own directing hand.

From 719 until 722 the two Englishmen worked together as father and son. Ruined churches were rebuilt, new ones were founded, clergy and monks were brought again into regular life, lapsed souls were revived, many converts were added to the Lord.

We have very little definite information concerning these years. Two letters, however, show that his friends in England had not forgotten Boniface.[54] A lady named Bugga, who will be found in later correspondence as abbess of a monastery in Kent, wrote to him of her happiness in the news he had sent her: of the consent of the Holy Father in Rome to his desire; of the "laying low at his feet of Radbod, enemy of the Catholic Church"; and of a dream in which the Lord had made known to him his true vocation for the reaping of souls into heavenly harvest. His prayers, she knows, have helped her herself to some haven of peace. Would he of his charity continue them and also deign to offer Masses for the soul of N., a specially beloved relative of hers? Yes, and would this most dear Father comfort her, all unworthy as she is, by sending her his excerpts from Holy Scripture, as he had promised in that delightful letter? She has not yet been able to get hold of those *Lives* of martyrs which he has asked her to send him, but she will do so as soon as possible. She is sending with this letter some money and an altar frontal, the best gifts she can manage. Small as they are, they are sent with very much love.

The second letter came from another abbess, called Eangyth. Her monastery was a double one, but we do not know where

[54] *Bonif. Epp.* Nos. 14f.

it was.[55] Her state of mind was indeed pathetic. She was overwhelmed by external troubles: poverty due to failure of the monastery's harvest of grain; terrible taxes and various payments, exacted by king and queen, by her bishop, by nobles of various degree, too many to count; envious persons who had misrepresented the income of her monastery to the royal exchequer. There was, too, the dreadful burden of all the souls, of men and women, under her guidance and governing; there was also the difficulty of maintaining order and peace within her house. It would be enough to shoulder all this responsibility, all these outward distractions, were her own heart tranquil within. But no! From within there rose day by day to torment her the vision of her innumerable sins, of her lack of confidence and trust, of her secret thoughts, witnessed by God alone. Added to all these troubles was the loss of friends and relations. "I have neither son nor brother, father nor uncle; only one daughter . . . there is no one else. God has taken them all in one way or another." She desperately needs some one on whom to rest her weary mind. "Long we have sought. And we trust that in you we have found that one for whom we have yearned and prayed and hoped. Oh, if only God would give it to us to reach those lands and come to that pilgrim way in which you dwell, to hear living words from your lips—sweeter would they be than honey and the honeycomb!"

[55] Eangyth mentions here her daughter, named Heaburg or Bugga. It seems safer (in spite of the index in Dümmler's edition of the *Letters s.v.* Bugga, Heaburg; Stubbs, *DCB* I, 355f.; Plummer II, xxxvi) not to identify either this Bugga or the abbess (also of Kent) who bears that name in the *Letters* Nos. 15, 27, 94, 105, 117, with the Eadburg mentioned above as abbess of Minster on Thanet. The two names are kept distinct in the *Letters,* and Eadburg, the learned director of Thanet, seems quite different from the troubled Bugga, longing to leave her monastery for pilgrimage and peace. The name Bugga was not an uncommon one; *cf.* the relative of Aldhelm (pp. 67f. *supra*), who also cannot be identified with these ladies. It is possible, however, that the daughter Heaburg-Bugga may have been the Bugga of *Letters* 15, 27, etc.; *cf.* Hahn, 111f. and 83 and Tangl, ed. 22, with Eckenstein, 131.

Since, however, her poor deserts have not merited this and she is far away across the sea in England, what would Boniface think of her going on pilgrimage to Rome? She is quite aware that many people vehemently oppose this practice, however sincerely purposed, on the ground that canon law bids each religious to abide and fulfil his vows to God in that place to which he was assigned when he made them. But she has wanted for so many years to see Rome, once mistress of the world, to ask forgiveness at its shrines for those many, many sins she has committed in her long life! And, after all, when the world is in such a troubled and uncertain state, who can tell what the secret will of Heaven may really be? Would not Boniface be her Aaron, her hill of strength, to lift up his hands for her as in the evening sacrifice? It would be very kind, also, if he would send an answer from abroad to this letter of hers, in spite of its bad writing and its clumsy style.

We do not know what came of this petition. But we know that some years later Boniface wrote to his friend Bugga, now definitely addressed as abbess, his opinion with regard to a similar request from her.[56] In view of the numberless men and women who craved in these days to see Rome and its churches, his counsel here is significant for its non-committal tone. "I cannot take the responsibility," he writes, "of either forbidding your pilgrimage on my own judgment or of over-confidently advising it. I will tell you just what I think. If you have left your monastery and the monastic life to seek quiet in the contemplation of God, why should you be through your travels at the mercy of worldly people and worldly things, with all the toil and worry which they bring? If things at home do really keep you from a free and quiet mind and you

[56] *Epp.* No. 27. The date is uncertain, probably c. 725 and before 738; see Dümmler, ed. 277, note 1, and *Epp.* No. 105; Hahn, *Bon. und Lul,* 114; pp. 445f. *infra.*

cannot find peace in your own country, then by all means seek this in pilgrimage, as our sister Wiethburg did.[57] She has written me that she has found in Saint Peter's the peaceful life which she had wanted so long. I wrote to her about your own desire, and she advised you to wait until the recent assaults and threats of the Saracens against Rome have quieted down and she can safely invite you to join her. That seems best to me, too. In the meantime you might get your things in order for the journey and wait on God's will. I am so sorry that I have not yet been able to finish the book of excerpts which you asked me to send; there has been so much work and so much travelling. But you shall have it, once it gets done. May God reward you for the gifts and the clothing you sent. Please, dear sister—or, rather, mother and most sweet lady—pray for me constantly. For my sins I am troubled by so many worries, far more of mind than of body. You know that the old friendship between us never fails. Good-bye in Christ."

In 722 Willibrord, increasingly aware of the burden of his years, begged Boniface to stay in Frisia and become its bishop. To him Frisia was all his life on earth; but for the younger man things were very different. He had been sent from Rome to convert the heathen Germanic peoples wheresoever the Pope should will; moreover, the Pope had not proposed the rank of bishop to him. After long discussion with Willibrord Boniface decided to leave Frisia for work among German people in Hesse, and set out with the blessing of the bishop with whom he had laboured so happily.[58]

In Hesse Boniface was at work in Frankland proper, and it may be well at this time to give some picture of its conditions, political, social, and religious, up to this period.

[57] *Soror nostra* is used, of course, in the religious sense. This Wiethburg was very probably the Wethburg of p. 361 *supra; cf.* Hahn, *ibid.,* 103.
[58] Hauck, 445f., 461f.

The whole political structure of life under the Franks, as carried forward from the rule of kings to the rule of the kings' "prime ministers" in Pepin of Heristal and in Charles Martel, was based on the possession of land. The Frankish rulers, of earlier and of later times, having gained vast territories by conquest, rewarded their supporters by gifts of land, tracts large and small, in return for their aid in war. As war was constantly going on, there inevitably grew up in the Frankish dominions an "aristocracy," not of blood, but of landed estate. The *leudes,* followers of the king, were thus attached to him by his generosity in the sharing of his spoils. In the course of years, therefore, the more favoured of these warriors and political henchmen became rich in landed estate, as their aid drew more and more reward from grateful sovereigns. Often, moreover, the king granted immunity from taxation to these landowners, who then lived luxuriously upon their broad acres, tilled by a multitude of miserable serfs. It was no wonder that cities in Frankish times crumbled away. The great estates, or villas, or farms of the kings and their chief supporters, the Frankish landed nobility, were communities in themselves, devoted to agriculture, from which came the revenues of their owners in produce of grain, milk, butter, cheese, farm animals, and, especially, of various wines and other fermented drink.

There was, however, another proprietor of land even more richly endowed than the Frankish king. This was the Frankish Church. So wide were its holdings that in the eighth century it owned not far short of a third of Frankish soil. Pious donors without number, as in England, sought forgiveness for their sins and hope of future happiness on earth and beyond this earth in gifts and legacies of estates; bishoprics and abbeys gradually covered the land, founded, endowed, and ceaselessly enriched by one after another of the souls who sought righteousness by way of mammon. And again here, in very many cases, immunity from taxation was granted by the king to these lands owned by the Church.

On the other side, constant raids, military service, and taxation impoverished the lesser men among these early mediaeval Franks. Many of the smaller landowners, who in addition to these evils also lacked immunity from taxes, found themselves no longer able to support themselves and their families. They were, therefore, obliged to do as their German forefathers had done in the days of the Roman Empire, long before the tide of German invasion overran it. They attached themselves to some neighbouring lord of far greater estate and power, by an act known in Roman days as *comitatus,* in mediaeval days as *commendatio,* in a relationship which bound the weaker to give free and honourable service in war and peace and the stronger, or patron, from the Roman term *patronicium,* to protect and care for his client. The same relationship occurred, of course, even more frequently in the case of men who had lost in these troubled times whatever land they once possessed.

Another step in such cases of need provided for temporary transfer of land to individuals from the great holdings of the Church or of lay nobles. The bankrupt head of a family, pressed by want, would make petition to the holder of wide tracts, bishop, abbot, or secular lord, for the "loan" of a piece of land or "farm," on condition that he tend it carefully, enjoy its produce and revenue, and return it in excellent working condition to its parent estate after a number of years, fixed by contract, or upon his own death. In this way both sides gained advantage, and the bishopric, abbey, or secular house did not lose its property in supporting the man who tilled its fields. Often, indeed, the owners made offer on their own side and farmed out their lands in this way for the sake of keeping them in good cultivation.

Sometimes the process was in reverse. The small landowner who had fallen on bad days voluntarily gave his little estate to the bishopric, or abbey, or secular chieftain, and received it back as a tenant, living henceforward in temporary possession upon the fields which had once been his own. Occasionally a small sum of money was paid by the tenant as a practical token of the bond.

In either case, whether the little man received or yielded land, this custom of its transfer was known as *precarium,* from the *preces,* or prayers of the suppliant, and the lands thus held were termed *precariae.*

Of greater importance was the bestowing by the patron upon his client of the *beneficium* (benefice). This was land either bestowed as unconditioned gift, usually in reward for services rendered, or in return for the solemn oath of the recipient that he would serve the giver on all occasions of need. Under either condition the recipient would naturally hold himself firmly attached to his patron.

In these institutions, nascent in Roman days, fostered under the Merovingian kings, and fully developed under the rule of the Mayors of the Palace, of Pepin and of Charles Martel, during the seventh and eighth centuries of Frankish dominion, we see the rising of feudal Europe. We have briefly noted their advantages for the little man. The disadvantages were also evident. The *precarium* did not provide for his children, whether he took over land from others or yielded others his own; moreover, the conditions of tenure were entirely in the hands of his patrons. The whole business, therefore, was temporary, required of him exacting and prolonged service and often obliged him to march off to war. Further, the altered status throughout the masses, from independence to this leaning upon a wealthy landlord, was bad for the State. The little people fell out of the reckoning; the king and great estate-owners decided between themselves for peace or for war. As the Frankish kings declined in character and gave way to Mayors of their respective Palaces, as the Frankish nobles increased in riches and power, we find the various parts of Frankish land, Austrasia, Neustria, and Burgundy, still struggling one against another as they had done so long before, while individuals in Church and State also struggled, each for his own pre-eminence.

So, in the seventh century, Grimoald as Mayor or "prime minister" of Austrasia raised his hand against royalty; so Ebroin, Mayor of Neustria, fought his long fight against Leodegar, bishop of Autun in Burgundy, as both in turn set up and overthrew puppet rulers upon Merovingian thrones; so Pepin of Heristal in 687 united his power over Austrasia with conquest of the Neustrian army at Tertry and made himself chief man in Frankland; and so, after his death in 714, fresh disorder and division arose, to be quelled by his son, Charles Martel. It was Charles who restored some measure of unity when he made himself master over these three realms of the Franks and threw his superior power around Aquitaine in the south.

To sum up then, land was craved by all as the ladder by which they might climb to noble ranking. The royal lands, however, were not boundless. Gradually Pepin and, more especially, Charles after him, as they saw their treasures drained by continual gifts and grants of *beneficia,* turned eager eyes for their replenishing upon the vast estates owned by the Church. Yet both these ministers, kings in all but name, acknowledged Catholic obedience. As Pepin had aided Willibrord by manifold gifts and strong support, so Charles was to aid Boniface.

Both were determined, nevertheless, above all and everything to keep and to extend their political power. If Christianity, as they believed, would further their political aims, they would support Christian missionaries and would work in accord with Rome and its Popes. When land or money was needed, their Catholic devotion, generous as it had been to the Church they acknowledged, did not stay them from transferring the property of the Church to their own names and their own ends.

Against Charles Martel in particular the Church levied for centuries her wrath on the charge of such "secularization" of her property. The warriors whom he thus rewarded had, it is true, aided him to bring about order and union throughout the disrupted Frankish realms. They had overcome the Saracens, the followers of Mahomet and terror of all faithful Catholics; they had brought peace into the land, a needful preliminary to missionary labour. But such service, as the Church judged it, did not give Charles Martel just cause for wholesale robbery when the dreaded order for transfer of their broad lands was heard by many a bishop and abbot—*precariae verbo regis.*

For such sin the Church of the eighth century at his death in 741 was to hold him eternally damned, a judgment which current rumour held proved by a vision of Eucharius, who as bishop of Orleans had dared to censure his conduct and who had, therefore, been banished from his see. One day, soon after Charles had died, the holy man was at prayer, when suddenly he was carried to the other world in a trance. There, among other awesome sights, he discerned Charles Martel tormented in the depths of hell. He asked the angel who was escorting him what this meant, and was told that by the sentence of the saints who would sit with the Lord hereafter to judge the world, and especially of those who had been robbed by him on earth, Charles had been assigned to everlasting punishment of body and soul, even before the Day of

Judgment. Moreover, he had been doomed to do penance, not only for his own sins, but for the sins of those good souls in Purgatory who had bequeathed to the Church and her poor the land he had so wickedly seized.

The spirit of Eucharius returned then to its body, still kneeling in his cell. At once, the story relates, he sent for Boniface and for Fulrad, abbot of St. Denis, where Charles had been buried. Would they please have the tomb opened in their presence? If they found no mortal remains lying within, they would know that Charles really was suffering the wrath of God in body and in soul. They quickly obeyed, and, to their horror, just as the lid of the tomb was raised, a serpent uncoiled and glided out; moreover, all the inner walls were found as black as if they had been burned. "This is written here," the narrative in the old records ends, "in order that all may learn of the just condemnation of this man who took the property of the Church." [59]

Charles, let it be said to his credit, did not always seize these ecclesiastical possessions outright. In many cases they remained as permanent property of the Church, and their recipients were only awarded by him tenure and enjoyment for the duration of their lives. Nevertheless, such practice led to other matters, and far greater. The warriors of Charles were laymen. And so not only small estates belonging to the Church, but entire bishoprics and abbeys were given into the charge of laymen who had fought for him, that they might be enriched by sacred revenue. Bishops, again, and abbots, duly consecrated, forsook their vows and their calling to march off for war, encouraged by such carnal return for services rendered. Plurality of holdings became common; it reached its extreme when Hugh, nephew of Charles, held at the same time

[59] See the (interpolated) account in the *Annales Fuldenses, ann.* 738: Pertz, *Script.* I, 345; Hincmar, *Vita S. Remigii,* PL CXXV, col. 1130; Bouquet III, 659; *Gest. Reg.* I, 255f.; Roth, *Beneficialwesen,* 327.

as bishop the sees of Paris, Rouen, and Bayeux, and as abbot the abbacies of Fleury-sur-Loire, of Saint-Wandrille, and of Jumièges. With plurality went, hand in hand, vacancy, and many sees and abbeys were left unserved, for the diverting of revenue into illegal use.

Lastly, wealth fathered luxury, and luxury fathered lust. Sport and feasting replaced fasting and prayer in many a holy place; tyranny and revolt flourished where single-hearted rule and prompt obedience had been the legacy of Columban and of Benedict; discipline fell before disorder in monastery and church and cathedral; sacred offices were bought and sold. Synods of bishops were forgotten; only three, we are told, were held between 639, year of the death of Dagobert I, and the time of Boniface.[60]

All this sad state of affairs concerned the west, the French, side of the Rhine rather than the east, or German, side, in which Boniface was so largely to labour. But, as the Frankish rule of Charles Martel extended over both sides, it is necessary to understand something of the conditions of the west. They explain why, through lack of Frankish missionaries, Boniface encountered so much ignorance and neglect of Christian faith and practice in the more distant countries where he began his work. Among their peoples such foundation as he could build upon had to a wide extent been laid by the Irish.[61]

He travelled, then, in 722 from Utrecht to the land of the Hessians, the ancient Chatti of the great forests, whom the Romans had had good reason to fear for their sinews of body, their sagacity of mind, their skill and endurance in fighting. "Other men go forth for a battle, but the Chatti go forth for war. . . . They distrust their luck; their courage they know."[62]

[60] Hauck, 402.
[61] Cf. W. Levison, "Die Iren und die Fränkische Kirche": HZ CIX, 1912, 1ff.
[62] Tacitus, Germ. cc. 30f.

From place to place he went with a few faithful companions, converting souls among trials and troubles almost unsurmountable. The people were overwhelmingly heathen; Saxon raiders were constantly throwing the country into panic of flight; and in this confusion and uncertainty it was very difficult to establish any settled centre for worship and instruction. At last, however, he came to Amöneburg on the river Ohm, near Marburg.[63] There twin brothers were chieftains, Dettic and Deorulf by name; they listened to his words of warning and exhortation, were baptized, and allowed him to set up in their rude town a little monastery and to gather within it some brethren for the perpetual offering of prayer. Thereupon, so we are told, his work grew apace, and "thousands were purged in baptism from their heathendom of old." [64]

Much more help, however, was needed for the progress of his campaign, so thrilling and yet so badly manned. The only thing to do was to inform Pope Gregory, as he had been bidden; and a messenger, Bynna, was sent off to Rome with a long letter, telling in detail all that so far had been brought about. There were many questions in this letter. The new work presented unending problems, and Boniface was immensely conscious of his responsibility to the Holy See. To his relief and delight in record time an answer arrived from Rome, calling him back to confer with Gregory in person. The Pope had decided that the young man had proved his worth and that the mission field in Germany should now have its much-needed bishop.

Across the territories occupied by the Franks and the Burgundians he slowly made his way, across the Alps into the land of the Lombards, down past Ravenna to the sight of Rome in the distance, and then once more to the guest-house of St.

[63] Amanaburch, in Willibald, c. 6.
[64] For the flowering of Benedictine monasticism on the continent, under Boniface, see Otto Zöckler, *Askese und Mönchtum*, 1897, 391f.

Peter's. The route, as can easily be seen, was not the nearest one, and it has been conjectured that he went out of his road to meet and talk with Charles Martel. But of this we have no convincing evidence.[65]

There was much discussion between the intrepid missionary and the Pope. It is interesting to read that Boniface, carefully trained in the comparatively classical Latin which we know from the pages of his contemporary, Bede, could not understand the vulgar and mediaeval variety spoken by Gregory and in common use for conversation in Rome. Pronunciation of Latin in Italy, different from that spoken in England at this time, as in the sermons of Bede and others, must also have caused trouble. As the Pope was purposing to raise Boniface to the order of bishop, it was necessary that the candidate in view should state very clearly and definitely his creed and knowledge of Christian doctrine. At last Boniface asked if he might present what the Pope was requiring in a written statement, and he did so after a short time "in cultured and learned Latin style." [66]

All proved to be in excellent ecclesiastical order, the details of missionary work were again heard and sanctioned, and it was decided that Boniface be consecrated on Saint Andrew's Day, the thirtieth of November. The Feast was, doubtless, convenient in date, but we need not forget that the name of Saint Andrew was especially dear in that Wessex where Boniface had spent his youth. Unfortunately the year is disputed. Argument has been advanced for both 722 and 723; the claim for 722 has perhaps the better support and is more generally followed by recent writers.[67]

The oath of loyalty to the Church taken by Boniface at this

[65] Cf. Hauck, 463, note 3.   [66] Willibald, ibid.
[67] For 722, see Jaffé, BRG III, 21; Hauck, 464, note 1; Kurth (French original), 37; Fischer, 42; Tangl, ed. 28, note 2; Dünzelmann, Forschungen XIII, 21f.; Hahn, Forschungen XV, 93; for 723 see Loofs, 8, note 1; Gregory Smith, DCB 325. Dümmler, ed. Epp. 228 "despairs of a decision"; Levison, ed. Vitae, 29, note 1, also leaves the matter open.

time followed the usual text, except in two important details: the customary promise of adherence to the Roman Emperor, reigning from Constantinople, was omitted, and in its place was written the vow to have no dealings with bishops who should break the law of the Church of Rome, to contend against their acts, and to inform the Pope thereof.[68] Gregory wrote in the next few days five letters of commendation for Boniface.[69] He informs "all Christians" in Germany that he is sending "our most reverend brother, the bishop bearing this message," to preach to the peoples wandering in the shadow of pagan death on the east side of the Rhine. "All who shall aid him shall be worthy to be counted among the saints and martyrs of Jesus Christ; if anyone (we pray not) shall try to hinder or oppose the mission entrusted to him, let him be struck down by Divine judgment, let him be bound by anathema and lie in eternal damnation."

In a second letter he declares to the clergy and laymen of the charge of Boniface that their bishop will live in accordance with canon law and explains certain details of that law for their instruction: Boniface may not ordain illegally; that is, he may not admit to the priesthood a man twice married, or one guilty of marrying a woman no longer virgin, or one uneducated, or maimed in body, or under penance, or debarred by any other legal or moral barrier. No African may be admitted to Holy Orders on any consideration; some of them are Manicheans and others have often been convicted of receiving a second baptism. He shall endeavour to augment the holy Offices and the adorning and endowment of the Church. Its revenue and the offerings of the faithful he shall divide into four parts: the first for himself; the second for the clergy, according as they shall show themselves diligent in

[68] *Epp.* No. 16; *cf.* Dümmler, ed. 265, note 1; Tangl, ed. 29.
[69] *Epp.* Nos. 17–21. The date of No. 21, however, is disputed; see Dümmler, 269, note 1; Hauck, 467, note 2. Tangl, 35, note 1, refers it to Gregory III.

duties; the third for the poor and for strangers; the fourth for the repair of Church buildings. For all this disbursement of funds he will give account at the Day of Judgment. Ordinations may be held, whether of priests or of deacons, only on the fasts of June, September, and December, at the beginning of Lent, and on the evening of the Saturday of Mid-Lent. Holy baptism is to be administered only at Easter and at Pentecost, except for those in danger of death.[70]

A third letter went to the Thuringian nobles who had already proved their loyalty to Boniface; a fourth announced to "the glorious lord, my son, Duke Charles, well-beloved in Christ," this official status of Boniface, and requested aid and protection for him in every need; a fifth warned the Old Saxons, those inveterate raiders upon Frankish lands, to depart from idolatry and listen for their profit to this new teacher. There seems no doubt that Boniface was being definitely commissioned by the Pope to form Hesse and Thuringia into a carefully organized centre of Catholicism and to do his best to convert the Saxon tribes in the north.

In 723 Boniface was travelling back to Hesse. On his way he visited Charles Martel and presented the letter from the Pope. As we have noted, Charles was no simple adherent of Rome; instead, he saw matters much as Clovis and his sons had seen them. He would obey, defend, and honour the Church so long as, under his profession of Christianity, he could conquer men and lands as missionary crusader; but it was he, as representing the nominal king, who must preside at the Church's councils and approve officially of her acts. The meeting which now took place between Boniface, the Anglo-Saxon, bred and matured in that spirit of deep devotion to the See of Rome which characterized the Anglo-Saxon Church of his time, and the independent Frankish conqueror was full of

[70] These instructions follow the formula of the *Liber Diurnus Romanorum Pontificum,* ed. Sickel, 1889, No. 6, pp. 5f.

prophecy for the future Frankish Church. It was the earnest and constant labour of Boniface as intermediary that gradually bound the Franks and the various peoples of the lands under their control into a nearer bond with Rome, and brought Frankish clergy nearer that loyalty to the mother Church which had been seen in the lives of Gregory of Tours and of Caesarius of Arles.

On the other hand, it has well been noted that there is a difference between the letter of Gregory II to Charles Martel and those written to Frankish royalty, such as Queen Brunhild, by Gregory the Great. The first Gregory was far more conscious of respect due to the Frankish throne in dealing with matters ecclesiastical than was his namesake of this eighth century, whose manner of writing to the chief power among the Franks was courteous, but entirely formal.[71]

Equally formal was Charles Martel's letter of commendation to Frankish dignities, ecclesiastical and secular, which resulted from his meeting with Boniface. There was no mention of the Church of Rome, and Charles requested protection and peace as for an individual bishop who at his own asking had been granted this safe-conduct wheresoever he should choose to labour in Frankish land.[72]

It was probably during this period of travelling that Boniface enjoyed for a brief while the hospitality of the nuns at Pfalzel on the bank of the Moselle near Trèves.[73] They were ruled at this time by an abbess named Addula, a very devout woman, who welcomed the Father gladly.[74] In the morning

---

[71] Hauck, 466.   [72] *Epp.* No. 22; Hauck, 470.

[73] See Fischer, 59; Liudger, *Vita Gregorii*, ed. Holder-Egger: Pertz, *Script.* XV, 67ff.; Hauck, 462.

[74] We have a letter (*Epp.* No. 8) in which Elfled, abbess of Whitby, commends to "Adola, abbess of Pfalzel," an unnamed abbess travelling to Rome. It has been thought that this "Adola" may have been the Addula mentioned here. A charter, probably spurious, mentions an abbess Adela as daughter of King Dagobert: Pertz, *Script.* XIV, 105. Another conjecture suggests that in the unnamed abbess here commended we have the Wethburg (Wiethburg) of *Epp.* 13 and 27; see Eckenstein, 124.

he said Mass, as he did almost every day, and then sat down to break his fast with the community. During the meal passages from holy Scripture were read aloud by a boy of fourteen or fifteen, named Gregory, who had lately come from school and was staying with the abbess, his grandmother. "You read well, my son," remarked Boniface at the end of the chapter, "if you understand what you read." The boy began again. "No," said Boniface, "don't read the Latin. Tell me in your own language and your own words the meaning of what you have read." This was beyond young Gregory's power. "Would you like me to explain it to you?" "Please." Then Boniface explained, and the boy hung on his words. When the new teacher was about to start out again, Gregory begged to go with him. He wanted to study; if his grandmother would not give him a horse to ride on, he would go on foot. After long argument the abbess realized that this was not a passing whim and sent him off, to begin a faithful discipleship which was to last as long as Boniface lived.

Soon Boniface was again in Hesse. The wild rites and heathen sacrifices, the spells of magic and the ancient gods, were all still there and flourishing mightily. But his courage now rose higher. He was a bishop, sent out by Rome to conquer the devil and all his works in this particular part of the world.

To this period belongs the famous narrative of the felling of the oak of Geismar, at one—we do not know which—of the several places thus named in the Hessian country.[75] Some of its people, we are told, had repudiated all pagan worship and would take no part in it. By their advice and after much thought Boniface decided to cut down an enormous tree known as the "Oak of Jupiter." Word flew all around the neighbourhood and a crowd of pagans gathered, furious in

[75] Levison, ed. *Vitae*, 31, note 1. It was probably near Fritzlar.

their anger against this sacrilege. Opposed to them and protecting the bishop, stood an even greater number of his friends and disciples. Boniface himself, doubtless of some experience in woodcraft, lifted the axe; at his first blow, so the story tells, there came a rushing mighty wind and the tree fell, miraculously cleft into four great trunks. Immediately, as in the similar wonder recorded of Saint Martin of Tours, the pagans turned from cursing to prayer. Boniface thereupon built a little chapel on the spot, to stand among the heathen as a perpetual warning of the power of the Christian God, and dedicated it to Saint Peter.

This bold act, of course, aroused intense wrath on the part of pagan priests and worshippers; and Boniface had full need of his guarantee of protection from Charles Martel. A letter sent about this time to him by his former bishop in England, Daniel of Winchester, shows that he must have poured out some of his difficulties in writing home.[76] Daniel recommends caution, patient discussing, and the bringing, by reasonable argument, of these heathen fanatics to admit their *reductio ad absurdum*. It is a rather pontifical epistle, somewhat superior in tone, as of a diocesan to one of his less experienced clergy. Boniface must have laid it down with a sigh of disappointment. Perhaps Daniel preferred Aldhelm's method of composing a treatise for the recalcitrant British to chopping down a numinous German tree!

Pope Gregory, also, heard from Boniface of these troubles, and of others as well. There were not only raging heathen; there were, it seems, Frankish clergy to contend with, who resented this sudden importation from Rome.[77] Boniface wrote

[76] *Epp.* No. 23. Dümmler dates it 723–725, Tangl 723–724, on account of the word *antistes,* addressed to Boniface; see Hauck, 445, note 5; Hahn, *Bon. und Lul,* 117.
[77] *Cf.* Heinz Vahle, *Die Widerstände gegen das Werk des Bonifatius,* 1934.

of one bishop in particular, doubtless Gerold, bishop of Mainz,[78] who had hitherto been too lazy to preach the Gospel in Hesse but was now claiming part of it as his own "diocese."

· In December, 724, the Pope wrote, "Well done! But press on. God promises salvation to those who persevere to the end. Let not their threats terrify you nor their terrors cast you down; hold fast your faith and preach the word of truth. If only your will to work be good, you shall attain the end, by the help of the Lord." Gregory went on to say that he had written to Charles Martel about the troublesome bishop and believed that he would be restrained from interfering.[79]

It was now time to return to Thuringia. Several years had passed since Boniface had worked there as a pioneer priest; he would now carry things further with his authority as bishop. The problems awaiting him, with young Gregory and other helpers, early in 725 were no less formidable than those of Hesse. The soil of Thuringia was so barren and the people so poor that there was never enough to eat; they managed to keep alive only by hard labour of their hands. From time to time a wild band of heathen would swoop down upon some Christian settlement in which Boniface was ministering at the moment, and he and his peasants would have to flee for their lives into a fortified town. They would remain there for many days, hungry and comfortless, until the Christians had collected an army strong enough to drive the raiders away.

Further hostility met them in the Celtic clergy, of whom we know four by name, Torchtwine, Berthere, Eanbert, and Hunrad. They were as tenacious of their ways as were their brethren in Ireland and in Britain. They could not have been very successful in Thuringia, it would seem, since Boniface

[78] *Epp.* No. 24; Hauck, 411, 471; Tangl, 42.
[79] *Epp., ibid.*

found its peasants in so wretched a state; and here again we may blame that lack of correlation in their work.[80]

In 726 the bishop sat down to describe, one after another, the problems which his own mind dared not solve. No man was less given than he to refer to another questions which should be decided by his own authority, as given him by Rome; and yet these were matters which he had never yet encountered. It was not only necessary at the moment but would be highly useful for the future to obtain a *corpus* of judgments in spiritual law, given by the Pope for these remote and barbarian sheep of the flock.

His letter was carried to Rome by a priest called Denual,[81] and on November 22 of the same year Gregory wrote back in clear and succinct paragraphs, each settling a difficulty, with not a superfluous word in the whole document.[82] The answers are still of interest, since they show what problems were confronting Boniface:

"Holy baptism and confirmation may not be received twice by the same person, with the possible exception of those who have been taken away from their parents in childhood and cannot give or find any evidence. Tradition of the Church orders the baptism of such. Persons who have been baptized in the Name of the Father, Son, and Holy Spirit may on no account be rebaptized, even though the holy rite were administered by a priest in foul sin, with no examination into the recipient's knowledge of the Catholic faith. This is the ancient custom of the Church; for grace is given in the Name of the Holy Trinity, not of him who baptizes. Such persons, however, must be instructed with special care.

"At Holy Mass the priest is to place, not two or three but

---

[80] Hauck, 472f.

[81] Perhaps the Denewald of *Epp.* Nos. 14 and 71; Hahn, *Bon. und Lul*, 106.

[82] *Epp.* No. 26.

one chalice upon the altar, following the example of our Lord, when He took the Cup and gave it to them, saying, 'This is the Cup of the New Testament in my Blood.' As to meats offered in sacrifice to idols, these may not be eaten by a Christian, even if he has made the sign of the Cross over them.

"Marriage should not, ideally, take place between any two related people. But, as it is better not to be too strict, especially toward those barbarians of yours, prohibition is only extended as far as third cousinship. A man may seek annullment of marriage if through sickness his wife be permanently incapable of her conjugal duty. It were better that he should not marry again; but since this is a very difficult matter, let him do so if he cannot help it. He must not, however, withdraw material support from his former wife unless she be guilty of some great sin.[83]

"You ask, further, whether young men and women who were dedicated to the religious life in a monastery as little children may leave this for marriage when they are old enough. Certainly not; it is in no way lawful that the reins of pleasure be made loose for those offered as children by their parents to God. Again, if an epidemic of disease or plague has attacked a church or monastery, may those who have not yet caught the infection flee from the place and its peril? My answer is No, for it would be exceedingly silly. No one can flee from the hands of God.

"Your last question deals with some priests and bishops deeply involved in crime, so wicked that their very lives stain their holy ordering. Is it right for you to eat and drink with them, granting that they are not heretics? Yes, you may do this, for in talking quietly you may be able to correct their ways. By all means you must use your apostolic authority to

[83] See Laux, 276f.

advise and warn such in order to bring them back to the discipline of the Church."

Slowly the earnest preaching, the ready help for body as well as soul, the determination coupled with the kindliness of Boniface, made their way among this people of Thuringia. More and more came to be prepared for baptism; numbers, at first from curiosity and then from attraction, came to listen, finally to worship. Churches were built, and a community of monks was settled at Ohrdruf, just to the north of the Thuringian Forest. Their monastery rose on land given by two chieftains, one named Hugo and the other Alvold, to whom Pope Gregory had commended Boniface in 722.[84] In all this time we hear of no aid from Charles Martel, such as he had given to Willibrord. No doubt the severe criticisms levied upon the Frankish clergy by this new and unwelcome bishop lay at the root of the neglect.[85]

In January, 731, the Pope died. He had been the constant friend of Boniface and his mission, a wise and far-seeing ruler, who, even in those days of Lombard fighting within Italy and of spiritual conflict with Constantinople, had given freely of his time and energy for the converting of the barbarians of central Europe. He was succeeded by Gregory III, the Pope whose name is always connected with that of Charles Martel.

Soon after the accession of the new Pope, Boniface sent to him, it would seem, two letters. The first assured him of humble loyalty on the part of the bishop and his fellow-workers and prayed that they might continue in intimate fellowship with Rome; the second gave the regular report on progress in Germany.[86] To this report we have an answer from Gregory, written about 732.[87] It entirely approved the work

---

[84] Willibald, c. 6: *Epp.* No. 19; Levison, ed. *Vitae* (*auct. Otloho*), 137.
[85] Hauck, 481f.
[86] *Ibid.*, 484, note 2. [87] *Epp.* No. 28.

and announced that Boniface was thereupon raised to the rank of Archbishop by the sending to him of the pallium. This long white band of lambs' wool, marked by crosses and worn around neck and shoulders, has been given from the fourth or fifth century (and is still given) to those to whom, as Archbishops, the Holy See accords a share in the highest pastoral office of the Church. In his letter of bestowal Gregory informed Boniface that he was to wear the pallium only when celebrating Mass or in consecrating a bishop-elect.[88] This last rite he was to solemnize, in union with two or three other bishops, wherever the number of converts had become too great for his own care.

Gregory then turned to deciding fresh problems of the German Church under Boniface:

"If you really are sure that some have received baptism from pagans, you must baptize them again. Also baptize in the Name of the Trinity those baptized by a priest of Christian ordering, if that priest at the same time made sacrifice to Jupiter and ate meats offered to heathen gods.

"Marriage, in my judgment, may not be solemnized between persons of the seventh degree of kinship. Moreover, if you can, see that a man who has lost two wives by death does not marry again.

"The penance proper for one who has murdered his father, mother, brother or sister is this: He shall eat no meat nor drink any wine for the rest of his life; he is to fast on the second, fourth, and sixth day of the week; he may never in all his days receive the Body of the Lord, except as *viaticum* when he is dying.

"Yes, anyone, and especially priests, may make intercession and offerings for the Christian dead, anyone, that is, who not only professes, but really leads a Christian life himself.

----

[88] *Cf.* Gregory the Great, *Epp.* ed. Ewald-Hartmann, V, No. 15: *MGH Epp.* I, 295.

"Two practices of which you write are certainly abhorrent and must be stopped; you must also impose heavy penance upon those found guilty of such. That any of the faithful should sell their slaves for pagan sacrifices is a crime against God and man; and that people should eat as food horses, whether wild or domestic, is a foul and accursed thing." [89]

The year 732 brought to a climax events which certainly turned the thoughts of Charles Martel away from this missionary bishop in his outlying dominions. It was now twelve years since the Arabs, the Muslim disciples of Mahomet, had crossed the Pyrenees. They had laid waste the many towns of Septimania and of Provence in the south, had advanced upon Aquitaine and threatened with invasion its ruler, Duke Eudes. For some time Eudes succeeded in holding them back, until in 732 the attack was reinforced by the energy of Abd-ar-Rahman, Arab governor of Spain. In this crisis he called upon Charles Martel for aid. The result is known to all in the great battle fought for several days near Tours and Poitiers. At last the Arabs withdrew again to the south, leaving Charles in high repute as defender of Christianity.

Meanwhile in his interest in Thuringia Boniface had not forgotten Hesse; he had constantly travelled to and from the two countries and fostered his work in both. Now, in the years between 732 and 735, encouraged by the letters from the Pope and by his new responsibility as Archbishop, he was busy with houses for the monks he hoped to gain. In Hesse the monastery he had already built at Amöneburg was enlarged by the addition of a church, that of Saint Michael the Archangel; at Fritzlar on the river Edder he founded another monastery, dedicated to Saint Peter.[90] Since it was impossible

[89] This was connected, of course, in the Pope's mind with pagan sacrifice.

[90] Willibald, c. 6. Fritzlar may, however, have been established during the earlier stay of Boniface in Hesse, in 724: see Flaskamp, *Das hess. Missionswerk* 71.

for him to govern these unaided, with the other foundations he had in mind, he decided to send home to various people in England invitations to come across and help in the work.

One of the earliest to arrive was Wigbert, a monk of Boniface's own monastery of Nursling in Hampshire. He came of an Anglo-Saxon family of high standing, was older than Boniface, and so greatly respected for his character and learning that he was installed as abbot of Fritzlar.[91] Apparently he had no easy experience there; monastic discipline was a thing by no means understood at this time in Hesse, and he spent enormous energy before he succeeded in getting his monks to observe the Benedictine Rule. This was, of course, the norm for all the religious houses of Boniface, following the custom already practised in England in the eighth century.

Another Wigbert also came from England to give his aid, we do not know exactly when. He was a priest, and he wrote back to the monks of Glastonbury Abbey an enthusiastic account of his reception.[92] "You must know, my dear friends, that Archbishop Boniface himself actually travelled a long way to meet me when he heard I was coming, and was most kind. Here I am in the lands of the pagan Hessians and Saxons; we are all working away hard, hungry, thirsty, and cold, besides always expecting an attack from these pagans. But God is giving us good success. Pray for us always, as we do for you."

First, however, in importance to Boniface among those who followed him from England was Lul, who was to carry on

[91] Lupus Servatus, *Vita Wigberti abb. Frites.* ed. Holder-Egger: Pertz, *Script.* XV, i, 36ff.; Hauck, 489, 493.
[92] *Epp.* No. 101. On the various Wigberts see Hahn, *Bon. und Lul,* 141ff.; Hauck, 489, note 4, and Holder-Egger, *ibid.,* 39, note 2. Dümmler dates *Epp.* No. 101 as c. 732–754. See also *Epp.* Nos. 55 and 40. "The priest Wigbert" of *Epp.* 101 and 40 may be one and the same man, but there is no reason to identify him with the "Witbert" of Bede V, c. 9 (Slover, *Speculum* X, 1935, 150): p. 344 *supra.*

his work after his death.[93] Lul's father seems to have been possessed of wealth, as we read of slaves freed by him. We know that he sent his boy to Malmesbury Abbey. Long afterwards, when Lul was a bishop in Germany, a monk, unknown to us by name, wrote to remind him of the time when they were friends together at Malmesbury and of how the abbot had called him "Lul, the Little." [94] Then he went on to Nursling, where he was taught by Boniface the art of writing Latin prose and verse in the extraordinary manner for which Aldhelm had been renowned. A serious illness sent him to convalesce at Rome, where he amused himself, when he was not at prayer or study, by writing "figured" acrostic forms of verse. One of these atrocities, in shape of an oval, with a letter composed in extreme Hisperic style embellished by runic script and high-flown metaphor, he sent to some English nuns who had been kind to him in his sickness at home. Would they please show it to no one without his permission? Some one might be jealous. He had been suffering horrid aches and pains in Rome, he wrote the Sisters, and was very, very sad because of the death of his father, who had been with him there.[95]

He appears next in Germany with Boniface. From there he writes with two English friends and fellow-workers an explanation of their doings to "Abbess Cuneburga, of royal blood." [96] Their relatives are dead, they tell her, and they have come to live under monastic rule with Boniface and help him

---

[93] See, for Lul, Hauck, 486ff., and Hahn, *ibid.*, 236ff. The *Life* written by Lambert of Hersfeld in the 11th century (ed. Holder-Egger: Pertz, *ibid.*, 132ff.) is almost entirely compiled from older records.

[94] *Epp.* No. 135.

[95] *Ibid.*, No. 98; *cf.* Dümmler, ed. 386, Tangl, ed. 220f.

[96] *Epp.* No. 49. This "Cuneburga" was perhaps the "Cuenburga" recorded as abbess of Wimborne, sister of King Ine of Wessex and of Cuthburga, foundress of Wimborne. *Cf.* the letter (*Epp.* No. 55) gratefully accepting a bond of mutual intercession between a Cuneburga (possibly the same), Coengils, abbot of Glastonbury, and Wigbert, priest, etc. See Hahn, 148f.; H. S. III, 342f.; *DCB* I, 720; *ASC ann.* 718.

so far as they can. Will she please remember them? They all would gladly be under her rule, were they in Britain, rather than that of any man, so great is their confidence in her kindly governing. They are sending her some gifts, incense, pepper, and cinnamon. . . .

Boniface sent Lul for further training to Thuringia, to the monastery of Ohrdruf, we may think, from which his novice wrote to him in very stilted prose, with some verses for good measure.[97] In due time Lul was ordained deacon and described himself as such in two letters he wrote home. One went to Eadburg, abbess of Thanet, bearing a present of a silver pen; another to one of his teachers in England, called Dealwin, probably a monk at Malmesbury. Lul asks him to send works of Aldhelm, both those in prose and those on the rules of metric and rhythm, "for my comfort in this foreign land and for the memory of that holy bishop."[98] Later on he became archdeacon and priest.[99]

Nor do we lose track of his two English friends. One of these was Denehard, whom Boniface sent more than once as confidential messenger to foreign countries. We still have a little note "from Boniface to Denehard, the priest": "Dear friend, please see to the bondman Athalhere, if he should need help. Give surety for him to his friends, just as if he were free-born. I am especially keen on this, now that he is getting married. Don't let him be afraid because he is a slave."[100] The second friend, Burchard, will be heard of later as bishop of Würzburg.

In the meantime Boniface needed further help, this time from a woman. Among his many women friends the nuns of the monastery of Thanet always held an honoured place. Two letters written to their Abbess Eadburg, about 735, tell of his

---

[97] *Epp.* No. 103.
[99] Nos. 85f.
[98] *Ibid.*, Nos. 70f.; Hahn, 243ff.
[100] No. 99.

love and his gratitude toward her. May the choir of angels who reward good works gladden this beloved sister, who has comforted his exile in Germany by her gift of sacred books and of clothing, so badly wanted! Could she possibly add to all her kindnesses one more, and write out for him in letters of gold a copy of the Epistles of his master, Saint Peter the Apostle, for the honouring of Holy Scripture in the eyes of men of fleshly mind? He is sending materials for this work by his messenger, the priest Eoban.[101] We have already noted the copy of the Four Gospels belonging to Wilfrid of York, written in gold upon purple parchment. Evidently women, as well as male scribes, were trained in the *scriptoria* of their monasteries.[102]

But the best gift that Abbess Eadburg made to Boniface was the early training of her nun Leobgyth, or Lioba, as she is usually called. Lioba was related to him, and wrote to him from Thanet a charming little letter. "Would you, of your charity, most revered and dear lord and kinsman, remember your friendship in the West country with my father Dynne, who died eight years ago? Would you pray for his soul, and pray, too, for my mother, of your own family, who is still living but very sick and sad? I am their only child. I wish I were good enough to call you brother, for there is no man living whom I trust and look up to as I do to you. I have sent you a little present, not at all a proper one, but only that you may not forget me, now that you are so far away. Please, dear brother, please protect me from the darts of the hidden enemy by the shield of your prayer. And would you correct this awkward, badly written letter, and send me as example a few of your own words? I am just longing to hear. I have tried hard to compose a few verses, and I send them with this, very humbly, as an exercise, in need of your correction. I have

[101] Nos. 30 and 35.   [102] Eckenstein, 122.

studied under Abbess Eadburg, who never stops poring over holy Scripture." There follow some four hexameters, made up very laboriously from the verses of Aldhelm and other precedent.[103]

From Thanet, Lioba went for further training as a nun to Wimborne Abbey in Dorsetshire, founded early in the eighth century by that Cuthburga who rejected *pro amore Dei* marriage with King Aldfrid of Northumbria.[104] The monastery was a double one, and the abbess of the time, Tetta, was very strict. High, strong walls surrounded its two parts, separate for monks and nuns. Each part had its own church. No man, not even a bishop, with the normal exception of the priest who administered holy sacraments, might ever set foot within the Sisters' enclosure, and even he withdrew immediately after his office was done. When it was necessary to issue rulings or give particular orders, the Mother spoke to her community through a window.[105]

But Tetta was a good woman, all the same. Lioba had a keen sense of humour and long afterward used to tell without malice all sorts of stories about the life at Wimborne under her rule. At one time there was a senior nun who was so harsh and overbearing toward the novices that she made their lives miserable. At last, to their unconcealed joy, she died, and they gathered round her grave, stood on top of it and beat it with their feet. The abbess, horrified by this unnunlike behaviour, went at once to see what they had done. Her horror was infinitely increased when she saw that the mound of the grave had sunk half a foot below the surface of the ground. She knew that this was a sign of Divine wrath against the austere Sister; but nevertheless she called all the nuns into chapter, preached them a lively sermon on the Christian duty

[103] *Epp.* No. 29.
[104] Dugdale II, 88ff.; Kemble I, No. 54.
[105] Rudolf of Fulda, *Vita Leobae,* ed. Waitz: Pertz, *Script.* XV, i, 118ff.

of forgiveness, and ordered three days of strict fast, with prayer and psalm and vigil for the departed soul. At the end of this period all the congregation of nuns walked in solemn procession into their own church with chanting of litanies and invocation of the saints. The abbess prostrated herself before the altar; and, even while she prayed, the earth over the grave slowly rose till it stood once more in a mound.

Another day the Sister who was sacristan, just as she had locked up the nuns' church after Compline, found to her dismay that she had lost her bunch of keys. In vain she hunted everywhere until it was time to open the church again for the Night Offices. There was nothing to do but to go and confess to Reverend Mother Tetta, who was already at her prayers in her cell. The Mother was wise; she knew the devil had once again been at his tricks. The Offices were chanted in one of the convent rooms, and before they ended a fox appeared at the door with the keys in his mouth. It must have been a relief in those days to call the devil openly to blame for all the sins and frailties of nature.

With all her wit and humour, Lioba was a model nun. She fasted and prayed and studied with great energy. When Boniface sent to Thanet and to Wimborne to ask for aid for his mission in Germany, she was, of course, far more eager to work under her kinsman, the revered bishop, than her abbess was to see her go. Yet women in barbarian Germany had souls and bodies as well as men, and English women were well accustomed to cross the Channel. Lioba did not travel alone. With her went Thecla, another of the community at Wimborne, and a relative of Lioba. In the company were also three more nuns: Chunitrud, Chunihildt, aunt of Lul, and her daughter, Berthgit.[106] After they had had time to become accustomed to their new surroundings, Boniface in courage

---

[106] Levison, ed. *Vitae* (*auct. Otloho*), 138; Hauck, 490ff.; Hahn, 132ff.; *Epp.* No. 67.

and hope founded several convents for nuns in the district near the river Main, where Christianity was of deeper growth than in Hesse. Lioba was made abbess at Tauberbischofsheim; Chunihildt and Berthgit, who were very learned ladies, presided over a school in Thuringia; Thecla ruled first a community at Kitzingen and was afterward transferred for the same duty at Ochsenfurt.

Tauberbischofsheim was happy in its Abbess Lioba. Here once again her cheerful spirit enlivened the Rule. "Her face was always gay, although she never burst into laughter." Her patience was as admirable as her clear-cut administration; her knowledge extended almost as far as her humility. These, of course, are commonplace descriptions in the *Lives* of the saints; but Lioba seems to have been gifted as well with much common sense, not always so prevalent. She made all her household, including herself, take a siesta after the midday meal in summer and would not hear of this rule being broken by any too ascetic a Sister. "If you do not rest," she warned them all, "you won't be able to read." The meals were liberally served, and her broad and friendly spirit made her dear to all. Naturally her biographer praised her own asceticism. "The nuns," he wrote, "used to call her special drinking-cup 'the little one of the Beloved'" (Lioba: *geliebte*).[107]

Boniface also wrote letters about the year 735 on other matters to friends in Britain. To Pecthelm, once a monk and deacon under Aldhelm and a friend of Bede, and now the first bishop of Whithorn (*Candida Casa*) off Galloway, Scotland, he sent gifts, a chasuble embroidered with a design in white and a towel to dry the feet of priests after the ceremonial washing. With them came a request for advice on a knotty problem. The Frankish priests, both in Germany and in Gaul, held guilty of grievous sin a man who married a widow when

[107] Rudolf, *ibid.*, c. 11; *cf.* also *Epp.* No. 96.

he was godfather to her child. Boniface had learned nothing of such sin, either in canon law or in the decrees of the Popes. Did Pecthelm know any place in the Fathers where such a matter was discussed? [108]

Probably no answer came from Pecthelm, since he died in the same year, 735. At any rate, two more appeals went to Britain concerning the same matter: one to Nothelm, Archbishop of Canterbury from 735 until 739, the other to Duddo, an abbot who had once been a student of Boniface, probably at Nursling.[109] From Nothelm Boniface also requested, for aid in the same problem, a copy of the *Responsa* which Gregory the Great had sent to Augustine when he, too, had been worried by various ecclesiastical difficulties on his first arrival in Kent.[110] "Moreover," the Archbishop continued, "would you *please* do your very best to find out whether holy Gregory really did write those answers? The keepers of the archives at Rome say they cannot be found there among his other papers. And just what year did those missionaries of his arrive in England?"

He asked Abbot Duddo also for books: "I have commentaries on Romans and on First Corinthians. Would you send me what I need for the other writings of Saint Paul? And, too, anything you have in the library of your monastery which you think would be useful to me, anything you think I don't know or do not have, please tell me about it, as a good son to his out-of-the-world Father. My priest Eoban will bring this letter and explain everything to you." [111]

It was very probably this same Eoban who brought to Boniface on the return journey from England a request that

---

[108] *HE* v, cc. 13, 18, 23. He was bishop c. 730–735: Flor. Worc. *MHB* 542. The letter is No. 32; *cf.* H. S. III, 310. For the gift of a towel *cf. Epp.* No. 75.

[109] Nos. 33f.; *cf.* Kemble, No. 92; Hahn, 164f.; Hauck, 495.

[110] *HE* I, c. 27; Plummer II, 45f.

[111] Eoban was another English missionary.

is rather interesting from a priest named Sigebald, of the diocese of Winchester: "I do beg and beseech you to grant me this prayer, that *you* will be my bishop, as well as my own diocesan, Daniel. If he had allowed this, I know you would. I had hoped that some word of comfort would come to me from you, my lord. I always include your name with those of our bishops here when I say Mass, and I shall go on doing so as long as I live." [112]

By this time the work of converting Hesse and Thuringia was progressing well. It is true that it was not ecclesiastically organized, and that Boniface was still Archbishop only in name.[113] Probably he felt that the Church in these countries was not yet ready and that he had better begin the necessary business of organizing Germany for spiritual purposes in a land more familiar with Christianity. He cast his eyes, therefore, upon the regions along the Danube and south of it, the ancient Raetia and Noricum.

Long before this time the Teutonic tribes that had dwelt in these regions had been conquered by the Romans, and Roman colonies, administered there under the Roman Empire, had been guarded by cities, such as Augusta Vindelicorum (Augsburg), Regina Castra (Regensburg), Batava (Passau), Juvavum (Salzburg). When the Empire declined in power, her provincials had been left to the mercy of nomadic marauders who swooped down from the north and west and east to ravage as they would. In the fifth century these unhappy colonists had found their only aid and comfort in the missionary Severinus, who had come from without to shepherd them in their troubles.[114]

After his death these lands near the river had been laid waste by the soldiers of Odovacar, the barbarian conqueror

[112] *Epp.* No. 36; Hahn, 128ff. [113] Hauck, 485.
[114] Duckett, *Gateway to the Middle Ages*, 1938, 360ff.

of Italy, in the years 487–488, and most of the inhabitants
had been killed or driven into exile. But soon fresh settlers
had streamed in, so that during the next thirty years Raetia
and Noricum had been more and more occupied by Germanic
migrants of various tribes who followed the Danube, hungrily
seeking a permanent home. Once established, they became
known as Baioarii. Like the people of Hesse, they were
heathen, worshipping their Germanic gods in the same cults
of magic and sacrifice and rites of the dead.

As the power of the Frankish kings grew, they naturally
controlled these inhabitants of the early mediaeval duchy of
Bavaria, comprising what is now the modern Bavaria, together with upper Austria and Salzburg, and ruled in hereditary succession by dukes of the Agilolfing line. Frankish dominion meant missionary teaching from the Catholic Frankish
Church, planted anew upon whatever remnant of faith and
practice remained among descendants of the few disciples of
Severinus who had escaped the hand of Odovacar.

As, again, the Frankish kings declined in power after the
death of Dagobert in 639, so the Bavarian dukes gained independence.[115] When this was reaching its highest point in the
time of Childebert III, nominal king of France, and of
Theodo I, one of the strongest dukes of Bavaria, there appeared about 696 among the Bavarians a Frankish missionary
bishop named Rupert, described in our records as coming
from Worms.[116] Theodo, it is said, welcomed him to the
Bavarian capital of Regensburg, listened to his preaching, and

[115] The line from c. 560 to 717 ran: Garibald I, Tassilo I, Garibald
II, Theodo I. For early mediaeval Bavaria see Riezler, *Geschichte Baierns*
I, 1878, 70ff.; Hauck, 357ff.; T. Hodgkin VII, 63ff.; Allen Leeper,
History of Medieval Austria, 1941, 82ff.
[116] For Rupert see *Breves Notitiae Salisburgenses*; *Gesta S. Hrodberti*:
Mayer, *Archiv f. österreich. Gesch.* LXIII, 606ff.; Pertz, *Script.* XI, 1ff.;
H. Widmann, *Geschichte Salzburgs* I, 1907, 58ff.; Levison, *Neues Archiv
f. ält. deutsch. Gesch.* XXVIII, 1903, 285ff., and in *MGH Script. rer.
Merov.* VI, 1913, 140ff.; Hauck, 372ff.

received baptism at his hands. In spite of urgent entreaty, Rupert then resumed his search for heathen souls and travelled along the Danube to Lorch, then to the mountains and lakes of the Salzkammergut, and at last to the south shore of the little Wallersee where Seekirchen was afterward to stand. Here once more he stayed awhile, ministered to the people of the salt districts and built for them a church, dedicated to Saint Peter.

The ruins of the old Roman city of Juvavum were only nine miles away. Rupert visited them and was immensely impressed by the scenery of river and mountain in which they lay. Moreover, here were mighty foundations of masonry upon which to build, caught though they were in a forest of wild growth. Here amid the glory of nature, where Severinus long before had taught, he would renew man's work for the worship of God. Duke Theodo gave him possession of the ruins and of land surrounding them, and soon another church of Saint Peter and a monastery for clergy were built upon the height still called the Mönchsberg, overlooking the river and the city which it divides. Later on, Rupert raised a convent for nuns on the Nonnberg, where fragments of a fallen castle remained, and placed at its head his niece Erindrud. From this centre, long since famous as Salzburg, he went out for many years on missionary journeys through Bavaria and Austria.

Two other bishops, wandering from Frankland proper on the same bent, also worked in these same regions before the coming of Boniface. Much legend has been told of one of them, Emmeram by name. All we really know is that he worked for some time in Regensburg, that he died by a murderer's hand, and that by his efforts or in his memory a monastery was founded there. The other was Corbinian, who made Freising his headquarters. Abundant and thrilling details concerning him and his somewhat unsaintly temper must also be enjoyed as fiction rather than fact. Yet he was valiant and fearless in the preaching of his faith.[117]

Duke Theodo did more than welcome Rupert, so keen was his desire to foster religion among his people. In 716 he travelled to Rome to consult Pope Gregory II on their education in its ways.[118] As a result, in the same year a little company of three, including a bishop named Martinian, set out from Rome as delegates of the Holy See appointed to bring Church discipline in Bavaria into regular order.

We still have the instructions given them by Gregory: on the examining and approving of its clergy, the celebrating of Holy Mass and the conducting of monastic Office; on its division into episcopal sees and the consecrating of worthy men as bishops; on the ordinances governing marriage; on the measures to be taken against pagan worship and superstitions among the people. One especially interesting clause empowered these commissioners, "if they shall find a man able by knowledge of doctrine and holy life to rule his clergy and layfolk in wisdom and prosper well his charge, to send him to Rome with a letter of commendation, or to escort him there themselves. Otherwise, an Italian shall be sent from the Holy See for this high matter."[119]

After Theodo's death his duchy was ruled by his sons, Theodebert and Grimoald, in two parts, with two capital cities. Theodebert, who governed from Salzburg in Austria, soon died and left his throne to his son Hucbert; Grimoald,

---

[117] Aribo (Arbeo), bishop of Freising, 764–784, wrote Lives of Emmeram and of Corbinian, but they are not trustworthy. See Krusch, *MGH Script. rer. Merov.* VI, 497ff., and in *Script. rer. Germ. in usum scholarum*, 1920, 1ff., 100ff.; Riezler, *Abhandl. d. k. bayer. Akad. d. Wiss. hist. Cl.* XVIII, Munich, 1888, 219ff., and *Gesch. Baierns* I, 95ff.; Hauck, 377f., 381f.

[118] Duchesne, *Lib. Pont.* I, 398.

[119] Pertz, *MGH Leges* III, ed. Merkel, 451ff.

who reigned over the second part at Freising in Bavaria, met a worse fate. His realm was invaded by Charles Martel. It was no declining Frankish monarchy that stood against him, but the master of France, even though still content to be called Mayor under a useless king. Grimoald was defeated, deprived of his possessions, and, it was said, killed by an assassin's dagger. The two parts of the Bavarian duchy were thereupon once more united under Hucbert, subject to control from Charles, until Hucbert himself died about 736.

Such, then, were the political circumstances in mediaeval Bavaria when Boniface decided, about 735, to enter it on missionary campaign. The three bishops were dead. Another, Vivilo, bishop in Passau, had been ordained by Gregory III at Rome. He, too, like them, had a "bishop's stool." We hear also of other missionary bishops, working here and there, up and down the land. But neither these four known to us, nor any one of the other episcopal figures now lost in the shadows of time, was a diocesan bishop in the modern sense of the words.[120] They did, indeed, make their headquarters at some place or other, generally in a monastery. From thence they went out to teach and to minister as monks ordained to episcopal office, returning to their cloisters between these journeys for the comfort of their brethren and the peace of prayer. They had no plan of organizing this land of their ministry into a unit which should be definitely linked throughout its various parts by superintendence and administration of its churches and clergy from a central disciplinary power, working by synod and by rule. There were also a goodly number of lower clergy. Many were of Frankish birth, but unlearned as well as undisciplined; many were Irish who had come, perhaps, to one or another of Columban's monasteries in France

[120] Hauck, 378f.

for training and who had then travelled further afield, or had
set out, like Maelduib of Malmesbury, on lonely pilgrimage.
They taught here and there their faith, Catholic and Celtic, as
they themselves had learned it. Yet the land held still a multitude untaught by any, pagans who had drifted from remote
places, seeking whereof they and and theirs might eat and live.
Lastly, the commission of Pope Gregory II had come to
nothing, perhaps because of Theodo's death and the division
of his rule. Undoubtedly Bavaria and the neighbouring territory of the Danube were barren soil for Boniface to plough
and sow.

Little is known to us of the beginning of this ministry. We
read that he preached in many places, visited and examined
many churches, expelled a heretic named Eremwulf, and
brought to conversion those who had absorbed evil teaching.[121]
The official permit of Charles Martel still protected and gave
him authority from the secular side, as the mandate renewed
by Pope Gregory III did from the spiritual. An event full of
interest for the future was the arrival of Sturm, a Bavarian
boy, born to Christian parents of high rank, who brought him
to Boniface that he might be reared by the Church.[122] Boniface sent him to school in the monastery of Fritzlar, where he
was studying when Abbot Wigbert died.[123] A letter, written
about this time to its community, shows the thought for detail
in the Archbishop's mind: "With fatherly love I beg you the
more eagerly to keep the Rule, now that our Father Wigbert
is dead. Let Wigbert, the priest, and Megingoz, the deacon,
see to observance of its details—the Hours and Church services, the admonishing and teaching of the monks, the discipline

[121] Willibald, c. 6.
[122] Eigil, *Vita Sturmi*: Pertz, *Script.* II, 365ff.
[123] If this Abbot Wigbert is the one described in the *Life* by Lupus
(*cf.* p. 394 *supra,* note 91), his death must have occurred before the date
given by tradition; see the notes of Holder-Egger, and of Hahn, *Bon. und
Lul,* 142, note 6.

and care of the children. Let Hiedde be Prior and superintend the servants, with the help of Hunfrid when necessary. Sturm is to do the cooking; Bernard is to be carpenter and see to needed repairs. In any difficulties consult Abbot Tatwin and carry out his rulings." [124]

As we have seen, about 736 Duke Hucbert died. He had neither actively opposed Boniface nor had he lent him open support. The rule of Bavaria now came by will of its overlord, Charles Martel, to Odilo, probably a grandson of Theodo I. He was of far different calibre from his predecessor; gradually, unable to bear submission to the Frankish yoke, he formed proud schemes. But he was a loyal son of the Church, endowing monasteries and giving generously of his wealth.[125]

Thus matters passed until the year 738 was well upon its way, when the Archbishop decided that for a third time he must visit Rome.[126] The burden was heavy to bear alone; the Holy Father would advise him what to do with these undisciplined Catholics, these Irish schismatics, these hordes of nomad pagans.

Once there, he made good use of his time, eight or nine months, talking all things over in turn. We may suspect that he begged permission to return to his heathen in Frisia.[127] He had passed his sixtieth year; his physical strength was no longer what it had been, especially after all the adventures and hardships, the mental and spiritual problems which had befallen him. After all, the work in Frisia had always been his chief desire; and his dear friend, his one-time colleague, Willibrord, was now no longer active, quietly awaiting in retirement at his beloved cloister of Echternach the death

[124] *Bonif. Epp.* No. 40, dated by Dümmler c. 735–737, by Tangl 737–738.
[125] *Brev. Not.* IX.
[126] Hauck, 497. Cf. *Epp.* 41, dated by Tangl 738.
[127] Hauck, *ibid.*

which was to release him the following year.[128] Or perhaps Boniface craved missionary work in any place, provided it were such, far more than the cold and logical business of administration. He would so far rather preach than arrange things in order.

In any case, the Pope would hear nothing of such purpose. He recognized the care for detail which, united with firmness and with courtesy, made of Boniface an able administrator. Now, when the Arab Muslims were still in Frankland, when Charles Martel was at the height of his power, despoiling abbeys and churches even while he threw back the invading enemies of the Faith, now was the time for a worker of skill and power, who might bring politics and schism and heathendom alike in Frankish dominions under submission to the Holy See.

We can still read in several letters despatched from Rome [129] of the matters discussed by Gregory and Boniface. Boniface himself wrote back to his monks and nuns in Germany that he had been welcomed with joy and honour; that the Pope wished him to carry on in Bavaria; that he was waiting for the convening of a synod of clergy which was to discuss and advise upon his future action. The Pope wrote to the nobles and people of Germany, admonishing them to abstain from all heathen rites, from the casting of lots, the sacrifices to the dead, the drawing of omens from groves or springs, the use of amulets, spells, magic, and sacrilege. In another letter he bade certain bishops of Bavaria and Alamannia [130] "to receive

---

[128] *HE* V, c. 11. He died Nov. 7, 739, at Echternach. For traces of his writing see Wilson, *op. cit.* (p. 349 *supra*, note 19), x, 42f.; Lowe II, xv. Possibly the "Moore Bede," the copy of Bede's *Ecclesiastical History* in the Cambridge University Library, dated c. 737, may have been written at Echternach during Willibrord's time; see Maunde Thompson, 386; *cf.* Lowe II, 7.

[129] *Epp.* Nos. 41 and 43f.

[130] Wiggo (Wicterp), of Augsburg or of Regensburg; Liudo (of Speyer?); Rydolt (of Constance?); Vivilo, of Passau; Adda, of Strassburg; see Hauck, 499, note 2.

Boniface, our brother and fellow-bishop, acting as our representative (*nostram agentem vicem*), with worthy and due honour in the Name of Christ; to refuse, forbid, and repulse the cult and doctrine of pagans, of the British, of all false and heretical priests from wheresoever they come; to be ready to meet with Boniface in synod, whether near the Danube or in the city of Augsburg or wheresover he may decide."

Among the "British," Gregory did not here include at least one of those "shadowy and ubiquitous missionary saints of the eighth century," Pirmin, preacher to the Alamanni who dwelt in the regions known afterward as Alsace and northern Switzerland. Pirmin may have been Anglo-Saxon by birth, or Spanish; he was surely another bishop possessed of no diocese.[131] He, also, was aided by Charles Martel, since the union of the Alamanni with the Franks in the Church was seen by Charles as furthering his own power in their country. He was working among Christians, for the land owed conversion to the Irishman, Saint Gall, and others who followed him. We may also remember that it was to his own conquest of the Alamanni that Clovis, founder of Frankland, owed his turning from paganism to Christianity.[132]

Pirmin is best known as the founder, in 724, of the Benedictine monastery on the island of Reichenau in Lake Constance. After a few years, however, he was forced to leave it through the hostility of the ruler of this region, who was no friend of the Franks and who could not abide the thought of Charles Martel. He then travelled to Alsace, still in Alamannian country, though beyond the reach of his enemy, and founded or reinvigorated a number of religious houses there.

[131] The 9th century *Vita S. Pirminii* (Pertz, *Script.* XV, i, 17ff.) is often misleading; *cf.* Hauck, 346ff. His origin is disputed; see Kenney, 518f., 783f.; Gougaud, 165; H. R. Bittermann, *AHR* XL, 1934, 235, note 11; H. Frank, 117.

[132] Gregory of Tours, *Hist. Franc.* II, 30.

He also laboured in the Black Forest, and his last days were spent in another cloister of his, at Hornbach near the Rhine in the Bavarian Palatinate. He was there in the neighbourhood of Boniface, and we may believe that his presence and his experience encouraged the Archbishop greatly in his work.[133]

In Rome Boniface had yet another matter on his mind. He wanted to find recruits for his mission in Germany, and this third visit brought him eventually two young men who were to be of great value. They belonged to an Anglo-Saxon family living in southern England, apparently noble, wealthy, and akin to Boniface himself.[134] The elder boy, Willibald, was a frail child. At the age of three his life had been saved, his parents declared, when they laid him at the foot of one of those beautifully wrought crosses which then hallowed the estates of noblemen or the public waysides, and vowed that he should be dedicated to the Lord.[135] Two years later they gave him to the keeping of the monks of Waltham Abbey in Essex, where he grew up with an increasing passion for travel abroad "to the ends of the earth and across the wildest seas." [136] When he was about twenty, he persuaded his father and his younger brother, Wynnebald, to go with him as far as Rome.[137] All went well till they reached Lucca in northern Italy, where the father, who had been extremely reluctant to leave his wife and his other children, fell sick and died. His sons buried him with

---

[133] Pirmin wrote a treatise, *Dicta abbatis Priminii de singulis libris canonicis scarapsus*, which contains the *textus receptus* of the Apostles' Creed, probably used by Boniface: A. E. Burn, *Facsimiles of the Creeds*, HBS XXXVI, 1909, 10f. See also PL LXXXIX, coll. 1029ff.; Jecker, 99ff.

[134] *Vitae Willibaldi et Wynnebaldi, auct. sanctimoniali Heidenheimensi*, ed. Holder-Egger: Pertz, *ibid.*, 80ff. They were written in 778 or shortly after; see 81 and note 5. The Willibald described here is not the priest of that name who wrote the *Life* of Boniface.

[135] Rock, *The Church of our Fathers* III, 13f.

[136] T. Wright, *Biog. Brit. liter.* I, 335ff.

[137] An 11th century *Life* of Willibald calls his father Richard; hence the tradition of Saint Richard: Butler-Thurston, *Lives of the Saints* II, 106f.; *cf.* Holder-Egger: Pertz, *Script.* XV, i, 90. A fictitious legend described him as a king of the Anglo-Saxons: *cf.* Hardy, *Cat.* I, 431.

due honour and reached Rome, after sundry perils from both Nature and man, to stay from Martinmas of 721 until Easter of 723, living there a life of strict religion in spite of a terrific attack of malarial fever in the summer heat of Italy.

They recovered from this illness, and in March, 723, Willibald, still keen on travel, decided to strike out for the Holy Land with two companions. The narrative of his *Life* becomes very thrilling as it tells of the marvels he declared he had seen and experienced there.[138] For nearly seven years he wandered —to Sicily, where the relics of Saint Agatha stayed the erupting of Mount Etna; to the Greek islands; to the shrine of Saint John upon Ephesus; on into Syria, where he was captured by Saracens; to Damascus and the spot of Saint Paul's conversion; to Cana, where he drank wine from one of the six vessels blessed by our Lord; to Mount Tabor and the Lake of Tiberias; to the springs of water, Jor and Dan, which, so he tells, unite to form the great river; to the holy places of Jerusalem, which he describes in detail; to Constantinople and to the island off the south coast of Italy where tradition held that the barbarian king, Theodoric the Great, for his wickedness was cast down into hell; [139] and at last to Naples. By this time it was 729, and Willibald felt he had wandered enough. It was time to begin to draw fruit from all that he had lived to see. Accordingly he settled down in Saint Benedict's monastery at Monte Cassino, where for the next ten years he followed its Rule with exemplary diligence.

In November, 739, chance, as it seemed, brought him again to Rome with a Spanish priest, a guest at Monte Cassino, who wanted a guide to the Holy City. In Saint Peter's they met the Pope himself and talked with him. In this Willibald the Pope

---

[138] *Cf.* (pp. 304f. *supra*) Adamnan's narrative of the travels of Arculf, written nearly a hundred years before. This story of Willibald's travels has been translated by T. Wright, *Early Travels in Palestine*, 1848, 13ff.

[139] Gregory the Great, *Dial.* IV, 30; *PL* LXXVII, col. 369.

saw just the right man for Boniface, one who had seen many lands and discussed much with many people, yet who knew well the daily rigour of monastic discipline. Boniface had already left Rome, in the spring of this same year; but the voice of the Holy Father was as persuasive as his own might have been. Indeed, he painted the joys of mission work under Boniface so vividly to this young man, hardly forty years old and still keen for adventure in distant places, that Willibald left Monte Cassino for Germany at Eastertide, 740.

The delighted Archbishop promptly assigned him as mission the district of Eichstätt in the valley of the Altmühl, between Nuremberg and Munich, lately presented to Boniface by the chieftain Suitgar. It was a wild and desert region; only a little church of Saint Mary was still standing to tell of Christianity among a heathen people. That they might receive the ministry of the Church, Boniface ordained Willibald priest on the Feast of Saint Mary Magdalene, July 22, 741, and there the young man worked amid all loneliness and difficulty for several months. However, as Boniface knew, a happy surprise was waiting for his new recruit. In October of the same year Willibald received word from his Archbishop to travel into Thuringia, where he was welcomed, to his joy, at the house of his brother Wynnebald.

Wynnebald had himself stayed on in Rome some years, had returned for a while to his home in England, and was once more in Rome when Boniface himself had captured him, also, for the work. With a few companions he had set out from Rome and had gone to Thuringia, destined as his special scene of action. There he, too, was ordained by the Archbishop and given the strenuous task of serving seven churches.

These ordinations took place, of course, after the return of Boniface to Bavaria in 739. He had been commended by the

Pope to "all bishops, priests, and abbots of every land," [140] his future designs had been approved by a synod of the clergy, and he had broken his journey at Pavia, once again at the court of the Lombard king Liutprand. His biographer describes the Archbishop as resting here, enfeebled by old age.[141] It would seem far more probable, however, that he discussed with tact, yet with his usual vigour, the international problems of the day. Liutprand was determined to extend his power throughout Italy, to be supreme over the great Italian dukes, and to end the domination of Constantinople over Rome. This was to be accomplished with all outward respect to the Papal See; but it was to be accomplished, even if it meant seizing Rome itself. Doubtless Gregory had instructed his Archbishop to stop over at Pavia and there to probe into Liutprand's mind.

But soon this rising ambition of Liutprand became too strong for the Pope. The Holy Father had in vain made common cause with Constantinople; and he had in vain supported dukes of Italy against Liutprand. The Papal land was harried in revenge by Lombard armies, and in this urgent crisis Gregory sent a call for help to Charles Martel. Charles was now triumphant. In recent years he had gone from glory to glory through his conquests of the Arabs and his despoiling of cities of southern France, Nîmes, Agde, Béziers;[142] he had been ruling without a king even as figure head of royalty, since the death in 737 of Theodoric IV. No wonder that the Pope wrote—twice, about 740—to "the Lord Charles, under-king" over the Franks.

They were very sad letters.[143] In the midst of all the tribulation that has come upon the Holy See, Gregory laments, no

[140] *Bonif. Epp.* No. 42.   [141] Willibald, c. 7.
[142] *Fredegar. Cont.* c. 20: *MGH Script. rer. Merov.* II, 177f.
[143] *Codex Carolinus: MGH Epp.* III, i, 476 f. (dates them 739 and 740); Bouquet IV, 92f. (dates them both 741).

help has arrived from Charles against the robbing and ravaging Lombards who are set upon Rome's destruction. Let this "most Christian son," for the sake of God and the salvation of his own soul, speed to the rescue of the Church of Saint Peter. The Pope sent also some filings from the chains of Saint Peter, enshrined in golden keys, and other "great and countless gifts," promising, too, that if Charles would free Rome from the Lombard menace, he should be given certain power there with the title of "Roman Consul" and that Rome would turn from Constantinople to alliance with him.

But Charles, although he received the Papal envoys with marked respect, would not hear of breaking with Liutprand, who had sent him aid against the Arabs in Provence and who had adopted as "son in arms" his own son Pepin. He would not, of course, be outdone in courtesy. He, too, sent magnificent presents to the Pope by the hands of Grimo, abbot of Corbie, and of Sigebert, monk of St. Denis. Promises, however, were not forthcoming, and the Pope's anxiety was only ended by death toward the close of 741.

And yet through this same Charles, robber of ecclesiastical properties, as indignant abbots and priests of his and of later generations held him, deaf to the Pope's appeal, and consigned to eternal damnation by the Church, the efforts of Boniface for Germany brought forth their first permanent fruits. Even as the menace in Italy was nearing the Papal estate, the Pope was writing to Bavaria to rejoice with Boniface over the great things that had come to pass "through your endeavour and that of Charles, prince of the Franks." [144] Boniface had been back only a few months—the Pope's letter was dated October, 739—but already he had followed the instructions received at Rome: he had divided Bavaria into four dioceses, had consecrated new bishops for three of them, and had pleased the

[144] *Epp.* No. 45.

Bavarians by confirming Vivilo, consecrated by Gregory himself, in his see of Passau. The other three bishops were carefully chosen to content the hearts of Bavarian Church people.
Two of them combined rule over monasteries in the cities
where they were to reside, Gaibald, chosen for a diocese of
Regensburg, and John, to direct another from Salzburg. The
third, Erembert, a brother of the beloved Corbinian, was
appointed to Freising.[145]

In all this fresh start Boniface had also the indispensable
support of Odilo, that duke of Bavaria whom we have seen
chafing under the Frankish overlordship but freely serving the
Church in his land. His cooperation was none the less useful
because there were motives less than ideal behind it, in that
he, like Charles Martel, saw the benefit to his power of an
alliance with the Catholic Church and its representative. If
there were to be bishops and sees and synods, he reasoned, he
had better be prominent in their midst, as had always been the
way of the Frankish kings.[146]

The Pope, in his letter of congratulation to the Archbishop,
touched upon other matters of which Boniface had written
him after his return. Had the bishop of his own election,
Vivilo of Passau, gone further than canonical rule allowed?
Well, Boniface must administer correction according to the
Pope's instructions given at Rome. Priests had baptized converts in all sorts and varieties of heathen dialect words? In
this case he must make sure that, whatever the language, they
really were baptized in the Name of the Trinity, and it would
be well to confirm them without delay with holy chrism and
laying on of hands. Boniface was going to hold a synod—
nostra vice, "as our representative"—near the Danube? That
was good; but the Archbishop must be there in all the power
of Apostolic authority. Finally, he must not think of staying

[145] Willibald, c. 7; *Epp. ibid.*   [146] Hauck, 504f.

on and enjoying the fruits of labour well done in any one place. He must travel on, here and there, converting souls, consecrating other bishops when needed, sharing thus in the world-wide office of the Holy See. 'For a man nearing his threescore years and ten, this vigorous counsel of the Pope must have drawn at times a sigh of resolution, difficult, even if entirely determined. So determined was it, in fact, that we find him about this time calling, as Archbishop and German legate of the Universal Church, upon all priests, deacons, canons, clerks, abbots, abbesses, monks, nuns and God-fearing layfolk, all Catholics of the English race, to pray God for the converting of the Saxons, those savage raiders from the north upon Hesse and Thuringia.[147]

The first synod of the Bavarian Church must have been held before long in one of the cities on the Danube. We know neither the place nor the date nor the matter discussed. Doubtless the Archbishop reported what he had done, with Papal consent, and announced his plans for the future under the same authority. There is, indeed, a copy of fifteen *Acts of a Synod of Ratisbon* (Regensburg) still extant, which, although the date of their making is energetically disputed, have been suggested as fruit of this first council of Boniface. In them priests warn their flocks that they "blush not to confess their sins in holy church in the presence of the priests who stand as witnesses between them and God . . . it is better to blush here and now in the presence of one man than before all nations in the judgment to come." [148] No one is to start upon the long road to eternity without confession and *viaticum*. All are to come often to church, and, when they get there, they are not to chatter idle tales but look to their prayer and work hard

---

[147] *Epp.* No. 46; *cf.* No. 47.
[148] Pertz, *Leges* III, ed. Merkel, 236ff., 455f.; Hefele-Leclercq III, ii, 811, 1109ff.; Watkins, *History of Penance* II, 640, 661f.; Riezler I, 108; Hauck, 507.

for the saving of their souls. They shall make accustomed
offerings for themselves and their kin, both alive and departed,
for herein lies occasion for forgiveness of sins. Careful preparation must be made for receiving the Holy Sacrifice; by keeping
of chastity in permanence, and of continence by the married
for several days before. Many people allow a whole year to go
by without making their communions, which they should do
at least every third or fourth Sunday. Fasting is the rule for
every Wednesday and Friday, and, accompanied by alms-
giving, for Ember Days four times in the year. Marriages must
be preceded by due notice to the priest, to relatives and to
friends. As for sins, drunkenness and dishonesty in business
transactions are especially to be banned.

The Christian life in Bavaria, however, was in need not
only of general admonition but of centres of prayer and practice where its priests should be trained. Accordingly, much of
the energy of Boniface was turned in these years, with the help
of Odilo, to the creation of new monasteries. Among many
others there rose now the cloister of Altaich, dedicated to
Saint Maurice during 741 in the diocese of Passau as a
daughter-house of Reichenau, and the still more famous Bene-
diktbeuern, founded about the same time on the spurs of the
Bavarian Alps near the Walchensee.[149]

While he thus spent his energy in Bavaria in fellowship
with its duke, Boniface did not forget the other regions under
his vast control. If a Christian Bavaria needed bishops, so did
the people of Thuringia and Hesse whom he had laboured so
hard to convert. Here Charles Martel gave support, the more
ready to show himself loyal to the Church in Frankland in that
he had refused succour to its Pope.[150] Three sees were founded
in 741, one, for Hesse, at Buraburg near the monastery of

[149] Annales Altah. maiores: Pertz, Script. XX, 782; Chronicon Bene-
dictoburanum: ibid., IX, 212f.; Hauck, 508; Riezler, 111f.
[150] Cf. Hauck, 512.

Fritzlar; two, for Thuringia, at Würzburg on the Main for the southern part and at Erfurt for the part stretching north of the Thuringian Forest. At Buraburg Boniface placed Witta, an Anglo-Saxon who had come from England to share his work; at Würzburg he installed Burchard, another Englishman, to labour where the Irish Kilian had witnessed to the Faith.[151] The name of the newly appointed bishop of Erfurt is unknown.[152]

One more consecration was added to those in Bavaria; for, probably in October, 741, Eichstätt became the headquarters of Willibald as "regionary" bishop. There is reason to think that the town and the district surrounding were not at first made an official diocese, as in other cases. Willibald's business was still rather to convert the heathen peoples of his outlying post than to organize Christian congregations. Certainly a bishop was badly needed there, and Willibald must have been consecrated directly his experience allowed it.[153]

On October 22, 741—tradition tells that it was the very day of Willibald's consecration—Charles Martel departed from this world to his destiny in the hereafter. Before he died, he decided the future of Frankland, with no thought of its royal Merovingian family. His elder son, Carloman, was to rule Austrasia, Thuringia, and Alamannia, with the supremacy over the Bavarians which Charles had held; the younger, Pepin, received Neustria, Burgundy, and Provence, with the overlordship of Aquitaine. There was also another son, Grifo, born to Charles by an irregular union with Swanhild, niece of Odilo of Bavaria. He received a small inheritance, carved out of his brothers' portions and to be ruled under their power.[154]

---

[151] The *Vita Burchardi*, ed. Holder-Egger (Pertz, *Script.* XV, i, 44ff.) is not reliable. See Hauck, 489, notes 2f.

[152] Hauck, 521, note 1, suggests the Dadanus who was present at the council of 742: *MGH Cap. Reg. Franc.* I, 24.

[153] Hauck, 536, note 1.

[154] *Einhardi Annales, ann.* 741: Pertz, *Script.* I, 135.

The characters of the two sons who succeeded Charles are pictured differently. Both Carloman and Pepin were ambitious, eager to uphold their father's achievement, like him to rule well and wisely. It was Pepin, however, who had inherited from Charles his deliberate and far-seeing patience and purpose for the desired end of dominion. Carloman was less determined, less calculating. To him, moreover, nothing mattered in the long run so much as his religion. He had been educated by the monks of St. Denis. So, too, had Pepin, who was deeply impressed by their judgment passed upon his father, and by the suffering which, inflicted by his father, had brought about that judgment. Both brothers were therefore ready to aid the Church, Pepin partly for the sake of politics, Carloman through a more devout allegiance.[155]

Boniface wrote to each of the three official acknowledgment of his accession. We have a copy of a letter addressed to Grifo as "son of Charles"; and the same document, perhaps with more elaborate salutation, appears to have been sent to his two half-brothers. It contains a plea for protection of the mission in Thuringia.[156]

Divided rule, however, soon bore evil consequence. Duke Odilo, so long the promoter of rebellion against the Franks, now instigated malcontents in Bavaria and Alamannia to rise in arms. Hunold, who had succeeded his father Eudes as duke of Aquitania, thought the time fit for trying to win independence. The Arabs on the borders of Spain and Gaul renewed their raids. Jealous nobles among the Franks asked why the sons of Charles Martel should usurp the Merovingian throne. Most jealous of all was Grifo, who probably made a convenient tool for Odilo's ambition. He raised open revolt, but was captured by his brothers and kept imprisoned for six years at Neufchâteau in the Ardennes.[157]

[155] T. Hodgkin VII, 95f.   [156] *Epp.* No. 48; Tangl, ed. 76, note 1.
[157] *Einhardi Ann.*: Pertz, *ibid.*, 135, 137; *Ann. Mettenses, ibid.,* 139, 327, 330f.

Swift uprising was as quickly suppressed. Duke Odilo was brought to submission and deprived of the Nordgau, the northern district of his Bavaria; his ally in arms, Hunold of Aquitaine, was driven to refuge in a cloister; the Alamanni were cowed; the Arabs, by feuds among themselves and by the growing power of the Berbers, were hindered from further worrying. Finally, the murmurs of the Frankish nobles were silenced by the nominal crowning in 743 of one of their royal line—we do not even know of what descent. He stands in the records as Childeric III. But he took no part in public affairs, and seven years later, in 750, was stripped of his decorations and sent to the monastery of Saint Bertin, near St. Omer, Pas de Calais.[158]

Such political confusion had its effect upon the work of Archbishop Boniface. Of even greater concern to him was the death of Pope Gregory in 741. He was succeeded at once by Zacharias, of Greek origin but Italian birth, a man of tact and diplomacy, notable for his rescue of the Papal estate around Rome and of the city of Ravenna, with its adjoining territory, from the hands of the Lombard Liutprand. He was as eager as his predecessors for the Church in Germany, where he seems to have tried to defend Odilo against the Franks, probably remembering the conduct of Charles Martel.[159] And yet between him and Boniface there was not the same warmth of personal friendship which had hitherto inspired and encouraged the missionaries. The Pope was zealous and the Archbishop was devoted; but on either side there appears a note of criticism.

Boniface wrote early in 742 to acknowledge with all reverence and loyalty this new Head; to ask confirmation of the three bishoprics in Hesse and Thuringia and advice on several pressing matters.[160] The usual gifts accompanied the letter.

---

[158] *Annales regni Franc. (Script. rer. German.)* 10.
[159] *Ann. Mett.* 328; Hauck, 533.　　　　[160] *Epp.* No. 50.

On this occasion they included a stout shaggy cloak and some gold and silver, with six hexameter verses composed by the scholarly Archbishop in a moment of spare time. But it is the troubled tone of the letter itself which is of most interest.

Boniface wrote: First, Carloman wants a synod for Austrasia, now under his government. He has promised to aid in reforming the state of affairs in the Church, in disorder these sixty or seventy years through lack of a controlling hand. Bishoprics in the cities are held by greedy laymen or by evil clerics, men of foul and avaricious character, all eager to enjoy their ill-gotten revenues. Will the Pope authorize this assembly?

And next—what is Boniface to do when he hears of deacons in the Church stained with every vice from boyhood onward, actually known to be evil when they were ordained, who stand up to read the Gospel in church as God's ministers when they have four or five mistresses to sleep with at night, who are advanced to the priesthood while yet in mortal sin, and in this state declare their right to intercede and offer Holy Mass for the people? Still worse, they are even consecrated as bishops although they drink and hunt and do no work, although they fight with sword and dagger in the army and shed the blood of men, heathen and Christian alike?

Again, a terrible thing has happened, concerning which the priests of the Frankish Church are scandalized and greatly perturbed. A layman of high rank wants to marry a woman who is not only his own uncle's widow, not only his own second cousin, but one who once took the veil and vow of chastity before God, broke her bond, was married to her own cousin, and deserted him. And he actually declares that Gregory of sainted memory, Pontiff of the Apostolic See, granted him permission for such a marriage! Of course, he is lying. Did not the Church of the Saxons beyond the sea, in which Boniface himself was born and reared, affirm such a marriage to be an incestuous, horrible, and damnable crime, on the authority of Scripture itself? [161]

Lastly, both the ignorant folk—Alamannians, Bavarians, Franks—and the very worst of the Frankish bishops and priests, whose children, born since they entered upon their holy ordering, declare their evil life, maintain that Rome, Rome herself, affords them example and encouragement! They say that at New Year's time near Saint Peter's, day and night, they have seen processions like those of pagans, people yelling unholy songs, tables weighed down with feasts, women offering for sale heathen amulets and bracelets. What *would* Saint Augustine think of this? And those evil Frankish priests and bishops come back from Rome saying that the Pope blesses their ministry in the Church. Such a thing has never been heard, that the Holy See should give judgment contrary to the canons! Will not the holy and beloved Father himself forbid such heathen doings at Rome for the sake of the Church universal? Will he not allow Boniface to condemn these wolves within the fold?

On April 21, 742, Carloman assembled a synod of clergy for the regulating of Church affairs and discipline in his land of Austrasia.[162] We do not know where it was held; but it was attended by Boniface and the chief bishops of the realm with their priests. The ruler issued afterward an official list of the decisions made in it under his presidency.[163] In substance, these declared that Boniface was Archbishop over Austrasia

[161] See, however, *HE* I, c. 27, *Resp.* V, in which Gregory the Great allows the marriage of the *tertia generatio,* i.e., of second cousins; *cf.* Plummer II, 47f.; H. S. III, 32f.; and the letters of Boniface to Pecthelm, Nothelm, and Duddo: pp. 400f. *supra.*

[162] The evidence for 742 (see for bibliography Hauck, 520, note 3) seems preferable to that for 743 (Loofs, *Zur Chron.* 9ff.). See also Hefele-Leclercq III, ii, 815, note 1; 818, note 3; Dümmler, ed. *Epp.* 50, 51, 56. The question turns on MS. witness and the position of Boniface as bishop in the realm of the Frankish king Carloman and as legate of the Papal See.

[163] *Cap. Reg. Franc.* I, 24ff.; Böhmer-Mühlbacher, *Regesta imperii* I, pp. 21f.; *Bonif. Epp.* No. 56.

and that the bishops consecrated by him were approved by royal acknowledgment. They decreed that a synod be held every year in the presence of the secular head; that revenues stolen from churches must be restored and false and evil clergy deprived of their holdings; that in Lent of every year each priest render account to his bishop concerning his ministry, his doctrine, and his personal life; that he receive his Father in God with due respect, with candidates all waiting, marshalled in order, when the bishop comes to administer confirmation, and ask from him year by year the new supply of oil for anointing, blessed on Holy Thursday; that strange and wandering bishops and priests shall not minister in Austrasia until they have been examined before the annual synod; that none in holy or monastic ordering be allowed to serve in the army or accompany it in the field, save only such as shall be appointed for saying Mass, hearing confessions, and carrying sacred relics; that none indulge in hunting or even in wandering through forests with dogs, or in keeping of hawks and falcons; that the clergy wear cassocks like monks, not cloaks like laymen; that monks and nuns live according to the Rule of Saint Benedict, that those who break their vow of chastity be imprisoned for at least a year on bread and water, and that the monks, further, be flogged and the nuns have their heads shaved bald; that all pagan rites be abolished, especially those which are celebrated by foolish folk in the churches as supposed honour to holy martyrs and confessors and which provoke God and His saints to wrath.

According to the ruling here enjoined, a second council of bishops, with secular nobles and magistrates, met the next year, 743, on March 1 at Estinnes in Hainaut, Belgium, again under the presidency of Carloman and at his will.[164] Here

---

[164] The year is again disputed. See Hauck, 530, note 1; Hefele-Leclercq, *ibid.*, 825, note 2.

the resolutions of 742 were re-read and confirmed, with one significant exception.[165] It had not proved possible for Carloman and his advisers to hand back all the properties taken from innumerable abbeys and churches as reward for those who had served Charles Martel faithfully in critical times. Wars, moreover, still remained, and Carloman, too, had need of soldiers. It simply would not do to deprive them all at one stroke of their ill-gotten gains. Therefore, doubtless prompted in conscience by Boniface, now formally acknowledged as his Archbishop, he decided upon a compromise. The churches and abbeys were declared as rightful owners of their lost properties; to those whose estates were still to be retained by their present holders, a sum of money, duly stipulated, was to be paid yearly by these holders;[166] on the death of each holder the property held by him might either return to the church or abbey to which it belonged or a similar arrangement might be made with his heir. Churches and abbeys, however, must not suffer want by this loss of the use of their land and possessions *in precario;* and if such want should be proved, the property must be restored entire to its rightful owner.

(We may remind ourselves here that the possessions of the Church were vast; that in countless cases abbeys and churches were well able to receive even a small sum in return for the occupancy of their wide lands, especially if the occupant for his own benefit kept them in good cultivation and repair.)

Boniface, we may imagine, felt that the resolutions were all to the good, so far as they went. Apparently, however, he did not think that a council called by Carloman was worth too much of the Pope's well-occupied time. We may be quite certain that his one aim was that all should be carried out, so

[165] Hauck, 532f.; A. Bondroit, *Revue d'histoire ecclés.* I, 1900, 41ff., 249ff.; Hefele-Leclercq, 827ff.
[166] Tangl, ed. *Epp.* No. 60, p. 123; No. 87, p. 199.

far as was possible, according to the Pope's wish; for never was any bishop more eager for the honouring of the Holy See. The very complaints which he had addressed to Zacharias on disorders reported from Rome were due to this anxiety that nothing be amiss, or be told amiss, concerning the mother Church of Christendom. When, therefore, the Pope wrote to him on April 1, 743, with no knowledge that the two synods had met and had decided upon their action, this ignorance on the part of Zacharias may be imputed to anything rather than his delegate's lack of responsibility or thought. That Carloman did not recognize the need of Papal authorization of a synod, that he, like the Frankish monarchy of old, held it rather to be his own prerogative to' call and to preside over Frankish Church councils, was no fault of the Papal delegate. Boniface did his best. Moreover, the Pope himself seems to have delayed till this moment, of April 1, 743, to answer the request for approval of a synod written to him by the Archbishop early in 742.[167]

Zacharias was of critical mind in his letter.[168] Boniface must be careful, he warns, not to appoint too many bishops; the canons forbid the name of bishop to be held lightly in that it is too often heard. However, the acts of Boniface in this matter are approved. A synod should certainly be held for the disciplining of sinful and disobedient clergy. What terrible crimes Boniface has reported! After much righteous wrath at this conduct, horror at the lying tale that the Holy See could permit incestuous marriages such as the one described, and stern denunciation of New Year's heathen practices at Rome or elsewhere—Zacharias with characteristic generosity shows no offence at the frank words of his delegate. He continues: "You say that the Pope, my predecessor, gave

[167] On this vexed question see Loofs, *Zur Chron.* 11f.; Hauck, 520, note 1; Tangl, *Neues Archiv* XL, 1916, 772ff.
[168] *Epp.* No. 51.

you permission to name your successor as bishop during your own lifetime. But no! We cannot possibly allow this; it is contrary to all the rules of the Church and the teachings of the Fathers. Certainly you may have an assistant, and if you should die before him and you really wish him to succeed you, then declare this at your last moment and let him come to Rome for consecration. Only please remember, this is a special privilege granted to you alone, because of our friendship for you; it is for no one else."

Austrasia was not the only land in need of reform. It was the turn next of Neustria and its lord, Pepin. On June 22, 744, Pope Zacharias wrote again to Boniface.[169] He rejoices that his most excellent sons Pepin and Carloman are aiding the work of the mission. He notes that Boniface has appointed three Archbishops, Grimo of Rouen, Abel of Reims, and Hartbert of Sens. He confirms these appointments and is sending each the pallium.[170] On November 5 of the same year the Pope sent off another letter. Since approving these symbols of office for the three Archbishops, he has been amazed to hear again from Boniface that only one is required, and for Grimo alone! Will he please explain this very confusing change of plan?[171]

The fault, it would seem, lay in the vacillating policy of Pepin and Carloman. Some years later Boniface wrote to Zacharias: "I know that much time has passed since I in-

[169] *Ibid.*, No. 57.

[170] The appointments of Abel and of Hartbert had been approved at the council of Soissons, held March 2, 744, under the presidency of Pepin, *dux et princeps Francorum* (*Cap. Reg. Franc.* I, 28ff.). The name of Grimo is not found in its minutes; for differing opinions on this matter see Hauck, 545, note 3; Hefele-Leclercq III, ii, 857, note 1. The presence of Boniface at the council is not proved, as his name is also absent; on this see also the conflicting theories of Hauck, 545, and H.-L. *ibid.*, 859f.

[171] *Epp.* No. 58. The dating of *Epp.* Nos. 57 and 58 is given here according to Dümmler and Tangl; *cf.* Whitney, *CMH* II, 540. For the dates June 22 and November 5, 743, see Hauck, 542, note 2; for September 22 and November 5, 743, see Loofs, 21ff.

formed your Holiness about the Archbishops and the request
of palliums for them in accordance with the promises of the
Frankish rulers, and I do beg the pardon of the Apostolic See
for this delay. The fact is that they have procrastinated and
have not kept their promises; discussion of the matter is still
dragging on, and we do not know what they may decide. If I
could have willed it, the promise would have been kept." [172]

The broken promise proved unfortunate. Nor was Zacharias comforted when Boniface went on practically to accuse
the Pope himself of simony in receiving reward for the
bestowal of these palliums. This charge, however delicately
hinted, Zacharias earnestly denied, imploring "his dearest
brother" never to write such insulting and unthinkable words
again. Nonetheless at the end of the letter, courteous as always,
he not only granted the request of Boniface for license to
preach in Bavaria but extended it to include the whole of Gaul.

For Boniface many troubles threatened and struck from
different quarters in these years: the determined hold of power
over Church matters by the Frankish rulers, the desire not
to offend them unnecessarily while maintaining on his own
part entire obedience to Rome, the jealousy of Frankish
bishops, the sins and errors of the clergy, the ignorance of
supposedly Christian laymen, the multitudes yet unbaptized.
He took his pen and sought comfort in writing home to England, once more to Daniel of Winchester.[173] Some of the
clergy preach abstinence from rightful food, he laments; others
live only on milk and honey; others tell their people that
morals have nothing to do with holy ordering. It is impossible
for him to keep aloof from these priests and bishops without
offending their Frankish rulers; and the aid and protection of
Carloman and Pepin are really necessary to his mission.

[172] *Epp.* No. 86 (dated 751 by Dümmler and Tangl).
[173] *Ibid.,* No. 63 (dated 742–746).

"Without them I can neither rule the layfolk nor the priests
and clerks, nor the monks and nuns of God; nor without their
command and the fear inspired by them am I strong enough
to stop the pagan rites and worship of idols prevalent in Germany." And yet, whenever he goes to court to obtain this
help, he is forced to associate with these men whom his
conscience so deeply condemns.

He is doing all he can, he assures Daniel. He will not give
consent to their ways and acts; he will not worship with them,
nor share with them communion of the Holy Mysteries. But
what about that oath he swore in Rome when Pope Gregory
consecrated him bishop, when he declared on the body of Saint
Peter that he would have no fellowship with wicked men,
save for their converting? Would Daniel, his Father in God,
tell him what he judges right and meet for his "sad and
worried son"?

There is one more favour he would ask. He is now growing
old and his eyes are troubling him; he cannot read books of
tiny and difficult script. He needs very badly a copy of the
Prophets. Would Daniel send him the one written out by
Abbot Winbert of Nursling in clear characters, with all the
words in full?

The answer of Daniel teems with long and pompous sentences, with references to authority both Scriptural and
patristic, in sharp contrast to the simplicity of his petitioner.[174]
He exhorts Boniface in counsel drawn from Jerome on doing
one's best in hard circumstances, and from Augustine in regard to the clean and the unclean that walked by one and
the same door into the ark. Moreover, does not Holy Scripture
tell of the wheat and the tares growing together? Does it not
bid men be subject to higher powers?

Worse, however, was in store for this harassed mission to

[174] No. 64.

Germany. A very real and pressing problem now reared its head, embodied in two of the most notorious of the "false priests," who especially were spreading poison far and wide through the land in their blasphemous words.

One was called Aldebert, a Frank by birth. He had won the hearts of the people by declaring that he was an intermediary between God and man for their comfort and salvation. An angel, he solemnly told, had given him sacred relics through which he could gain from God whatsoever he asked. Gradually his fame had spread among the ignorant and simple-minded, not only layfolk but priests and even bishops, till at last certain of these were induced to consecrate him to the episcopate. His own belief in his divine mission and mystic calling so increased that he counted himself one of the apostles of Christ; he dedicated crosses and chapels in the fields and beside springs of water, where unnumbered crowds flocked to pray in the name of "Saint Aldebert." He gave to his followers filings from his nails and hairs from his head which should protect them on their way; and when peasants, thrilled by his fanatic power, threw themselves at his feet to confess their sins, he said: "I know it all, your secret doings are open to me. There is no need to confess; the evil past is put away. Go home, absolved and in peace." [175]

The other offender, Clement by name, was one of those Celtic bishops who wandered on missionary work in Germany without any diocese.[176] He was distinguished by intellectual and moral heresy, claiming that he was entitled, although a bishop, to be father of ill-begotten children, and, Christian though he was, to marry his brother's widow. He rejected not only the canons of the Church, but also her doctrines and precepts as set forth by the Fathers, Jerome, Augustine, Greg-

[175] No. 59.
[176] *Scottus*: i.e., either Irish, from Ireland, or of Irish descent but Scottish in birth or residence.

ory. He declared that Christ, when He descended to the world of imprisoned spirits, set free all who were there, the believing and the unbelieving, the worshippers of God and of idols alike. His teaching on predestination was horrible and utterly opposed to the Catholic faith. Much of his doctrine he claimed to derive from Jewish law as put forward in the Old Testament.[177]

Before June, 744, Boniface had condemned these sinners and had consigned them, with the cooperation of Carloman and Pepin, to monastic prison and penance. At the council of Soissons, held in March, 744, Pepin had also approved the judgment of twenty-three bishops against Aldebert, who was working in Neustria. A General Synod of representatives from both Austrasia and Neustria, meeting under both rulers in 745, confirmed the sentence in each case.[178] It is, then, of great significance that the Frankish Church, with all the energy of Boniface, was not able to restrain these two men, who escaped from their cells and renewed their former teaching. Carloman and Pepin either could not, or would not, compel them by force; and Boniface had to refer the matter to Rome.

A council met in the Lateran on October 25, 745, to hear the accusations, forwarded in writing by this Archbishop and Papal Legate in Germany, and brought by the hand of Denehard, that trusted messenger. In the ears of the assembled prelates and priests all the grevious details were declared. At the end of the evidence the Pope, who was presiding, asked whether Denehard had any further documents? The clerk and keeper of records then read aloud a letter, which Aldebert affirmed had been written by the Lord Christ and had fallen from Heaven, together with a prayer addressed by him (Alde-

[177] *Epp. ibid.*
[178] Levison, ed. *Vitae (auct. Otloho)* 154; Hauck, 560; Hefele-Leclercq, 862.

bert) by name to eight angels of God. It was enough. Re-
marking that doubtless Aldebert was mad and that those
who listened to him were as brainless as infants and silly
women, Zacharias called for judgment. All present declared
that they knew by name no angels save three, Michael, Gabriel, and Raphael, and that surely Aldebert must hold con-
verse with demons. They then voted unanimously to prohibit
both him and Clement from all priestly office and communion
with the Church, together with any who should follow their
counsel and doctrine.[179] It is to be noted that we hear nothing
of the appearance of either criminal in Rome for his defence.

Boniface might appeal to Rome for condemnation of men
already condemned by Frankish rulers. Yet these rulers retained independence; and the sentence of the Papal Council
does not seem to have been carried out with any force under
them.[180] Sixteen months later, in January, 747, we find
Zacharias advising that Aldebert and Clement be once more
brought before a Frankish synod.[181] There the Archbishop is
to deal with them in union with the secular power; if they
still prove obdurate, he must send them under escort to Rome
for final judgment.

The Frankish General Council of 745 had yet further
offence to examine. The accused in this case was an important
personage, Gewilip, bishop of Mainz. His father, Gerold, one
of the less estimable prelates of that time, but a great friend
of Carloman, had ruled the same diocese. When Carloman
had marched out against the Saxons in 743, Gerold had gone
with him and had been killed in the thick of the fight. The
son, Gewilip, comforted in his grief by the bestowal of his
father's see, was also dear to Carloman. He was, it was said,
a very honourable gentleman, but he loved to sport with

[179] *Epp.* Nos. 57, 59, 60, 62; Hauck, 553ff.; J. Laux, *CHR* XXI, 1935,
190ff.
[180] Hauck, 564.   [181] No. 77.

falcons and dogs. Once again, in 744, Carloman took the field against the Saxons, and this time Gewilip accompanied him. When the two armies pitched camp on opposite banks of the river Weser, Gewilip opportunely thought of that Saxon who had slain his father Gerold. "He is here again, in the enemy's ranks," he was told. "Ask him," replied the bishop, "to come and have a talk with me in the middle of the river." The Saxon hurried to the meeting. "Ho!" said Gewilip. "Take the sword of vengeance!" and drove it through his heart. Neither the bishop himself nor his ruler Carloman had any thought but that a chivalrous deed had been done, especially as they returned triumphant in victory.[182]

But Boniface knew otherwise. Had he not accused bishops of this sort to Pope Zacharias? He chanced about this time, guided by the Lord, as the chronicler has it, to visit Mainz in his round of inspection, where he at once heard the story. His horror could find no rest until Gewilip had been deposed from the see of Mainz by his authority, confirmed by that of the powers spiritual and secular in this assembly of 745. Unfortunately we know neither the place of meeting nor the day, although some other details reach us from the Pope's letters. In one, dated 745, shortly after the synod, he writes: "You told me in your letter about one called Gewilip, who leads men astray and misuses the office of bishop—that he is hastening to Rome entirely on his own impulse. When he comes, God's will be done with him!" [183]

That Gewilip appealed to Rome is significant for Rome's growing power in Germany.

Another matter weighing upon the mind of Boniface was the question of a see for himself. He had been Archbishop in Germany by approval of its rulers since 742; by decision

---

[182] Levison, ed. *Vitae,* 90ff., 154f.
[183] *Epp.* Nos. 6of.

of the Pope, some ten years earlier. And yet there was nothing permanent about this office unless it were embodied in a see which could be handed on to a successor. To Boniface himself the city of Cologne seemed far the best location; it was in the north of Austrasia, near Hesse and Thuringia, and provided an excellent base for future mission work among the still heathen Saxons. Pepin and Carloman gave their approval, and the Pope his glad blessing. All seemed well.[184]

Then the Frankish chiefs changed their minds, for reasons now obscure. Probably they were keen on their own power; they may have been influenced also by the many clergy of whom Boniface disapproved, who could not have borne to see him in this important centre.[185] Whatever the direct cause, the fact remains that the bishopric of Mainz was vacant and that, after some time had passed, Boniface was appointed its bishop. The see of Cologne was given to one named Agilulf.[186]

The position of Boniface in 748, when he was well past his seventieth year, presented therefore grievous difficulty. He was still Archbishop, still Papal Legate in Germany. But he was not Archbishop of Mainz, only its bishop; nor was Mainz to be raised to the dignity of a metropolitan see until 780. The Pope apparently felt obliged to comply with necessity. "Your letter, my brother," he wrote Boniface, "tells me again that the Franks have not kept their promise about Cologne and that you are still at Mainz." [187]

This same letter tells us of another man accused of heresy. Two years before, he had come into notice by appealing, like Gewilip, to Rome from the judgment of Boniface.[188] "Virgil

---

[184] No. 60. No. 88 (spurious) may be reminiscent of a bull destined for Cologne: Hauck, 562, note 2.

[185] *Cf.* Hauck, 567f.; Fischer, 189.

[186] *Annales Lauriss. min.*: Pertz, *Script.* I, 115; *Epp.* No. 82 (in the superscription). Oelsner, 31 (*cf.* H. Böhmer, 215) gives 748; Dünzelmann, *Forschungen* XIII, 32, gives 747.

[187] Tangl, ed. *Epp.* 179f.   [188] *Epp.* No. 68.

and Sidonius have written, reverend brother, to inform us that you have ordered them to re-baptize persons already Christian. We are much worried and surprised by this report, if it really is true. They said that there was a priest in Bavaria who, because he knew no Latin, made a mistake in the service, saying, *Baptizo te in Nomine Patria et Filia et Spiritus Sancti;* and that because of this bad Latin, you decided that baptism must be administered a second time.

"But, most holy brother, if the officiating priest introduced into the rite no error of heresy and carried out the correct procedure, with only some mistakes in his Latin, we cannot allow re-baptism. You know very well that even persons receiving the rite from heretics in the Name of the Father and of the Son and of the Holy Spirit are truly baptized and need nothing more, save cleansing through the laying on of hands. Please, if I hear aright, do not issue any more such instruction, but keep to the words and doctrine of the Fathers of the Church."

This Virgil was an interesting character. He was an Irishman, once abbot of a monastery at the modern Aghaboe, in county Leix, Irish Free State; his native name was Ferghil. He had crossed to Frankland and had been for more than a year a welcome guest of Pepin himself, at Quierzy-sur-Oise, near Noyon. He was learned, witty, and very entertaining. At last Pepin, in what was probably a gesture of reconciliation, had sent him on to that Duke of Bavaria, Odilo, whom the Franks had lately defeated. Odilo, in any case, had also felt the charm of his Irish originality and had made him abbot of St. Peter's, built by Rupert in Salzburg. He had done more, for after the death of John, whom Boniface had placed as bishop of Salzburg, he had appointed Virgil, who was no bishop, ruler of its diocese.

Here, then, is an instance of the Irish custom of rule of

abbots over the "dioceses" surrounding their monasteries. Such abbots, if they were not themselves of episcopal ordering, regularly held within their community a bishop who would function when his office was needed. The name of Virgil's bishop has come down to us as Dobdagrec.[189]

Naturally such an arrangement did not suit the ideas of Boniface on organization of dioceses, and here, once more, we have the Irish conflicting with the Anglo-Saxon. That admonition of the Pope on baptism must have been hard for him to digest. However, he kept hard upon the trail, and was finally rewarded. The letter of Zacharias in 748 contained a different note.[190] "You have also told us, holy brother, that that man Virgil—we do not know whether he should be called priest—is showing spite against you because you proved him wrong in regard to Catholic doctrine; that he is telling stories to Duke Odilo in order to sow enmity between the Duke and you; that he is saying also that he was appointed by us to enter upon one of those four dioceses established by you in Bavaria, as soon as it falls vacant. That is a wicked lie. . . . I note, moreover, that he is charged with perverse and wicked teaching. If it really shall be proved that he believes in an- other world, and in other men, below this earth, as well as in another sun and moon, then do you assemble a council, inhibit him from his priestly office, cast him from the Church. We, too, have written to the Duke, and we are writing to this Virgil to summon him before us for strict inquiry."

The theory of Virgil was not new; it had been put forward in the fifth century by Martianus Capella. Irish annals of a later time call him "the Geometer," and he has gained a great repute for erudition. Yet all we really know of his scientific doctrine is contained in this letter of Zacharias. Did

[189] Kenney, 523ff.: "no doubt an Irishman named Dub-dá-chrich." See *ibid.* for bibliography.
[190] Tangl, ed. 178f.; *Epp.* No. 80.

he talk of the Antipodes, or did he believe, as well might one who came from a land of saints and pixies, in a wonderful folk that lived below its green fields?[191] At any rate, Boniface could not prevail against him, in the long run. He was consecrated bishop for Salzburg in 755,[192] the year after Boniface died, and ministered to his diocese for almost forty years, so well, indeed, that in the thirteenth century he was canonized.

Another errant Celt against whom the Archbishop drew forth his pen in accusation to Zacharias was the priest Samson, who was misled enough to believe that the sacrament of confirmation, without the necessity of baptism, opened the way to the Christian life.[193]

Again and again the Pope found himself giving judgment on strange Germanic customs referred to him by this same perplexed scribe of God:[194]

"Birds—jackdaws, crows, storks? No, certainly not. They are no food for Christians. And to eat of beavers, hares, and forest ponies is far worse. But, most holy brother, you yourself know your Bible very well.

"About the Easter fire? This shall be lighted on Holy Saturday by the bishop for the rite of holy baptism, from a flame that has been burning since Holy Thursday on wicks in three large vessels, filled with oil from the different lamps in the church."

Boniface was asking the Pope here about the lighting of the Paschal candle. He knew well the danger of the "Easter fire";

---

[191] M. R. James, *CMH* III, 512f. The Pope's reason for condemning Virgil's teaching was probably the fear that "the other race of men" would be held free from original sin and from the necessary sharing in redemption. See H. Krabbo "Bischof Virgil von Salzburg und seine kosmologischen Ideen," *Mitth. d. Inst. f. österr. Geschichtsforschung* XXIV, Innsbruck, 1903, 1ff.; Krusch, *MGH Script. rer. Merov.* VI, 1913, 517ff., 545; cf. Kurth (French original), 148; Kuhlmann, 253f.
[192] See Krusch *MGH ibid.*, 519, against the date 767, given by the *Annales Salisburgenses*: Pertz, *Script.* I, 89.
[193] Tangl, 177. [194] *Epp.* No. 87.

438 ANGLO-SAXON SAINTS AND SCHOLARS

fire was one of the most important elements in the pagan
ritual against which he fought so long. The "need-fire" was
used by heathen men in times of plague upon their farms;
sick oxen and swine were driven through a huge flaming pile,
kindled upon some open ground, in hope of their cleansing
from disease. The practice was repeatedly forbidden by the
Church in the eighth century. Then there were the pagan
Fire-Festivals, held in honour of the sun, especially at the
time of the summer solstice, and also the fire lighted in the
spring, perhaps as greeting of Eostre, goddess of the sun's
growing warmth and light. The Christian feasts of Easter in
the spring and of Saint John at midsummer were naturally
connected in the memory of pagans and of converts alike with
these old heathen rejoicings.[195]

The Pope continues: "Concerning flints we have no tradition." This may be a reference to an Irish custom of the
"Easter fire," introduced by Irish missionaries to the continent
in these early days and perhaps struck from flints.[196]

The next question—they occur one after another in the
same letter and in this order—deals with "the plague of
kings," leprosy. The Pope rules that those who are victims
of leprosy from birth or through heredity must be banished
from towns, but may receive alms of charity; those who have
contracted it through other illness are to be allowed to stay,
in hope of cure. Should they present themselves in church at
the altar, they shall receive communion last of all the congre-

---

[195] *Cap. Reg. Franc.* I, pp. 25 (5); 223 (*Indic. super. et pag.* 15);
Grimm, *Teutonic Mythology* II, 1883, 616; Frazer, *Golden Bough* VII, i,
1913, 106ff. *Cf.* R. M. Meyer, *Altgermanische Religionsgeschichte*, 1910,
404.

[196] Duchesne, *Christian Worship*, 1910, 250f. *Cf.* the story of the
Paschal fire lighted by St. Patrick on the hill of Slane above the river
Boyne. "The idea is that Easter is to replace Beltane, the Christian to
overcome the heathen fire; and it is a matter of no import that the day
of Beltane was the first day of summer, which could never fall on Easter
Eve": Bury, *St. Patrick*, 104ff. For Beltane fires see Frazer, *ibid.*, 146ff.

gation. Horses infected with the same disease must be thrown into pits, if they are beyond cure. Horses or other domestic animals that have been injured by mad wolves or dogs must be segregated, in case they, too, become mad and bite others.

"You ask me, brother, whether nuns, like men, should wash one another's feet on Holy Thursday and other days. Of course. God, Who is in heaven, is one and the same for men and for women.

"Should a man be ordained priest before he is thirty? It were well, dear friend, if such may be found, that men of ripe years and of good report be ordained priests, as canon law prescribes. But if men are lacking and there is serious need, then let them be ordained deacon and priest from the age of twenty-five.

"How long should bacon fat be kept before eating? The Church Fathers tell us nothing about this. But, as you have asked me, I advise that it should not be eaten before it has been smoked or cooked by fire. If, however, it be preferred raw, at any rate it should not be eaten until after Easter.

"Are you at all to blame, you want to know, for having ordained priests and deacons at times not prescribed by Church law, for yielding to their pleas of poverty or other special circumstances? My brother, you know very well the proper seasons for ordination! All the same, because you acted through zeal for the faith, we will ask God to forgive you.

"You are not sure where the sign of the Cross should be made in the saying of the Canon? We have given to your priest Lul a roll of manuscript on which the proper places are marked."

In another letter, written some years before, the question of a successor to Boniface had again been discussed: [197] "You say that you are old and frail, full of days, and ask to

[197] *Epp.* No. 80: May 1, 748.

be allowed to place a successor in your see, if you can find one, while you yourself remain Legate of the Apostolic See as before. But we, God helping us, counsel you for the sake of the souls of men by no means to forsake that see of Mainz which you hold under the favour of Christ, in order that the word of the Lord, 'He who endureth to the end, the same shall be saved,' may be fulfilled in you. But, if the Lord shall have granted to your prayer a perfect man, who can exercise thought and care for the saving of souls, you will consecrate him bishop with you, as your representative, and he shall work in the preaching and the ministry of Christ committed unto you."

There were, however, many joys to place against these troubles and problems; and not the least of these was the growing power of Rome at Frankish headquarters. In 747 the elder brother, Carloman, like so many Anglo-Saxon kings and nobles, had decided to leave his rule for a monastery. Bearing gifts, rich and numerous, so the old records tell,[198] he arrived in Rome, received the habit from Pope Zacharias, entered a cloister founded by himself upon Mount Soracte, and later, weary of notoriety, left it to become an unknown monk at Monte Cassino.

Pepin was now sole master of Frankland. In 751 he felt the time had come to end this mockery of the Merovingian kings. According to the story so familiar to students, he sent Burchard, bishop of Würzburg, and Fulrad, abbot of St. Denis, as envoys to Rome with this question: "Was it well in these times that there should be kings in Frankland who had not kingly power?" And—so the old narrative goes on— "Pope Zacharias sent word back to Pepin that it were better that he who had the power should be called king, and by his

---

[198] *Annales Mettens.*: Pertz, *Script.* I, 329; *Einhardi Ann., ibid.,* 136; *Ann. regni Franc.,* 6; Regino of Prüm, *Chronicon*: Pertz, *ibid.,* 555.

Apostolic authority he bade that Pepin assume the crown." [199]

Pepin, it was clear, did not venture to take this final step without the sanction of the Pope, whom he, in spite of all his independence, held to be Vicar of Christ upon the earth. Once he had received that sanction, a general assembly of clergy, nobles, and people of the Franks declared the deposition of Childeric III, last of the Merovingian line. Pepin was raised, according to ancestral custom, upon the shield, and at his crowning in November, 751, Boniface himself as Archbishop and Papal Legate anointed with holy oil this Frankish monarch, first of the Carolingian kings.[200] By this act he brought to reality that which for so long had been his great desire—union, consummated in this homage, between the Frankish realms for which he laboured and the Holy See for which he lived. Pepin was now *rex Dei gratia*. Herein Boniface was making ready for the days of Charles the Great.[201]

Even a deeper happiness was his over the foundation of that monastery which was to foster through the ages the learning, sacred and secular, for which he had hungered all his life. Again and again in his letters sent from Germany we find him begging for books, and yet more books. The raising of the monastery of Fulda in Hesse-Nassau, where the valley of the Fulda runs between the Vogelsgebirge and the hills of the Rhön, was due, under Boniface, to his disciple Sturm.

We left young Sturm cooking dinners for the monks of Fritzlar.[202] There in due time he was ordained priest, and then carried on mission work for nearly three years, in spite of a growing wish to lead a life even more remote from the world, as the hermits had done on whose lives he meditated.

[199] *Annales Lauriss. min.*: Pertz, *ibid.*, 116.
[200] *Annales regni Franc.*, 8, 10; Hauck, 577.
[201] See J. P. Whitney, "The Earlier Growth of Papal Jurisdiction," *CHJ* IV, 1932, 22f. We should not see in this act of Boniface any personal triumph; he was merely acting as representative of the Pope.
[202] P. 408 *supra*.

At last Boniface had given the word; Sturm might now make his way into the Hessian wilds to find some possible retreat.

With two companions he promptly started from Fritzlar, pushed his way through the forest, dark with oak and beech and matted briars, until he came upon a large clearing by the side of a stream. It was a place of many waters, where the rivers Haune and Geis pour into the Fulda; in later days it was known as Hersfeld. The pilgrims thought that perhaps this would answer their purpose and built a rough cluster of huts from the bark of trees. Thus this year, 743, saw the beginning of the cloister of Hersfeld, famous in the earlier Middle Ages.

But in the eighth century Hersfeld was not far enough from the raids of the Saxon freebooters, and therefore Sturm struggled on still deeper into the forest. His biographer Eigil, himself a Bavarian, a disciple of Sturm for twenty years,[203] seems to have been too young to be one of his companions on this adventure, but he must have heard from Sturm the many details of his narrative. He describes very vividly the three men passing by boat along the Fulda, anxiously scanning its banks for likely ground;[204] then forward again by land, up hill and down dale. Presently Sturm left his weary brethren and rode alone upon his ass. By day he forged ahead, looking right and left, stopping now and again for rest and prayer; as night drew on, he swung his axe and built a stout rampart for himself and his beast against the perils of the dark. Once they were both alarmed by a crowd of Slavs swimming at a ford over the river; once he spent the night with a friendly woodsman who knew every path and trail.

At last he found his journey's end, a place that Boniface might reasonably bless, and filled with hope he returned. The

---

[203] Eigil was abbot of Fulda 818–822.
[204] Eigil, *Vita Sturmi*: Pertz, *Script.* II, 367.

Father did approve, and at his petition Carloman gave the necessary land. Some of the brethren immediately set off to work; trees were felled, undergrowth was cut away, the first chapel and cells gradually rose. It was now 744.

Fulda became to Boniface what Echternach had been to Willibrord, his beloved place of peace and refreshment. Sturm was made its abbot; and there the Father himself would return year by year, to pore over his Bible, to meditate in its quiet, to find recreation as he joined the brethren in their work in house and field. Especially he would climb one of the hills near the monastery to be alone with his books and his thoughts, a hill which the monks called "Bishop's Mount." [205]

In 751 he wrote to Pope Zacharias: "There is a place in the forest, wild and very lonely, at the very centre of our work here. We are building a monastery in it and settling monks to live under the Rule of our holy Father Benedict, men of very strict life, who eat no meat, drink no wine or cider, and have no servants, content in the labour of their own hands. It has come to me by honest effort, through religious and God-fearing men, especially through Carloman, formerly ruler of the Franks. There, if you allow, I hope to rest awhile my tired old body and to lie there after my death. The four peoples to whom by God's grace we have declared the word of Christ dwell around there, as all men know. With your aid I can be useful to them, so long as my mind and my body let me work."

The end of this letter is lost to us, but undoubtedly it held a request for privilege for Fulda. In the same year Zacharias wrote back that a privilege had been granted "according to your desire and petition." The Papal charter for the monastery is still extant, declaring that it was to be under the jurisdiction of the Holy See alone, that no bishop of any other church

[205] *Ibid.*, 371. It was called afterward the Frauenberg.

should have any authority therein, and that no one might even say Mass within it save by invitation of the abbot alone. This charter marks the first time that a monastery of the Frankish Church had been placed directly under Rome.[206]

During this same year of privilege for Fulda another house of prayer was founded amid the silence of virgin forest, the monastery of Heidenheim, built by Wynnebald.[207] We last saw him labouring as priest among the heathen of Thuringia.[208] From there he had gone to stay with Duke Odilo, had remained in Bavaria, it seems, for some three years, and then, about 747, had travelled to Mainz, where Boniface was in charge as bishop. He had preached with success in the city for some time. But that longing for solitude which Sturm had known had also prevailed in him; in Mainz, among the crowds that frequented its cathedral church, the world was far too near. At last, after consulting his brother, now regularly installed as bishop of the see of Eichstätt,[209] he gained by his own purchase and by the gifts of pious Churchmen the retreat he sought, where the river Brenz runs through the hills, between Aalen and Ulm.

It was a double cloister; for we read that a sister of Willibald and Wynnebald, named Walburg, came from England with other nuns to work in Germany and ruled this house of Heidenheim for a while after Wynnebald's death in 761.[210] No doubt she was already in charge of the nuns while he was presiding over all as abbot.

Another feminine member of this community of Heiden-

---

[206] *Epp.* Nos. 86f., 89. See on this much disputed matter Hauck, 582f. and notes. He observes that Boniface feared to leave the brethren to the jurisdiction of some Frankish bishop. Fulda lay in the diocese of Würzburg. *Cf.* Tangl, *Mitth. d. Inst. f. österr. Gesch.* XX, 1899, 193ff.; also in ed. *Die Briefe* (1916), 203, note 1.

[207] *Vita Wynnebaldi*: Pertz, *Script.* XV, i, 111.

[208] P. 413 *supra.*   [209] *Cf.* p. 419.

[210] Levison, ed. *Vitae*, 138; Bateson (*op. cit.*, p. 60 *supra*, note 155), 184f.; Hauck, 537.

heim is of special interest.[211] She, also, had been brought up in England, a distant relative of these two brothers and their sister, and had come to Heidenheim after Wynnebald's death.[212] There she lived as nun under Abbess Walburg and wrote the *Lives* of Willibald and Wynnebald, largely from the dictation of Willibald in his old age. Her pride in her task, especially in dealing with the travels of Willibald, was only equalled by her consciousness of inferiority: "I am frail and prone to error through the weakness of my sex, supported by no gift of wisdom, upheld by no great strength. I am driven on only by the force of my own will, to pluck like an ignoramus a few flowers and fruits of wisdom from many a laden tree." [213] Her Latin is indeed flowery with ungrammatical rhetoric whenever she waxes eloquent. She seems, however, to have had some of the training regularly given to Anglo-Saxon nuns; and several times she reflects Gregory the Great.[214] Her name is unknown. Modern students call her "the Anonymous Nun of Heidenheim."

The friends of Boniface across the sea were never far from his mind. When Abbess Bugga won her desire to visit Rome, Boniface met her there, probably in his third visit of 738–739. Although they were both intent upon visiting its shrines, he was kind enough to spend some time in friendly talk with her, of course on matters quite necessary. These things she reported on her return to that monastery in Kent which she had left in hope of peaceful contemplation.[215] Apparently, however, she had found worse worries lying in wait without its walls, for Boniface wrote her a letter of sympathy in "the tempests of troubles which God has allowed to come upon you

---

[211] Holder-Egger: Pertz, *ibid.*, 8of.
[212] *Vita Wynn.* c. 10: *ibid.*, 114; *cf.* 80, note 6.
[213] Prologue, *Vita Will.*: *ibid.*, 86f.
[214] *E.g. Vita Wynn.*: *ibid.*, 110, 112. She also imitated the *Life of Boniface* by the priest Willibald, and thus helps to date that work: Holder-Egger, *ibid.*, 91, 105, 107, 111; Levison, ed. *Vitae,* ix.
[215] *Epp.* No. 105.

in your old age." "But," he goes on, "let this old age be lovely; let it finish building to the glory of God that tower of the Gospel begun in goodly youth." [216]

The anxious Bugga had plenty of time for the work. For, long afterward, Bregwin, Archbishop of Canterbury (759–765), wrote to Lul in Mainz: "We are keeping the day of the death of Abbess Bugga, December 27th. She asked me so eagerly to let you know when she died. As she hoped and believed, so do you, since Boniface, your bishop, was her father and her friend in Christ." [217]

Four letters of the Archbishop sent to England are concerned with Ethelbald, king of Mercia (716–757).[218] We saw him in the time of Bede as a friend of the hermit Guthlac and as overlord of England from the south to the river Humber.[219] Men knew him not only as "king of the southern English," but also as "king of Britain," *rex Britanniae,* titles which he gained largely by conquests in Wessex.[220] His character was a mixture of good and evil. He was generous in gifts to the Church, especially—so far as our records go—in Worcestershire and Berkshire.[221] But as his long reign progressed and he grew to middle age, his vices balanced his virtues, and Boniface, who knew him, felt forced to write rebuke.

One letter merely expressed friendship and affection and as a token of remembrance announced gifts, a hawk and two falcons, two shields and two lances. Boniface was probably trying to pave the way for less pleasant address, for at the end he observed, " 'Fear God and obey His commandments.' We ask, also, that if letters reach you from us by another messenger, you will be kind enough to hearken to them with all care."

[216] No. 94.   [217] No. 117.
[218] Nos. 69, 73ff.; H. S. III, 35off.
[219] P. 297 *supra.*   [220] Stenton, 202ff.
[221] Kemble I, Nos. 65ff.; Birch, Nos. 134, 137ff.

About 746 he wrote again, in union with five other bishops working among the Franks.[222] "We have heard that you give generously in alms, that you sternly repress thefts and unjust deeds, false oaths and robbery, that you are known as a protector of widows and the poor, and that you have established peace in your realm. And for this we give praise to God. . . . But we have heard from many sides, and we would it were not true, that you have never married a lawful wife nor have kept chastity, but have been overcome by lust of foul indulgence. Moreover, what is worse, it is told that you do your evil deeds in cloisters, with holy nuns and virgins vowed to God."

A vivid picture, recalling that of Tacitus,[223] then describes the punishment for unfaithful wives in Germany. Boniface had heard of the loose state of morals in the England of this time, so bitterly denounced by Bede to Egbert of York. He wrote: "If the English people are living in wanton lust, like those of Sodom, a race degenerate and low must rise of them— a nation given to passion and murder, neither brave in war nor steadfast in faith, knowing neither honour of men nor love of God." He reminded Ethelbald of other sins against the Church: "It has also been told us that you have broken many rights of churches and monasteries and have taken away certain possessions; that your ealdormen and your nobles inflict more savage violence and tyranny upon monks and priests than Christian kings have ever done before." Let Ethelbald remember the terrible end of Ceolred, ruler of his own Mercia, and of Osred, king of Northumbria: "Beware, most dear son, of that pit into which you have seen others fall!"[224]

The reason for the indictment of the five bishops was ex-

---

[222] *Epp.* No. 73.   [223] *Germania*, c. 19.
[224] The letter abridged in *Gest. Reg.* I, 8off. ends differently, although its general tenor is the same; see Stubbs, ed. 82, note 1; Dümmler, ed. *Epp.* 344, note 5; 345, note 1. Cf. the reference to this censure by Boniface in John Bromyard, *Summa Predicantium*, 1518, *s.v. Adulterium*, fol. XXI.

plained in another letter, addressed to Herefrid, a priest [225] : "Be sure, dear brother, that the only motive underlying our rebuke was of pure friendship; we wrote because we ourselves are sons of that same English race, though now, in obedience to the Apostolic See, we live in a foreign land. In the well-being and praises of our race we rejoice and are glad; in its sins and their scandal among men we are overcome with sorrow." And still further explanation was sent by Boniface to Egbert, now Archbishop of York: that his oath, pledged in Rome, had bound him to do all he could to recall any whom he might anywhere find guilty of breach of Church discipline.[226]

Another letter asked Egbert to send him some of the writings of Bede, "a lantern given you by the Lord." With the letter went two little casks of wine, that "you may have a holiday with your brethren." Books by Bede were also asked by him from Hwaetbert, still abbot of Wearmouth and Jarrow when Boniface was writing, about 747. He also prayed the abbot, if it would not give very much trouble, to send him a cloak, which would be such a comfort in travelling. In return he was sending, with his love, a couch-cover of goats' hair.[227]

The bishops apparently made an impression upon Ethelbald, an impression heightened by resolutions against evil passed this same year in an English council held at Clovesho.[228] Soon afterward, in 749, he signed a charter, declaring in the usual phrase, *pro expiatione delictorum suorum,* that he freed the monasteries and churches in his realm from all taxation and public services, except the repair of bridges and guarding of forts.[229] About seven years later he was murdered by his own bodyguard at his residence, Seckington in Warwick-

[225] *Epp.* No. 74. *Cf. Baedae Cont. ann.* 747: Plummer I, 362.
[226] No. 75.
[227] Nos. 91 and 76.   [228] *Cf.* Stenton, 204.
[229] Kemble I, No. 99; Birch, No. 178 (*cf.* No. 140); H. S. III, 386f.

shire.[230] It is to be feared that his purgatory was hard; for a fragment written after his death, describing a holy woman's vision of the world beyond, tells of Ethelbald, once a royal tyrant, enduring torment in the pits of penance.[231]

There are letters received by Boniface from two other kings of England. Elfwald of East Anglia, who died in 749, assures the Archbishop that his name will be held in perpetual remembrance by the religious of the realm as they meet in their various houses for the sevenfold Office, that Boniface is to be Warden of these monasteries and to direct the spending of the royal alms for their benefit. He asks, also, that the dead for whom he and Boniface desire prayer be remembered in both East Anglia and in Germany.[232] Some years later Ethelbert II of Kent, who lived until 762, sent to Germany the story of Abbess Bugga's meeting with Boniface in Rome, as told him by her. He was a stranger to Boniface, but he wrote a very friendly letter, appreciating the work of the mission abroad, and he added some gifts, "with no thought of any worldly return." In the last lines, however, he begs for a special favour—not at all difficult to grant, so far as he has heard. Would Boniface send him two falcons, bold and clever enough to seize cranes on the flight and bring them to earth? There are so few birds of this kind in Kent, such as can be tamed and trained for sport. A reply would be much appreciated.[233]

In 747 Boniface presided over another general council of Frankish bishops, his last. It was called to debate and pass resolutions concerning reform in the Frankish Church.[234] These resolutions, duly approved by the council and by the

[230] Earle and Plummer II, 47; *Baedae Cont. ann.* 757.
[231] *Epp.* No. 115; Plummer II, 342.
[232] No. 81.
[233] No. 105.
[234] Hauck, 571ff. *Cf.* the request sent by Pepin to the Pope for details of Church law, and the Pope's answer: *Epp.* No. 77; *Codex Carol.* III: *MGH Epp.* III, i, 479ff.

Papal See, to which he had reported them, Boniface then sent to Cuthbert, Archbishop of Canterbury (740–758).[235] They dealt with the same recurring matters of administration and discipline.

To his account of what had been done to improve the state of the Frankish Church he added some courteous words of warning: "The labour of our ministry is for one and the same cause; equal watchfulness over churches and peoples is ours to fulfil, whether we teach or discipline or admonish or defend the orders of the ministry or the laypeople. . . . And therefore, my dear friend—not that you in your wisdom need to hear and read the resolutions made by us, who lack high learning—we believe that of your humble and holy desire you will want to know what our bishops and clergy here have decreed, so that you may correct and improve upon the same . . . I must tell you that all the clergy here who are most experienced in Scripture and the fear of God agree that it would be good for the honour and purity of your Church and would give some protection against foul sin if your bishops and your rulers would forbid women, including nuns, to travel to and from Rome so frequently. Many of them are lost; few remain untouched by evil. To tell the truth, there are very few cities in Lombardy or Frankland or Gaul where a prostitute of English birth may not be found. This is a scandal and a dishonour to your whole Church." Other crimes are also declared, exactly similar to those prevalent among clergy and lay people in Germany and France.

This letter, we may think, did its part toward the assembling, in September of this same year, 747, of Cuthbert and the bishops of his Province at Clovesho, now unidentified.[236]

---

[235] *Epp.* No. 78; H.S. III, 376ff. Tangl dates this Ep. 78 in 747.
[236] *Cf.* Hauck, 571, note 1; Hefele-Leclercq III, ii, 903ff.; Hahn, *Bon. und Lul,* 219ff.; Loofs, *Zur Chron.* 36; Dümmler, ed. *Epp.* 350, note 1; Stubbs, ed. *Gest. Reg.* I, 82f.; Fischer, 289. See also for divers theories H. S. III, 382f.; Stenton, 235; Whitney, *CHJ* IV, 1932, 21.

Moreover, Boniface may well have furthered this event by writing to the Pope, for Zacharias certainly stirred up the English in two letters of rebuke which threatened to excommunicate all who paid no attention. The list of reforms determined upon at Clovesho was long; its details show evident relation to those of the Frankish synod described by Boniface to Cuthbert.[237]

And now the many activities of this Archbishop in Germany were drawing to their close; yet even his last days were not those of peace. In March, 752, Zacharias died. His successor-elect died three days after election, and another was at once chosen and consecrated, known to history as Stephen II.[238] The greeting of Boniface to his new Pope was delayed on account of heathen raids; more than thirty churches had been robbed and burned, and he had been working hard on their restoration.[239]

To the end he thought of his followers. A letter to Abbot Fulrad of St. Denis begged him to support a petition sent by Boniface to Pepin for the care and protection in years to come of the missionaries from England: "I pray our high King, in the Name of Christ, Son of God, that he will tell me while I am yet living what he will do for them hereafter. They are nearly all of foreign race. Some are working as priests, with charge of church and people in many places; some are monks in our monasteries, studying their books as children; others are now growing old, those who have toiled long with me and have helped me in my work. I am troubled about all of them, praying that after my death they may not be scattered here and there."[240]

It may be remembered that Pope Zacharias had given Boni-

[237] *Gest. Pont.* I, 9ff.; H. S. III, 362ff.
[238] Also called by some historians Stephen III, as the Pope-elect who had died was also named Stephen.
[239] *Epp.* No. 108.　　[240] No. 93.

face permission to choose a bishop to help him at Mainz;[241] in 752 he consecrated Lul for this office.[242] He asked afterward—in this same petition to King Pepin—that the royal assent be given to his desire that Lul succeed him in the overseeing of the mission in Germany. His prayer was granted; and Lul assumed charge of the diocese of Mainz and of the work of Boniface in general. "Take thought for Fulda," the old man bade him as they talked together for the last time, "and finish the building there which I began. See, dear son, that my body be buried there when I have gone. And take care of Lioba and her nuns at Taubersbischofsheim with all love and reverence. Let her body be laid beside mine in that same place of burial when she, too, has departed hence, so that we, who with a like desire and devotion have served Christ here, may side by side await the day of resurrection." Then he said goodbye to this abbess, his kinswoman, who had revered and loved him since her novice days under Eadburg in Thanet, and told her to follow with all her might this pilgrimage to its end.[243]

Once, years before, he had planned to rest in his last days amid the peace of prayer and reading at Fulda. But when now the moment came, he found his thoughts turning irresistibly to that land which had been the longing of his youth, the Frisia of his life's work, as he had once believed. Willibrord had been dead since 739, and Carloman, as ruler of the Franks, had entrusted to Boniface the appointing of a bishop of Utrecht, centre of the Frisian mission. He had done this at the time, but the see was now once more vacant.

There was trouble, too, regarding this bishopric, and he could not leave things in disorder there. The bishop of

[241] Pp. 439f. supra.
[242] Hauck, 584, note 1; cf. Levison, ed. Vitae, 45, note 2 (dates the consecration between 751 and 753); Hahn, 250ff.
[243] Epp. No. 107; Levison, 45f.; Rudolf, Vita Leobae, c. 17: Pertz, Script. XV, i, 129.

Cologne was claiming Utrecht as part of his own charge, on the ground that the Frankish king Dagobert, who had died in 639, had given its fortress and the ruins of the little Christian church within its walls to the diocese of Cologne, on condition that Cologne's bishop should work for the conversion of the Frisian heathen. Boniface wrote to Pope Stephen in protest. The bishop of Cologne, he declared, had *not* converted the Frisians, had not even preached to them. It was Willibrord who had done this, who had made the ruins once more into a house of God and consecrated it in honor of Saint Martin.[244]

Here was clearly good reason for going to Utrecht. But first Boniface went to Neustria to see King Pepin on this weighty matter, and there gained his end. The Frankish king placed the bishopric of Utrecht under his direction, so that for the time, at least, it was not absorbed by Cologne.[245]

In 753 he reached Utrecht and promptly put one of his assistant bishops, Eoban, at the head of its cathedral and diocese.[246] Now, once again in the midst of the old work, he found it impossible to rest apart from it. As long as the milder weather lasted, he journeyed to this place and that, as far northward as the shore of the Ijssel Meer. His friend, Gregory of Bavaria, who had been with him amid the hardships of Thuringia and Hesse, was now at the monastery of Saint Martin in Utrecht. There, perhaps, Boniface spent the winter days of 753–754, when travel was not possible for him; or, it may be, he went back for a brief visit to his people in Mainz.[247] With gladness he saw the spring return; again he set to work in Frisia, for the last time. On the fifth of June,

[244] *Epp.* No. 109.

[245] Hauck, 589, note 3; Böhmer-Mühlbacher I, 33f. (the date is given as May 23, 753); *MGH Dipl. Karol.* I, No. 4.

[246] This may be the priest of *Epp.* Nos. 34ff., 41; Hahn, *Bon. und Lul,* 130f.

[247] Cf. Eigil, *Vita Sturmi* (*op. cit.,* p. 407 *supra,* note 122), c. 15; Hauck, 590.

754, at dawn, as he was about to lay his hands in blessing of confirmation upon a company of Christian converts at Dokkum, near Leeuwarden, a rush of fanatic pagans, enraged at the sight, suddenly struck down both him and Eoban. With them died many of their fellow-workers.[248]

Monks from Utrecht hastened to the place and brought his body across the water to their cathedral. They longed to keep it with them, but the will of Lul prevailed, and the journey was continued to Mainz. There, so the story goes, desire was sharply divided regarding its burial. Lul contended for Mainz, the seat of the bishopric of Boniface; Sturm for Fulda, supported by the Father's own wish. At length Fulda prevailed. In its monastic church the last rites for this apostle to the Germans were solemnized, and the sepulchre of his relics remained for the solace of his brethren and the hope of the multitudes who came there to pray.[249]

In describing the raid which caused the death of Boniface, his biographer, the priest Willibald, tells that barbarians searched here and there in hope of treasure, but found nothing that they valued, only books. Some of these they threw away into the marshes; some, however, were saved and placed in safe keeping at Fulda or elsewhere.[250] There is still in the Landesbibliothek at Fulda a manuscript, *Codex Bonifatianus* 3, a copy of the Gospels in early Irish script which may well have belonged to Boniface.[251]

[248] The year of the death of Boniface is given in the tradition of Mainz as 755, in that of Fulda as 754: Hauck, 590, note 7; Levison, ed. *Vitae*, 55, note 2. The date 754 is accepted here, as by Hauck and Levison and others, on the ground of the arguments of Tangl, "Das Todesjahr des Bonifatius," *Zeitschrift des Vereins f. hess. Geschichte und Landeskunde*, *N. F.* XXVII, Kassel, 1903, 223ff.

[249] *Martyrologium Fuldense*: Levison, ed. *Vitae*, 60; Eigil, c. 15.

[250] Levison, 51.

[251] Lindsay, *Early Irish Minuscule Script*, 4ff. He suggests that *Codex Bonifatianus* I (*Codex Fuldensis*: "Victor-Codex"), a New Testament in 6th century uncial script, may show the actual writing of Boniface in its marginalia (insular minuscules): *ibid.*, 10f. At least, it, too, surely be-

BONIFACE OF DEVON 455

In this same year of 754 Archbishop Cuthbert of Canterbury wrote to his fellow-countryman, Lul, bishop of Mainz: "Our hearts, it is true, are torn by bitter grief; yet at the same time a joy, new and triumphant, constantly comes to mind for our comforting. We give thanks to God that this was vouchsafed the English, a people from another land, to send out so splendid a searcher into sacred learning, so excellent a soldier of Christ, with many trained and well-instructed followers, for spiritual wrestlings in distant places, for the sowing unto harvest among many souls through the grace of Almighty God." [252]

longed to him; cf. Leclercq, *DACL s.v.* Fulda, col. 2691. For the three *Codices Bonifatiani* at Fulda see Carl Scherer, *Festgabe zum Bonifatius-Jubiläum,* Fulda, 1905, II, pp. 1ff.; Nürnberger, 15ff. For the theory that Boniface took the *Codex Fuldensis* from Wearmouth-Jarrow to Germany see J. Chapman, *Early History of the Vulgate Gospels,* 157f.; cf. p. 266 *supra,* note 102; Scherer, pp. 10, 12, 33, and Laistner, *HTR* XXX, 1937, 43, note 15.

[252] *Epp.* No. 111. On the influence of Anglo-Saxon missionaries upon German language and culture see W. Braune, "Althoch-deutsch und Angelsächsisch": *Beiträge zur Gesch. d. deutschen Sprache und Lit.* XLIII, 1918, 379ff.

EPILOGUE

WE HAVE now traced from youth to old age the lives of these four men, each in his individual circumstances and vocation; it may be well at the end to bind them together by the things they owned in common.

They were all Anglo-Saxon, born of that warrior race which had descended on the coasts of Britain to conquer and to hold. The characteristics that marked the life and literature of early England were found in them, children of her soil. They shared in the feeling toward their own people which had been the heritage of every Germanic tribe from the time of Tacitus. As monks and as scholars they wrote, of course, formally and informally, in Latin; they preached and conversed in Latin. Yet in the seventh century Aldhelm sang native songs from his bridge over the Avon; in the eighth, Bede could proudly write the Church history "of the English nation," and his last hours found him translating the Gospel of St. John "into our tongue." Boniface called in their own speech—*patria voce*— to his fellow-Englishmen as their assassins bore down upon them in foreign Friesland. Not even the poet of the *Wanderer* can have felt exile more than Boniface in Germany, than Wilfrid in Frisia, in Mercia, and on Selsey Island.[253]

Saxon, too, was their love of their kin, natural and spiritual, of sib and fellow-bedesman alike, witnessed constantly in their letters from abroad, in the little gifts they delighted to send home and overseas. Most marked in this human bond

[253] For bibliography of texts and for discussion and translations of the O. E. poetry mentioned here see Charles W. Kennedy, *Old English Elegies*, 1936; *Beowulf*, 1940; *The Earliest English Poetry*, 1943.

between them and theirs was their bearing toward women, so different from that of continental monks and Fathers. They looked upon woman with the respect given her among the Germans who dwelt in ancient days beyond the Rhine. As to the pagan Germans woman was mysteriously gifted with the power of prophecy, so to these Anglo-Saxons there seemed nothing amiss in the rule of spiritually-gifted women over men, in the learning of women in literature both sacred and pagan, in the simplicity of affection, gladly welcomed and gladly told. Theirs was the loyalty, above all, which bound them one to another in new birth within their Church, which set the Holy Father in place of liege lord, the saints and martyrs of spiritual fellowship in place of the heroes of pagan reverence.

Theirs, again from their Saxon birth, was sympathy with the spirit of mystery, of joy and sadness, that brooded over Nature. As the *scop* felt, while he sang the wonders of creation in Hrothgar's hall, so they felt as they chanted *Benedicite* in chapel. Aldhelm as he walked in Selwood Forest, Boniface and Sturm as they traced the Fulda river, Cuthbert and Wilfrid upon their island shores, Guthlac in the silent marshes, were all akin to the poet of the *Beowulf,* as he told of the haunted mere of Grendel and Grendel's mother. As Beowulf grappled with the monsters from the deep, dread tarn, dimly seen shapes red with claw and tusk, as he fought the great dragon to death, so Bede in the church at Jarrow warned his brethren to put on the whole armour of God, for the battle against ghostly powers of hell in their evil hour. To these monks, as to the poets of old English literature, the earth was lightened by the glory of the Lord, dark with the shadow of the Guardian of sins and his demon followers. From fairies and trolls they turned to angels, good and evil, presences unseen but apprehended, that protected or led astray. They understood with the writers of Old English elegy the mystic bitterness of winter, ice and hail and snow, the terror of black waters and lonely places. As the spring came flowing back in Old English poetry to drown the sorrow of winter, so it was for Bede, who knew that God created the earth in the days of an English April. So Aldhelm was glad in renewed life, cuckoos in the distance, beavers on the brook, bees among the flowers.

From their race they drew, too, their strong and ruling purpose. The poet of the *Seafarer* fears the sea which he has known in all its rage and cruelty; yet he must return once more to ride its paths before the wind, for his yearning gives him no rest. So Bede persevered in his little cell, year after year, relentlessly writing for the light of ignorant folk, through troubles without and within, till the pen dropped from his hand in his last sickness; so Aldhelm worked all his life to spread a pall of words and their rhythms over the mysteries of heaven and earth; so Wilfrid journeyed again and again to uphold his cause at Rome, and as an old man faced his enemies in his own land, unafraid; so Boniface endured to pass from scholarship to mission labours, from preaching to the care of churches, from churches to a murderer's arm.

And, lastly, they were one with their race in passion of craftsmanship. As the Anglo-Saxon loved to spin and weave his designs of strange and intricate fancy, so did they: Aldhelm in verses and Wilfrid in stones; Bede in allegory and the "melodies of Scripture"; Boniface after plainer pattern but not less engaging, in dreams and plans for monastery and bishopric.

The years of their working in England were full of uncertainty. Battle and murder, turmoil and treason in Church and in State, disease of body, mind, and soul struck their world again and again in many forms. They laboured on among the changing shadows, knowing that all things in time must pass, that the One and the Eternal was all that mattered. Suffering, whether in himself or in others, was each man's inheritance from Adam; it was the part of each to redeem his little world in his own measure of power and to leave the rest to hope. Each knew the way appointed him and, once it grew clear, followed it with all his might. The old Saxon driving of *wyrd*, of Fate, was to them the will of God; nothing to them could be more terrible than the misery of the Wanderer, cut off from his Lord. It is this thought that sounds its solemn note so often in the sermons and commentaries of Bede, who loved so well his fellow-men.

Thus they paved in their time a road straight and shining, that should lead the peoples of Europe, old and new, from the gateway of the sixth century to that house of many windows which we call the Middle Ages.

BIBLIOGRAPHY AND ABBREVIATIONS

(For extensive bibliographies see the works marked *)

Abbott, W. C.: *Conflicts with Oblivion,* 1935.

Acta SS. Boll.: *Acta Sanctorum Bollandiana,* November III, 1910 (Willibrord).

Acta SS. O.S.B.: see Mabillon.

A H R: *American Historical Review,* New York.

Aldhelm, Saint, *Opera*: ed. Ehwald, *M G H Auct. Ant.* XV, 1919; ed. Giles, 1844 (see *P E A*), reprinted in *P L* LXXXIX, coll. 87ff.

Allison, Thomas: *English Religious Life in the Eighth Century,* 1929.

Analecta Hymnica Medii Aevi: ed. G. M. Dreves, C. Blume, and H. M. Bannister, vols. I-LV, 1886-1922.

Annales Fuldenses: ed. F. Kurze: *Scriptores Rerum Germanicarum in usum scholarum,* 1891.

Annales Regni Francorum, qui dicuntur Ann. Laur. maj. et Einhardi, ed. F. Kurze: *Scriptores* (as above), 1895.

Antiphonary of Bangor: see *H B S.*

Archiv: *Archiv für das Studium der neueren Sprachen und Literaturen,* Berlin.

Arnold-Forster, Frances: *Studies in Church Dedications,* vols. I-III, 1899.

A S C: *Anglo-Saxon Chronicle*: ed. J. Earle and C. Plummer, *Two of the Saxon Chronicles, parallel,* vols. I-II, 1892-1899; ed. B. Thorpe, *Rolls Series* XXIII, vols. I-II, 1861.

Attenborough, F. L.: ed. and trans. *The Laws of the Earliest English Kings,* 1922.

Aubrey, John: *The Natural History of Wiltshire,* ed. Britton, 1847.

Bardenhewer, Otto: *Geschichte der altkirchlichen Literatur,* vols. I-IV, 1913-1924.

Bede, the Venerable, *Opera:* see Jaager, Jones, King, Laistner,

P E A (Giles), *P L* XC-XCV, Plummer, Sellar, Smith, Stevenson.

Betten, F. S.: "St. Bede the Venerable": *Church Historians,* ed. Peter Guilday, 1926, pp. 71ff.;
—— *St. Boniface and St. Virgil, Benedictine Historical Monographs* II, 1927.

Birch, W. de Gray: *Cartularium Saxonicum: a Collection of Charters Relating to Anglo-Saxon History,* vol. I, 1885 (Birch);
—— *Memorials of Saint Guthlac of Crowland,* 1881.

Böhmer, Heinrich: *Zur Geschichte des Bonifatius: Zeitschrift des Vereins für hessische Geschichte und Landeskunde,* N.F. XL, 1917, pp. 171ff.

Böhmer, J. F.: *Regesta Imperii* I: *Die Regesten des Kaiserreichs unter den Karolingern,* ed. E. Mühlbacher, 1908.

Bönhoff, Leo: *Aldhelm von Malmesbury,* 1894.

Boissonade, P.: *Life and Work in Medieval Europe (Fifth to Fifteenth Centuries),* trans. Eileen Power, 1927 (reprinted 1937).

Bond, F. B.: *Dedications and Patron Saints of English Churches,* 1914.

Bondroit, A.: "Les *precariae verbo regis* avant le concile de Leptinnes": *Revue d'Histoire Ecclésiastique* I, 1900, pp. 41ff., 249ff., 430ff.

Boniface, Saint, *Epistulae:* see Dümmler, Emerton, Jaffé, Kylie, *P E A* (Giles), *P L* LXXXIX, Tangl.

Bouquet, M., and Delisle, L.: ed. *Recueil des Historiens des Gaules et de la France,* vols. III-V, 1869.

Breves Notitiae Salisburgenses: Salzburger Urkundenbuch, ed. W. Hauthaler, 1910, pp. 17ff.

Breysig, Theodor: *Jahrbücher des fränkischen Reiches,* 714-741, 1869.

B R G: See Jaffé, P.

Bright, William: *Chapters of Early English Church History,* 1897.

Brittain, F.: *The Medieval Latin and Romance Lyric to A.D. 1300,* 1937.

Brønsted, J.: *Early English Ornament,* trans. A. F. Major, 1924.

Brown, G. Baldwin: *The Arts in Early England,* vols. I-VI, 1903-1937.*

Browne, G. F.: *Aldhelm, Saint: His Life and Times,* 1903;
—— *The Venerable Bede,* 1919;
——*Boniface of Credition and His Companions,* 1910;
—— *Theodore and Wilfrith,* 1897 (Theodore) ;
—— *The Importance of Women in Anglo-Saxon Times,* 1919.
Bury, J. B.: *The Life of St. Patrick and His Place in History,*
1905.
Buss, F. J. von: *Winfrid-Bonifacius,* 1880.

Cabrol, F.: *L'Angleterre Chrétienne avant les Normands,* 1909.
Cambridge Bibliography of English Literature, vol. I, 600-1660,
ed. F. W. Bateson, 1941.*
Camden, William: *Britannia,* 1607.
Capitularia Regum Francorum: see *M G H.*
Carmody, F. J.: ed. *Physiologus Latinus Versio y:* University
of California, 1941.
Caspar, Erich: *Geschichte des Papsttums,* vol. II, 1933.
Ceolfrid, Life of, by an unknown author of the eighth century:
ed. and trans. D. S. Boutflower, 1912 (see also *V A A*).
Chadwick, H. M.: *Studies on Anglo-Saxon Institutions,* 1905;
—— and Chadwick, N. K.: *The Growth of Literature,* 1932.
Chambers, R. W.: *Man's Unconquerable Mind,* 1939, pp. 23ff.
(reprinted from *Proceedings of the British Academy,* 1937).
Chapman, J.: *Notes on the Early History of the Vulgate Gos-
pels,* 1908.
C H E L: Cambridge History of English Literature, vol. I, 1907.*
Chevalier, C. V. J.: *Répertoire des Sources Historiques du Moyen
Âge: Bio-Bibliographie,* vols. I-II, 1905-1907; *Topo-Biblio-
graphie, vols.* I-II, 1894-1903.*
C H J: Cambridge Historical Journal, Cambridge, England.
C H R: Catholic Historical Review, Washington.
C L A: see Lowe.
Clapham, A. W.: *English Romanesque Architecture before the
Conquest,* 1930 (*E R A*).*
Clay, R. M.: *The Hermits and Anchorites of England,* 1914.
C M H: Cambridge Medieval History, vols. II-III, 1913-1922.*
Colgrave, Bertram: ed. *Eddius Stephanus, Life of Bishop Wil-
frid:* text, translation, and notes, 1927;
—— *Two Lives of Saint Cuthbert:* texts, translations, and notes,
1940.

Collingwood, R. G., and Myres, J. N. L.: *Roman Britain and the English Settlements,* 1936.

Collingwood, W. G.: *Northumbrian Crosses of the pre-Norman Age,* 1927.

Cook, A. S.: ed. *The Old English Elene, Phoenix, and Physiologus,* 1919;

——and Pitman, J. H.: *The Old English Physiologus: Yale Studies in English* LXIII, 1921.

Coulton, G. G.: *Five Centuries of Religion,* vol. I, 1923.

C R: Classical Review, London.

Cram, R. A.: *The Ruined Abbeys of Great Britain,* 1927.

Crawford, S. J.: *Anglo-Saxon Influence on Western Christendom* (600-800), 1933.

C S E L: Corpus Scriptorum Ecclesiasticorum Latinorum.

Cuthbert, Saint: see Colgrave and Jaager.

D A C L: Dictionnaire d'Archéologie Chrétienne et de Liturgie, ed. Cabrol and Leclercq.

Dahlmann, F. C., and Waitz, G.: *Quellenkunde der deutschen Geschichte,* hrsg. von Hermann Haering, 1931, Nos. 5157ff.

Dahn, Felix: *Die Könige der Germanen,* vols. VIII-X, 1897-1907.

Dawson, Christopher: *The Making of Europe,* 1932 (6th printing, 1939).

D C A: Dictionary of Christian Antiquities, ed. Smith and Cheetham.

D C B: Dictionary of Christian Biography (to about A.D. 800), ed. Smith and Wace.

Deanesly, Margaret: *A History of the Medieval Church* (590-1500), 1925.*

D H G E: Dictionnaire d'Histoire et de Géographie Ecclésiastiques, ed. Baudrillart and others.

D N B: Dictionary of National Biography, ed. Leslie Stephen and Sidney Lee.

Dobbie, E. V. K.: *The Anglo-Saxon Minor Poems,* 1942;

——*The Manuscripts of Caedmon's Hymn and Bede's Death Song, with a critical text of the Epistola Cuthberti de obitu Bedae: Columbia University Studies in English and Comparative Literature* CXXVIII, 1937.

Dopsch, A.: *Wirtschaftliche und Soziale Grundlagen der Eu-*

ropäischen Kulturentwicklung aus der Zeit von Caesar bis auf Karl den Grossen, 2nd ed. 1923-1924, condensed by Erna Patzelt and trans. by M. G. Beard and Nadine Marshall, 1937.

Drane, Augusta T.: *Christian Schools and Scholars*, 1881 (reprinted 1910).

D T C: *Dictionnaire de Théologie Catholique*, ed. Vacant and Mangenot.

Duchesne, Louis: *Les Origines du Culte Chrétien*, 1910, trans. *Christian Worship: Its Origin and Evolution*, 1910; *
—— ed. *Liber Pontificalis* I (to 795), 1886.

Dudden, F. Homes: *Gregory the Great*, vols. I-II, 1905.

Dümmler, Ernst: ed. *S. Bonifatii et Lulli Epistolae, M G H Epp.* III, 1892, pp. 215ff. (Dümmler);
——ed. *S. Bonifatii Aenigmata, M G H Poetae Latini Aevi Carolini*, 1881.

Dugdale, William: *Monasticon Anglicanum*, ed. J. Caley, H. Ellis, B. Bandinel, vols. I-VI, 1817-1830, reprinted 1846.

Earle and Plummer: see *A S C*.

Ebert, Adolf: *Allgemeine Geschichte der Literatur des Mittelalters im Abendlande*, vol. I, 1889.

Ebrard, J. H. A.: *Die iroschottische Missionskirche des sechtens, siebenten, und achten Jahrhunderts*, 1873;
—— *Bonifatius*, 1882.

Eckenstein, Lina: *Woman under Monasticism*, 1896.

Eddius: see *Wilfrid, Saint*.

E E T S: *Early English Text Society*, London.

E H R: *English Historical Review*, London.

Ehwald, Rudolf: ed. *Aldhelmi Opera: M G H Auct. Ant.* XV, 1919.

Ekwall, Eilert: *The Concise Oxford Dictionary of English Place-Names*, 1936 (*E P N*);
—— *English River-Names*, 1928 (*E R N*).

Elmham: see Thomas of Elmham.

Emerton, Ephraim: trans. *The Letters of Saint Boniface, Columbia University Records of Civilization* XXXI, 1940 * (cf. La Piana, *Speculum* XVIII, 1942, p. 272).

E R E: *Encyclopaedia of Religion and Ethics*, ed. J. Hastings.

Erhardt-Siebold, Erika von: *Die lateinischen Rätsel der Angelsachsen: Anglistische Forschungen* LXI, 1925.

Eulogium: *Eulogium historiarum sive temporis,* by a monk of Malmesbury, ed. F. S. Haydon, *Rolls Series* IX, vols. I-III, 1858-1863.

Faricius: *Life of Aldhelm: P E A* ed. Giles, *Opera Aldhelmi,* pp. 354ff.; *P L* LXXXIV, coll. 63ff.

Farmer, H. G.: *The Organ of the Ancients from Eastern Sources,* 1931.

Festgabe zum Bonifatius-Jubiläum, Fulda, 1905 (studies by G. Richter and C. Scherer).

Fischer, Otto: *Bonifatius, der Apostel der Deutschen,* 1881.

Flaskamp, Franz: *Das hessische Missionswerk des heiligen Bonifatius,* 1926; *

—— *Die homiletische Wirksamkeit des heiligen Bonifatius,* 1926; *

—— *Die Missionsmethode des heiligen Bonifatius,* 1929; *

—— *Die Anfänge friesischen und sächsischen Christentums,* 1929;*

Flick, A. C.: *The Rise of the Mediaeval Church,* 1909.

Florence of Worcester: *Chronicon ex Chronicis (A.D. 450-1117),* ed. B. Thorpe, *English Historical Society,* vols. I-II, 1848-1849;

—— ed. in Petrie, *Monumenta* (see *M H B*), 1848.

Foligno, Cesare: *Latin Thought during the Middle Ages,* 1929.

Forschungen: *Forschungen zur deutschen Geschichte* (Göttingen).

Frank, H.: *Die Klosterbischöfe des Frankenreiches: Beiträge zur Geschichte des alten Mönchtums und des Benediktinerordens* XVII, 1932.

Fuhrmann, J. P.: *Irish Medieval Monasteries on the Continent,* 1927.

Fuller, Thomas: *The Church History of Britain (to 1648),* 1655: ed. J. S. Brewer, vol. I, 1845.

Furst, Clyde: *A Group of Old Authors,* 1899: *Aldhelm,* pp. 131ff.

Gallia Christiana in Provincias Ecclesiasticas Distributa, ed. Congregation O.S.B. of St. Maur: ed. P. Piolin, IV, 1876.

Gest. Pont.: William of Malmesbury: De Gestis Pontificum Anglorum, ed. N. E. S. A. Hamilton, *Rolls Series* LII, 1870.

Gest. Reg.: *William of Malmesbury: De Gestis Regum Anglorum,* ed. W. Stubbs, vols. I-II, *Rolls Series* XC, 1887-1889.

Ghellinck, J. de: *Littérature latine au Moyen Âge, depuis les Origines jusqu'à la Fin de la Renaissance carolingienne,* 1939.

Giles, J. A.: see *P E A;*

——ed. *Anecdota Bedae, Lanfranci et aliorum, Caxton Society,* No. 7, 1851;

——trans. *The Minor Historical Works of Bede,* in: *The Biographical Writings and Letters,* 1845.

Goodwin, C. W.: ed. *Anglo-Saxon Life of St. Guthlac,* 1848 (with Eng. trans.)

Gougaud, Louis: *Les Chrétientés Celtiques,* 1911; revised and trans. as *Christianity in Celtic Lands,* 1932 * (Gougaud);

——*Ermites et Reclus*: *Études sur d'Anciennes Formes de Vie Religieuse,* 1928;

——*Les Saints irlandais hors d'Irelande, étudiés dans la devotion traditionelle,* 1936.

Gover, J. E. B., and Mawer, Allen, and Stenton, F. M.: *The Place-Names of Wiltshire,* 1939 (Gover).

Green, J. R.: *The Making of England,* 1903.

Grein, C. W. M., and Wülker, R. P.: *Bibliothek der angelsächsischen Poesie,* vol. II, i, 1888.

Grieve, Alexander: *Willibrord,* 1923.*

Gross, Charles: *The Sources and Literature of English History (from the earliest times to about 1485),* 1915.*

Gummere, F. B.: *Founders of England,* with supplementary notes by F. P. Magoun Jr., 1930.

Hahn, H.: *Bonifaz und Lul,* 1883 (Hahn);

——*Jahrbücher des fränkischen Reiches* (741-752), 1863.

Hahn, Karl F. von: *Rhetores Latini Minores,* 1863.

Hardy, T. D.: *Descriptive Catalogue of Materials Relating to the History of Great Britain and Ireland,* vol. I, i and ii, *Rolls Series* XXVI, 1862.*

Hauck, A.: *Kirchengeschichte Deutschlands,* vols. I-V, 1887-1920 (vol. I, 1904).*

H B S: *Henry Bradshaw Society, Publications of:* Nos. IV and X: *The Antiphonary of Bangor,* ed. F. E. Warren, 1893-1895; Nos. XIII and XIV: *The Irish Liber Hymnorum,* ed. J. H. Bernard and R. Atkinson, 1898; No. XXXVI: *Facsimiles of the Creeds,* ed. A. E. Burn (with notes by L. Traube), 1909; No. LV: *The Calendar of St. Willibrord,* ed. H. A. Wilson, 1918.

H D B: Hastings, James, ed. *Dictionary of the Bible.*

H E: Bede, *Historia Ecclesiastica Gentis Anglorum.*

Healy, John: *Insula Sanctorum et Doctorum,* 6th ed. 1912.*

Hefele, Karl J. von: *Conciliengeschichte;* ed. in French by H. Leclercq, *Histoire des Conciles,* vol. III, 1909-1910.

Hepple, R. B.: "The Monastery School of Jarrow": *History* VII, 1922, pp. 92ff.

Hilpisch, P. S.: *Die Doppelklöster, Entstehung und Organisation: Beiträge zur Geschichte des alten Mönchtums und des Benediktinerordens* XV, 1928, pp. 25ff.

History: *Quarterly Journal of the Historical Association,* London.

H J: *Hibbert Journal,* London.

H-L: see Hefele, K. J. von.

Hodgkin, R. H.: *A History of the Anglo-Saxons,* vols. I-II, 1939.*

Hodgkin, Thomas: *Italy and Her Invaders,* vol. VI, 1916, vol. VII, 1899.*

Horstman, Carl: see *N L A.*

Howorth, H. H.: *The Golden Days of the Early English Church, from the Arrival of Theodore to the Death of Bede,* vols. I-III, 1917.

H. S.: Haddan, A. W., and Stubbs, W.: ed. *Councils and Ecclesiastical Documents Relating to Great Britain and Ireland,* vols. I-III, 1869-1878.

H T R: *Harvard Theological Review,* Cambridge.

Hunt, William: *History of the English Church* I (597-1066), 1901.

Hutton, Edward: *Highways and Byways in Wiltshire,* 1928.

Hutton, W. H.: *The Influence of Christianity upon National Character, illustrated by the Lives and Legends of the English Saints:* Bampton Lectures for 1903.

H Z: *Historische Zeitschrift,* Munich.

I C C: *International Critical Commentary.*

I L H: *Irish Liber Hymnorum:* see *H B S.*

Jaager, Werner: ed. *Bedas metrische Vita Sancti Cuthberti: Palaestra* CXCVIII, 1935.

Jaffé, Philipp: ed. *Bibliotheca Rerum Germanicarum:* vol. III, *Monumenta Moguntina,* 1866; vol. VI, *Monumenta Alcuiniana,* ed. W. Wattenbach and E. Dümmler, 1873;
—— ed. *Regesta Pontificum Romanorum,* vol. I, revised W. Wattenbach, 1885.

Jecker, Gall: *Die Heimat des hl. Pirmin: Beiträge zur Geschichte des alten Mönchtums und des Benediktinerordens* XIII, 1927.

J E G P: Journal of English and Germanic Philology, Urbana, Illinois.

Jenkinson, F. J. H.: *The Hisperica Famina,* 1908.

Jones, C. W.: *O D T:* ed. *Bedae Opera de Temporibus: Publications, Medieval Academy of America* XLI, 1943; *

——*Bedae pseudigrapha: scientific writings falsely attributed to Bede,* 1939.

Jones, P. F.: *A Concordance to the Historia Ecclesiastica of Bede: Publications, M A A* II, 1929.

J T S: Journal of Theological Studies, London.

Jung-Diefenbach, Josef: *Die Friesenbekehrung im Frühmittelalter,* 1931.

Keil, H.: *Grammatici Latini,* vol. VII, 1880.

Keitz, A. von: *Die Codices Bonifatiani in der Landesbibliothek zu Fulda: Hessenland* IV, 1890, pp. 197f., 211f.

Kemble, J. M.: *Codex Diplomaticus Aevi Saxonici,* vol. I, 1839; vol. V, 1847, *English Historical Society.*

Kendrick, T. D.: *Anglo-Saxon Art to A.D. 900,* 1938.

Kennedy, C. W.: *The Earliest English Poetry,* 1943.

Kenney, J. F.: *The Sources for the Early History of Ireland,* vol. I: *Columbia University Records of Civilization* XI, i, 1929.*

Ker, N. R.: *Medieval Libraries of Great Britain: A list of surviving books,* 1941.

Ker, W. P.: *The Dark Ages,* 1911.

Kimble, G. H. T.: *Geography in the Middle Ages,* 1938.

King, J. E.: ed. *Bedae Opera Historica,* vols. I-II, 1930 (Loeb edition: text and translation based on the version of Thomas Stapleton, 1565).

Kittredge, G. L.: *Witchcraft in Old and New England,* 1929.

Knowles, David: *The Monastic Order in England: a History of* *its Development from the Times of St. Dunstan to the Fourth Lateran Council, 943-1216,* 1940 (Knowles); *

—— *The Religious Houses of Medieval England,* 1940.

Köhler, W.: "Bonifatius in Hessen und das hessische Bistum Buraburg"; *Zeitschrift für Kirchengeschichte* XXV, 1904, pp. 197ff.

Krapp, G. P., and Dobbie, E. V. K.: *The Exeter Book,* 1936.

Kuhlmann, Bernhard: *Der heilige Bonifatius,* 1895.

Kurth, Godefroid: *Saint Boniface,* 1924.*

Kylie, Edward, *The English Correspondence of Saint Boniface,* 1911.

Laistner, M. L. W.: *Thought and Letters in Western Europe A.D. 500 to 900,* 1931; *

—— "Bede as a Classical and Patristic Scholar": *Transactions of the Royal Historical Society* XVI, 1933, pp. 69ff.;

—— *Bedae Venerabilis Expositio Actuum Apostolorum et Retractatio: Publications M A A* XXXV, 1939;

—— *A Hand-List of Bede Manuscripts* (with the collaboration of H. H. King), 1943 (*Hand-List*).

Lappenberg, J. M.: *Geschichte von England,* vol. I, 1834; trans. B. Thorpe, 1845: revised E. C. Otté, 1894.

Latourette, K. S.: *The Thousand Years of Uncertainty, A.D. 500-1500* (*History of the Expansion of Christianity* II), 1938.*

Lau, Hermann: *Die angelsächsische Missionsweise im Zeitalter des Bonifaz,* 1909.

Laudate: Quarterly Review of the Benedictines of Nashdom Abbey, Burnham, Bucks, England.

Laux, J. J.: *Der heilige Bonifatius,* 1922.

Leach, A. F.: *Educational Charters and Documents (598-1909),* 1911.

Le Bras, G.: art. "Pénitentiels": *Dictionnaire de Théologie Catholique* XII, 116off.

Leeds, E. T.: *Early Anglo-Saxon Art and Archaeology,* 1936.

Leland, John: *Collectanea,* 1770.

Lesne, Emile: *Histoire de la Propriété Ecclésiastique en France,* vol. II, i, 1922.

Levison, Wilhelm: ed. Stephanus, *Vita Wilfridi: M G H Script. Rer. Merov.* VI, 1913, pp. 163ff.;

—— ed. *Vitae Sancti Bonifatii: M G H Scriptores Rerum Germanicarum in usum scholarum,* 1905;

—— *Die Zeit der Karolinger: Handbuch der deutschen Geschichte,* ed. Gebhardt and Holtzmann, vol. I, 1930, pp. 132ff.;

——*Willibrordiana: Neues Archiv:* XXXIII, 1908, pp. 517ff.;

—— ed. *Alcuin, Vita Willibrordi: M G H Script. Rer. Merov.* VII, 1919, pp. 81ff.

Liber Eliensis: ed. D. J. Stewart, *Publications, Anglia Christiana,* 1848.

Lightfoot, J. B.: *Leaders in the Northern Church,* 1891.

Lindsay, W. M.: *Early Irish Minuscule Script,* 1910.

Lingard, John: *The Antiquities of the Anglo-Saxon Church,* 1854.

Lloyd, J. E.: *A History of Wales,* vol. I, 1911.

Loofs, F.: *Zur Chronologie der auf die fränkischen Synoden des hl. Bonifatius bezüglichen Briefe,* 1881.

Lot, F., Pfister, C., and Ganshof, F. L.: *Histoire du Moyen Âge* (ed. G. Glotz) vol. I (*Les destinées de l'empire en occident de 395 à 888*), 1928.

Lowe, E. A.: ed. *Codices Latini Antiquiores: a Paleographical Guide to Latin MSS. prior to the Ninth Century,* Parts I-III, 1934-1938 (*C L A*).

Lumby, J. R.: *Greek Learning in the Western Church during the Seventh and Eighth Centuries,* 1878.

M A A: Mediaeval Academy of America.

Mabillon, J.: ed. *Acta Sanctorum Ordinis Sancti Benedicti;* ed. by the monks of Solesmes, vol. II, 1936; vol. III, Fasc. 1-3, 1939-1940.

MacDonald, A. J. M.: *Authority and Reason in the Early Middle Ages,* 1933.

McIlwain, C. H.: *The Growth of Political Thought in the West,* 1932.

MacNaught, J. C.: *The Celtic Church and the See of Peter,* 1927.

McNeill, John T., and Gamer, Helena M.: *Medieval Handbooks of Penance: Columbia University Records of Civilization* XXIX, 1938.*

Mai, Cardinal Angelo: *Auctores Classici* VII, 1835.

Manitius, Max: *Geschichte der lateinischen Literatur des Mittelalters,* vol. I, 1911 (Manitius, *Gesch.*); *

—— *Geschichte der christlich-lateinischen Poesie bis zur Mitte des VIII Jahrhunderts,* 1891;

—— *Zu Aldhelm und Baeda,* 1886 (see also *Wiener Sitzungsber.* CXII, 1886, pp. 535ff.).

Mann, H. K.: *The Lives of the Popes in the Early Middle Ages,* vol. I, 1902-1903.

Maunde Thompson, E.: *An Introduction to Greek and Latin Palaeography,* 1912.

Mawer, Allen: *The Place-Names of Northumberland and Durham,* 1920 (*Northumberland*);

—— Stenton, F. M., and Gover, J. E. B.: *The Place-Names of Sussex,* vols. I-II, 1929-1930.

Meissner, J. L. G.: *The Celtic Church in England after the Synod of Whitby,* 1929.

Meyer, Kuno: *Learning in Ireland in the Fifth Century,* 1913.

Meyer, R. M.: *Altgermanische Religionsgeschichte,* 1910.

M G H: Monumenta Germaniae Historica, ed. Pertz and others: *Auctores Antiquissimi; Scriptores Rerum Merovingicarum; Scriptores Rerum Langobardicarum; Scriptores Rerum Germanicarum* (Pertz, *Scriptores*); *Leges* (vol. I: *Capitularia Regum Francorum*); *Diplomata; Epistolae; Poetae Latini Aevi Carolini; Scriptores Rerum Germanicarum in usum scholarum.*

M H B: Monumenta Historica Britannica, vol. I, ed. H. Petrie and J. Sharpe, 1848.

M L N: Modern Language Notes, Baltimore.

Molinier, Auguste: *Les Sources de l'Histoire de France,* vol. I, 1901.

Mommsen, T.: ed. *Chronica majora ad. ann. 725;* ed. *Chronica minora ad ann. 703: M G H Auct. Ant.* XIII, 1898, pp. 223ff.

Montalembert, Comte de: *Les Moines d'Occident depuis S. Benoît jusqu'à S. Bernard,* trans. *The Monks of the West,* vols. IV-V, 1867.

Mühlbacher, E.: *Deutsche Geschichte unter den Karolingern,* 1896.

Neues Archiv: *Neues Archiv der Gesellschaft für ältere deutsche Geschichtskunde,* Hanover.

N L A: Nova Legenda Anglie, ed. Carl Horstman, vols. I-II, 1901.

Norden, Eduard: *Die antike Kunstprosa*, 1909.
Nottarp, H.: *Die Bistumserrichtung in Deutschland im achten Jahrhundert: Kirchenrechtliche Abhandlungen*, hrsg. von Ulrich Stutz, XCVI, 1920.
Nürnberger, A. J.: *Aus der litterarischen Hinterlassenschaft des hl. Bonifatius: Bericht d. wiss. Gesell. Phil. in Neisse*, XXIV, 1888, pp. 133ff.
—— ed. *Dicta Bonifatii: Theologische Quartalschrift* LXX, Tübingen, 1888, pp. 287ff.

Oakley, T. P.: *English Penitential Discipline and Anglo-Saxon Law in their Joint Influence: Columbia University Studies in History* CVII, 2, 1923.
Oelsner, L.: *Jahrbücher des fränkischen Reiches unter König Pippin*, 1871.
Ogilvy, J. D. A.: *Anglo-Saxon Scholarship, 597-780: University of Colorado Studies* XXII, 1935, pp. 327ff.;
—— *Books known to Anglo-Latin Writers from Aldhelm to Alcuin, 670-804: M A A Studies and Documents* 2, 1936.
Oman, Charles: *England before the Norman Conquest*, 1913.

Paetow, L. J.: ed. *Guide to the Study of Medieval History*, 1931.
Payne, J. F.: *English Medicine in the Anglo-Saxon Times*, 1904.
P B A: Proceedings of the British Academy.
P E A: Patres Ecclesiae Anglicanae, ed. J. A. Giles: *Aldhelm, Opera*, vol. I, 1844; *Bede, Opera*, vols. I-XII, 1843-1844; *Boniface, Opera*, vols. I-II, 1844.
Pertz, *Scriptores:* see *M G H.*
Pfahler, Georg: *St. Bonifatius und seine Zeit*, 1880.
Phillips, W. A.: ed. *History of the Church of Ireland*, vol. I, 1933.
Pitman, J. H.: *The Riddles of Aldhelm, text and translation: Yale Studies in English* LXVII, 1925.
P Q: Philological Quarterly, Iowa City.
P L: Patrologia Latina, ed. J. Migne: vol. LXXXIX, *Aldhelm, Opera*, coll. 87ff.; *Boniface, Opera*, ibid. coll. 687ff.; *Bede, Opera*, vols. XC-XCV.
P L M: Poetae Latini Minores.
Plummer, Alfred: *The Churches in Britain before 1000 A.D.*, vols. I-II, 1911-1912.

Plummer, Charles: *Bedae Opera Historica,* vols. I-II, 1896 (Plummer).

Poole, Reginald Lane: *Studies in Chronology and History,* 1934 (including "St. Wilfred and the See of Ripon": *E H R* XXXIV, 1919, pp. 1ff.)

Potthast, August: *Bibliotheca Historica Medii Aevi,* vols. I-II, 1896.

P R I A: *Proceedings of the Royal Irish Academy,* Dublin.

Quentin, Henri: *Les Martyrologes Historiques du Moyen Âge,* 1908;
—— "Bède le Vénérable," *D A C L* II, i, coll. 632ff.

Raby, F. J. E.: *A History of Christian-Latin Poetry from the Beginnings to the Close of the Middle Ages,* 1927 (*C L P*);
—— *A History of Secular Latin Poetry in the Middle Ages,* vols. I-II, 1934 (*S L P*);
—— "Bède le Vénérable," *D H G E* VII, 1934, coll. 395ff.;
—— "Bede, 735-1935": *Laudate* XIII, 1935, pp. 140ff.

Raine, James, Sr.: *Saint Cuthbert,* 1828.

Raine, James, Jr.: ed. *The Historians of the Church of York and its Archbishops,* vol. I, *Rolls Series* LXXI, 1879 (*H Y*), containing the *Life of Saint Wilfrid by Eddius Stephanus;*
—— ed. *The Priory of Hexham, SS* 44-46, 1864-1865.

Ramsey, J. H.: *The Foundations of England* I, 1898.

Rand, Edward Kennard: *The Irish flavor of Hisperica Famina: Ehrengabe für Karl Strecker,* 1931, pp. 134ff.

R B: *Revue Bénédictine,* Maredsous, Belgium.

R C: *Revue Celtique,* Paris, France.

Rees, W. J.: *Lives of the Cambro-British Saints,* 1853.

Reeves, William: ed. Adamnan, *Life of Saint Columba: Historians of the Church of Scotland* VI, 1874.

Registrum Malmesburiense: ed. J. S. Brewer and C. T. Martin, vols. I-II, *Rolls Series* LXXII, 1879-1880.

Rettberg, F. W.: *Kirchengeschichte Deutschlands,* vols. I-II, 1846-1848.

Rhys, John: *Celtic Britain,* 1908.

Riese, A.: ed. *Riddles of Symphosius, Anthologia Latina* I, i, 1894, pp. 221ff.

Riezler, S.: *Geschichte Baierns* I, 1878.

R M: *Rheinisches Museum für Philologie*, Frankfurt-am-Main.

Robertson, A. J.: ed. *Anglo-Saxon Charters*, 1939.

Robinson, C. H.: *The Conversion of Europe*, 1917.

Robinson, G. W.: trans. Willibald, *Life of Boniface*, 1916; *

—— "Letters of Saint Boniface to the Popes and others: First English translation": *Papers of the American Society of Church History, Second Series* VII, 1923, pp. 163ff.

Robinson, J. Armitage: *Somerset Historical Essays*, 1921.

Rock, Daniel: *The Church of our Fathers*: ed. G. W. Hart and W. H. Frere, vols. I-IV, 1905.

Rösler, Margarete: "Erziehung in England vor der normannischen Eroberung": *Englische Studien* XLVIII, 1914, pp. 1ff.

Roger, M.: *L'Enseignement des Lettres Classiques d'Ausone à Alcuin*, 1905.

Roth, Paul: *Geschichte des Beneficialwesens von den ältesten Zeiten bis ins zehnte Jahrhundert*, 1850.

R S: *Rolls Series: Chronicles and Memorials of Great Britain and Ireland during the Middle Ages*, 1858-1911.

Ryan, Alice M.: *A Map of Old English Monasteries and Related Ecclesiastical Foundations, A.D. 400-1066; Cornell Studies in English* XXVIII, 1939.

Ryan, John: *Irish Monasticism*, 1931 (Ryan).

Scherer, Carl: *Die Codices Bonifatiani in der Landesbibliothek zu Fulda* (see *Festgabe*), 1905.

Schmitz, H. J.: *Die Bussbücher und die Bussdisciplin der Kirche*: I, 1883; II, 1898.

Schnürer, Gustav: *Bonifatius: die Bekehrung der Deutschen zum Christentum*, 1909 (interesting illustrations).

Schubert, Hans von: *Geschichte der christlichen Kirche im Frühmittelalter*, 1921.*

Schultze, Walther: *Deutsche Geschichte von der Urzeit bis zu den Karolingern*, vol. II, 1896.

Searle, W. G.: *Anglo-Saxon Bishops, Kings, and Nobles*, 1899.

Sellar, A. M.: *Bede's Ecclesiastical History of England*, trans. 1912 (based on trans. of J. A. Giles).

Sheldon, Gilbert: *The Transition from Roman Britain to Christian England, A.D. 368-664*, 1932.

Short, E. H.: *A History of Religious Architecture,* 1936.
Sim. Durh.: Simeon of Durham: *Opera omnia,* ed. T. Arnold, vols. I-II, *Rolls Series* LXXV, 1882-1885;
——*Opera et Collectanea,* ed. J. H. Hinde, vol. I, *Surtees Society* LI, 1868.
Skene, W. F.: *Celtic Scotland,* vol. II, 1887.
Slover, Clark H.: *Early Literary Channels between Britain and Ireland: University of Texas Studies in English* VI-VII, 1926-1927.
Smalley, Beryl: *The Study of the Bible in the Middle Ages,* 1941.
Smith, A. H.: *Three Northumbrian Poems: Caedmon's Hymn, Bede's Death Song, and the Leiden Riddle,* 1933.
Smith, J.: ed. Bede, *Historia Ecclesiastica,* 1722.
Speculum: A Journal of Mediaeval Studies, Cambridge, Massachusetts.
S S: Surtees Society, Publications of the, Durham, England.
Stenton, F. M.: *Anglo-Saxon England,* 1943 (Stenton).
Stephanus, Eddius: see *Wilfrid, Saint.*
Stevenson, Joseph: ed. Bede, *Historia Ecclesiastica, English Historical Society,* 1838;
——ed. Bede, *Opera Historica Minora, ibid.* 1841.
Stokes, Whitley: *Lives of Saints from the Book of Lismore,* 1890;
—— ed., with translations, *The Tripartite Life of St. Patrick,* vols. I-II, *Rolls Series* LXXXIX, 1887.
Stutz, Ulrich: *Geschichte des kirchlichen Benefizialwesens* I, i, 1895.

Tangl, Michael: ed. *Die Briefe des heiligen Bonifatius und Lullus,* 1916 (Tangl);
—— *Bonifatiusfragen: Abhandlungen der preussischen Akademie der Wissenschaften, Phil.-hist. Klasse,* Berlin, 1919, 2;
——*Die Fuldaer Privilegienfrage: Mittheilungen des Instituts für oesterreichische Geschichtsforschung,* Innsbruck, XX, 1899;
—— *Neues Archiv* XL, 1916, pp. 639ff.; XLI, 1917, pp. 23ff.
T A P A: Transactions of the American Philological Association.
Taylor, H. O.: *The Classical Heritage of the Middle Ages,* 1911 (reissued 1925);
——*The Mediaeval Mind,* vols. I-II, 1925 (reprinted 1927).
T C A S: Transactions of the Connecticut Academy of Arts and Sciences, New Haven.

Thomas of Elmham: *Historia Monasterii S. Augustini Cantuariensis*, ed. C. Hardwick, *Rolls Series* VIII, 1858.

Thompson, Alexander Hamilton: ed. *Bede, his Life, Times, and Writings*, 1935 (Thompson);
—— *English Monasteries*, 1913.

Thompson, J. W.: *An Economic and Social History of the Middle Ages (300-1300)*, 1928;
—— *The Middle Ages (300-1500)*, vols. I-II, 1931;
—— *The Medieval Library* (with essays by his students), 1939.

Thorndike, Lynn: *A History of Magic and Experimental Science*, vol. I, 1923.

Thorpe: see *A S C*.

Timerding, Heinrich: ed. *Die christliche Frühzeit Deutschlands in den Berichten über die Bekehrer: Erste Gruppe, Die irischfränkische Mission*, 1929.

Traill, H. D., and Mann, J. S.: *Social England*, vol. I, 1901.

T R H S: *Transactions of the Royal Historical Society*, London.

Traub, Gottfried: *Bonifatius*, 1894.

Traube, Ludwig: *Karolingische Dichtungen*, 1888 (Traube);
—— *Perrona Scottorum: Sitzungsberichte, Hist. Kl., Akad. der Wiss.*, Munich, 1900.

Tupper, Frederick: *The Riddles of the Exeter Book*, 1910.

V A: *Bede, Vita beatorum abbatum Benedicti, Ceolfridi, Eosterwini, Sigfridi atque Hwaetberhti: Plummer I, pp. 364ff.

V A A: *Vita sanctissimi Ceolfridi abbatis auctore anonymo*: Plummer I, pp. 388ff.

Verbist, G. H.: *Saint Willibrord*, 1939.

V H D: *Victoria History of Dorset* II, 1908, pp. 1ff. (M. M. C. Calthrop).

V H S: *Victoria History of Somerset* II, 1906, pp. 1ff. (T. Scott Holmes).

V H Suss.: *Victoria History of Sussex* II, 1907, pp. 1ff. (L. F. Salzmann).

Vinogradoff, Paul: *The Growth of the Manor*, 1920.

Waddell, Helen: *The Wandering Scholars*, 1927.

Wasserschleben, F. W. H.: *Die Bussordnungen der abendländischen Kirche nebst einer rechtsgeschichtlichen Einleitung*, 1851.

Watkins, O. D.: *A History of Penance,* vols. I-II, 1920.

Werminghoff, A.: *Verfassungsgeschichte der deutschen Kirche im Mittelalter* I, 1913.

Werner, August: *Bonifacius, der Apostel der Deutschen,* 1875.

Werner, Karl: *Beda der Ehrwürdige und seine Zeit,* 1881.

Westwood, J. O.: *Facsimiles of the Miniatures and Ornaments of Anglo-Saxon and Irish MSS.,* 1868.

Wildman, W. B.: *Life of St. Ealdhelm,* 1905.

Wilfrid, Saint: Life, by Eddius Stephanus: ed. B. Colgrave, 1927; ed. W. Levison, 1913; ed. J. Raine Jr., 1879: see these authors.

Williams, Hugh: ed. and trans. *Gildas, Works: Cymmrodorion Record Series* III, 1899.

Willibald: see Levison, ed. *Vitae S. Bonifatii.*

Wright, Thomas: *Biographia Britannica Literaria* I, 1842; —— ed. *Aldhelmi Aenigmata, Rolls Series* LIX, ii, 1872, Appendix II; ed. *Tatwini Aenigmata, ibid.* Appendix I.

Y A J: Yorkshire Archaeological Journal.

Zöckler, Otto: *Askese und Mönchtum* I, 1897.

INDEX OF PERSONS AND PLACES

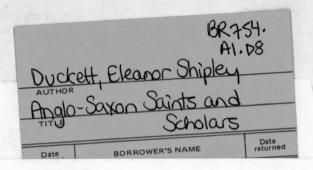

INDEX OF SUBJECTS

815 **WINTER SCENE, Niagara Falls,**   ILL. P. CARD CO., 116 CHAMBERS ST., N. Y.

This is pretty; but I like the moonlight scene more, don't you?

Charles Stetson.

ecored $2.50

"SCENE ON FALLS RIVER" NEAR SHEFFIELD. TAS.

91 Victoria Falls — The Falls and Chasm, from
Livingstone Island

There are nearly 150 different
views taken of the falls & the
scenery surrounding them.

E.M.

2/4/08.

The Whirlpool Rapids.   Niagara Falls, N. Y.

This is below the falls, magnificent and awful I hope you will come to see them sometime as well as that I may see the beautiful scenes on your card, your royal cousin. marguerite S—

91   Victoria Falls — The Falls and Chasm, from
Livingstone Island

There are nearly 150 different
views taken of the falls & the
scenery surrounding them.

Published by E. Peters, Cape Town (Copyright)   E. M.

1/4/08.

The Whirlpool Rapids. Niagara Falls, N. Y.

This is below the Falls magnificent and
awful I hope you will come to see them
sometime as well as that I may see the beautiful scenes on your cards your royal cousin
marguerite S-